# HOWARD HUGHES

## THE SECRET LIFE

## ALSO BY CHARLES HIGHAM

*Theater and Film*

Hollywood in the Forties (with Joel Greenberg)
The Celluloid Muse: Hollywood Directors Speak
(with Joel Greenberg)
The Films of Orson Welles
Hollywood Cameramen: Sources of Light
Warner Brothers
Ziegfeld
Cecil B. DeMille: A Biography
The Art of the American Film
Kate: The Life of Katharine Hepburn
Charles Laughton: An Intimate Biography
Marlene: The Life of Marlene Dietrich
Celebrity Circus: *New York Times* Profiles
Errol Flynn: The Untold Story
Bette: The Life of Bette Davis
Princess Merle: The Romantic Life of Merle Oberon
(with Roy Moseley)
Audrey: The Life of Audrey Hepburn
Orson Welles: The Rise and Fall of an American Genius
Brando: The Unauthorized Biography
Cary Grant: The Lonely Heart (with Roy Moseley)
Merchant of Dreams: Louis B. Mayer, MGM and the Secret Hollywood

*Literary Biography*

The Adventures of Conan Doyle:
The Life of the Creator of Sherlock Holmes

*History and Politics*

Trading with the Enemy: An Exposé of the Nazi-American Money Plot, 1933–1949
American Swastika
Elizabeth and Philip (with Roy Moseley)

*Poetry*

A Distant Star
Spring and Death
The Earthbound and Other Poems
Noonday Country
The Voyage to Brindisi

*Anthologies*

Penguin Australian Writing Today
They Came to Australia (with Alan Brissenden)
Australians Abroad (with Alan Brissenden)

# HOWARD
# HUGHES
## The Secret Life

### Charles Higham

SIDGWICK & JACKSON
LONDON

First published in the United States by Putnam Berkley Group Inc., New York

First published in Great Britain 1993 by Sidgwick & Jackson Limited
a division of Pan Macmillan Publishers Limited
Cavaye Place London SW10 9PG
and Basingstoke

ISBN 0-283-06157-X

1  3  5  7  9  8  6  4  2

A CIP catalogue record for this book is available from
the British Library

Printed by MacKays of Chatham PLC

*This book is*
*dedicated to*
*Richard V. Palafox*

# Contents

Preface *11*

**One** Dark, Tangled Roots *13*

**Two** Growing Up *23*

**Three** Taking Off *35*

**Four** New Adventures *48*

**Five** Airman *64*

**Six** Around the World *73*

**Seven** Wartime Years *91*

**Eight** Of Sex and Corruption *107*

**Nine** Crash! *120*

**Ten** From *Hercules* to Hollywood *130*

**Eleven** More Misadventures *151*

**Twelve** Troubled Years *163*

**Thirteen** Withdrawals *180*

**Fourteen** Sealed Rooms *196*

**Fifteen** Buying Las Vegas *224*

**Sixteen** Buying Nixon *242*

**Seventeen** From Nassau to Watergate *260*

**Eighteen** The Cuban Connection *279*

**Nineteen** How to Burgle Yourself *306*

Postscript *325*

**Author's Note and Acknowledgments** *331*

**Notes on Sources** *337*

**Bibliography** *351*

**Index** *357*

"I can buy any man in the world."

*Howard Hughes*


"There is no inconsistency in trying to earn money from Hughes while serving the interests of the [Central Intelligence] Agency and the nation; after all, the interests of the Hughes organization are so intertwined as to be almost symbolic."

*Raymond Price*
*Former Special Assistant to*
*President Richard M. Nixon*
*1976*

# Preface

On a certain day in March, 1974, ill and in pain in his penthouse at the Xanadu Princess Hotel in Freeport, Bahamas, Howard Hughes dictated an instruction to his high-powered New York lawyer, Chester Davis. He was nervous, fretful; his former right-hand man, Robert Maheu, was demanding papers in connection with a multimillion-dollar libel suit against him; the Watergate Committee was about to sit, and might, perhaps, expose his or certain of his executive employees' involvement in the decade's most famous burglary; the Securities and Exchange Commission wanted to send him to prison because he had criminally taken over Air West, stripping the shareholders of $60 million.

He made clear in that aides' memorandum he wanted his files on his CIA connections destroyed. Hughes was secretly earning tens of millions a year from contracts with the Agency, supplying spying devices, satellites, lasers, X rays, buggings, and a vessel that would soon bring up the codes from a sunken nuclear submarine. These documents revealed his hidden relationship with President Richard Nixon, showing the monies Hughes had contributed to Nixon's brother Donald and, illegally, to the 1972 campaign to gain him favors in Washington; tapes, too, of conversations with the people at the highest level with whom he was in touch were also to be shredded.

Soon afterward, a series of fake burglaries of Hughes's offices were staged, under orders from Chester Davis, culminating in a staged raid on Summa, the vast corporation that controlled the empire. The headquarters building on Romaine Street, Hollywood, was stripped of incriminating papers and tapes.

Hughes was protecting himself and his legend: the legend that persists till this day, of the former hero and inventor of the Spruce Goose who, in later years, became a mindless zombie, out of control, ruled like a puppet by a group of Mormons, unable to think or act for himself. Nothing could be further from the truth; he was drug-ridden and he had periods of listlessness and hopeless apathy, but his memoranda, unearthed from files in Texas, show that, up to his death in 1976, he was constantly wheeling and dealing, feisty, manipulative, and power-hungry as he had always been.

His favorite doctors, among them Howard House and Wilbur Thain, his friend, aircraft honcho Jack Real, and aides Gordon Margulis and Mell Stewart confirm that Hughes was completely alert in his later years. This fact makes all the more clear his role in some of the great events of the time, i.e., Watergate, of which he is supposed to have had no knowledge. It is to correct this view, to show that Hughes played a crucial role not only in aviation and movie-making but in major political affairs, that I have written this book.

# Dark, Tangled Roots

Even his birth details were falsified. He was not born in Houston, Texas, on Christmas Eve, December 24, 1905, but in the oil town of Humble, in the same state, on September 24. The date survives today in the baptismal registration of the parish ledger of St. John's, Keokuk, Iowa.

No birth certificate was entered for him; the day he was born, there was a thunderstorm, and the doctor and midwife were unable to make the journey to Houston through washed-out roads to register him. So they let the matter lie; at risk to his immortal soul, since Episcopalians believed an unbaptized baby went to hell, he was not taken to his grandfather's home in Keokuk for baptism until months later, apparently because his nervous mother feared he might die on the train.

Lie after lie surrounded his infancy. He was supposed to be one of triplets, the other two brothers exchanged for him, for sinister reasons, throughout his lifetime; he was supposed to be his mother's sister's illegitimate child, but she was only eleven at the time; he was supposed to be a substitute baby, brought in at midnight to Houston by rail to replace one who had died or been murdered. He delighted in these tall tales, which persist until today.

His father was the outlaw wildcatter Howard Robard Hughes; his mother, the neurotic Dallas heiress Allene Gano. He would always be half outlaw, defying justice; half fragile, self-centered neurasthenic. Two men helped shape him also: his grandfather, the monomaniac Iowa judge Felix Hughes, and his brilliant Jekyll-and-Hyde uncle, the celebrated best-selling novelist and Broadway playwright Rupert Hughes.

Judge Hughes had several children, the two youngest of whom died in infancy. His only daughter, Greta, and his youngest son, Felix, were musical; Greta became an opera singer, and Felix the founder of the Cleveland Orchestra and the top singing coach of the early days of talking pictures. Rupert was said to be a sadist, murderer, and committer of incest. He was accused of physically torturing his wife, whom he spectacularly divorced in 1903 in the most notorious case of a decade; the New York papers headlined the story on the front pages for weeks as Rupert accused his wife of ten adulteries and she charged him with bedding as many women.

In later years, as Howard Jr. grew up, Rupert was said to own a circular graveyard in New England, filled with the bodies of people he had murdered; he was supposed to have drowned his daughter and replaced her with a double, and to have made love to his sister Greta.

Howard's father, "Bo" Hughes, was almost as colorful as Rupert. Unlike Howard in looks, which gave rise to the usual number of suspicions, he was oval-faced and dreamy-eyed, tall, and strapping compared with his more delicate son. Like Rupert, he was brutal; as a boy, he beat up young girls, slashed male children with knives, and staged cockfights, illegal at the time, in which the spurred roosters tore each other to pieces. Dismissed for bad behavior from college after college, he sank to being a ticket collector on his grandpa Hughes's railroad. He bummed his way around Europe, and was in the Midwest and South as telegraph operator, reporter, and zinc miner.

Bo Hughes wound up penniless in Joplin, Missouri, in 1899, sweating eighteen hours a day, stripped to the waist, in a lead mine. Run out of town on a rail by the angry father of a girl he had seduced, he dreamed of striking oil. He caught the fever that seized tens of thousands of Americans in those days; and then something amazing happened.

On January 10, 1901, at Spindletop, Texas, near Beaumont, oil burst up through the ground in a thousand-foot spume. The rush was on. Bo was among the first to grab up leases.

At Beaumont's only "hotel," a glorified shack called the Crosby House, he caroused with fellow wildcatters Walter Sharp, soon to be his closest friend and partner, and Walter's half-brother Jim. Walter was tall, over six feet three, raw-boned and rangy, with red hair, burning eyes, and a wide frog mouth. Shorter, handsomer, dark and swarthy, Jim was part Mexican, and a small-time Billy the Kid.

The three outlaws grabbed up land at a few dollars an acre, selling it days later for hundreds. They often reneged on their payments and were pursued by angry creditors, whom they disposed of with their fists.

Squandering his money on prostitutes and gambling, Bo rode around town with a Winchester rifle and a hickory stick strapped to his saddle, using both so frequently on his rival wildcatters that he was run out of town.

Bo moved with the Sharps to Houston. Using Walter's money, Bo founded the Texas Fuel Oil Company in 1903, which later became Texaco.

He was broke within six months. When he built a new derrick at Spindletop, he had to barter his diamond tie pin and watch to make a down payment.

On a visit to Dallas in 1903, he fell in love with the darkly pretty Allene Gano; high-strung, a hypochondriac, she was terrified of small animals, especially cats. She was obsessed with the perils of mosquitos, flies, roaches, and beetles.

The couple fell in love. They were ill-matched. The Ganos were monarchs of Dallas society, rich from Kentucky horse farms, wheat lands, and city real estate. Bo Hughes had little. But his relationship to his illustrious father the judge and to his brother Rupert, who was publishing one best-seller after another, proved influential. The Ganos yielded, and the couple were married after five months' courtship, during which Bo was frequently absent in Houston. The couple was wed at the bride's parents' house at the intersection of Masten and San Jacinto streets in Dallas, at 8:30 on the evening of May 24, 1904.

The Ganos spared no expense for the ceremony, which was featured in the social columns. The living room was decorated with arches of bride roses and sweet peas; the couple entered through an aisle of American Beauty roses hung with red and pink ribbons. The large, airy reception rooms were crowded with pink and white flowers; flower baskets clustered in the chandeliers. Allene made a picture in Bruges lace and *mousseline de soie,* with a lace-and-tulle veil, carrying a bouquet of lilies of the valley. The groom's sister, Greta, sang "Memories." So great was Judge Hughes's influence that his friend the Reverend R. C. McIlwain was brought all the way from Keokuk, with three changes of train, to preside; General Gano remarried the couple in the Baptist faith.

The Hugheses traveled to St. Louis to visit friends, continuing to Europe for an extended six-month honeymoon. Bo bragged later that he spent $10,000 (it was his wife's money) on a journey that stretched to 10,000 miles. The couple came back to Houston, where they took rooms at the expensive and fashionable Rice Hotel. But they had run out of cash; no sooner were they settled than the manager asked them to quit for nonpayment. Charlie Lane, Walter Sharp's secretary and bookkeeper, was dispatched to the hotel to pay the $150 owing, as the unhappy newlyweds sat on their luggage in the lobby. Again they fell behind, and again they were forced to leave. They moved to an airy, white wooden house at 1404 Crawford Street, a fashionable but still unpaved street where many socially prominent families lived.

Allene was afraid of germs spreading from the dreaded Buffalo Bayou, an immense and loathsome pool of filth, the water link between Houston and the Gulf of Mexico. Brown and brackish, the Bayou was littered with putrefying cattle that had been discarded for lack of quality from the nearby stockyards. No one bothered to sweep up the dead birds and fish that lay stinking with corruption in the water and mud. Frequently, people would find their pipes blocked by drifting snakes or eels.

Filters did not exist then, and often, when a tap was turned on, brown water coughed out of it, emitting a stench; anyone who took the chance of drinking it could be poisoned. Even the milk tended to be contaminated, and smallpox and typhoid epidemics were frequent. Not only was Houston slovenly to the point that no one took care of the water problem, and hung over with constant banks of smoky clouds that seemed to sweat the rain, but it was a moral cesspool as well. Prostitutes roamed the streets of the squalid districts, drunkenness was endemic, and there were constant fistfights. To escape, Bo and Allene moved to Humble in 1905, where Howard Jr., known as Sonny, was born.

Following his son's birth, Bo learned of a strike at Shreveport, Louisiana. He took off with wife and baby to that city, putting up at the Caddo Hotel. Howard Jr.'s earliest memories were (he claimed) the sounds of whistles and the sirens of the Red River steamboats, with their echoes of the great days of King Cotton. For decades, prospectors had threaded through the inlets and bayous, squandering fortunes on derrick after derrick that collapsed in soft soil, cursing as gushers turned to salt water, watching slicks of green-gold liquid sweating out into the shallows. When Bo Hughes and his family arrived in Shreveport in early 1907, the stench of sulfur from the tidal marshes blended with the odor of mud and silt and oil: the tarry, unmistakable smell of new strikes. Not even flowers and trees could survive for long in that region: black rot, canker, and elm disease were everywhere.

It was a nightmare for Allene, with her sensitivity, delicacy, and fear of contagion. Cases of yellow fever were reported at the time; as she took Sonny out in a carriage, the first words they saw were QUARANTINED—KEEP OUT, painted on the doors of houses. Allene and her baby found it difficult to sleep at night: from dusk to dawn, the sky was lit a garish orange-crimson as brilliant as at high noon, from the gas-lake fires lit for miles and burned away because nobody saw gas as having any value in an age when electric light was taking over. Not even the thickest curtains at the Caddo Hotel could blot out the light. And the noise of drills, as men worked all night to lay down new streets or build new buildings and mud was churned up for asphalt, added to her misery.

Bo became Postmaster and Deputy Sheriff of nearby Oil City on July 1, 1907. Since there was no jail, he chained prisoners to trees before shipping them off to Shreveport. He put roughnecks in charge of the post office and the arrest details; the result was rampant thievery. When Sonny was two, Bo rushed off to Pierce Junction, Texas, following an oil strike; he continued on to Goose Creek. His fishtail drilling bits broke off, and he was seized by an obsession: he must fashion a bit that would cut through rock and quicksand.

In 1908, on one of his visits to Houston, he got wind of two recently patented bits: one designed by Erich Hoffner, a German in Providence, Rhode Island, and the other by oilman John S. Wynn in Beaumont. He borrowed $12,000 from Walter Sharp, took off to Rhode Island, and bought the first bit for $2,500; Wynn sold him the second one for $9,000. He spent weeks setting up a machine shop in a dirt-floored, rented shack in Houston, testing out the bits. He and Walter Sharp worked eighteen hours a day, trying to blend the two patents. Sharp would stretch out his long legs on the leather office couch, dreaming up ideas, while Bo would pace up and down, then rush to his drawing board with a new concept.

In a Shreveport saloon in October, 1908, Hughes ran into a millwright, Granville (Granny) Humasson, who showed him a sketch for a drill formed like two pine cones, one part moving clockwise and the other counterclockwise, and based on the concept of a coffee grinder. Hughes bought the patent for a mere $1,200, and sold it to his partner for $1,500. Then he took off to Keokuk, where, at dinner one night, he noticed the butter pats on a silver dish. The ribbing on the pats gave him an idea. Suppose he could create a bit that not only had two cone-shaped sections revolving in opposite directions, but could be ribbed like the butter pats? When dinner was over, he cleared the table, sketched away furiously, and then yelled, "Eureka!", so that the whole family came running out to see what he had done. He had provided the cones with 166 cutting edges. The cook walked in, carrying an egg beater. He yelled with joy when he saw it. By November 20, 1908, he had invented the Hughes tool bit, which, improved yearly for most of a decade, marketed all over the world, formed the basis of the countless millions of the Hughes fortune.

He brought his family back to Houston, moving them into 916 Crawford Street. No sooner had he settled into offices than the sheriff arrived at his office with a warrant for his arrest. The Oil City Post Office account was $450 short. Walter Sharp paid the money out of the office safe, plus a bribe, and the sheriff went home.

In 1909, when Sonny Hughes was four, Bo formed the Sharp-Hughes Tool Company. The problem was marketing the new bit. Resistance to it was strong. Jim Sharp came in handy; he shot the ground from under reluctant buyers' feet until they gave in. Once a prospector bought a bit, Hughes sent him an engraved gold cigarette case. But even though the bit began to take off, Hughes lost his money again in gambling, whoring, and ordering expensive equipment on the company accounts. When he bought an expensive Pierce Arrow automobile, he lost it in a bet to Jim Sharp. He was $10,000 in the red by 1910.

By the time he was four, Bo and Allene Hughes knew that delicate, nervous Sonny was afflicted. He had inherited deafness, as his Uncle Rupert had, from generations of Hugheses. Hereditary otosclerosis was a condition of the ear that would grow progressively worse for a lifetime. The result of a child's finding he had that condition was that he would become introspective, isolated, and feel a piercing sense of inferiority. It is remarkable that Hughes overcame the handicap as strongly as he did, in the rough and tumble world of childhood. He was, and remained, controlling of his tiny universe.

At the age of five, Sonny was sent by his mother to kindergarten. Jenny M. Eichler's University, a comical name for the tiny school, was located in Christ Church Episcopal's parish house. The German Mrs. Eichler, with her strict discipline, fascinated the child. Among his fellow students in a class of thirteen were Dudley Sharp, his best friend, Walter's second son; and the pretty young Ella Rice, daughter of Peter Rice, of the poorer branch of the wealthy Houston family which had founded the Rice Institute. A skeleton rattled in the Rice family closet. There was talk among the children of Ella's great-uncle William Rice's being murdered in 1900 by his valet and his lawyer. One day, Ella would marry Sonny.

Young Howard was always late for school; this annoyed Mrs. Eichler, who tried in vain to make him wear a watch. He was shy, handsome, polite; a "perfect little gentleman," as another fellow pupil, the radio playwright Elizabeth Dillingham, remembered him years later.

Both Allene and Estelle Sharp were strict, recalls Mary Cullinan, the daughter of Hughes's partner Joe Cullinan. Much of young Howard's time was spent with Mary and Dudley Sharp at the Walter Sharp home on Main and Elgin, a romantic house, covered in creeping vines, filled with the delicious scent of sandalwood. There Howard, Mary, and Dudley built a shed; he was always inventing things in it. Mary says, "Howard had to be ahead in everything; he constantly challenged himself. We'd be at the back of the estate; he'd have us jump off a high swing and see who would jump the furthest and it was usually him! We'd race each other; he'd always come first. But I was a tomboy and gave him a good run for his money!"

At age eight, Sonny attended Dr. James Richardson's exclusive school, Prosser's Academy. Richardson wasn't impressed with him; years later, when asked by another head teacher for a report, Richardson stated that Sonny was uppity, snobbish, refused to join in manly pursuits, and preferred to spend most of his time with the little girls, resulting in the boys calling him a "sissy." He showed an unhealthy interest in his mother's diamonds, and would borrow them to show his schoolgirl friends. It is a safe bet he received kicks in the behind from the boys for his behavior.

That year, the family suffered a shock: Walter Sharp, who had been ailing for some time, died in Chicago of kidney disease, brought on by years of drinking. The solemn funeral gave Sonny his first taste of the meaning of death. He was afraid of it for the rest of his life.

Walter Sharp's partners struggled over the company. Two resigned in protest over Bo Hughes's controlling methods. But his inventive genius, as he obsessively produced newer and better oil bits, propelled them into wealth. When partner Joseph Cullinan walked out on February 8, 1913, after several quarrels with Bo, Hughes Sr. became the dominant figure of the company. On October 30, 1914, he moved his wife and son into Apartment Three of the expensive and lavish Burlington Apartments, whose owners rolled out a red carpet when the occupants arrived. Allene, housed in her first comfortable residence to date, was at last able to face up to her family in Dallas, found herself in the Houston Blue Book, and joined the Country Club.

Bo was still incorrigible. Again, he ran through all his money, so that on December 8, 1915, the Burlington's manager, E. C. Lambagh, was compelled to threaten him with eviction. Hughes scraped up a loan on his collateral, paid the rent, and took off with his family to New York, pulling his son out of Prosser's before graduation. They stayed at the expensive Biltmore Hotel. There, they enjoyed the Broadway shows of the day, which gave the ten-year-old Sonny a lifelong love of showgirls, glamour, and music.

In January 1916, when they were back in Houston, a friend suggested to the Hughes that it was time to make a man of Sonny. He was altogether too over-refined, nervous, and sissified. The Boy Scout movement had recently swept America. Problem children were packed off to camps for rugged training; the most popular of these was Camp Dan Beard Outdoor School at Lake Teedyuskung, in the pine forest of the Pohokopa Mountains in Pike County, Pennsylvania.

The camp was run by the eager beaver "General" Dan Beard, a grizzled, peppery dynamo who had been a friend, years before, of Mark Twain. Beard bombarded the Hugheses with brochures and pleading letters as soon as he got wind of their interest. In one letter, citing the principles of manhood training exemplified by ex-

President Teddy Roosevelt, he boasted of having 140 boy "wood-crafters" who were as hard as nails, bright-eyed and strong mentally and physically from healthy outdoor living.

Allene was nervous about sending Sonny so far away. She had heard that one of the scouts had infantile paralysis and was presently in a hospital in Brooklyn. Would there not be a danger of Sonny's being stricken with the disease? Beard reassured her, and Sonny begged her for the chance to go to the camp. On May 30, 1916, she tearfully bade him goodbye; he had to change trains three times before he reached the Pennsylvania wilderness. He was met by his close friend and fellow scout, Russell ("Rush") Hughes, stepson of Uncle Rupert Hughes, who was still writing successful novels in New York.

Sonny was shocked, on arrival at the forest retreat made up of log cabins and tents, to see a sign painted with that dreaded word from his infancy: QUARANTINED. Instead of being able to roam freely through the countryside, the boys, because another pupil had been stricken with polio, were confined to the camp for the entire term, which stretched until August. It rained almost constantly, so that the scouts had to tramp through the downpour and heavy, slippery mud when out for hikes in the forest.

But, despite sheltering at home, young Sonny was quite athletic and fit. He was assigned to a "stockade," a team of eight boys led by thirteen-year-old Lt. Victor Aures of Baltimore, all dressed in matching green Robin Hood–like uniforms with caps, and equipped individually with totem poles and bows and arrows. He quickly became an expert at whittling, carpentry, building huts out of two-by-fours; he learned the names of birds, flowers, and plants, Indian signs, secret codes, and animal lore. Each morning, a trumpet blast awoke him in his narrow cot in an Indian tepee; he plunged into an icy shower, then marched in military style to the mess hall, where Dan Beard spoke grace. Along with the other boys, Sonny would sit with arms folded and back straight until it was time to eat. The mornings were filled with lessons, the afternoons in digging up Indian pottery, joining in paper chases, and shooting rabbits or deer.

The outdoor life, even in the rain, turned out a lean, muscled Sonny at the end of his first term. He shook off the effeminacy he had shown at Prosser. But no sooner had he joined his parents at the Vanderbilt Hotel in New York than he was seized by what appeared to be infantile paralysis. Actually, the "sickness" was no more than a spoiled boy's contrivance to obtain sympathy when he was losing an argument. Allene fussed hysterically, as the Vanderbilt suite was turned into a hospital room, with doctors and nurses round the clock. Sonny "recovered" and was packed off to winter school at Sanford, Redding Ridge, Connecticut, with young Dudley Sharp, son of Walter. By February, 1917, the eleven-year-old boy's plans were uncertain: he might stay home, under his mother's wing, go to a military academy, or (his dearest wish) return to Camp Dan Beard. One characteristic letter, addressed to Lt. Victor Aures and written on Valentine's Day, shows a fierce poetic streak in him: a burning nostalgia for the moan of the whippoorwill and the rich, green-clad forests of Lake Teedyuskung.

When Dudley Sharp promised to join him at the camp, his mind was made up: following a brief yachting trip aboard his father's sloop, off the Houston ship canal, he returned to his stockade. When he left Houston, his parents were busy building a mansion that was commensurate with their now considerable financial status. Designed by William Ward Watkin, first chairman of Rice University's Department of Architecture, it was a handsome Georgian residence of fifteen rooms. The floors were marble, the furniture of Haitian mahogany. In the back there was a landscaped garden, alive with fountains and sculptures of naked Greek gods.

## CHAPTER TWO

# Growing Up

B y May, Sonny was back in the lake-and-forest paradise of Camp Dan Beard. Typically, he put on a theatrical performance in letters to his mother, knowing how sensitive she was, and complaining, in a neurotic manner, of nightmares, insomnia, and exhaustion. Allene, in a series of letters written in an enormous, slanting, overwrought hand, besieged Dan Beard and Victor Aures, insisting on a medical checkup for Sonny, demanding he be looked at for digestive problems, constipation, and irregular heartbeat. Wearily, Beard, who knew that Sonny was healthy, wrote back, reassuring her that there was nothing wrong with the boy.

Allene wrote again, charging that Sonny was being teased by Dudley Sharp; that he was a victim of the other boys. Beard refuted these allegations and, risking the loss of an expensive pupil, even dared to reprimand Allene in a letter dated July 28: "I am glad to say that I have noticed very few of [Sonny's] faults to which you have called my attention. However, I shall make every effort to rid [Woodcrafter Hughes] of his sensitiveness as soon as possible." If Sonny was tired at times, it was understandable in view of his strenuous physical activity. Beard reported to Allene that the boy was attentive in scoutcraft and bird study, lacked reasoning power in arithmetic, and was only fair at drawing. He added, daringly, that Sonny was much better off away from overprotective parenting.

At term's end, in late August, Sonny, Dudley, and Rush Hughes took off to Cleveland to stay with his Uncle Felix in his music-filled house in Euclid Heights. Uncle Felix taught Sonny the saxophone. The boy's tootlings drove everyone mad, from that moment on, for several years.

In March, 1918, with America at war, Dan Beard lost several of his pupils, who were put into military colleges to train as cadets. He had to plead to Allene to let Sonny come back for a third term. He promised the boy that he would be an officer now, with three stars on his shoulder. No sooner had Allene yielded to these pleas when Sonny was "stricken" again, talking once more of infantile paralysis. The frantic parents tried to get the famous Dr. Simon Flexner to come from the Rockefeller Institute to Houston, but Flexner instead sent Dr. Henry Chickering, who on arrival informed the Hugheses, to humor them, that the boy's was "an abortive case, with good chances of recovery." He carted Sonny off to his summer home and clinic at Mackinack Island, New York, where Sonny cast off his "illness" and learned to sail his own yacht.

On his return to Houston, Sonny went on plane rides with his father. He fell in love with flying, a lifelong obsession. He was not allowed to go back to Dan Beard's, and instead was sent off to the expensive Fessenden School, near Boston, Massachusetts, for the September, 1920, term. He arrived shortly before his fifteenth birthday, sporting his own invention: an electric motorcycle, with which he was photographed in the pages of *The Houston Post*.

Sonny matured at Fessenden. He edited the school paper, *The Albermarle,* and compelled his father to buy a full page on which to advertise the tool bit; he excelled at geology and physics; he played a mean game of golf; he was substitute tight end on the football team and blew on his saxophone in the school band. Pushed by his parents, he started in the ninth grade, known as the Seventh Form, and had to be put back quickly into the Sixth; he scored a hundred out of a hundred in algebra at term's end, but his poor spelling pulled him down to ninth in his class. He formed friendships with athletes: Charlie Borah, who was to achieve fame as an Olympic hurdler, and star footballer Chauncey Hubbard, who later played for Yale. His chief weakness was, as Fessenden's head teacher wrote to Hughes Sr. on October 27, that he lacked the ability to concentrate on one thing at a time: "It is not easy for a boy who has never attended boarding school and has been indulged at home to get adjusted to so many conditions. He has ability, but finds it somewhat hard to get down to business from day to day."

At the end of the fall term, the boys were required to read a poem to the school. Sonny chose a poem by Oliver Wendell Holmes, entitled "Old Ironsides." He rehearsed with one of the masters, John Fife, in the empty gym. He had trouble with the words, "I tear that tattered ensign down." Finally, Fife screamed at him, "I can't hear you!" And Sonny hitched up his oversized, drooping gray pants, took a deep breath, and almost knocked Fife's head off with his yells. Fife burst into laughter. The story is a legend at Fessenden until this day.

In Houston for the winter vacation, Sonny really fell ill at last: with mumps. This was a serious matter at his age; he was just out of puberty, and the disease in many cases causes near or actual sterility (but not impotence) in males. Only two of the countless women who slept with Hughes claimed to be pregnant from him. Those exceptions were Rita Hayworth and Terry Moore.

Following a pattern begun with his infant school, Bo and Allene foolishly pulled Howard away from Fessenden before he could graduate. They seemed to be incapable of letting him have a sustained education anywhere. They packed him off, of all places, to far-away Ojai, a sleepy country town in southern California, where he was admitted to the Thacher School.

The reason for the move was that the Hugheses were spending a great deal of time in Los Angeles. The previous December, Bo had shipped his brand-new, fifty-foot gas-screw yacht, the Milwaukee-built *Ranger,* in two halves from Houston by freight train to sail her at Newport and San Pedro. The couple had found a home on Coronado Island, San Diego, where they mingled with the navy society set, both at the naval base and at the famous Coronado Hotel. When in Los Angeles itself, they were housed in a suite of the exclusive Ambassador Hotel on Wilshire Boulevard, a fashionable center of social events with rambling tropical grounds filled with palm trees.

There, during a party, Bo met the darkly pretty young actress Eleanor Boardman, who had briefly been involved with his brother Rupert. They entered into a fierce and committed love affair that caused Allene severe jealousy and pain. For appearances' sake, and for Sonny's, the couple did not separate; but this situation, along with the parents' continuing excessive overprotectiveness, upset the growing boy.

It was at that time that Rupert exacted a heavy price for his helpfulness to the fifteen-year-old Sonny. The late *Photoplay* magazine publisher James Quirk, who had a unique grasp of inside Hollywood affairs, and was a close friend of Rupert Hughes, told his nephew, the author Lawrence Quirk, that Rupert put great pressure on Sonny to go to bed with him. Already leaning toward homosexuality, and painfully frustrated in the presence of the handsome young Boy Scouts, Sonny cannot have been attracted to Rupert, who was round, dumpy, and unhandsome. But perhaps curiosity and pubertal sexual tension drove him to the edge and he succumbed. A fire was awakened in him that would never be quenched. And along with it, self-disgust, guilt, misery, a sense of being less than a man; a feeling that he must somehow compensate for his fate by being dominant, utterly masculine in his personal behavior.

If Adelaide Hughes found out about this incestuous seduction, and there are indications that she did, she was undoubtedly driven further into alcoholism and despair. Fortunately, Sonny's parents did not find out. Bo might have killed his brother if he had known.

Sonny was admitted to Thacher School in March, 1921. It was situated, as Camp Dan Beard was, in territory haunted by the memories of the Indian settlements. In the surroundings of the punchbowl-shaped valley of Ojai, there were tales of ghosts, emerging from pillars of smoke, reminiscent of the old tribal fires, to haunt the occupants of houses built over the ancient graveyards. Once again, Sonny, still naturally solitary, was a commanding, haughty, and spoiled figure of the school. One of his few friends there, Anson Thacher, now aged eighty-six, son of then-principal Sherman Thacher, recalls Sonny well. He says that Sonny was the brightest student in physics the school had had in years and that he was fond of going hiking on trails, checking out nests and eggs. His idol was the physics teacher, Owen McBride, who led him into many scientific mysteries and solved them.

Anson Thacher recalls that Sonny was inventive and built his own radio transmitter, a copy of one he used at his house in Houston, which picked up ham signals from all over the North and South American continents.

Each afternoon, the boys were allowed to choose their own favorite form of exercise. This freedom was very rare in those days.

Typically, Sonny chose the solitary athletic occupation of horse riding. His father had bought him a black horse (it is painful to report that its name was Coon), and he would trot the stallion up the high, rambling bridle trails; as at his previous schools, he excelled at golf, but was mediocre at tennis and football. His main achievement, apart from obtaining full marks in mathematics (algebra and geometry), was building a handsome woodland cabin hideaway with his bare hands, roofing it with one-by-twelve boards, and fitting it up with pipes, without the help of a plumber.

On his school vacation late that summer, Sonny spent a great deal of time at his Uncle Rupert's Spanish-style mansion on the then-fashionable South Western Avenue. Whatever Sonny thought of his bisexual relative, Rupert had one great advantage: he offered Sonny access to the magic world of motion pictures. He drove the boy in his super-deluxe Cord automobile day after day to the Goldwyn studio, where several films of his authorship had been shot, and where he was presently preparing *Souls for Sale*, which had odd elements of autobiography and which he would direct: the story of a despotic husband who ill-treats his wife, forcing her to leave him; jumping off a train, she meets a movie sheik on horseback, who romantically abducts her and carts her off to Hollywood, where she becomes an extra and rises to featured status, seeing the stars at work.

Rupert was equally cruel to his wife. Prohibition annoyed her; Rupert confiscated the bootleg liquor that she bought on the sly. Sonny witnessed agonizing scenes in which the unhappy Adelaide would, in desperation, drink perfume from a bottle or steal her husband's hair tonic, which would result in stomach attacks and days in bed.

Sonny was prepared to put up with anything to be able to stand on the sidelines of a picture in production, feasting his eyes on the handsome performers, invading the projection room to make copious notes which he would hand to his astonished uncle, or besieging crew members with countless questions about lighting, set construction, and location shooting.

For the rest of his life, even into old age, Howard was a voyeur in love with movies. With Rupert's stepson Rush and Dudley Sharp on visits from Houston and the East Coast, he spent countless hours in motion picture theaters.

An influence on him was the dashing, handsome young John

Monk Saunders, the fiancé of Rush's sister Avis. Dressed to the teeth, suntanned, athletically built, Saunders was the heterosexual idol of Hughes's life. But Saunders had a flaw: he was filled with guilt because, although he had trained as a flyer in World War I, the conflict had ended before he could join his young companions and serve in the American flying corps in France. He had taken to drink to assuage his misery at not having proved himself a man in aerial combat; he overcompensated by describing imaginary scenes of his wartime heroism to Sonny. He was emerging as an author, writing stories about the kind of hero he longed to have been.

On January 8, 1922, there was a big family event: Saunders and Avis were married in a society wedding at politician George Creel's estate in Ossining, New York. Rupert gave the bride away. Oddly, neither Howard Sr. nor Allene nor Sonny made their way to New York for the ceremony.

Then Sonny, who was back at Thacher, received devastating news. His mother had suffered a hemorrhage from her womb, which, given her hypochondriac nature, may have suggested to her that she had cancer. (An earlier problem, following Sonny's birth, had resulted in a diagnosis that she would never have another child.) On March 29, Bo Hughes cabled his son that Allene was desperately sick and that he was to meet up with Uncle Rupert in Los Angeles and then come to Houston at once.

That morning, Allene was admitted to Houston's Baptist Hospital for a curettement of her womb. It was risky, because she had a shaky heart, although before she was put under the anesthetic, it was found that there was no evidence of the pulmonary or nephritic diseases that she had suspected. As the gas anesthesia was administered, her pulse stopped. At the age of thirty-eight, she was dead.

Sonny didn't find out until he reached Los Angeles. Busy shooting *Souls for Sale,* Rupert was unable to accompany the devastated Howard to Houston, but instead sent his wife with the boy. Aunt Adelaide's drunkenness cannot have been a consolation in Sonny's grief, but he loved her, and she was sweet and motherly to him on the agonizing train journey.

As many family members as could be mustered at short notice attended the funeral. Bo was handed a note by Allene's lawyer, which she had left in the event she should not survive surgery. It read: "If I die, please remember I have loved you. I forgive you for your affair with Eleanor Boardman." At that moment, Eleanor Boardman was starring in Rupert Hughes's *Souls for Sale*.

Bo was out of his mind with grief and guilt. He was appalled by the idea of Sonny's being left without a mother. Since 1919, Allene's youngest sister, Annette, had been living with the couple during their stays in Houston, housesitting for them in their frequent absences in Los Angeles. In Sonny's presence, Bo asked Annette if she would do him a great kindness. Would she postpone her marriage to her fiancé, the thriving young doctor Frederick Lummis, and help to raise the boy? This would mean separating from the man she loved for over a year and moving to California. With almost saintly selflessness, Annette agreed.

Sonny adored her, and was happy to accept her as his surrogate mother. But now Bo acted badly. Back at the Ambassador Hotel, he decided to take Sonny out of Thacher. This removal from yet another school was extremely damaging to the boy's education. But in his misery Bo forgot that consideration. He wrote pleading letters to Sherman Thacher, begging him to understand, saying that his loneliness was unbearable and that he must have Sonny as his companion, with Aunt Annette as foster parent.

Thacher was annoyed as well as sympathetic: He felt, correctly, that this withdrawal was a serious mistake. Bo tried to bribe him with a radio set and other gifts, but they were sternly refused. Finally, Bo paid an entire year of school fees as an acceptable compensation.

Instead of holing up at the Ambassador in a state of mourning, Bo decided to take his son off on an elaborate grief-assuaging trip with Annette. Accompanied by Judge Felix Hughes and his wife Jean and, briefly, Frederick Lummis, they took the train to San Antonio to visit friends, and thence to Del Monte, California, where they stopped at the luxurious Del Monte Lodge, for the golfing tournament. Back in Los Angeles, Annette moved into the Vista Del Arroyo Hotel in Pasadena to be close to Sonny, who was admitted to the California Institute of Technology. Since he had not graduated from any school, nor was he of sufficient age, his admission had to be arranged through a bribe. Bo made a handsome donation under the table; the Institute's official records only show that Howard took extramural courses with a teacher in solid geometry.

By the late summer of 1923, Rupert and Adelaide Hughes were locked in bitter quarrels, which greatly distressed Sonny. Had she found out about his incestuous relationship with his uncle? Adelaide was operated on for cancer in August. Accompanied by a nurse, she left on a freighter for a recuperative cruise to the Orient. A typhoon struck the vessel en route to Yokohama, and she became hysterical. When she was in Japan, an earthquake wrecked her hotel, and she barely escaped. At midnight on December 13, after writing out a long, affectionate message to her husband, complaining of severe earache from a mastoid condition, she hanged herself from a luggage strap in her cabin. The real reason for her suicide was that Rupert was having an affair with a much younger woman, the actress Elizabeth Patterson Dial, to whom he had given a small part in *Souls for Sale.*

Sonny was shattered; this was a blow that came all too soon after his mother's death. Then came an even worse shock. On January 14, 1924, while conferring with his sales manager, S. T. Brown, at his office in Houston, Bo stood up at his desk, clutching his arm in intense pain. He crashed to the floor. A doctor was fetched, but it was too late. He had died of an embolism of an artery. He was fifty-three years old.

Once again, Sonny had to make a ghastly, depressing trip to a funeral in Houston. But, saddened though he was after this third death in a row, he acted with typical swiftness once his father was buried. Commanding as ever, he decided that, though only eighteen, he would assume control of the Hughes Tool Company (as it was called now) and the production of the Hughes tool bit, which was now earning the company substantial returns; he would tolerate no interference with his ambitions. Bo had not altered his will since 1913. He left one quarter to his wife, whose share, automatically, would now go to Sonny, one quarter to Sonny himself, and one twelfth each to Judge Hughes, Jean, and his sister Greta Witherspoon, who actually had been dead for almost five years. (A small codicil, made in 1919, accorded her twelfth to Bo's brother Felix.) He left nothing, pointedly, to his detested brother Rupert.

For the purposes of probate, the total amount of the estate was, surprisingly, less than a million dollars: $871,518. Sonny filed a petition with the court, insisting that his disabilities as a minor be removed. It was, he stated, desirable to increase the fixed capital by improving the capital stock and declaring a dividend. He hired attorney R. C. Kuldell to handle the matter. Drawn up right away, but not filed until December 26, 1924, the petition stated: "Howard Hughes,

Jr., represents himself as sober, studious, a non-drinker and smoker, and as moral. His chief desire is to build up his father's business and help worthy enterprises and to assist in the education of deserving young men and women.''

While he was waiting for the authorization to act as administrator, Sonny had to pay off a large number of his father's debts. The accounts showed colossal sums expended on jewelry, clothes, and other indulgences, probably for Eleanor Boardman. Sonny also had to fight Rupert, who, as the oldest surviving sibling, demanded that he be allowed to run the estate. This disillusioned Sonny, although actually Rupert's request was reasonable, and he fought Rupert to the last ditch, finally winning on December 26. He decided to buy out his grandparents and his uncle Felix, all of whom held him for ransom for every last cent.

It was important to him to cement his position as a responsible young man. He hit on the bold decision to get married. After surveying the available crop of Houston belles, he decided on his school companion, Ella Rice. She was ideally eligible, since she had money, was good-looking, was an expert on a dance floor, and didn't drink. She was pliable, submissive, sweet. With great shrewdness, Sonny left Cal Tech, Pasadena, enrolled at Houston's Rice Institute, which had been founded by Ella's ill-fated great-uncle, and installed Annette and her husband, Dr. Frederick Lummis, in his father's Yoakum mansion, ostensibly so that they could be his surrogate parents while he attended Rice. This series of chess moves shows that, by his late teens Sonny, now known to everyone as Howard, had learned the executive art of manipulating people for his own advantage. He was already a user.

The Rices were no less keen to arrange the match than the Hugheses. The linking of two dynasties would be highly advantageous. Furthermore, Ella's sister Libby was married to William S. Farish, a friend of Bo's in the early oil-boom days, and the wealthy founder of Standard Oil of New Jersey. Thus, no less than three major dynasties of money and power would be linked in one go.

Howard had to introduce his fiancée to an astonishing ménage which had established itself in a sprawling, T-shaped Spanish house at 204 North Rossmore Avenue, Los Angeles. His stern grandfather, retired Judge Felix, and his grandmother Jean, the terrifying "Mimi," owned it, occupying separate bedrooms and addressing each other with grim formality as "Judge Hughes" and "Mrs.

Hughes." Mimi, who was in her eighties, spent most of her time tending to her collection of stuffed parrots or learning Portuguese loudly. The couple quarreled constantly. Mimi snarled at Sonny that his two favorite subjects, movies and airplanes, must never be discussed in her home.

To the fury of Rush and Avis Hughes, Rupert conducted his affair with Elizabeth Patterson Dial flagrantly under his parents' roof. The walls rang with his lectures on every subject under the sun. Uncle Felix was there, too; he was messily divorcing his wife Adella, had moved permanently from Cleveland, and was sleeping with the movie star Ruth Stonehouse. Felix filled the air with song as he trained boys and girls for the concert stage; to add to the din of quarrels, rages, singing bouts, perpetual scales being played, and slamming doors, Avis was always arguing with her husband John Monk Saunders over his drunkenness, and Rush, who was involved with the singer Marion Harris, was souping up automobiles noisily in the garage. Marion was forbidden entrée to the house. She had been divorced and—horror of horrors—performed in nightclubs. Is it any wonder that, stuck in this expensive bedlam of family quarrels, Howard Hughes, Jr., longed for the isolation and seclusion that would later mark his life?

There was opposition from Annette and Frederick Lummis to Sonny's getting married. They seemed to be the only holdouts in the family, finally yielding because of fear (Annette said later) that Howard would yield to "vampire" movie actresses.

The wedding was set for June 4, 1925. The ever-restless, manic Howard pulled out of Rice without graduating. He signed a will on May 31, leaving his fiancée half a million dollars and his aunt Annette $100,000 and the house on Yoakum. The other members of his family were left smaller legacies, with the notable exception of Uncle Rupert and Rupert's new bride (since December), Patterson Dial. Ever mindful of his mother's concern over contagious disease, he laid it down that a Howard Hughes Research Laboratory should be built in her memory, devoted to developing antitoxins and other cures, with Dr. Frederick Lummis heading up the board of trustees.

In bowers of roses, Howard Hughes, Jr., married Ella Rice in William and Libby Farish's newly built mansion at 10 Remington Lane, Houston. Dudley Sharp was best man; Libby was matron of honor. With typical eccentricity, no inhabitant of the Hughes zoo on

North Rossmore Avenue bothered to attend. Dr. Peter Gray Sears of Christ Church presided.

The arranged marriage dissolved into a miserable relationship. Howard was neglectful, irritable, cross, critical, and fault-finding. The honeymoon in New York was wretched. Exactly why, having achieved his purpose in convincing everyone that he was an adult by virtue of marrying at a tender age, Howard so ill-treated his wife is unclear. It is possible that he had entered into an agreement with her that the marriage would be platonic, and then she made certain demands. Significantly, when he bought a Rolls-Royce in Manhattan, he didn't allow her to share it, but bought her a separate one; with great extravagance, since he could easily have obtained the vehicles in Los Angeles, he had them shipped out to the West Coast. On arrival, he decided to sell his own Rolls because he was aware of air pollution and didn't wish to add to it. He rebuilt a 1907 water-driven Stanley Steamer, and rode it around proudly, shouting at automobile drivers that they should abandon gasoline and flying a pirate flag with a skull and crossbones.

He had developed a sharp, hectoring voice, which, apparently, was caused by the increasing deafness inherited from his father and paternal grandfather. His yellings added to the cacophony of the North Rossmore zoo, where Ella was understandably unhappy. By the late fall of 1925, even he had had enough. He moved with Ella, requesting a twin-bedded suite, into the Ambassador Hotel.

His habits were clearly formed. Perhaps because of the misery of seeing his beloved Aunt Adelaide drunk all the time, he refused to touch a drop of liquor, even beer or wine. If forced to attend a party, he would carry the wineglass with him to the bathroom and empty it into the toilet. He declined to smoke; in those days, in society, the ladies and gentlemen parted after dinner, the men to enjoy cigars and the ladies to engage in light conversation. He would sit among the men, coughing at the fumes, and then find an excuse to withdraw early from the room. As a result, he was a laughing-stock, and there were those who dared declare him less than a man.

He became exceedingly finicky over his food. He stuck religiously to a certain diet. In the morning, he would have three eggs scrambled in milk; he would nibble at a sandwich at lunchtime, before he took off to the Wilshire Country Club golf course; at teatime he devoured chocolate chip cookies; and for dinner he would have a butterfly steak, cooked medium rare, twelve peas, no more and no less, which he would thread through a fork; if one pea were too large for it, he would send for the waiter and have it replaced from the kitchen. Dessert was always a single scoop of vanilla ice cream. He did not indulge in coffee; his refusal to take caffeine, combined with his rejection of all leafy vegetables, caused him lifelong constipation. He would spend an alarming number of hours on the toilet, reading *The Wall Street Journal* or company reports, current newspapers and magazines, but never books. To the annoyance of his various assistants, he would insist on having business conferences in the bathroom, where their olfactory senses were assaulted.

His sexual habits were various. He preferred intermamary intercourse—making love between a woman's breasts—or fellatio to vaginal intromission. With men, he also preferred oral sex. He was a thoughtless, dispassionate lover, seeking only control. His sexual partners were not so much lovers as hostages, prisoners, or victims of his will; he had to dominate in everything. His boyish, vulnerable charm, handsome, underfed, lanky look, and atmosphere of power and money captivated all of his sexual partners, but he left no echoes behind.

## CHAPTER THREE

# Taking Off

O n Thanksgiving Day, 1925, Hughes hired a Man Friday. The sharp, bright, muscular young Noah Dietrich was the son of an itinerant Lutheran minister; dropping out of high school at fourteen, the energetic youth had traveled the country as cashier, auditor, and real estate salesman, becoming a certified accountant in 1923. He answered Hughes's advertisement for a bookkeeper and general factotum. Hughes liked him immediately, seeing a willing servant, and hired him as his executive assistant on the spot, without references, moving him, his wife, and his daughter into an adjoining suite at the Ambassador.

He immediately assigned Dietrich a task. He had become irritated by the limitations of the stockbroking services supplied by the hotel, and decided he must have a ticker-tape machine of his own, which could bring him the quotations from Wall Street. Individuals in those days were forbidden to have ticker tapes. Dietrich applied to Western Union and was told the installation was out of the question. The Bell Telephone Company was equally adamant. Hughes told Dietrich to disregard these restrictions and do what he asked. The accountant, feeling extremely stressed, suddenly had a brain wave: looking up at the Wilshire Boulevard streetcar poles, he noticed that they had unused insulators. Observed with a team of electricians up ladders in the middle of the night, he was ordered by the police to desist. In desperation, he went to the streetcar administrators to get a permit. At first, they refused him. But after some greasing of palms he was able to join the citizens' telegraph pole line association, and began stringing the lines. Again, he was blocked by red tape. Desperate by now, he tried to set up a direct telephone link across the street to a specially rented office, but this plan also fell down. Finally, he was forced to admit failure. Irritably, Hughes got through to a Western Union executive, promised him a parcel of shares in the Hughes Tool Company, and a special ticker-tape machine was put, against the law, into his suite.

Hughes fretted constantly over whether he should file his tax returns in California or Texas. Finally, he settled on Texas and moved with Ella to Houston. They stayed with Dr. Frederick and Annette Lummis at the Hughes family house on Yoakum until spring.

Days after he returned to Los Angeles, Hughes, now twenty, was stricken with spinal meningitis. Ella had gone to New York, to stay with her sister Libby and brother-in-law Bill Farish, in their Park Avenue apartment. Noah Dietrich telephoned her, begging her to come back. Reluctantly, since Hughes had beaten her black and blue in a recent quarrel, she did. By now, Dietrich had moved the sick man into a newly rented home, a big, handsome Spanish-style house at 211 Muirfield Road, a short distance from North Rossmore, and next door to the Wilshire Country Club. No sooner had Ella arrived, nervously saying to Dietrich, "Am I safe?", than she saw an actress running out the back door. Despite the fact that he was recovering from meningitis, Hughes had been bedding a young girl.

Who was she? Noah Dietrich was discreet about this in his memoirs, but in 1971 he told this author that she was a teenaged future star, the blonde and slender Carole Lombard. She was making her name as a comedienne, and would soon be busy throwing custard pies for the movie-maker Mack Sennett. Lombard was ambitious, humorous, wittily diffident; she used the F-word like a longshoreman, and was known as a slangy, sisterly mate to men, as well as sexy lover; Hughes, as always, liked oral sex, and she was noted for her skill at fellatio.

At the time, Hughes deepened his friendship with John Monk Saunders and his wife Avis. Encouraged by the publisher George Putnam of G. P. Putnam's Sons, who later married the flyer Amelia

Earhart, Saunders was writing stories about flying in which Howard took a keen interest. Spurred on by Putnam, Saunders embarked on a screen story which would influence Hughes more than any other: *Wings.* Putnam's World War I experiences as an aviator were poured into the story, which dealt with the friendly rivalry between two men in heroic exploits and the pursuit of a pretty girl. Paramount production chief Jesse L. Lasky bought Saunders's property (without knowing that Saunders was having an affair with Mrs. Lasky) and embarked on the subject as the most elaborate and expensive picture in the studio's history.

Hughes was furious that Saunders had not brought him the material, as he himself was possessed by the idea of making an aviation movie. He was determined to get revenge by fashioning a picture that would go beyond the limits of *Wings.*

That summer, Hughes met another keen golfer at the Wilshire Country Club, the handsome and powerfully-built young movie star Ralph Graves. They liked to skeet-shoot together as well as golf. Graves had just messily divorced the actress Marjorie Seaman, and he, the incorrigible Rush, and Howard, despite his romantic involvement with Carole Lombard, all chased girls together.

Graves wanted to become a director of his own films. One day at the club, he made Hughes fall over laughing as he acted out all of the parts in a story he had written, *Swell Hogan,* about a tramp who helps orphan children in the Bowery. When Graves, who had expertly imitated a dog, a cat, and several male and female children, successfully mimicked a crying baby, Hughes was delighted and asked Graves how much the picture would cost to make. Graves replied, "Fifty grand."

Hughes told him to go ahead. The idea of being a producer thrilled him. He could get his feet wet while he was planning his aerial epic. He took over a run-down studio and, when Graves found it difficult to direct himself, cranked the camera himself. "He was like a kid with a new toy," Noah Dietrich said later.

According to Dietrich, Hughes appeared in one scene dressed as a hobo, unshaven, in rags. His fantasy as a rich young man was to be a tramp, to ride the rails in freight cars, to stop worrying about the stock market, to be a man among free men. It was a dream he would fulfill one day.

The budget on *Swell Hogan* escalated rapidly and, finally, doubled; Graves was completely at sea, and Hughes, when he saw the rough cut, realized he had made a mistake. He scrapped the picture. But he had learned much: he could take a camera apart and put it together again; he knew about lighting; he discovered he had an unexpected skill in the editing room.

*Wings* continued to obsess him. He ran into a sex-mad Irish-American charmer, director Marshall Neilan, who had risen from itinerant orange-picker to successful handler of Mary Pickford and other major stars. Neilan told Hughes that in 1916 in Havana, Cuba, he had heard a story about two brothers fighting over a woman in the World War I air force. Hughes asked him to sketch out a draft of the story. Meanwhile, the two men whipped up a nonsensical movie about five New York actors who adopt a baby girl, called it *Everybody's Acting,* and rushed it out with record speed. Surprisingly, it did quite well.

In the last months of 1926, Hughes's relationship with Ella deteriorated still further. She spent more and more time with her sister Libby in New York; she traveled to Houston to be with her family there; in Los Angeles, she joined the Junior League and the Pasadena Country Club, having nothing in common with the film world and deeply offended (despite her platonic relationship with Hughes) by Carole Lombard's presence on the scene. Hughes acted with absurd possessiveness toward her; though he had established no genuine rights over her, he had insisted, from the days at the Ambassador Hotel, that she be accompanied everywhere by a female chaperone. When she finally refused this arrangement, he fretted and bullied.

At the beginning of 1927, at a Charleston party at the Ambassador Hotel, Hughes met, and became fascinated by, the pink-cheeked, plump young Russian-American director Lewis Milestone. Milestone had served in the aerial camera division of the U.S. Army Air Corps, and was able to give Hughes and Neilan many tips on their aviation story in progress. He talked Hughes into letting him make *Two Arabian Knights,* a story about a pair of roughnecks who escape, disguised as Arabs, from a World War I German prison camp and are shipped off to Arabia; they meet a gorgeous Tunisian girl on the boat.

Hughes liked the knockabout comedy of the story and made a deal with Jesse L. Lasky to release the picture. He plunged $500,000 of his company's money into the production, and cast in it Louis Wolheim, William Boyd, and Mary Astor. According to Milestone,

Hughes inserted certain off-color sexual gags into the film. At one stage, Wolheim is seen milking a goat; when the white liquid squirts out, he announces, with a swishy hand gesture, "It's a *male* goat!" Boyd kisses a veiled figure in a sultan's harem; he pulls off the veil, and it's a eunuch. In a title, Wolheim says to Boyd, "This sultan guy sure is strange. Not all the girls in his harem are girls!"

Hughes insisted on tough realism in making the movie. There is a scene in which Mary Astor almost drowns. Instead of shooting it in a studio tank, he had Milestone set the scene in the freezing, oil-slicked waters of San Pedro harbor, so he could use his yacht, the *Ranger,* as a floating studio. Mary Astor's gold-beaded gown weighed her heavily, and she could barely swim. Cruelly, Hughes insisted she be dunked off the boat again and again, gurgling as though she were about to drown, until she almost did drown. The crew pulled her back, time and time again, dripping wet; they gave her shots of brandy, and Hughes massaged her—with understandable enthusiasm, since she was gorgeous—and then dunked her again.

Milestone told me, many years later, that Hughes showed an abnormal degree of interest in the sequence, running it in his private screening room between two and four A.M., dwelling voyeuristically on Mary Astor's body as her gown, soaking, clung to it. It was the beginning of his lifelong approach to movie-making. This was his way of indulging his sexual fantasies; by making movies himself, he could actually create his own wet dreams.

By the time *Two Arabian Knights* was finished, Neilan was completing the script for the aviation picture, which he called *Hell's Angels.* Harry Behn, who had written King Vidor's masterpiece *The Big Parade,* came in to rewrite some scenes and add others. Hughes introduced an unexpected element into the story: whereas in *Wings,* which was in the final stages of production, dealt with clean-cut, uncomplicated American heroes, *Hell's Angels* would show more complex characters. One brother, Monte Rutledge, is shown as weak, cowardly and selfish; the other, Roy, is a deadly prig and a snob. Their lady love, illustrative of Hughes's attitude to women, was a worthless, cruel teaser and layabout who plays one brother against the other and betrays them both with another man. Hughes also, to avoid too close a comparison with *Wings,* switched the locale to England, making the characters British and using the Royal Flying Corps' attacks on Germany as the theme.

Hughes realized that, if he was going to earn the aviators' respect, he would have to be a flyer himself. So he began lessons at Clover Field. Assigned the twenty-one-year-old Chuck La Jotte, he took one look at this fresh-faced boy and groaned, "He can't train me. He's too young!" The more experienced pilot Moye Stephens trained him instead. He spent several months in lessons every morning, yelling out above the propeller and engine noise, constantly insisting on answers to technical questions and irritating Stephens with his deafness.

Through J. B. Alexander, sales manager for the American Aircraft Company, which owned Clover Field, Hughes met the legendary Frank Tomick, the great and fearless pilot and aerial stunt coordinator for *Wings*. Hughes put Tomick in charge of obtaining, on an open budget, every British and German aircraft he could get his hands on. The *Wings* production crew had, of course, commandeered most of the American planes.

It was no easy matter to find foreign aircraft in the United States in those days. In many cases, planes had to be repainted or remodeled to provide simulated versions of the actual craft. Curtiss Jennies were designed to look like British Avros; a Sikorsky had to be faked to resemble a German Gotha bomber.

By August, Hughes owned about forty-five airplanes. He bought a cow pasture near Van Nuys and named it Caddo Field, after his father's company at Shreveport and the Caddo Hotel, where he had spent so much of his babyhood. He hired a ground crew of some thirty-five men; he built hangars in administration buildings, whose design he personally supervised. He was a boy again, as fired with enthusiasm as he had been when he built the cabins in the woods at Camp Dan Beard and at the Thacher School at Ojai.

He snapped up land at Inglewood Field, today the site of the Los Angeles airport. There, he built an imitation headquarters of the British Royal Flying Corps. A vast acreage at Chatsworth, in the remote north of the San Fernando Valley, became the German flying base. He bought real estate in San Diego, Oakland, Santa Cruz, and other locations.

He began negotiations with German Zeppelin experts to come to Hollywood and build sets which would be exact replicas of the airships' interiors. They would bring with them charts of dirigibles, which could be used to create scale models of the exteriors.

Hughes worked nonstop, day and night, drafting storyboards on huge sheets of architect's paper for the aerial combat scenes. He fought with insurance companies to give him coverage, knowing full well the dangers many pilots would be subjected to. He began casting; he needed fearless men for the leading roles who would be able to do some of the flying themselves, with doubles performing the more difficult stunts. He borrowed Ben Lyon, currently under contract to First National, a handsome, witty, secretly bisexual (according to Quirk), devil-may-care man about town who was in the papers because he had spectacularly split with the Broadway musical star Marilyn Miller. Lyon was cast as the cowardly, insecure older brother; James Hall, a stolid, unexciting man, was cast as the priggish sibling. The beautiful Norwegian actress Greta Nissen would play the British aristocrat in love with both men.

It was unfortunate that Hughes did not have Lewis Milestone, with all of his rich experience of World War I, direct the movie. Instead, he unwisely took on Marshall Neilan, and then the inept Luther Reed, for the absurd reason that Reed had once been the aviation editor of a newspaper. Reed proved incompetent, and Hughes fired him, but scarcely improved on his clumsy technique. Shooting of *Hell's Angels* began on October 31, 1927, at the Metropolitan Studios in Hollywood. There was a thunderstorm that night; Hughes altered the script so that the scene took place in rain, and the actors were drenched. Hughes sadistically made them go through the scene again and again. Ben Lyon laughed the whole thing off, but James Hall was furious and came close to punching Hughes in the nose.

Hughes became a close friend of Ben Lyon. Lyon was a man after his own heart: free, immoral, irresponsible, always playing practical jokes. Lyon whisked Hughes off to parties, leaving his own romantic interest, Bebe Daniels, as stranded as Hughes's Carole Lombard. They picked up women, took them to Lyon's home, and made love to them as a foursome. Lyon took Hughes up to San Simeon, William Randolph Hearst's fabled ranch, where, again, they had the pick of gorgeous girls looking for screen breaks. At night, their sexual bouts were interrupted by loud roars . . . from the lions housed in the ranch's zoo.

Often, Hughes and Ben Lyon would go to Agua Caliente, just over the Mexican border, or to the gambling ships to play roulette and blackjack, sharing rooms. They loved to clown around. At one party, Hughes was photographed sitting coyly on Lyon's lap. They would photograph each other playing tennis or golf, and race each other in their Packard automobiles on dirt valley roads.

In shooting the picture, Hughes made sure that there were an extraordinary number of body and face shots of a glowing Adonis, John Darrow, the gay actor who played the part of a young German Zeppelin crew member in the story. According to Noah Dietrich, they were constantly in each other's company when Hughes was not with Ben Lyon; there is no evidence of an affair, but, given the fact that Darrow was a magnificent physical specimen, clear-skinned, broad-shouldered, muscular, an American dream of masculinity, Hughes, as a bisexual, would have to have been superhuman to have resisted this golden youth. A source told the author he is sure Darrow was Hughes's lover.

Hughes enjoyed the company of the *Hell's Angels* pilots. He spent evening after evening at the Caddo Field mess, exchanging dirty stories with the men, pitching horseshoes and playing poker. While the others drank bootleg liquor out of coffee cups, he would sip, to general friendly derision, lemonade. He built an outdoor wooden privy with his bare hands. Constipated as ever, he would sit in it for hours, sketching away at his plans for the combat scenes. One time, the pilots revved up an engine of a fighter plane and blew the hut over, leaving Howard furiously trouserless. In revenge, he set up a hydraulic device that would shoot water through a pipe into the septic tank and blast the waste upwards into the squatting men's rectums. In further revenge, the pilots drilled three joke penis holes in the wooden wall, a big one for flyer Frank Clarke, a medium-sized one for Frank Tomick, and a tiny one for Hughes. When he saw his name on the smallest one, Hughes was livid.

Since virtually all of the pilots were heterosexual, Hughes would never have dared approach them. But, according to biographer Lawrence Quirk, he would compel very young and inexperienced mechanics or their aides, men whose sexual desires were inhibited, to give him sexual satisfaction; he had a mania for the typical aircraft mechanic, who was muscular, clean-cut, athletic, and buyable. He must have paid them, in cash or advancement, because the likelihood is that accepting payment would (paradoxically) assuage their guilt.

Despite the fact that he was a novice, he insisted on showing off his prowess as a pilot. The men would try not to laugh as he showed them how to make particular flights. On one occasion, he was ir-

ritated when a pilot failed to lift a plane off the ground (the terrain
was too rough). Hughes screamed at him, "Goddammit, get out. I'll
show you how to do it!" He climbed into the cockpit, grabbed the
joystick, and the plane soared—only a hundred feet. Then it
crashed; Hughes got out, nursing a broken nose. The pilot took the
plane up and deliberately nosedived on Hughes, missing him by
inches. "He's trying to kill me!" Hughes screamed. Frank Tomick
said, "He's proving he's a good pilot. He could have killed you and
he didn't!" Hughes had to laugh.

Hughes used the pilots to fly him down to Palm Springs, where
Carole Lombard was staying, to continue his affair with her. He used
them for assignations in Santa Barbara and further north. At one
stage, he wanted to see two things in the same afternoon: a San
Gabriel Country Club golf tournament and an aerial stunt in which
a flyer would narrowly miss high-tension wires. His coach, Moye
Stephens, rushed him through the wild, far-flung expedition, and the
whole time Hughes was screaming his irritation at Stephens's slowness.

Shooting continued into 1928. In May, pilot Al Wilson had a
narrow escape. His plane, a Fokker D.VII, ran into thick fog. With
visibility nonexistent, Wilson had to bail out. He landed on the roof
of a house in Hollywood, spraining his back. The airplane crashed on
an open lot next to movie mogul Joseph Schenck's house at 7280
Hollywood Boulevard.

Hughes insisted on having massive cumulus cloud formations.
Lewis Milestone said, "He wanted to show the planes fucking the
clouds. The clouds full of rain reminded him of breasts full of milk."
Because the San Fernando Valley skies were clear, he shifted fifteen
planes to Oakland in June. It was November before the correct
formations appeared, but Hughes refused to withdraw the unit, a
decision which added enormously to the cost of the film.

There were several major accidents on the picture. One pilot
was killed when he hit high-tension wires; another ran out of gas and
flip-flopped into a field. A third tried to show off in a straight dive,
and his joystick got jammed. He was smashed to pieces. The worst
accident occurred when Hughes staged the crash of the Sikorsky
bomber. It was a very difficult stunt. The huge plane had to tailspin
to only a few feet from the ground; the pullout could be fearsomely
difficult. The leading stunt aviator, Dick Grace, refused to risk his
life for Hughes for less than $10,000; Frank Clarke also refused. Al

Wilson took on the task. The problem was that smoke had to pour from the tail. Wilson couldn't operate the controls and release the smoke pot at the same time. The eager young Phil Jones, who needed money for syphilis treatments, said he would undertake the task. The two men climbed in and took off in the plane to an altitude of 7,000 feet. Hughes watched intently.

Wilson nosedived the Sikorsky. But the wind pressure was too strong and tore off the fabric from the right wing and an engine cowl. Wilson managed to parachute out, but Jones was unable to struggle loose and was killed. Wilson was blamed for the accident. Hughes showed no emotional reaction: war, even in the movies, was war.

Meanwhile, Hughes was busy making other pictures. Despite his exhausting schedule, driving out to Caddo Field and other locations every morning, shooting from dawn to dusk, supervising the Zeppelin sequences at the studio, partying with Ben Lyon, making love with Carole Lombard on the weekends, Hughes found the energy— he was only twenty-three—to make *The Racket,* directed by Lewis Milestone, an exposé of Chicago gangsterdom, its villain, Scarsi, based on the scarred Al Capone. It was a forceful, violent movie that was cut to ribbons by censorship. Hughes fought with Will Hays, guardian of movie morals, and charged Paramount and Jesse Lasky with yielding to Hays's absurd restrictions: in telegram after telegram to the Paramount head offices in New York, he denounced the movie's mutilation and emasculation. He even carried the fight into court, charging that Hays was in the pay of corrupt politicians exposed by the movie and that the cutting of the picture created a dangerous political precedent. Paramount refused to support him, and he was forced to give up. The picture did well, but not sufficiently well to recoup his investment, and he had equally disappointing results with a subsequent picture, *The Mating Call,* based on a story by Rex Beach.

A further irritation occurred that June. Hughes took a picture of Ben Lyon seated on a log which had a sawn-off branch emerging, almost vertically, between his legs in the form of an erect penis. Hughes jokingly had Lyon send this picture to his female fans. One of them turned out to be a fourteen-year-old girl, Caroline Black, of San Bernardino. The girl's father was angry, charging Hughes and Lyon with attempting to corrupt an innocent child; he called every woman's club in Southern California, demanding that they embargo Hughes productions, and took the matter directly to the District

Attorney of San Bernardino County, who, in turn, sent an angry letter to the defendants. Black sued Hughes, who settled for over $100,000. The obscene pictures were discontinued.

A furor blew up when Albert Marco, Los Angeles vice king, copied a plot element in the picture. In the movie, the criminal played by Louis Wolheim forces his chauffeur to take a rap for a murder charge. When Marco slew Santa Monica businessman Dominic Conterno and café entertainer Henry Judson, he also framed his chauffeur. Hughes was berated by the legal establishment for having put ideas in the minds of gangsters. He mustered support from San Francisco police chief Daniel J. O'Brien and from the Los Angeles authorities, while at the same time he formed connections with mobsters, who guaranteed him protection when he was threatened with being murdered for having presented the Mafia in an unfavorable light in the picture.

He began planning a movie version of the sinking of the *Titanic* in 1912, but became exhausted by efforts to lick the script into shape, and gave up the project. He became possessed by the idea that *Hell's Angels* would fail. Talkies had come in, following the huge success of Al Jolson in *The Jazz Singer,* and Hughes realized he would have to reshoot much of the picture with sound. *Wings* had been a great success with only some music and sound effects, but *Hell's Angels* would have to have talking characters. He scrapped all of his own silent dramatic footage and hired the currently successful homosexual British theater director James Whale to come to Hollywood to ensure authenticity in the scenes set in London and Oxford. He fired Greta Nissen because her Norwegian accent would make her part as a British aristocrat ludicrous. He replaced her with somebody almost equally inappropriate: the very young, slangy, coarsegrained, utterly American Jean Harlow, whom Ben Lyon had noticed as an extra in a new picture. Hughes wasn't impressed with her when he met her: her soon-to-be-legendary sexual allure did nothing for him. But she came over at the screen test with considerable erotic impact. She exuded a crude appeal that he instinctively knew would arouse men all over the world.

In his personal life, Hughes was as promiscuous as his movie hero, and considerably more adventurous. The rangy, handsome Randolph Scott arrived from Virginia with a letter of introduction to the Hugheses from his father, who had connections to the Gano family through stud farm ownerships. A footballer and engineer,

Scott was interested in becoming a member of Hughes's aeronautics staff. Hughes took one look at this beefy, six-foot, 195-pound athlete with the horsey face and lazy, self-indulgent awareness of his own beauty and decided he had to have him. He moved him, cruelly, into the house he shared with Ella. He risked his masculine image with the *Hell's Angels* pilots, whose attitude was that any "fairy" should be given a gun and an empty room to dispose of himself, and he risked a colossal scandal if Ella should mention this in the now pending divorce proceedings.

But he went ahead; he visited Scott often when Scott moved into a West Hollywood apartment. Scott was coolly indifferent to most people, using men and women to get ahead, but he seems to have felt at least some affection for Hughes, who pushed him into a movie career. Hughes—who was having some differences with Jesse Lasky at the time—asked Lasky if he would look the young man over at Paramount. Lasky saw what Hughes was talking about and hired him, figuring that his sex appeal and physique would compensate for the fact that he had all of the acting ability of a weighing machine.

Hughes had writer Howard Estabrook concoct new scenes for Harlow, including one in which she would seduce Ben Lyon in a flimsy negligee. He hired the poet Joseph Moncure March to write much of the dialogue. He had become fascinated by March's current best-seller made up of two narrative poems, "The Wild Party," the sensation of New York, which featured, daringly for the time, an orgy with both gay and straight sex, and "The Set-Up," an anti-Semitic picture of the boxing racket. "The Wild Party" fully reflected his own interest in kinky forms of sex, and the text illustrations of women with bare breasts profoundly stimulated him. A passage like this was amazingly daring for the time:

> Now Jackie stood back of Phil
> And his hands just wouldn't be still!
> One clutched Phil's shoulder:
> The other was bolder:
> It ran white fingers through his long, black hair
> Then fondled his throat
> And rested there . . .
> He bent down and kissed Phil on the lips.
>
> © Random House, Inc. 1993

In October, with the talkie version progressing slowly because of Jean Harlow's ineptitude and James Whale's painstaking but ill-fated attempts to give the British scenes some measure of realism (Harlow's American accent could not be corrected in time), Ella Hughes walked out of Howard's life for good. She came back from a long trip to Houston and found a woman's clothes (Carole Lombard's?) in her closet. Disgusted, furious, she went back to Houston and filed for divorce.

Hughes couldn't endure the fact that she had gone. Even though he had never loved her, had consistently betrayed her with other women, and had treated her with heartless contempt and indifference, the blow to his ego was considerable. He made a theatrical gesture. He sealed up her bedroom suite, which was at the other end of the house from his own, and left it in that condition for decades. Occasionally, he would send an aide in to check the plumbing, but then the suite would be sealed up again. It was as though he refused to acknowledge that Ella had ever left the house; even the few items of clothing, the china she used, and the pieces of soap and the perfume bottle she had left behind remained in the exact position they were in the day she moved out.

In the midst of shooting *Hell's Angels,* John Monk Saunders committed what Hughes felt was an act of betrayal by a friend and step-cousin. He sold a story of World War I pilots, *Dawn Patrol,* to Warner Bros. Hughes berated him for this; the two men exchanged punches, and Hughes, who was only 145 pounds to Saunders's strapping 186, wound up nursing a battered face. Hughes called Warners producer Hal Wallis at three or four A.M., morning after morning, yelling that Wallis had no right to be hiring planes he hadn't finished using, offering twice the money to the owners. He was determined to get hold of the script.

He bribed one of Wallis's secretaries to steal a copy. Another secretary tipped off Wallis that she was to deliver the script to Randolph Scott's apartment—a very daring and reckless choice of location. Wallis hired two private eyes to slip into the apartment with the manager's collusion and hide in a closet. Noah Dietrich arrived and the girl walked in. The detectives grabbed both Dietrich and the girl. Wallis sued Hughes for theft; Hughes counteracted with a plagiarism suit. Both cases were settled out of court.

## CHAPTER FOUR

# New Adventures

By 1929, Hughes had become established as a filmmaker of great enterprise and daring, even before *Hell's Angels* was finished, but only with the public; the heads of the film industry, dominated by the great studios MGM, Warners, and Paramount, as a whole detested him, not least because of his gross anti-Semitism, his refusal to succumb to the controlling interests, and his mania for independence. Though his publicists strove to give the impression he was a master of money and a captain of industry, he was incapable of handling his tool factories and left Noah Dietrich to build his empire from the newly revamped oil drilling tool bit. Dietrich, not he, marketed the bit and its derivations worldwide with amazing skill and ruthlessness, persuading the Arab nations to adopt it without exception, slicing through competitors in the bidding, even making deals with the Russians, whose Communist system Hughes abhorred.

Hughes spent the money like water, refusing to listen to Dietrich's anxious urgings to compromise. Planes, sex, and partying in those pre-reclusive years absorbed his energies as Dietrich raised the less than a million he had inherited to some $50, then $75, million between 1925 and 1930. When balance sheets and tax charges reached him, he tossed them impatiently aside. Had he been the industrialist he was credited with being, he would have lost everything; had he refused to pay taxes as he wished, he would have been imprisoned. Not even the Wall Street crash, which cost Hughes about $5 million, could interrupt his headlong work on *Hell's Angels*. It continued until December, 1929; at the last minute, he decided to splurge several hundred thousand dollars on a previously unplanned sequence showing the successful advance of the American Sixth Brigade, toward the end of World War I. He snapped up as many as 1,700 extras for the scene, which took up less than half a minute on the screen.

He plunged into editing. James Whale was already off the picture: he began work on a screen version of *Journey's End*. So Hughes worked with his team of editors, learning as he went along. They were astonished by Hughes's grasp of screen construction. He mastered, almost overnight, the techniques of simultaneous sound recording, so that the roar of the Zeppelin over London, the crunch of bombs, the throbbing engines of a mass formation take-off of German airplanes, all were dubbed brilliantly under his and the technicians' guidance. The total cost of the picture, including the promotional campaign, turned out to be $4 million, making *Hell's Angels* one of the two most expensive pictures in history up to that time (the other was MGM's *Ben-Hur*).

The movie ran for several hours; in the long run, only a fraction of it was used. But the result was splendid: Hughes ran the finished cut over and over again, narcissistically marveling at his own creation. He seemed oblivious to the improbable re-creation of British society, the awkward scenes in a German beer hall, with a waitress speaking in a French accent, the clumsiness of the still amateurish Jean Harlow. The aerial sequences, he knew, lifted the picture into greatness. The Zeppelin nosing its way through artificially simulated clouds, the crew dropping through a hatch to their deaths to lighten the ballast when the British fighter planes were in pursuit, the massive dogfight in the second half, the crash of the Sikorsky/Gotha bomber—all of these surpassed his expectations. He brimmed over with congratulations to both his friends the pilots and the technical crew.

In this exciting period, Hughes split with Carole Lombard, who had never forgiven him for not casting her in the Harlow role in the picture. They had a series of violent quarrels, startling the servants at Muirfield Road with the sound of shattering glass. On one of his trips to San Simeon with Ben Lyon, William Randolph Hearst's mistress, Marion Davies, introduced him to the stunning star Billie Dove. She was twenty-eight years old, a former artist's model and Ziegfeld Follies dancer, and was regarded as the most beautiful woman in the movies. She had dark hair, enormous, lustrous eyes and cupid-bow lips; her body was regarded as perfect by directors and cinematographers. She had made a particular splash in Douglas Fairbanks, Sr.'s, early color movie, *The Black Pirate.* She had recently been appearing in a series of pictures for Alexander Korda.

When she met and fell in love with Hughes, she was inconveniently married to the rough and tough director Irvin Willat. Brutish, muscular, an expert boxer and wrestler, Willat had no finesse, charm, or social graces. He imposed on her constantly; like Hughes, he was a control freak who believed no woman was capable of making decisions for herself. The moment Dove began dating Hughes, she separated from Willat; at the same time, Ella announced her official separation from Hughes in Houston.

When Willat discovered that Billie Dove was determined to marry Hughes (who proposed to her at the Del Monte Lodge, scene of his childhood visits, that winter), Willat decided he would not grant her a divorce. He would, he told her, fight her to the last ditch in the courts; Hughes was appalled, dreading the publicity and realizing that if Ella successfully charged him with adultery, she could possibly walk off with half his fortune. He settled on a characteristic solution. He decided he would buy Billie Dove from Willat. He called Willat, asking him how much he wanted to allow a divorce to go through on the grounds of mental and physical cruelty. Willat asked for half a million dollars. Hughes, after an ugly, protracted negotiation, got him down to $325,000. Willat said he would not take a check; the money must be delivered to him in cash in thousand-dollar bills.

Hughes told Noah Dietrich to get the money. He obtained a cashier's check and took it to the Federal Reserve Bank, packed the bills into a large suitcase and drove to the office of Hughes's lawyer Neil McCarthy. McCarthy counted them, and then called Willat, who arrived to pick up the cash.

Despite the fact that he had gotten what he wanted, Hughes despised Willat to the end of his life as less than a man. When this author asked Willat in 1971 if he had any remorse over the matter, Willat said, "I should have stuck Hughes for a half million."

Not content with buying Billie Dove from her husband, Hughes bought her contract from Jack Warner at the First National studios. Nervous about Billie Dove's rather high-pitched voice, which might ruin her in talkies, Warner was happy to let her go, but held out for $250,000. He deceived Hughes into thinking she had great value and he was about to renew her contract. Hughes paid Warner the money and her agent $85,000 for her services for five movies. It was a decision he would have cause to regret.

Billie Dove announced she liked to go sailing. Hughes had recently sold the *Ranger,* and instructed Dietrich to find him another boat immediately. The 171-foot, diesel-motored *Hilda* was ideally suitable. Owned by Charles Boldt, a New York multimillionaire, who had originally named it for Eleanor Boardman's husband King Vidor, it had been given to Boldt's wife in a divorce settlement. The asking price was just under half a million dollars. Hughes haggled with Mrs. Boldt through Dietrich; when Billie Dove announced that she particularly wanted to take a weekend trip, Hughes gave in and paid $350,000 through the Caddo Company, although he later learned he could have gotten the boat for $75,000 less if he had waited until Monday.

Skeet shooting, swimming off the boat, lying in the sun, Hughes relaxed with Billie after the enormous strain of completing *Hell's Angels.* The following Monday, he was back at the office, planning the premiere. He decided to stage the most lavish opening of any movie to date; he made a deal with showman Sid Grauman, owner of Grauman's Chinese Theater, not only to open the picture, but to handle its nationwide exhibition. He confirmed an earlier deal with Joe Schenck at United Artists to distribute the movie.

Hughes was as feverishly involved in the advertising and promotion of the picture as he had been in its production. He slashed through contact sheets of photographs in their entirety, and tore lobby display posters in half if they did not appeal to him. Not a still went through for newspaper or magazine use without his personal approval. He forbade any advance previews, any interviews with the stars before the movie was released, and every detail of the plot was hidden from reporters. When the zealous editor of the Los Angeles *Examiner* insisted on invading the Metropolitan studios in person to pick up information, Hughes called the newspaper's owner, William Randolph Hearst, and had the man removed.

The giant premiere took place on May 27, 1930. Hughes and Sid Grauman had been meeting for weeks to work out the details of this spectacular event. Hughes and Billie Dove (he in black tie, she in a clinging white dress) preceded a galaxy of stars into the theater, which was flanked by airplanes. Searchlights pierced the night sky. Fifty planes flew in formation overhead, drastically affecting the on-the-spot radio broadcasts as gushing announcers interviewed Ben Lyon, James Hall, Jean Harlow, Douglas Fairbanks, Sr., Mary Pickford, Charlie Chaplin, and the other celebrities.

The theater curtain had been painted with a replica of a fighter aircraft. An elaborate stage show preceded the main attraction. The Abbott Dancers, the Albertina Rasch Dance Company, and numerous comic and musical performers had the audience cheering through a series of high-powered scenes.

At last, the picture began. The Hollywood audience, on its best behavior because of the presence of the national press, could scarcely resist titters during the labored and ridiculous scenes in Germany and at Oxford. Reporters scribbled unfavorable notes. But once the bombing raid on London began, and the Zeppelin emerged, the crowd gasped and there were sporadic outbursts of clapping.

When the German crew dropped rigidly, one by one, into the night, the audience was riveted. To increase the effect, Hughes had arranged for the screen to open out for the whole sequence. When the intermission came, there was a hubbub of excited comment. People walked over to shout their congratulations to Hughes across the seats.

Part Two started. Once again, there was much feeble-minded material in which the British aristocrat acted by Jean Harlow played the two airmen brothers against each other. But from the moment when James Hall and Ben Lyon took off in the Sikorsky/Gotha to bomb the German ammunition dump, the picture soared again. The audience cried out with excitement as the German Flying Air Circus took off in V-formation, and when the bomber crashed in flames. The ending, in which one brother shoots the other to prevent certain secrets from leaking to the Germans, was a knockout. As soon as the curtains closed, the audience leapt to its feet and cheered for twenty minutes.

It was the greatest night of Howard Hughes's life. But instead of partying in celebration, he worked all night, making notes, calling in his editors to make trims and tighten certain scenes that had brought giggles. A week later he ran the picture, alone, at Grauman's. He had bought every seat in the house. Now he was satisfied.

Feeling his oats, he decided to secure a partnership in United Artists itself. He offered Joe Schenck $3 million to buy in, but ran into much irritating red tape in the negotiations and finally gave up. He took off to Seattle for another spectacular premiere. He laid the ground rules for the New York opening of *Hell's Angels*, which also proved to be colossal. On June 15, he and Billie Dove attended the second major event of the Hollywood year: Ben Lyon's marriage to Bebe Daniels. Over a thousand people were present at the dazzling nuptials at the Beverly Wilshire Hotel; scarcely a Hollywood name was absent. Hughes loaned the couple a plane so that Lyon could fly his bride to Del Monte for the honeymoon.

Everywhere *Hell's Angels* opened, there were brass bands and banners, searchlights and cheers. Almost overnight, Hughes was the most famous picture-maker in America. His greatest triumph was exhibiting the planes, diagrams, and photographs of *Hell's Angels* at the International Aeronautics Exhibition in Manhattan. Hughes sent publicist Lincoln Quarberg to every large and small town in the nation, plugging it relentlessly.

In October, Hughes moved into new facilities at the United Artists studio; he was too busy with the transfer of his furnishings and files to attend the opening in London. The premiere, on October 28, 1930, at the London Pavilion in Piccadilly Circus, was the most sensational in a decade. So vast was the crowd struggling to get in, that traffic was stopped for miles. The Duke and Duchess of York, later King George VI and Queen Elizabeth, the Prince of Wales, members of the nobility, and British air aces packed the theater to the last inch. The standing-room sections were filled six deep. Although the absurd American accents and false picture of Oxford brought gusts of laughter, the aerial scenes threw the normally restrained British audience into an uproar.

But despite the international success of Hughes's flawed masterpiece, it never earned its money back. Four million dollars was too much to recoup when ticket costs, away from the big cities, were a mere twenty-five cents. Soon, Hughes knew, the truth that he was a money-loser would come out. That would be the unforgivable sin in the motion picture industry. Therefore, he decided to try immediately to make outright winners on medium budgets. Overlooking her tinny voice, Hughes committed himself to turning Billie Dove into a major talkie star. He hired writers to cook up vehicles for her.

The first of these, *The Age for Love,* was a poorly written concoction dealing with the over-familiar theme of a woman torn between career and love. The second, *Cock of the Air,* was not much of an improvement. Hughes chuckled constantly over the title, mischieviously aware that he was taking on an army of puritans by using it. The original story was as weird as the title. Billie Dove would play an actress appearing in a stage production of *Joan of Arc.* When a young man, reminiscent of Hughes in his arrogant womanizing, suggests they go to a bedroom, she walks out and returns wearing a suit of armor in which she appears on the stage. He takes a can opener to her, and she skittishly disappears. Later, returning to his bed late one night, he is delighted to find a suit of armor in it. When he succeeds in opening it up, it is empty. Having taught the Don Juan a lesson, the star yields to his embraces. Censors reduced these intensely personal scenes.

Right afterward, Hughes made a picture, *Sky Devils,* which, in many ways, was as bizarre as his other movies. It starred Spencer Tracy and William Boyd; it was the story of two lifeguards who get mixed up with the Air Corps, and was full of off-color bisexual references. Tracy's nickname throughout the story is Hortense, there are drag scenes, and during a boxing match, Tracy calls out to the athletes, "Why don't you guys kiss?" At one stage, Tracy says to Boyd, "Be careful wearing that perfume around sailors." The movie was the last made by Hughes for several years, and was a failure at the box office.

By contrast with such childish ventures, Hughes embarked on two ambitious projects that year. The first of these was *The Front Page,* based on the celebrated stage play by Ben Hecht and Charles MacArthur. It evoked the vicious, unprincipled, dynamic life of a top newspaper; Hughes hired Lewis Milestone to match up the direction to Jed Harris's sensational production on Broadway. The picture was shot at record speed, in barely a month, on cramped, carefully authentic sets. Hughes was present throughout the shooting, worked with Milestone on the editing, and insisted on a driving, breakneck pace throughout. Starring Pat O'Brien and Adolphe Menjou, the movie came out to rapturous reviews. Hughes was furious when censor Will Hays insisted on certain trims when the dialogue became too racy, and when it was banned outright in Chicago (because of critical statements about Chicago politicians in the text).

Hughes quarreled violently with Joe Schenck for failing to give the picture sufficient weight in promotion. He charged that Schenck was favoring Sam Goldwyn's more heavyweight prestige productions. He and Lincoln Quarberg were of one mind as they screamed in telegrams and notes about "peanut politicians and racketing promoters" and "people of low mental and moral calibre" who were at United Artists' offices in New York. Never satisfied, Hughes plunged several hundred thousand dollars of his own money into additional advertising and electrical displays for the New York opening. He fussed endlessly over arrangements for the British release.

He embarked on an even more ambitious project: *Scarface*. He hired Ben Hecht to write the script. It was in many ways a spin-off from *The Racket*, though it was ostensibly drawn from a dime novel by the pseudonymous Armitage Traill. Originally, the book, like *Hell's Angels*, was about the conflict of two brothers, in this case a policeman and a crook. Hughes and Hecht decided instead to have only one protagonist: the Al Capone–like Tony Camonte, who rises from criminal's bodyguard to czar of the Chicago underworld. Camonte would be shown slaughtering everyone who stood in his way as he ran the beer rackets in South Chicago. Hughes hired the tough young Howard Hawks to direct the movie. Hard-bitten, cold, as detached and smart as Hughes himself, Hawks had much in common with the young tycoon. And he had the additional advantage that he knew several Chicago gangsters.

Hawks was a typical figure of the movie world, living out a fantasy life, the greatest spinner of lies in town, a Baron Munchausen in a city of compulsive liars. For years, he claimed that he was a great cocksman, when in fact he was inept, thoughtless, and inadequate in bed, and finally became impotent. He asserted that he swapped airplanes with Hughes and that Hughes let him pilot his planes: totally false. But one thing about him that was genuine about him was his talent. He made lean, tough pictures whose heroes, or anti-heroes, were flawed male animals asserting themselves against heavy odds with women or in acts of violence; they achieved on the screen what he could never achieve in bed.

Hughes hired the great Jewish theater star Paul Muni to play Camonte. He gave Ann Dvorak the role of Camonte's sister, and Karen Morley the part of Camonte's girlfriend.

Ben Hecht wrote the script in eleven days, for $11,000; Hughes had promised him a thousand dollars a day, and Hecht, instead of dragging out the schedule, foolishly rushed the writing through, thereby losing a small fortune. But Hecht won several thousand more from Hughes in games of backgammon on the train to New York.

Hecht, with Hughes's approval, based the story on the allegedly incestuous relationship between Cesare and Lucretia Borgia: Camonte's kid sister is terrified of his jealous rages when anyone touches her, and of his own far too sensual interest in her body. This was a daring theme for any period, and in 1931 it was sheer effrontery. It was typical of Hughes that, once again, he felt he could get away with anything; he himself was, of course, a victim of incest, and it is believed by many in the Hughes family that his bisexual Uncle Rupert had had an affair with Rupert's sister and Hughes's aunt, Greta; when Greta died, Rupert had gone into a coma from shock for three days and nights, scarcely the normal reaction of a brother.

Hughes and Hecht portrayed Camonte as a vain, anarchic, viciously contemptuous mass murderer. As his counterpart in a symphony of blood and bullets, Hughes and Howard Hawks cast the former professional dancing partner, crook, and gigolo George Raft (who had recently been in the sensational *Quick Millions*) as his oily-haired sidekick. Constantly tossing a nickel coin, smirking in the face of disaster, Raft would prove to be as unforgettable as Muni himself.

Releasing a sadistic desire for violence, Hughes egged Hawks on to add scene after scene of bloody slayings; he insisted on real bullets being used in the machine guns, one of which richocheted and injured a set visitor; Hughes had to pay a fortune to the man on top of the hospital bills. Hawks, who was equally filled with blood lust, was happy to carry out Hughes's wishes. Voyeuristic as ever, Hughes brought in three extra writers to add more suggestive sex scenes between Muni and his sister, played by Ann Dvorak. He brooded with intense erotic interest in the dark hours of the early morning over a sequence in which the two danced, very close, Dvorak's breasts almost bare. Later, he was forced to cut this and replace it with a scene in which Raft danced with Dvorak.

The timing of the picture was lucky: Al Capone was in the news almost every day. He had been arrested shortly after the movie commenced shooting for income tax evasion, and was in prison for weeks. He was tried and found guilty, and sent off to Leavenworth Prison; it is doubtful that he ever saw *Scarface*. For years Howard Hawks boasted that Capone so liked the movie he entertained him at dinner in Chicago to express his appreciation. Since Capone was behind bars at the time, it is easy to judge the veracity of this tale.

While Hughes attacked bootlegging illegal liquor in the picture, he was, ironically, doing some of his own. According to Noah Dietrich, he used his yacht to run liquor up and down the coast. In fact, he went a step further than that. He found that the Rice Hotel in Houston had never disposed of its cellar of fine wines, which had been locked and barred with the outset of Prohibition. Despite the fact that transporting liquor across a state line was a federal offense, Hughes, not as violent but certainly as crooked as Al Capone, smuggled the thousands of bottles, for which he paid several hundred thousand dollars, to Los Angeles in an armored freight car marked UNEXPOSED FILM. Noah Dietrich drove down to the Los Angeles depot to retrieve them. But he was out of luck: the car contained bales of cotton and a fumigation team was present inspecting for boll weevils. Their leader announced that they must inspect the film cans in case they concealed more cotton.

Dietrich was frantic. He begged the men not to open the cans, as priceless film would be ruined. When it was obvious they would not desist, he drew the team leader aside. Seven hundred dollars took care of the problem. The bootleg liquor made its way to Hughes's house; when Hughes had drinking associates in for dinner, they found themselves enjoying 100-year-old French champagne.

Toward the end of the shooting of *Scarface*, George Raft became involved in an affair with his boss's lover, Billie Dove. Hughes got wind of this and flew into an hysterical rage. The idea of Billie's going to bed with a mere actor, who was on his payroll, infuriated him even more than what he took to be her betrayal. His anger was fueled by the fact that Raft was a famous stud, an expert, passionate lover. Hughes arrived in the lobby of the Ambassador Hotel as Raft stripped and got into bed with Billie. Hughes noticed that Raft's friend, the gangster Owney Madden, was standing near the reception desk. He asked Madden if the story was true. Madden gave a rather shaky answer. Hughes started toward the elevator. Madden called the suite and warned Raft, who was actually making love to Billie at that moment. Naked, Raft ran for his clothes, flung them on, and fled out the back door. Hughes burst in and berated Billie, only to forgive her later and continue to see her.

Not content with having broken every Hollywood code by showing incest on the screen, Hughes bought a viciously anti-Semitic novel, *Queer People,* for immediate production following it. The story of a reporter who invades the Hollywood of 1931 and finds the community run by squalid Jewish executives appealed to him strongly, and he seems to have been stupidly blind to the effect such a purchase would have on the movie moguls with whom he was associated, most notably Joe Schenck. He pressed ahead, but no actor would appear in the picture; they knew they would never work again if they did. Anonymous phone callers threatened Hughes's life; studio chiefs offered him fortunes to desist. He begged Ben Lyon and Paul Muni (despite the fact that Muni was Jewish) to appear in the picture; both refused. He even went to New York when Muni was appearing in a play to try to change his mind. Muni ordered him out of his dressing room and said he would never work with him again. On August 22, 1931, after Hughes had cast the homosexual William Haines in the lead, borrowing him from Louis B. Mayer, who was grossly caricatured in the script, Hughes was forced to announce that *Queer People* was suspended indefinitely. Petulantly, his press release added, "*Queer People* would have taken the public behind the scenes of Hollywood . . . I regret we were not allowed to make [it] immediately."

Not a single American newspaper commented on the suppression; but the London *Daily Mail* printed a startling series of articles giving the inside story on the matter. As a result, Will Hays, head of the Motion Picture Producers Association and the chief arbiter of movie morals, a close friend of Louis B. Mayer, turned on Hughes with anger, definitively and for good. Despite the fact that Warner Bros. had made the bloodily violent *Little Caesar,* which Hays had given kid-glove treatment, Hays set out, implacably, to wreck *Scarface.* At the same moment that he began planning its destruction, there was new grist for his mill: it leaked through the secret movie grapevine that Jean Harlow, who was still under contract to Hughes, had become a gangster's moll. With Capone's imprisonment, Abe (Longy) Zwillman, an East Coast racketeer, was in and out of Los Angeles to organize the West Coast mobs. He had fallen in love with Harlow when she toured to promote *Hell's Angels,* and they were having an intensely passionate affair. Zwillman became Topic A in Hollywood social circles when, at an elaborate dinner for the various mob members at the Ambassador Hotel, he took out his pocket watch and removed from the back of it a strand of dark hair. He announced that it was Harlow's pubic hair, which she hadn't bothered to dye platinum blond.

Zwillman forced Hughes to loan Harlow to Harry Cohn, who was in the pay of the mob, at Columbia. Then Hughes defied Zwillman: he sold Harlow to Louis B. Mayer for $60,000. Mayer, who had the Hays office sewn up through inside influence and virtually controlled the press, had no fear of the Harlow-Zwillman affair's becoming publicly known. By letting her go, Hughes assured Harlow a stunning future at MGM.

On October 1, 1931, Will Hays ran *Scarface.* He informed Hughes it was unacceptable and guaranteed that it would be banned in Ohio, Pennsylvania, and New York State. He insisted on a new ending: Hughes and Hawks had shown Camonte shot down in the street, under the ironical travel agents' advertisement THE WORLD IS YOURS. Hays wanted Camonte to be shown turning yellow, pleading for his life, and then being shot down, whimpering with fear. Later, Hays changed his mind and decided the ending should have Camonte put in handcuffs, rushed through a trial, and sent to the hangman's noose.

Hughes had not only to face Hays's demands. Contrary to Howard Hawks's self-advertising statements, Hughes's gangster contacts were furious because Camonte was made to look like a coward. They warned Hughes, who took the threats with sufficient seriousness to order publicist Lincoln Quarberg to remove the Caponeish scars from Paul Muni's face in every advertisement and poster. In many cases, the scar had to be painted out; for the larger color sheets, Muni was rephotographed with normal makeup. This absurd attempt to assuage mob feeling (after all, anyone could go into a movie theater once the picture was released and see the scar on Muni's cheek) failed to achieve its purpose.

Instead of fighting with all guns blazing, emulating his gangster subject, Hughes proved shiftless and panicky over the next few weeks. He and Quarberg began making charges that Hays himself was in the pay of the mob and that the industry was afraid of exposing government corruption. When this failed, he was forced by Hays to put together a clumsy prologue in which newspaper tycoon William Randolph Hearst called attention to the evils of crime. Hays felt this was simply Hearst selling his own newspapers, forbade the prologue, and had a new one inserted in which the New York Police

Commissioner called for legislation forbidding the sale and shipment of guns.

Hughes shot a new ending on October 25 and 26, using second-unit director Richard Rowland. Muni refused to appear going to the scaffold; a double had to be used. Then, in mid-November, Hays decided the title *Scarface* was unacceptable, and that it should be called by a title that would draw attention to Capone's disgrace and imprisonment. Hughes fought against this. But with $800,000 tied up in it, he dared not risk the picture's being nationally banned. On January 3, 1932, the title *The Shame of a Nation* was settled on. On January 12, on Hays's orders, Hughes had Rowland direct a dreadful scene, inserted into the middle of the picture, in which a Hearst-like newspaper publisher addresses a civic-minded group in his office to discuss the necessity for wiping out crime. As a result, the mob threatened Hughes's life. Immediately after filming this absurd sequence, Hughes left with Billie Dove for New York. The picture was still without an official production seal, and all theater chains refused it until that seal was granted.

There was nothing Hughes could do. He was forced to put his staff on half-salary. The Depression was seriously affecting the Hughes Tool Company. Irrationally, he feared he would run out of money. The disasters of *The Age for Love* and *Cock of the Air* and fear of the mob's killing him shattered him still further. In a last-ditch effort to save *Cock of the Air*, Hughes ordered a poster in which Billie and Chester Morris would be seen suggestively astride the erect tail of an airplane. When the Hays office dismissed the idea, Hughes gave up any attempt to promote Billie. He was forced to remove her name from advertisements of *Cock of the Air* because she was waning in popularity, and their affair began to fall apart.

Weeks went by while Billie stayed at the Warwick Hotel and Hughes (for appearances' sake) at the Ambassador. At the end of January, with more title changes, they took off for West Palm Beach aboard the *Hilda*. Hughes fired off telegrams calling for further salary cuts in Hollywood. Quarberg begged Hughes to resign from the Motion Picture Producers and Distributors of America, make *Queer People*, and, though not in so many words, tell everyone in Hollywood to go fuck themselves.

Spurred by Quarberg, Hughes took up an interesting idea. Certain states did not have local censorship boards. If Hughes defiantly opened *Scarface* in one of those states, and invited the press to see a brilliant picture, maybe the Hays office would be shamed into allowing the picture a production seal? Throughout February, Hughes sailed through Caribbean waters; he arrived in Havana, where he established connections with the rising young political demagogue Fulgencio Batista, who would soon become the fascist dictator of Cuba. Then, by telegram from Havana, Hughes confirmed an earlier arrangement with Joe Schenck to open *Scarface* in New Orleans on March 26 under its original title. Quarberg lined up some powerful support: the playwright Robert Sherwood, who was overwhelmed by the picture when he saw it at a private screening in New York, and used his newspaper columns to denounce Hays and Senator La Follette, who introduced the issue into the Congressional Record.

Hughes was delighted. He moved back to Palm Beach, shifting from hotel to hotel to avoid the press, then, leaving Billie Dove behind, sailed the *Hilda* to Galveston, drove over to Houston to see old friends and family and to talk to theater owners about releasing *Scarface* in that city, and continued through the Panama Canal. On March 7, he telegraphed Hays from Mexico that nothing would stop *Scarface* now.

More supporters rallied to Hughes's cause. Columnist Walter Winchell gave radio broadcasts supporting him. Morris L. Ernst of the National Council of Freedom from Censorship condemned Hays's actions. When Joe Schenck proved nervous about pouring money into a promotional campaign, Hughes fired off $10,000 to pay for advertisements. Hughes had to sign promissory notes when money was needed for the picture's distribution costs. Lewis Milestone was in New York cutting and recutting sequences; he was handicapped by the fact that Hughes could not be reached aboard the *Hilda*. *Scarface*'s structure changed from day to day.

By late April, Hughes was in Mazatlan. Lincoln Quarberg flew there to see him, begging him not to let the picture be shown anywhere in any other than its original form. He told Hughes that the trade organ *Film Daily* had refused to support him; as a result, Hughes canceled all advertising in that publication. Suddenly, Hughes scored his first major victory. On April 21, 1932, Wilton A. Barrett, Executive Secretary of the National Board of Review, a special citizens' committee set up to represent appropriate moral views, cabled Hughes: WE ENDORSE *SCARFACE*. This was a smack in the eye for Will Hays, and at last assured Hughes that he would not be publicly vilified if he went ahead and showed the picture. Back in Hollywood on April 23, he cabled Al Lichtman of United Artists in Manhattan that he very much wanted his film to open in Manhattan in an unadulterated version and wouldn't accept any interference with the cut he had approved. He also issued a statement to the press in which he openly defied interference with the film.

Hughes opened *Scarface* to standing ovations in New Orleans. He showed the picture to the Hollywood press at a screening at Grauman's Chinese Theater; again there was a standing ovation. He flew with Ann Dvorak and Howard Hawks, who was bedding her, to Houston for the opening. So overwhelming was public opinion that Hays was forced to give the picture a seal; the only major compromise was that the picture, in New York State, ended with Camonte's hanging, and all of the incestuous scenes were removed everywhere.

The reviews were excellent. Mordaunt Hall in *The New York Times* compared the film to a Shakespearean tragedy, and called it "a stirring picture, efficiently directed and capably acted . . . an excellent diversion for those who like to take an afternoon or an evening off to study the activities of cowardly thugs." Hall praised Paul Muni for his "compelling portrayal" of Camonte. *Variety* described the picture as "powerful and gripping," and said, "[Muni] is tough enough here to make Capone his errand boy." The *Motion Picture Herald*, which had not been supportive up to then, and the *Los Angeles Times* also ran rave reviews. By June, *Scarface* was a hit.

But there was a bitter aftermath. Billie Dove left Hughes definitively after just over three years. Soon afterward, she married the handsome and wealthy Robert Kenaston and retired from the screen.

Hughes was consoled by his friendship with Marian Marsh, a major discovery of Jack Warner who had made a sensation as a hypnotized girl in *Svengali*, a film starring John Barrymore. Blonde, with enormous blue eyes, Marian Marsh fascinated Hughes, but he didn't place her under contract.

Hughes was with Marian one night at the Coconut Grove when he felt a light, sharp blow to the head. He looked up. A beautiful girl, the actress June Vlasek (later Lang), had tossed a sugar cube on his head to attract his attention. Fascinated, he left Marian, went upstairs, and took June down to the dance floor.

He saw her regularly, and Marian didn't seem to object. "I felt he was sexless," June Lang says today. "He never even tried to kiss me." One night, rather boldly, she asked him in for a drink. He asked for a cocktail—a rare example of his wanting alcohol—with a lime twist. "We don't have any limes in the kitchen," she said.

Next day, a messenger arrived staggering under a huge package. It was a lime tree. From then on, Hughes had lime twists with his cocktails at her house.

Hughes had become exhausted by the long struggle with Will Hays and had begun to feel that he should follow Quarberg's suggestion and resign from the Motion Picture Producers and Distributors of America. The news was greeted with relief, and in some cases, rapture, by the association's members. His hatred of paying his workers and his reckless disregard of human safety were hypocritically disapproved of by many studio bosses who did exactly the same every day in their nefarious dealings. But the fact that he was an outsider, a pigheaded independent, branded him permanently; and his snappish remarks about such moguls as the Warner Brothers and Louis B. Mayer ("king kikes") did him in. He got out of the MPPDA in the summer of 1932, and went a step further: he abandoned motion pictures altogether, disbanded his team, let Quarberg go, and pursued a greater love than movies: flying.

# Airman

Hughes closed up his offices and dismissed his staff, with the exception of Noah Dietrich. Early in 1933, he bought an S-43 Sikorsky Amphibian, as capable on land as on water, and engaged a brilliant engineer, the handsome and charismatic Glenn (Odie) Odekirk, who became one of his closest friends, to revamp it. He harassed Odekirk constantly during the reconstruction, at one stage obsessively taking eight hours to approve the fitting of three wood screws. When Odekirk finished the job, Hughes decided to take his plane out on a series of trial hops across America. Odie left his wife for months to go with Hughes. (Asked by a reporter how he could do such a thing, Odie gave a vivid picture of his marriage by replying, "She won't mind; we don't have children.")

Early in March, the two men left Glendale in the S-43 for Houston, where Hughes drove Odie to his house to see Aunt Annette and Uncle Frederick Lummis, and took him on a tour of the Hughes Tool Company. Then they flew on to one of Hughes's favorite cities, New Orleans, for the Mardi Gras.

Determined not to be late for the opening of the festivities, Hughes ignored storm warnings. The plane ran into turbulence and was shaken by thunder and threatened by zig-zags of lightning. The faulty left engine failed, leaving only one. When that, too, began to sputter, Hughes, navigating with great skill, dropped the S-43 through black clouds and pancaked into the Mississippi. He and Odie bobbed around for hours in the damaged aircraft, in drenching rain, branches and logs hitting the plane violently. At long last, Hughes was able to get through to the Coast Guard, and a cutter arrived and towed the two men back to New Orleans.

As detached as ever, Hughes slept in the back of the plane through the journey. When he arrived at the wharf, he jumped up and ran, in his goggles, through the excited reporters and photographers, scattering them as he went. He refused all interviews. Later he vanished for a week, apparently pursuing the sexual possibilities of Mardi Gras.

He and Odekirk flew on to Long Island in the damaged plane, arriving in time for the summer social season. They would turn up at glamorous parties at the last minute, often without an invitation (but who would refuse entrée to Howard Hughes?). Few would forget the sight of them, skimming in the S-43 through the Atlantic waters, mooring it at a pier, two tall and wildly attractive men in black leather, striding leggily up the sloping lawns, then changing in the hosts' bedrooms into black tie for the evening. Apart from Joe and Rose Kennedy, who detested Hughes (Hughes had tried to wrest control of RKO Radio Pictures from Kennedy in 1929), everyone else in society was excited to have Hughes as a houseguest. Few women, or gay men, could resist him; most knew that his income from the tool bit was over $1 million a *month,* even in the Depression. He would stand, smiling crookedly, in the corner of expensive living rooms, nursing a glass and waiting for the inevitable passes from rich singles. He calmly enjoyed a world of cocktails and laughter when most of the nation was starving.

It was his custom, once given a hint by a houseguest, to simply raise an eyebrow. Then, in the small hours of the morning, he would arrive at the appropriate person's door, tap twice as a signal, go in, make love, and return without a word to his bedroom.

He got wind, while staying at Newport, that the world's most glamorous motor yacht, the *Rover,* had just been built by Stephens and Company in Glasgow, Scotland. Three hundred and twenty feet long, accommodating a crew of thirty, with a built-in radio station, the white-painted, oil-fueled twin-screw yacht was the world's seventh largest ocean-going vessel in private hands and was a masterpiece of marine engineering. He had to have it: it would be the ultimate toy. The asking price was $850,000, or about $15 million in 1990s currency. The canny Scots wouldn't budge, and Hughes was forced to pay the full amount. He took a ship to Southampton and a train to Scotland, snapped up the vessel, and hired the Irish captain Carl ("Jock") Flynn to sail her across the Atlantic to Newport.

One of his problems was registry; he would be subject to heavy taxes if the vessel were of American ownership, and, since he planned to transport liquor illegally in her, and might accommodate gangsters and prostitutes, he put the vessel under Panamanian registry—the umbrella for all sins. Many criminals used that cover for their boats, since Panamanian vessels could not be seized or even boarded at sea by U.S. Coast Guard or drug enforcement officers. He changed the name of the boat to *Southern Cross;* he hoped to sail her to the South Pacific. In the southern hemisphere, the Great Bear constellation of stars was seen upside down as the Southern Cross.

He sold the *Hilda,* with all of its romantic memories of Billie Dove, and sailed the *Southern Cross* up and down Long Island Sound, showing her off to such wealthy friends as Sherman Fairchild, of the Fairchild plane fortune. Then he had Flynn sail the craft to her berth in San Pedro, California, to await his pleasure.

Elaborately refitted, with sumptuous furnishings of white and gold, and solid gold taps and fixtures in the bathrooms, the *Southern Cross* boasted a master stateroom with a vast double bed covered in wolf skins in which the owner could enjoy the company of his various companions.

Hughes now decided that he would break the continental air speed record. He gave Glenn Odekirk instructions to come up with a totally new and revolutionary style of aircraft, the Hughes Racer, also known as the H-1.

Breaking with Marian Marsh, he ruthlessly dumped her, and began a romance with the actress Ida Lupino. British, fiercely intense, tough, ambitious, and at the same time insecure (she used to run from previews when she saw her face on the screen), she was a member of a leading London theatrical family. She was just beginning to make her mark in Hollywood as a gifted performer who would soon emerge at the top of the heap as a Warner Bros. star. He was seen frequently with her in Palm Springs, but, as with all his other women, he was incapable of emotional commitment. It is not even likely that the pair were physical lovers.

While work continued on the Hughes Racer, the ever-restless owner tired of the day-and-night work of checking every detail and took off on a whim in an entirely different direction. Having tasted the pleasures of movie-making, flying, sailing, partying, he would find out what it was like to be poor. Years later, one of his his friends, the director Preston Sturges, based a film, *Sullivan's Travels,* on his adventures. He ordered Noah Dietrich to give him no more than a tiny stake of $100, and he closed up his house and made his way in his cheapest clothes, a frayed white cotton shirt, denims, and sneakers, to the Los Angeles Union Depot.

He managed to sneak into the freight car for a free ride to Houston, where he was picked up as a bum in the street and was barely able to talk his way out of jail. He never gave away his identity. Traveling the country, he met many of the homeless, vagabonds who managed to exist by riding the rails and stealing food from the trains' kitchens. He was thrilled by the experience, and felt released from all pressure.

Tiring of this romantic escapade, he suddenly enlisted as a baggage handler with American Airways under the name of Charles Howard. He went on to become a part-time pilot for the same airline, but he was found out in New York and fired.

Turning up in Huntsville, Texas, he checked into a cheap hotel, again in disguise. The good-looking young night clerk, Harry G. Reed, befriended him. Hughes pretended that he had little experience with women and was afraid he couldn't afford to date them. Reed told him that, for a mere fifty cents for the evening, a presentable male could take a girl out, buy her a hamburger and a Coke, take her to a movie (for twenty-five cents) and, after getting her excited in the dark of the theater, be assured of bedding her into the bargain. Hughes was thrilled by the idea.

The problem was, how was Hughes going to earn enough money to have even fifty cents? As a child, he had proved to be an excellent photographer. He got Reed to lend him money to buy a camera and some equipment and set himself up under the name R. Wayne Rector, a gag version of "erector," and he began putting cards in windows. As a result, he was hired to take wedding pictures. He would, again voyeuristically, photograph attractive young couples, no doubt imagining the sexual pleasures that would follow on the honeymoon.

He decided to go for bigger game. He took Reed on as a partner and began to travel the country, as far east as Miami. Reed would wait in his car outside expensive schools and write down license plate numbers of the wealthy parents in their Rolls-Royces or Duesenbergs, and then trace the owners. Then a girlfriend of Reed's would call up the parents and tell them that a Mr. Wayne Rector would like to photograph their offspring, that he was in partnership with a famous British firm and only the most distinguished families would be honored by his artistry. The ploy worked; in a matter of months, Hughes was established as a society and child photographer. He kept this existence up on and off for years.

As well as having affairs with handsome mechanics or other hired hands, he was ruthless in his womanizing. He used his skills as a photographer to secure models for sex. He had an arrangement with Reed: he would always have a woman first. As before in his life, he was devoted to the idea of foursomes. He liked to watch.

Toward the end of 1933, Hughes tired of this existence for a time and began to lust for further successes in the air. On January 14, 1934, in a souped-up Boeing he had bought in New York, he entered the All-American Air Races at Miami's municipal airport. He thrilled the crowd with his loop-the-loops, his daring nosedives to within a few feet of the grandstands, and his snakings through the sky. He and other pilots joined in a fake air raid, dropping imitation incendiary bombs on a miniature version of Miami. Then he flew on a wave of cheers and awards to Palm Beach to party at the Breakers Hotel, in Palm Beach, night after night until dawn.

He flew the Boeing to California to check on Odekirk's top-secret, security-guarded progress on his beloved H-1 Racer. He was dismayed to learn it would not be ready until August. But throughout the spring he was continually overjoyed by Odie and comechanic Dick Palmer's brilliant work. An amazing new aircraft was emerging.

The four-cabin monoplane powered by 550 horsepower Pratt and Whitney engines was equipped with unusually small wings, which were streamlined and structured to allow for very rapid take-offs. Its construction was of the lightest possible metal, duraluminin, and of the lightest wood, plywood. The very large fuel tank took up an unusual amount of space and could accommodate 250 gallons. In trial runs at Glendale, the Racer managed an astonishing 352 miles per hour, more than half of the average achieved by a 1993 jet.

Dumping Ida Lupino, Hughes found a new woman that summer, the gorgeous silent screen star, Corinne Griffith; he enjoyed occasional forays into the bedroom of the British actress Lilian Bond. Corinne Griffith was not, she claimed, Corinne Griffith at all: she was really Corinne's near-twin, Mary Griffith. Corinne had died of a sudden heart attack during the shooting of a movie in Mexico. To save the studio a fortune, Mary had taken over at a moment's notice without acting experience, and nobody knew the difference. When anybody asked Corinne where the real star was buried, she said, "In an unmarked grave in Mexico." She fought personal income tax (as Hughes did) and, taking a leaf out of the automobile millionairess Mrs. Horace Dodge's book, kept all of her money in tax-free bonds in steel boxes in her house. When the IRS officials arrived at the door, she showed them the boxes. They were forced to creep meekly away.

The only man allowed into Hughes's secret Glendale workshop other than Palmer and Odekirk and their trusted team was Cary Grant. Three years earlier, Grant had succeeded Hughes as Randolph Scott's lover. They were living together in a West Hollywood apartment building, La Ronda. At weekends, Hughes took Cary sailing aboard the *Southern Cross* to Ensenada and thence north to San Francisco. It is believed that on these voyages the two men became involved in a sexual affair. They were well suited; neither was romantic (despite Grant's image on the screen), passionate, or committed. They were cool, detached, impersonal in their liaisons. It seems to have occurred to neither that they had commitments, Hughes to Corinne Griffith and Cary Grant to Randolph Scott. Nor did they complain when the high-powered *Hollywood Reporter* columnist Edyth Gwynne reported one of their supposedly secret voyages. When Hughes visited with Grant and Scott at their apartment, it was on a friendly basis. Soon afterward, Scott took off to his hometown, Orange, Virginia, and married money: the man-hungry, tweedy heiress to the multimillion-dollar Du Pont textile fortune, Marian Du Pont.

That left Cary open to Hughes's interest in him. The relationship of the pair was to continue on and off until the 1950s. In August, 1935, Grant was shooting the picture *Sylvia Scarlett*, a cross-dressing romantic comedy filled with off-color references. In it, Grant acted with astonishing effeminacy, and his costar, Katharine Hepburn, was dressed as a boy. Hughes was fascinated when he learned that, at one stage, a maid kissed Hepburn on the lips, telling her, "You're very attractive," and at another stage, actor Brian Aherne was drawn to Kate as a "boy." Aherne says, in a very suggestive scene, "There's something very queer going on."

Hughes flew one of his airplanes to Trancas Beach, north of Los Angeles, where the picture was shooting, and landed on a nearby golf course. The noise of his engine ruined a shot, and the prissy gay director George Cukor, who told this author that he hated Hughes, was furious. Katharine Hepburn exclaimed, "What a nerve!" Hughes jumped down from the cockpit in black leather coat and flying goggles, and insisted on joining cast and crew in a picnic lunch. Hepburn had brought hampers with sandwiches and thermos flasks of coffee and tea, as well as expensive china, to entertain like royalty on location.

Irritated by Hughes's intrusion, and knowing he was deaf, Hepburn arranged with Cukor, Grant, and Brian Aherne to irritate him. They whispered all through lunch, making unflattering remarks, until Hughes grew red in the face with irritation. When he asked them to speak up, they opened their mouths very wide, as though they were shouting, and nothing came out. Hughes strode off to his plane to mocking laughter and applause.

But, maddening though Hughes's intrusion may have been, Hepburn found herself as attracted to him as Grant was. She was no stronger than any other woman when it came to meeting an immensely powerful and wealthy young man with stunning good looks and a lean, hard body who looked vulnerable and anxious to be mothered. She made up her mind she would see more of him. And she did. It never seems to have occurred to her, in her extraordinary state of self-centeredness, that she would be sharing Hughes with Cary Grant, Corinne Griffith, and any number of unnamed beauties of both sexes.

Returning from Trancas, Hughes was delighted to find that the H-1 Hughes Racer was at last completed. The final cost was $120,000. On August 10, he had Noah Dietrich give a press conference announcing that he would be trying for the world speed record on September 12. The Hughes Tool Company executives panicked, convinced the flight might cost him his life, and insisted he make out a new will. They twisted his arm to make sure he would leave them the company, but he left the will unsigned. He apparently wrote a secret will which left everything to form a Hughes medical foundation. That will disappeared.

On the appointed morning, Hughes drove down to Martin Field, Santa Ana, for the epoch-making flight. The airborne judges were Amelia Earhart (Mrs. George Putnam), the famed pilot Paul Mantz, and the National Aviation Association's Lawrence Thorkelson. They watched from an observation aircraft.

Towards sunset, Hughes taxied the Racer down the runway and made a brisk takeoff. In his first rapid circle, he only managed a disappointing 302 miles per hour, due to wind pressure. Then, with his customary eccentricity, instead of gradually increasing speed to break the record, he went into a nosedive at 346 miles per hour, which, he must have known, was not on the required schedule. This unnecessary stunt lost him several points.

He pulled out, and, banking steeply, made a normal flight at full throttle at a record-breaking 352 miles per hour. Night fell, precluding any accurate photography or speed checking of his performance.

He tried again the next day, the 13th; it was his lucky number. And his luck was in: this time, he had a tail wind, and he was able to repeat his 352 miles per hour in ideal test conditions. After a perfect landing, he received his trophy from the judges. But he got overexcited and ran off to the Racer. He jumped into the cockpit, manipulated the wheel, and flew south—against the wind. Then something happened. One of the tanks cut out. He tried the auxiliary; it, too, puttered out. To his horror, he found himself gliding.

He kept calm as always; realizing that if he lowered speed and dropped his landing gear for an immediate touchdown he would crash into a traffic-filled highway and kill several people as well as himself, he knew he would have to pancake at 100 miles an hour into a bean field. He achieved the forced landing brilliantly. The Racer slammed down into the hard earth and skidded hundreds of feet before tilting forward in a sudden stop. The hundreds gathered at the air field ran to see if he was injured. An ambulance screamed up. When it arrived, he was sitting calmly on the propeller shaft, chewing a stick of gum.

He immediately ordered an investigation to see what had gone wrong. Palmer and Odekirk stripped the Racer down to the last nut and bolt. Hughes was appalled to find that somehow, when the plane was being checked after the successful test flight, one of his team of mechanics had tried to sabotage him. Someone had jammed steel wool into both his gas lines. One jamming could possibly have been accidental; not two. Who could have done it? Was it possible that one of the executives who would inherit his millions had bribed a team member to kill him? He never found out; the mystery remains unsolved to this day.

# Around the World

H ughes's friendship with Hepburn quickened into an antic romance. They were opposites: she was talkative, opinionated—she issued streams of opinions!—bossy, pushy, funny, charming, overpowering. He was, as always, taciturn, tight-lipped, cut off by his deafness to the point that he was socially uncomfortable, and guilty of a dreadful schoolboy humor. Yet they also had much in common: singlemindedness, courage, enterprise, a refusal to be denied or crossed, a passion for airplanes, automobiles, golf, being alive.

They were both angular and prone to wear leather; they were like brothers. It is hard to believe theirs was a wild Romeo and Juliet relationship. They were chums; he was more at ease covered in grease under a car or a plane than in a bedroom, she was very much the same. To them, the top of the list of available people in the world, it was amusing to be a pair.

He gave her a wonderful time. He taught her to fly; he allowed her to pilot his plane, at one hair-raising moment underneath New York's 59th Street bridge. He landed on the Bel-Air Country Club golf course, scattering the golfers as she approached the ninth tee, ruining somebody's hole-in-one. He wasn't foolish enough to take her on at tennis.

She was the best, and he knew it. He also decided he would have the best aircraft in the world. His own Racer was outclassed by the celebrated pilot Jacqueline Cochran's Northrop Gamma, a controversial plane that had blown up twice in the workshop during construction and had been constantly fussed over and souped up by its determined owner.

He had to have it, at any cost. Finding out that Cochran, who was engaged to the multimillionaire Floyd Odlum, was staying in Los Angeles, he called her up at 11:30 P.M. She couldn't believe the famous Howard Hughes was on the phone. He had to talk almost nonstop to convince her he wasn't a practical joker.

When he offered to buy the Northrop, she turned him down. He invited her out to see the Racer; she was thrilled, but disappointed when he wouldn't let her take the Racer up. She wouldn't yield on the sale; in desperation, Hughes offered to lease the plane instead. Since the figure he suggested, a staggering $65,000, was more than the cost of building the Gamma, she gave in. Later, he got his way and bought it anyway.

He also bought a DC-1 from Douglas Aircraft, using the Northrop for test flights only and the DC-1 to take him from place to place. After weeks in his machine shop at Glendale, he was ready to take off on the transcontinental record-breaker from Los Angeles to New York in the Gamma, which he had refitted with a 925 horsepower Wright G-Cyclone engine, originally designed for army use. Hepburn, busy with *Mary of Scotland,* in which she played Mary, Queen of Scots, was unable to be present when, at 11:30 A.M., on January 13, 1936, wearing a Palm Beach suit and sneakers, Hughes climbed into the cockpit, the mechanic twirled the propeller, and he took off for Sante Fe, New Mexico.

So violent was the turbulence on takeoff that his radio antenna snapped and for the rest of the journey he was unable to contact the ground. He ran into a storm over the Sierras that pushed him down from 15,000 feet. He had to fly blind over the Colorado River into Arizona, looking nervously at his fuel level, but somehow managed to find El Paso in the murk. He ran into trouble again north of Wichita, Kansas, the storm weather so severe that he almost blacked out and his compass needle was knocked off. Using the moon and stars for celestial navigation, he flew on from Indianapolis to Columbus, Ohio, thence to Pittsburgh, and finally to Newark, arriving to a cheering crowd in a light sprinkle of rain at forty-two minutes past midnight. "I don't think there's anything sensational about it," he said, as he staggered out, grinning wearily. He was overjoyed to find that, at nine hours, twenty-seven minutes, he had broken Colonel Roscoe Turner's record of just over ten hours.

On April 21, he broke another record, flying the Northrop into difficult crosswinds from Miami to New York in four hours, twenty-one minutes. Again, his radio broke down and he had to fly by landmarks after Raleigh, North Carolina. He made a fast descent over Coney Island, landing with a thud on Floyd Bennett Field. The story of his triumph broke on the nation's front pages and he was swamped with fan mail and besieged by hundreds at the Drake Hotel.

On May 15, 1936, he was in Chicago; a man he met in a North Beach bar bet him $50 that he couldn't fly between the Windy City and Los Angeles between the hours of lunch and dinner. What the man didn't realize was that Hughes always had his dinner very late.

Because he acted so quickly on the bet, he left Chicago without the necessary maps. He had to beat a head wind of forty-five miles per hour that forced him up to 20,000 feet. He followed the Great Circle Route to Kingman and dashed in over steep mountain ranges. He almost died when the airspeed indicator dropped to zero, the oxygen tank connections were fouled, and he had to breathe rarified air. He started to black out. He screamed loudly to release pressure in his lungs. Then ice formed on the wings; for five hours, he flew in desperate peril. He never enjoyed a steak dinner more.

In June, he was busy preparing a flight around the world, when he had a serious automobile accident. He was driving from east to west on Wilshire Boulevard when he reached a streetcar zone. Instead of observing the signal to stop he veered impatiently around the streetcar and struck and killed a pedestrian who was leaving work as a sales clerk at the May Company. His passenger was a Pasadena heiress, with whom he was apparently conducting a light-hearted romance despite the continuing presence in his life of Katharine Hepburn. The heiress fled the scene. Arrested and charged with manslaughter, Hughes was questioned for hours but refused to reveal the heiress's name. Despite the fact that pedestrians had right-of-way in Los Angeles, and that he had broken the law through reckless driving, Hughes got off. In those days, the District Attorney could be bought and sold, and anyone with sufficient money could get away with almost anything.

In the late summer, Hughes was at New York's Drake Hotel

again; he heard that the dancing star, Ginger Rogers, a strong, romantic woman, was in town and he renewed an earlier interest in her. It seemed to not be of the slightest concern to him that she was already married to the actor Lew Ayres, or that he was supposed to be emotionally committed to Hepburn. Hepburn, hearing of this in Los Angeles, and later at her home in Connecticut, was absolutely furious.

Hughes knew that the way to Ginger's heart was through her formidable mother, Lela. He overcame Lela with his boyish charm and took mother and daughter aboard the *Southern Cross* to his friend Sherman Fairchild's estate at Lloyd's Neck, Huntington, Long Island.

They played tennis, visited the Sikorsky helicopter plant and danced in fashionable nightclubs, especially at the St. Regis Roof. He suggested to Ginger that they should get married as he flew her home in the Racer to Los Angeles.

Sturdily independent, she was amazed at the suddenness of the invitation. The papers were full of his dating Hepburn and their only serious dates had been in public. She turned him down.

Hepburn detested her. When she saw Rogers standing in a mink coat below her dressing room window at the RKO Radio Pictures studio, she tossed a jug of water on her head. When Rogers sent Hepburn a birthday gift of a platinum pin, Hepburn gave it to someone else. In her memoirs, Ms. Rogers records Ms. Hepburn's acts of vengeance without giving the reason for them.

In the fall of 1936, Hepburn accepted from the Theater Guild an invitation to appear in a national tour of Helen Jerome's play version of Charlotte Brontë's *Jane Eyre*. Hughes supported her in the idea, but she was miscast; she couldn't play a mousy orphan too shy to admit her feelings for the landowner Edward Rochester. She was too bold, and could not subdue her nature in the performance, which was first seen in New Haven on December 26, 1936.

Hughes followed her romantically by plane to several points on the tour, leaving ruby or diamond bracelets on her dressing tables. She was unable to resist these romantic gestures.

On March 3, 1937, President Roosevelt presented the Harmon International Trophy for best aviator of the year to Hughes in a celebration at the White House. Hughes was only the third individual to win the coveted award; the others were Charles Lindbergh and Wiley Post. Soon afterward, in a luncheon in his honor at the Advertising Club of New York, Hughes held the audience spellbound with an account of the difficulties encountered in his latest transcontinental flight, in which he had broken his own record. "It will be a hard battle with nature to gain greater speed," he said in closing.

While Ginger Rogers was starring in Hollywood in the film *Vivacious Lady*, Hughes worked harder than ever on his proposed world flight. He was asked by Mayor La Guardia to name the plane he would use for the flight, an L-14 Lockheed, *The 1939 New York World's Fair.*

The problem was that the L-14 was too small to carry enormous amounts of fuel. By equipping the plane with extra tanks, Hughes risked overweighting it, and indeed was denied a certificate of airworthiness, which precluded his flying over Great Britain. He went to England and argued in vain with the British government that fuel consumption across the Atlantic would reduce the weight. The Department of Commerce only granted him permission to fly across American territory on the return journey after considerable argument. But he had to delay the flight for a year.

While he was in London, he enjoyed a brief affair with the delicate and insecure Woolworth heiress, Barbara Hutton, who would later marry Cary Grant. They stayed at the Savoy Hotel. In her diary, Barbara Hutton wrote of his impatience as a lover; his inability to help her over her problems in obtaining a climax; and how he finally just gave himself pleasure—a complaint others had made, and would again.

When Hepburn ended her tour in *Jane Eyre*, she began work in Hollywood in the film *Stage Door* on June 1, 1937. She was very annoyed when she was billed below Ginger Rogers, especially since Hughes continued his romance with both women. Angered, Hepburn jealously snubbed Rogers throughout the production.

Perhaps to consolidate her position in Hughes's life, Hepburn moved in to Hughes's house at 211 Muirfield Road in August. Later, in December, she brought in her own staff, including her maid, Johanna Madsen; Madsen and her chauffeur and cook, Louis and Ranghild Preyssing, were all brisk, close-mouthed, coolly reliable Scandinavian types. They meshed easily with Hughes's devoted housekeeper, Beatrice Dowling, and his majordomo, Richard Dreher.

Hepburn, with typical curiosity, explored the house from top to bottom, from Hughes's monk's cell of a bedroom with its iron single bed, too short for his six feet three, so his feet hung over the end, to the cellar, a converted film vault crammed with the contents of the Rice Hotel liquor store, which had scarcely been touched: 300 wine bottles, 100 of vintage champagne, gallon jugs of whiskey and massive barrels of beer; cases of scotch and gin: an Arabian Nights cave of alcohol.

She was fascinated by the garage with its Stanley and Dobie steamers, nostalgically kept up on blocks and still fully driveable, his Buick four-door saloon, his Packard 120—she moved it out to make room for her Model A Ford roadster—and his grand old Duesenberg.

They established their routines. For the first months in the house, from August 16 to January 10, 1938, Hepburn was involved in the slow, protracted shooting of *Bringing Up Baby,* a comedy in which she costarred with Hughes's other romantic interest, Cary Grant (it seemed that the major stars of RKO were all mixed up with Hughes's life—and the studio's owner, Floyd Odlum's wife, Jacqueline Cochran, still remained a close friend, ensuring him unlimited access to the studio).

Despite her heavy schedule on the picture, directed by Howard Hawks, yet another Hughesian link in incestuous Hollywood, Hepburn would rise at dawn and take long walks or march out onto the golf course at the back of the house to practice her strokes. Hughes hated to get up before late afternoon. She wolfed down enormous breakfasts of kidneys, eggs and bacon, coffee, lashings of toast; when she returned at night, he would have his usual dinner of butterfly steak and peas, or well-done lamb chops, ice cream, and oatmeal cookies; she would have a big, hearty meal. Yet she remained as thin as he did (the cook called her "Hollow-legs").

They weathered a burglary; when she was at the studio and he was sleeping, a thief crawled through a lower window, stared directly at Louis Preyssing, who was vacuuming the dining room, and, without a word, went to Hepburn's bedroom (he knew where it was) and took diamond and ruby bracelets and a fur coat, all gifts from Hughes. As a result, Hughes installed an elaborate alarm system of his own invention, a Rube Goldberg contraption that was often triggered off by the three dogs or by straying neighborhood cats; it was so loud (because of his deafness) that it would often bring neighbors running out of their homes in the middle of the night.

Hughes fixed up a telephone system at the time that rang like fire alarm bells; Hepburn found it irritating. She abhorred the phone, preferring the Victorian custom of letter writing; he had telephones everywhere in the house, including two in the bathroom, and with push buttons on them—a recent invention. He still liked to do most of his business in the bathroom.

They added new staff members: a part-time barber, to cut their hair; a laundress, Mrs. Foster, who, instead of hanging the laundry to dry in the cellar, the custom of those days, hung it on a line in the yard. Snoops could see, over the wall, Hughes's undershorts hanging next to Katharine Hepburn's slips and panties.

Hepburn was baffled by Hughes's concern with germs—inherited from his mother and his paternal grandmother, Mimi. He had Mrs. Preyssing serve guests dinner on the cheapest china plates and wine in inexpensive glasses, then he had the lot smashed to pieces in his presence, wrapped, and placed in the trash cans.

He refused to use toothpaste because he feared the chemicals in it, rinsed with mouthwash day and night, and chewed on mysterious black seeds that were supposed to relieve constipation as well as keep off bugs. When Johanna Madsen, the maid, found seeds on his toothbrush, he told her to destroy it.

If a fly, moth, or winged cockroach entered the house, the staff had orders to catch them and swat them; they must not use a Flit gun or flypaper as both would poison the air.

Most nights he was up until close to dawn at Burbank's Union Air Terminal working on the L-14, which he was preparing for the flight around the world. He redesigned the aircraft with Glenn Odekirk and his team; the problem from the beginning was that the L-14 was not large enough, but he stubbornly refused to abandon it. In order to have sufficient fuel to last for the long first hop across the Atlantic, he had to stow very large vertical gas tanks in the cabin itself, leaving very little room for the crew. To insure his and his men's safety, he had to house five parachutes equipped with water and food; to obtain flotation should the plane crash into water, he had to squeeze in an inflatable life raft and stow Ping-Pong balls into every inch between the fixtures. He even had the fuselage's highpolish paint sandpapered so that the sunlight wouldn't flash in his eyes. He built a commode with air suction to blow out human waste.

In February, while Hepburn was in the picture *Holiday*, again with Cary Grant, at RKO, Hughes, completely without conscience, began to date Bette Davis. He was still seeing Ginger Rogers as well as Grant, and living with Hepburn. Davis, fierce and neurotic, compulsive in her hunger for attractive men (though she posed as hard-to-get), was fascinated by Hughes; for him, she was another very famous name in the world's best sexual shopping list.

How Hughes found time for this new romance is a puzzle, what with three other affairs going on at the same time and working all night at Burbank, but he did, by her own boast, have a very intense sexual relationship with Bette Davis. For years he had tended to be an impatient and clumsy lover, who ignored his own up-and-down sexual cycles and insisted on having sex whenever the whim, rather than the desire, took hold of him. Even though he was only thirty-two, he was never a highly-sexed man, and with Davis, who was challenging, fierce, and bitchy as a lover, he couldn't keep up the pace. He repeatedly, and embarrassingly, failed to climax after he had penetrated her.

She used various stroking techniques until he was able to consummate intercourse, and for years she boasted about that to her friends, saying that she had achieved something no other woman had done. It was probably untrue, and a very rude slap at her chief rival, Katharine Hepburn. When Bette's husband Ham Nelson found out that his wife was involved with Hughes, he moved out of the house, and hired a sound truck and a sound technician to eavesdrop. He bugged Davis's bedroom, parking the truck up Coldwater Canyon, hoping to catch her in flagrante delicto.

That night, Bette fulfilled a sexual fantasy; she covered her big double bed with gardenias. Hughes entered her and climaxed easily. Ham listened to the groans and cries and the subsequent sleepy conversation of the happy lovers. He burst into the house and stormed the bedroom.

Hughes put one of Bette's big, fluffy bedroom slippers in front of his genitals. He stood there like a big, thin, overgrown schoolboy caught with his hand in a cookie jar, while Bette, furious, screamed abuse at her husband. Looking at the absurdly naked adulterer, Ham coldly stated that it would cost $70,000 to buy his silence. One word of adultery to the women's clubs and Bette's pictures, in those puritanical days, would have been banned.

Hughes found a checkbook and wrote out the sum of $70,000. But Bette Davis insisted on paying the money back herself through her business managers, Vernon and Carlyn Wood. It took most of her life savings; she claimed that Hughes sent her a rose (some say, a gardenia) every year on the anniversary of the payment.

Did Hepburn know about this episode? It is possible she got wind of it, because, after buying out her RKO contract, she took off abruptly to New York and Connecticut, where her family home was—Fenwick, at Old Saybrook, at the mouth of the Connecticut River.

That Hughes cared for Hepburn is proven by the fact that, with work progressing on the L-14, which was to leave on the round the world flight in July, he managed to tear himself away to fly to Connecticut to visit with her and her energetic family. Her brother Richard, an unsuccessful playwright and the family failure, unwisely dashed off a play about Hughes's and Hepburn's love affair, which he insisted on reading aloud to Katharine's clan. The family was furious.

At the end of June, Hughes let Hepburn fly his S-43 Sikorsky amphibian under the 59th Street bridge—the thrill of her lifetime. Then he returned to Los Angeles to fly the L-14 to New York.

A crowd cheered him as he landed at Grand Central Airport on July 4, where official greeter and mayor's assistant Grover Whalen was waiting with a group of officials and a loud brass band. With Hepburn's help—she had forgiven him for his other affairs—he spent the next days in Manhattan, stocking up guns, fishing tackle, a hunting knife, snake bite remedies, water, and thirty days of rations, in case the plane should land in dangerous terrain.

She helped him select the sandwiches, testing fifteen kinds of bread for nutritional value, cold cuts of turkey and ham, cheese and frozen milk. She fretted with him as he worried about the excessive weight of the cargo in the super-light fuselage.

After three days and nights with Hepburn at her friend Lana Harding's apartment on East 52nd Street, he went up with her in her chauffeur-driven Lincoln to Old Saybrook. They returned two days later, the publicity-shy Hughes hiding on his hands and knees at the back while she rode in front with the driver. In an effort to reach Floyd Bennett Field, where an exhausted Glenn Odekirk and a team of six had worked without sleep for seventy-two hours on the L-14, Hepburn's chauffeur exceeded the speed limit. A motorcycle cop roared up. Hepburn told the driver, "Take the ticket, don't argue." Hughes was not detected.

The eccentric couple would have been far more sensible to have accepted Grover Whalen's offer of a police escort from Connecticut to Floyd Bennett. As it was, as soon as they reached the airfield, they had to run a gauntlet; several fans tried to pluck off Hughes's lucky brown felt hat. When they grabbed at Hepburn, she told her chauffeur to turn around and leave.

Hughes was dismayed to find Odekirk many pounds lighter, unshaven and trembling. This man who more than any other had made the L-14 fully airworthy had to state, in tears, that he wasn't up to making the flight.

Hughes accepted the situation, gripped Odekirk's shoulder, and told him to take a vacation with his wife at his expense. Luckily, the other members of the team were sufficiently fit to continue.

Hughes was dismayed to find that there were severe problems with the struts and fuselage. He had to work all night and much of the next day before he was done. Many of the crowd of thousands refused to leave, and, along with a mob of reporters and press photographers, camped out in the sweltering heat for seventeen hours.

The worst part of the ordeal for Hughes was not the long drawn-out struggle to fix up the plane but having to give a farewell speech. At 7:00 P.M., his cheekbones hollow with exhaustion, stubble on his chin, his eyelids fluttering almost shut, he stood up for the microphones. He pushed his lucky brown felt hat up to the top of his head and spread his lanky legs wide; he shifted nervously from foot to foot. He delivered a few halting words, apologizing for dodging the reporters so rudely, and announcing the importance of binding, through flight, a troubled world into one unity. He looked like a country farmer about to climb on a mechanical plough, not the most famous aviator next to Charles Lindbergh taking off on an epic adventure.

It was 7:19 P.M. on July 10, 1938 that the amazing journey began. To wild cheering and numerous hats flying in the air, the weary Hughes took the controls. He and his crew, alone in the world, knew they were risking their lives. At the last minute, Hughes had discovered the shocking fact that the Floyd Bennett Field runway was too short. The L-14, with its too-heavy load of fuel and equipment, was barely large enough to sustain a takeoff. Instead of smoothly rolling forward, the plane lumbered frighteningly. It did not lift up as it reached the end of the tarmac. Would Hughes crash to his death in front of 3,000 people and the world's newsreel cameras?

He was forced to do the unthinkable: he had to plough on, well beyond the runway, into baked mud and thick summer grass. The plane jarred badly as it hit a bump, and there was a snapping sound at the back. Because of his deafness, he didn't hear it, and the others of his crew, not wanting to unsettle him, did not report it to him. At last, he managed to raise up the L-14, not realizing that the all-important metal strut fusing the left tail wheel to the rear bulkhead had broken its mooring.

Hughes lost precious time in the next hour by keeping a romantic promise: he flew over Hepburn's Connecticut house and dipped his wings as she and her family ran out, waving frantically. Then he put the plane on automatic pilot, and the L-14 streaked out beyond the last winking lights of the coast into the inky darkness that covered the Atlantic.

Hughes, in his high-pitched Texan deaf man's voice, kept up a rat-tat-tat series of bulletins to the special short-wave station set up at the New York World's Fair building. His mental state was far removed from the confident, cocky character the world listened to in those next hours; he was nervous the fuel supply would not last as far as Paris, and headwinds slowed him down alarmingly. With the greatest weight per wing size carried by any pilot up to that time, forty-seven pounds per square foot, he had visions of pancaking into the ocean at any moment.

Keeping up a steady 175 miles per hour, he was still using up forty-five gallons of fuel per hour per engine. He had to cut down to thirty-two gallons, then drop to 375 horsepower per motor. Even if he survived, how would he ever make the speed record?

His fears were groundless. He made it to Paris in a record-breaking sixteen hours, thirty-five minutes—less than half the time made by Charles Lindbergh. After streaking in for a flawless point landing at 9:55 A.M., the sleepless captain and crew climbed out of their bucket seats, grinning groggily, as U.S. ambassador William Bullitt poked his head through the open cabin door and said, as though the aviators had been merely on a fishing expedition, "Did you have a nice trip?"

They had barely the energy to respond. While the other men walked through driving rain to the airport building to feast on steaks and coffee, Hughes had no time to waste. As soon as the French mechanics told him about the broken strut, he crawled under the plane in the mud, examined the wheel, noted that a stabilizer was buckled, and emerged to ask for an immediate, extra American mechanic in Paris. Miraculously, a man was found in less than an hour.

Hughes worked tirelessly for hours with the auxiliary help; at last, the strut was repaired and soldered. Hughes double-checked that American ethyl, not French fuel, was used as the 735 gallons were pumped into the tank. He personally went over items of stock, including food, taken on for the next lap of the journey: frozen lamb chops for him, roast chicken for the others—and only then, with great excitement, he ran through the storm to radio Hepburn at Fenwick that he was safe and sound.

The takeoff from Paris was hazardous because of severe crosswinds. The still top-heavy plane actually began to plummet onto the runway, but Hughes pulled it out at the last minute and managed a trembling takeoff. He headed into almost twelve hours of nonstop buffeting by electrical storms over Germany. Because Hitler was nervous about his arming for war being observed and photographed, Field Marshal Goering had issued instructions that Hughes was to fly at a very high ceiling level. This meant that he could not make major changes to escape turbulence and the plane was strained to the utmost.

Nevertheless, he made excellent time, and, at 11:10 A.M. the following day, he managed a perfect landing at the Civil Air Fleet Aerodrome in Moscow. The Russian Ambassador to the United States was on leave, and, with the heroes of a recent Russian transpolar flight, was there to greet him with a product of capitalism: a box of Kellogg's Corn Flakes.

Setting aside his ingrained hatred of Communism, Hughes gave a radio speech of praise, expressing his admiration for the airport designers who had built the structure so conveniently close to the heart of the city. Then he strode with his team to the dining room for the luncheon in his honor.

In the middle of the meal, a messenger walked in with a telegram from comedian Buster Keaton, which read, BE SURE TO BRING BACK A POT OF CAVIAR. Hughes burst out laughing. While the tanks were being refueled, he pored over maps supplied to him in New York, and obtained radio weather reports on conditions that he might expect in Siberia. They were not encouraging. He took off at 1:31 P.M.

He flew over the immense, freezing, and poorly-charted terrain of Siberia. He had to fly blind over huge rain clouds before making a bumpy descent into Omsk. Driving wind and rain had turned the runway into a sea of mud. The L-14 skidded to a halt at the very end. One foot more, and it would have foundered. Hughes jumped out and began issuing instructions to the ground crew, only to discover that they understood no English. Every time he tried to explain he wanted more fuel and mechanical adjustments, the men merely nodded their heads, held their stomachs, and pointed to the building, indicating that dinner was ready. In desperation, Hughes was forced to draw a diagram of the plane and of gasoline containers. Once the containers were brought, he was shocked to see that the ethyl he required was not available and he would have to fly on low-grade octane. This was a serious handicap.

Over Siberia, Hughes had another problem to face. Flying through murky clouds, black and threatening, he saw an enormous cliff looming directly ahead. He made a perilous 3,000 foot ascent, barely clearing the jagged top of a mountain. As the plane bumped through the updrafts to Yakutsk, Hughes looked at his chart. He was appalled to note that it showed the mountain range as only 3,500 feet high, whereas, in fact, it was 9,500 feet.

For the next 1,000 miles, the airplane's wings were coated in ice. Conditions were dangerous all the way to the Bering Straits. But the sturdy, undamaged plane made it magnificently to Fairbanks, Alaska, arriving at 2:17 P.M. A large and excited crowd ran up with hot dogs, bursting through the police cordon. Mrs. Wiley Post, widow of the last great aviator, was there with warmest greetings. She examined the tail, on which she had placed a good luck gob of chewing gum just before the plane left Floyd Bennett Field. It was still there.

Hughes jettisoned every last item at Fairbanks that could weigh the plane down: the life raft, most of the food supplies, sleeping bags, personal items of luggage. He tossed the Ping-Pong balls onto the tarmac and the crowd scrambled desperately for them. Most of them were retrieved by children. Then, to cheers, Hughes took off again.

He circled over Floyd Bennett Field at 2:35 P.M. the next day. The officials clocked up the record: he had circled the globe, a distance of 14,716 miles, in exactly three days, nineteen hours, and eight minutes.

Seeing the thousands below waiting to greet him, Hughes, for the first time, lost his nerve, and deliberately, not to say rudely, landed on the wrong runway.

It was a useless effort to avoid being mobbed. In fact, it made it more difficult for the two dozen motorcycle policemen scheduled by Grover Whalen to form a protective circle around the flyers. They stepped out awkwardly, blinking against the harsh light and temporarily stunned by the waves of heat that came up from the ground. Hughes was still wearing his battered brown felt hat. His companions' wives ran up; mechanic Ed Lund's fiancée fainted from the excitement. The yells from the 3,000 present were shattering.

Hughes stood uncomfortably alone. Not one of his family or friends was there to greet him. There could have been no more painful illustration of the way he disconnected himself from people than that. Not even Katharine Hepburn was on the tarmac; she was waiting for him at her town house at Turtle Bay. Eyes baggy with exhaustion, Hughes said gratingly into the nation's microphones: "The flight was wonderful and this is the world's best crew. All I can say is, this crowd frightens me more than anything in the last three days!"

Stretching his cramped limbs, Hughes added, wearily, "I'm glad it's all over. I expect to get as much sleep this week as possible. I want to bathe and eat, get a massage and a good shave."

Grover Whalen took Hughes in his car to his town house—two stables knocked together in Washington Mews. Whalen said, "I guess the first thing you'll want, Howard, is a hot bath." Hughes sighed in agreement. The bath refreshed him, but he lacked a clean shirt. Whalen offered him one of his own, but, though it had been shrunk repeatedly in the laundry, it was much too big. So Whalen's Filipino houseboy ran out and grabbed one at Wanamaker's.

Whalen and Mayor La Guardia had organized a press conference for late afternoon. But Hughes failed to appear. He ducked out into the backyard, through a small gate, and hotfooted it by cab to Katharine Hepburn's Turtle Bay town house. La Guardia was furious and addressed the press in a stream of four-letter words describing his view of America's hero. Hughes returned very late at night, waking up the household, unforgiven.

He had to face up to the biggest ordeal of all the following day: the ticker-tape parade. Whalen drove him to the Battery, where the parade began. It was almost noon as, in record heat, almost every human being who could move, from children to the very old, jammed the sidewalks and windows. Many fought the police cordons, composed of one-third of the entire Manhattan force. Hughes sat on the top of the back seat, still wearing his favorite hat, and a white shirt and baggy pants, grinning for once and waving. People were hanging from windows, tossing down a snowstorm of tape, and even complete telephone books weighing over two pounds each, one of which almost knocked him out. Sirens went off all the way down to the river, motor horns made a colossal din. Slowly, the motorcade crawled to City Hall. Mayor La Guardia was there to preside over the official reception. Hughes clumsily managed a brief speech about world unification before an audience of dignitaries.

The parade continued along Broadway, where the crowd became totally hysterical. Hughes was, overnight, America's idol. His youth, his good looks, his rangy physique, his unpretentious clothes and boyish grin captivated everyone. He was the symbol of American bravery and enterprise in the midst of the Depression. And the fact that he was one of the richest young men in the world added to an instant legend.

Drenched with sweat, Hughes showered at the Drake Hotel the moment the parade was over. Stubbornly, he tried to reach Katharine Hepburn's town house, and this time the crowds stopped his cab. When he yelled out to the people to let him in, nobody heard him. They were too busy cheering to attend to what he was saying.

It was not until the early hours of the following morning that at last the sightseers dispersed and he and Hepburn made their way through her street entrance, where her driver was waiting to take them to Fenwick. There, Kate's clan greeted him joyfully.

He dodged four lunches and dinners in his honor, and even a weekend party organized by Sherman Fairchild at Lloyd's Neck. But, on July 17th, he did turn up at the estate of multimillionaire F. Trubee Davison in Locust Valley, for a luncheon given for his flight companions. From there, he drove to North Hills, where Grover Whalen had his summer residence, for a dinner of seventy-five people. He continued to Flushing Meadows for lunch at the Terrace Club, to celebrate the first buildings of the forthcoming World's Fair.

He had promised to spend the following weekend with Hepburn at Fenwick. But instead, and quite inconsiderately, he broke the appointment and instead spent three days with the wealthy and socially prominent Jock Whitneys. Among the guests was the dark-haired, quietly subdued, movie and stage actress Fay Wray, whose greatest claim to fame was being gripped in King Kong's hand. She was presently on a theater tour.

Fay Wray was married to Hughes's former mentor, friend, and step-cousin by marriage, John Monk Saunders, whose first wife had been Rupert Hughes's daughter Avis. That fact alone provided a basis for conversation. Also, the pair shared a dislike of society people and were happy to withdraw onto the patio to talk.

They were attracted to each other. Hughes's callousness towards Katharine Hepburn, who was so deeply in love with him, as well as toward Fay Wray's prospective feelings, was shown by the fact that he made no mention of Hepburn to Miss Wray, and she, wrapped up in her career, seemingly knew nothing of his involvement. As for her husband, his drinking had alienated her from him, and she apparently felt no twinge of conscience in encouraging Hughes's advances.

That night, after a late party, she climbed into the antique four-poster of one of the guest rooms. The door opened at the end of the room. Howard Hughes was standing there. She invited him in.

They began seeing each other regularly. It could only have been painful to Hepburn when snippets began to appear in gossip columns. On July 28th, reporters trailed Hughes to Stamford, Connecticut, where he arrived by speedboat. He drove to the train station. Fay Wray got off the train. He kissed her. One columnist reported that he had expected to see him kissing Hepburn.

An International News Service reporter dogged the couple as they made their way to the pier to go by speedboat to the Fairchilds. "Does that kiss mean anything?" the snoop asked. "Are you and Mr. Hughes engaged?" "*Is this* Mr. Hughes?" the actress coyly replied as they climbed aboard.

Night after night, in order to avoid similar incidents, Hughes drove Fay Wray home to the Pierre Hotel in New York. He attended her constantly during her stage appearances. The novelist Sinclair Lewis was pursuing her at the time; Hughes insisted she see nothing of Lewis. Sometimes, Hughes would make romantic air trips with her; he would pick her up at the East River pier on 34th Street and fly her in his amphibian up to various friends on Long Island Sound. He would insult his previous lovers by inference: just as he had slept in a bed full of gardenias with Bette Davis, he gave Fay Wray 100 of the same flower. And he mimicked his friendship with Hepburn by flying with Wray under the 59th Street bridge.

John Monk Saunders was shattered by the news stories. Hepburn finally learned to take them in her stride. But Saunders began drinking more heavily than ever. Eventually, he hanged himself in his cottage in Miami.

Hughes took off to Houston for more speeches, parties, and parades. He tired of Fay Wray and, with typical ruthlessness, dropped her.

Back in Hollywood, he resumed his earlier interest in the long-suffering Ginger Rogers, while at the same time deciding he would befriend the very young and beautiful Olivia de Havilland. Finding out that de Havilland was making a picture entitled *Wings of the Navy*, he called his old friend from *Hell's Angels* days, Paul Mantz, and asked Mantz to arrange an introduction. As it turned out, Olivia, in common with millions of other American girls, was already in love with the great airman and America's hero, and would have given anything to meet him.

She was finishing up the picture when she met Hughes through Mantz. He took her for joyrides in his various planes—so often that gossip columnist Louella Parsons announced that they were engaged. This was a considerable shock to Ginger Rogers.

Hughes took off to Key West to work with Howard Hawks on a script for a planned version of Ernest Hemingway's *To Have and Have Not*. He mingled with a raffish group of beachboys, male and female prostitutes, Mafia figures, and amateur spies. Each Sunday he would sail in from the Keys with a boatload of assorted riffraff and call Olivia in Hollywood on the ship to shore line. She could barely understand him as his high-pitched deaf man's voice crackled through the static. When she complained about his deserting her, he oddly offered her a gift of thirteen (his lucky number) orchids per week. She was superstitious and only reluctantly accepted the offer.

Then he offered to marry her—when he was fifty years old. He told her that as a teenager he had planned his life in four acts: the first for flying, the second for building planes, the third for planning the future of aviation, and the fourth for marriage and retirement. He would marry her seventeen years hence; she didn't want to wait. When Hughes returned, he invited her to his house and told her he definitely couldn't marry her until late middle age. "I won't marry you—ever!" she exclaimed.

When the severe 1938 hurricane struck Connecticut in September, Hughes didn't fly back to Connecticut or help engineer a rescue mission for the stranded Hepburn family. Fenwick was almost completely wrecked by the wind. In her memoirs, Hepburn wrote that it was then she realized that her love for him had turned to water. She was too discreet to mention the real reason. But they remained friends. When she wanted to act in Philip Barry's play *The Philadelphia Story,* he put up some of the money and bought the screen rights for her.

Back in Hollywood, Hughes continued to romance Olivia de Havilland without concern for Ginger Rogers. The virginal young girl, who had easily resisted the more obviously predatory Errol Flynn, found it difficult to resist Hughes's act of being boyish, vulnerable, and sweetly shy. He kept telling her about his world flight—the dangerous takeoff from Floyd Bennett Field, the near crash in Siberia, the ice on the wings, and she was captivated. He was, in real life, everything Errol Flynn pretended to be on the screen.

While still dating Olivia, Hughes met her smarter sister, Joan Fontaine. De Havilland was giving a tea party when Joan appeared. Olivia was furious, believing that Joan was hoping to take Hughes away from her. Later, Olivia announced that Joan was to be honored by a party at the Trocadero nightclub; she was to come alone. Thinking Olivia was giving the party, or perhaps her fiancée Brian Aherne, Joan turned up in an elegant evening gown; she was astonished to find that Hughes was the host.

They danced; Hughes told her she should not marry Aherne, but that she should marry him. He had only just proposed to Olivia, and he was waiting for an answer from Ginger Rogers. "I've been in love with you ever since Olivia's tea party," he said.

She turned him down; he gave her his phone number at Muirfield Road. She arranged to meet him at Don the Beachcomber's restaurant. He repeated his proposal. She returned home and told Olivia everything. Olivia was furious; she broke off the romance with Hughes at once. On August 19, 1939, Joan married Aherne.

## CHAPTER SEVEN

# Wartime Years

In the wake of his world flight, Hughes, now worth about $60 million, began to fret about the fact that, in contrast with Hughes Tool, which was still thriving under the single-minded control of Noah Dietrich and a succession of harried executives, Hughes Aircraft was being outpaced by every other aircraft company, including Lockheed and Douglas. His neglect of management had left Hughes Aircraft in a hole, and Noah Dietrich showed little interest in it. The Army Air Corps refused to do business with him; even though he was America's hero, the brass knew what a wretched businessman and spendthrift playboy he was, and that the planes he designed were useless for military purposes, including the revamped H-1. He filed blueprints and specifications again and again, blissfully ignoring the requirements laid down in Washington and at Ohio's Wright Field base. He scarcely helped matters by accusing the authorities of indulging in a "Hate Hughes" campaign, and he began to brood on how to buy the bigwigs with women and money.

If he couldn't make it in military aircraft, why couldn't he use his fame and money to exploit a civilian airline?

Late in 1938, Hughes began to take an interest in TWA. He had flown the airline's DC-1 and DC-2 airplanes and liked them. Popular airline president Jack Frye, a rags-to-riches daredevil of the time, flew to Los Angeles to discuss Hughes's buying Pacific Air Transport, which flew between his city and Seattle. After dinner at Muirfield Road, Frye and his colleague Paul Richter brought up the subject. Finally, Hughes said, "Why don't we buy TWA instead?"

The two men said it would cost a lot of money. "I've got the money," Hughes replied. Hughes asked for a stockholders' list. Frye mailed Hughes the list. In January, 1939, Hughes bought 12 percent of the stock, then 13 percent more. Eventually, he had 78 percent.

On September 3, 1939, war broke out in Europe. Hughes at once found himself in an odd position vis-à-vis the *Southern Cross*. In 1938, he had formed a secret partnership with Axel Wenner-Gren, one of his rivals as the world's richest man, the founder of Electrolux and the inventor of the modern refrigerator, who was a friend of Field Marshal Goering and an arch-negotiator behind the scenes, with the Duke and Duchess of Windsor, for a permanent peace with Nazi Germany and a *cordon sanitaire* against the Soviet Union.

Wenner-Gren had become Hughes's partner in the Rover Steamship Company, named for the original title registration of the yacht; the company was still headquartered in Panama, with an office in Nassau, the Bahamas. Hughes's interests spread like a spider's web through the Caribbean region, and he kept in touch, via his little-known shipping interests, with the fascist dictators Batista in Cuba and Trujillo in the Dominican Republic.

For Hughes to be in partnership (his press office via Russell Birdwell kept lying that he had *sold* the yacht to Wenner-Gren) with a Nazi collaborator was reckless and indicated his questionable international connections. Shortly after war broke out, Wenner-Gren was linked to the sinking of the *Athenia,* by German torpedo, with many British and Americans on board, and Hughes had to at once dispose of his share in the *Southern Cross,* which was said to be guiding U-boats with its private radio station. The Rover Steamship Company, in which he still had an interest, was moved to Stockholm for the duration of the war.

Hughes began making overtures to the government to be allowed to build fighter and reconnaissance planes for a potential conflict. Meanwhile, ironically, the Japanese were using the models for his H-1 and H-2 craft for their own Zeros, and the Germans were employing the Sperry gyroscope, which he had used for his world flight—in both cases, secrets had been leaked from the various government departments, which had offered as much security as the average chicken coop.

Concurrently, in the early 1940s, Hughes set out to capture the two reigning young beauties of Hollywood: the gorgeous Gene Tierney and the equally beautiful Tyrone Power. Both dark, sultry, with carved features and flawless bone structures, their bodies ideally proportioned, they were sweet, pliable, self-adoring, spoiled, and highly sexed. Hughes conveniently ignored the fact that Tierney was involved with Count Oleg Cassini, the intense and passionate Russian high-fashion designer who would soon marry her, and who created the classically simple clothes that helped her to become a legend. Ignored, too, was the fact that Tyrone Power was married to the French actress Annabella, while also sleeping with a famous Hollywood male Latin lover.

Both stars were provocative of wild fantasies; in both, Hughes typically found a fulfillment of those fantasies.

Gene Tierney—famous for her sexy overbite—was the daughter of a wealthy insurance broker, expensively schooled at St. Margaret's, Connecticut, as well as Miss Porter's Finishing School and Brillamant in Switzerland. She made her theatrical debut on Broadway in *Mrs. O'Brien Entertains*, on February 8, 1939; she was in another play, *Ring Two*, later that year; when Hughes met her she had just completed a run in *The Male Animal*, for which she received a very good review from Brooks Atkinson. Darryl F. Zanuck, head of 20th Century–Fox, had therefore given her a contract and she was rehearsing for a western, *The Return of Frank James*.

Hughes was fascinated by her: she had Hepburn's breeding as well as a sweet, innocent purity combined with a certain steely strength and determination; she was well-read, intelligent, cultivated. The aphrodisiac of money worked again. She found Hughes fascinating, wrote poems to him, and enjoyed trips to Mexico with him—but she took her mother along as a chaperone. The sturdily macho, dashing, and handsome Cassini despised Hughes and longed to beat him up, "just to see if he had any red blood in him."

For Tierney, Hughes staged a small drama which he imposed on his successive women, famous or unknown. He took her to a place in the Hollywood Hills, where he had bought an unfinished house that he had left deliberately in a semi-constructed state. He told her she must kneel with him and agree to marry him under heaven, submitting to copulation on the spot on the understanding the house would be hers. In Tierney's case, this was a fatal mistake: she was prepared to indulge herself in a lazy, casual affair, but not to marry a master in a ritual of dominance. Cassini would make a more reliable and faithful husband. Realizing Hughes was trying to buy her (and he had forgotten she wasn't poor) she ran off down the hill and broke with him at once. Three years later, she returned to his bed.

Tyrone Power was, at the time, a much bigger name. The great star of 20th Century–Fox had already made his mark in such classics as *Lloyds of London* and *The Rains Came.* He was innocently sensual, vain, and laid-back, a kind of Polynesian WASP who believed that if anyone handsome, ugly, trim, or heavy wanted him badly enough he should grant them the pleasure of his body. He was a committed and tender lover who flung himself into affairs with the innocence of a child. A narcissist, he insisted on having scenes written in his scripts in which he was stripped to the waist; his square shoulders and well-defined pectoral muscles thrilled countless women and gays all over the free world in *Blood and Sand,* which he was shooting when Hughes enjoyed his body. He was much more open and untortured than, for example, Cary Grant, who was miserable in his off-again, on-again sleeping with Hughes.

As if having affairs with Tierney and Power (who would one day unforgettably costar in *The Razor's Edge*) were not enough, Hughes also had a relationship at the same time with Lana Turner. The beautiful blonde actress, feisty, strong-willed, wildly ambitious, was a far cry from the placid, pliable stars he was sharing his busy bed with. In fact, she made it clear she had no interest in having a physical affair with him, that she didn't like oral sex, that she was offended by his failure to use deodorants, a razor to remove his stubble, or a laundry to wash his shirts. She found it amusing, rather than sexy, when he sheepishly admitted his pants were torn and asked her to sew them up; he had brought needle and thread. In short, she was far too shrewd to consider even sleeping with him, and far too much her own person to risk emotional involvement or pregnancy for the sake of money and power—she was already making her mark at MGM, in *Ziegfeld Girl.*

Disappointed, Hughes consoled himself by dating a very pretty and famous actress of that time; that sensible young woman interviewed by this author also made it clear that she found him unappealing—his third strikeout following Joan Fontaine and Lana.

Thinking he could arouse the woman, he suggested he tie her up for sex; she refused. But she was prepared to be friends. She had a strong, fine character and didn't want to be compromised. Hughes was furious; pretending to be calm, he invited her to an apartment he had rented for a final drink. He asked her to come into the bedroom; she declined. To her amazement, he walked in there, leaving the door open, and she saw, on the bed, a life-sized rubber copy of herself, with breasts and a vagina. She watched as he mounted the figure, stroked it, thrust deeply into it, and, after a few minutes, climaxed. Yawning at the absurdity and boredom of it all, she left without a word.

Whether out of frustration or a simple yearning to be a movie tycoon again, Hughes decided to return to the motion picture business. He would make the sexiest picture ever made: the fulfillment of his wet dreams. He decided he would dare to suggest sexual intercourse on the screen, then the final taboo. Still the total voyeur, he would cast unknowns who would epitomize male and female beauty. He would put them under long-term contract and make sure no other producer could use them. Since they would yearn for a break, they would accept anything. He would impose his masterful will on them.

His ideal male had always been the moodily dark, lean, tall, handsome, and Latin-looking Jim Sharp, of his earliest days, and he settled on the idea of making a picture of the life of Billy the Kid, based more upon Sharp's exploits than upon the original Billy's murderous banditry. Unfortunately for him, Louis B. Mayer had already embarked on the same subject at MGM, so Hughes was forced, yet again, to see himself upstaged by one of the established Jewish figures he hated.

But Hughes went ahead anyway, and hired the writer Jules Furthman, who specialized in telling raunchy, off-color stories, and Howard Hawks, still a super-cool voyeur like himself, to put together *The Outlaw,* for release through United Artists. Like almost all of Hughes's previous pictures, his script contained off-color elements: the half-breed girl, Rio, who falls in love with Billy the Kid, is raped in a barn and found bound in ropes and gagged, struggling voluptuously, in a remote part of a desert. This was pure S and M bondage, astonishing in an American movie of the time. In another scene, Billy is ill, and Rio strips him naked and places burning-hot stones on his thighs and chest to revive him; she succeeds, and when she suggests to him he isn't strong enough to make love to her, his fierce eyes deny it and there is a fadeout.

There is also a strange bisexual undercurrent in the story, a male bondage/jealousy pattern established between two older men and Billy and Rio. A scene in a men's washroom, cut by censors, was especially crude and suggestive.

The feverish screenplay was finished in March, 1940. Hughes and Howard Hawks discussed it with Geoffrey Shurlock, movie censor. Hughes told Shurlock nothing of what was in the script, only that he wanted an ending that left Billy the Kid unpunished. Shurlock ruled this out completely.

Hughes was furious: even when he pointed out that Billy was obviously going to die at the end, Shurlock insisted that Billy must be killed. In seven months of constant battling, the censors decided that the entire project was impossible, but Hughes, as defiant as ever, went ahead anyway.

He cast the picture with attractive unknowns. He found, in questionable circumstances, a slender, darkly handsome insurance clerk, Jack Beutel, in a sleazy walk-up on Gower Street in Hollywood, spread on one of two beds with three other out-of-work young men he was sharing the flat with. What was the great Howard Hughes doing in such a place? Since Beutel was almost certainly heterosexual, the most likely explanation is that Hughes was pursuing one of the other youths.

He signed him, and according to author Lawrence Quirk and *Outlaw* assistant cameraman Lucien Ballard, urged Beutel into a sexual relationship.

Hughes's treatment of Buetel (he changed the spelling of his name) can only be described as brutal, heartless, a sultan's handling of a slave; movie-mad, hungry, Buetel was one of an army of handsome and physically perfect youths who were virtually on the street and would do anything for a break in Hollywood. Buetel was glad to have a job even if he had to do what were to him disgusting things to preserve it. It is doubtful that Hughes felt a similar guilt in exploiting Buetel as he enjoyed the young man's body. He was always callous, indifferent, buying what he wanted and then throwing it away.

Bizarrely, Buetel's agent was a Marx Brother: Gummo, one of the brothers of Groucho, Harpo, and Chico. Gummo Marx, presumably unaware of Buetel's affair with Hughes, was unable to arrange for his client more than a miserable $150 a week contract. And Hughes, for all his millions, never increased it. It was another way of ensuring Buetel's slavery.

Hughes had Buetel's photographic tests done by Ballard; in them, Buetel was dressed in tight-fitting, revealing cowboy jackets, jeans, and buckskins, which emphasized his good shoulders, trim waist, and muscular but slim arms and legs. Jane Russell, Hughes's choice as Rio, was maternal and warm, but with a sturdy, almost masculine air of self-confidence that belied her almost excessively female body. A struggling model, she was decent, very religious, tough, nobody's fool, with sultry good looks and huge breasts; she was humorous, and very ambitious under a laid-back front.

Hughes, Ballard remembered years later, ran the tests over and over again through the dark hours after midnight, feasting his eyes on the gorgeous couple. He didn't approach Russell for a physical affair; he may have sensed that she would refuse him. He gained his satisfaction by seeing her in the love scenes with Buetel.

Howard Hawks began filming the picture in Tuba City, Arizona, in November, 1940. While he handled the action scenes with Walter Huston, Thomas Mitchell, and Jack Buetel, Hughes's publicist, Russell Birdwell, had the stills cameraman shoot Russell in sexy shots against rocks or cactus or in a hayloft, her lips opening in a sensual snarl, her blouse cut low to reveal her cleavage, her powerful thighs raised in welcome. Soon afterward, Birdwell designed rousing slogans for her: "Mean, moody, and magnificent," and (under a shot of her breasts swelling up) "Two good reasons for seeing *The Outlaw.*" Her photographs appeared in magazines all over the world. Jane Russell became famous overnight, stimulating millions of erections from Alaska to Australia.

One shot of Russell bending over and picking up a milk pail was pinned up in countless GIs' dormitories or in ships' canteens, stuck in airplane cabins and fixed inside schoolbooks. She herself balked at one shot Birdwell had planned, showing her in a plunging, semi-transparent nightgown. Her psychology seems odd: she was prepared to become the world's leading sex object, made love to in fantasy by two-thirds of the world's men, yet she was decent, prissy, and puritanical in private.

Hawks proved to be the wrong choice as director. Not only was he painfully slow, he refused to allow Hughes to ride roughshod over him by telephone, interfering and fussing when the rushes—the scenes shot each day—were flown back to Hollywood. Hughes waited for a day, December 20, when Hawks had laid off the unit for a rest; he piled the cast and crew into a train and brought them home, leaving Hawks and Ballard stranded. Hughes took over the direction himself, which was what he had wanted to do all along; he neglected the action scenes, which were written feebly anyway, and concentrated, with a voyeur's intensity, on such sequences as Rio placing the hot stones on Billy's naked thighs, and Billy tying Rio up in a stretched-out state of bondage in burning desert rocks.

With his usual feverish interest in private lives, he asked Russell if she would mind shooting at night—would this interfere with her love life with a football jock to whom she was about to be engaged? She said, with the proper air of a Victorian gentlewoman, that the nocturnal schedule would be just fine.

Hughes hired a great cameraman, Gregg Toland, soon to be famous for *Citizen Kane,* and then forced that genius to descend to making countless shots of Buetel in tight pants and Russell in her blouse. He beat Buetel down as firmly in directing him as he presumably did in the bedroom: he made him reduce his insolence, his cocky self-assurance and dominating masculinity, to a passive, sleepy obedience and gentleness totally unsuitable for Billy the Kid but entirely suitable for an S and M slave. He even made Buetel call him "Sir."

He took countless takes of Buetel's hands, dwelling on their hairy slimness as he forced him to exhaustion, making him alter even the movement of a thumb or finger; as for Russell, he made her masterful, shooting her always in a dominant position, especially in the big bedroom scene, angling her shoulders so they looked bigger than Buetel's. She was an earth goddess, her breasts, like the cumulus clouds the planes penetrated in *Hell's Angels,* bursting with health as Buetel gazed at them, not with the powerful lust of a grown male animal, but with the puling longing of a sexual baby.

The masturbatory frenzy of making the film continued. No other individual in commercial Hollywood had so completely released his sexual urges on the screen, and nobody would for decades. The movie was one long, slow, drawn-out, sensually charged dream: a vision of a lean, pliant, soft man still handy with guns, and a woman who could offer him health, succor, and sex.

So obsessive was Hughes that he controlled the actual cut of

Jane Russell's brassiere. When he saw her seams showing through her blouse in one shot, several days into the shooting, he apparently found they reduced his degree of arousal and he sat up night after night designing a very tight brassiere that thrust her breasts higher and did not show seams. He sent it to her with orders she wear it. She tried it on and it was agonizingly painful. Refusing to be part of an S and M ritual, she put it away and redid her own brassiere so that it looked like the one he designed. He didn't know the difference. He approved—and was aroused.

Just before Christmas, with the picture a month into shooting, Hughes was heading for home after a very late night, no doubt masturbatory, session in his soundproofed, cork-lined screening room at the Goldwyn studio when he crashed into a car turning off North Rossmore Avenue onto Beverly Boulevard. He was laid up in the hospital for days, paid thousands to the other motorists to keep the accident out of the papers, and directed the movie by telephone, with writer Jules Furthman taking orders obediently at the other end of the line. He had the movie projected onto the wall of the hospital room, telling Furthman when a breast was insufficiently emphasized (he cannot have dared suggest equally attentive treatment for Buetel). Now he was directing the picture actually, as well as metaphorically, in bed.

On Christmas Eve, he was reluctantly at home: even Buetel threatened to walk off the picture, lawsuit or not, if he could not spend the time with his girlfriend, and Jane Russell was equally adamant. There was a ring at the doorbell. He was amazed to see Santa Claus walking in, complete with cotton beard, red velvet suit trimmed with more cotton, and big boots. A voice boomed out: Santa placed a bag filled with gifts on a table.

As he stood looking at it, the figure threw off its hat and removed its beard: according to a staff member, it was Ginger Rogers. Unfortunately—Hughes's life resembled a French farce—another actress (Gene Tierney?) was in the house at that moment and made a rather clumsy escape. Rogers and Hughes plunged into an argument. Santa picked up her cap and beard and made an undignified exit into the night. The romance with Ginger was over. He repossessed the car he had given her.

*The Outlaw* was finished on February 8, 1941. Hughes submitted it to censor Joe Breen on March 28. Breen was horrified. The countless shots of Jack Buetel's face and figure never crossed his mind as questionable, but as for the shots of Russell . . . he was appalled by the constant exposure of her mammaries.

He banned the picture outright. Hughes was furious. After a series of meetings between Hughes and Breen, Breen agreed he might issue a seal of approval if Hughes sliced up the breast shots— the notes to Hughes resembled instructions in a slaughterhouse. Hughes refused to deny the world his biggest wet dream. He put the cans away in a vault. Every few months he fiddled with the sound-track or added shots. But he refused to let anybody see the picture. Instead, he let Russell Birdwell build a constant groundswell of ex-citement in the potential audience by stating that *The Outlaw* was a victim of censorship, that he was fighting for freedom of expres-sion, and that one day the public would be able to see Jane Russell's healthy American womanhood in all its glory. Her pictures, particu-larly those of her stretched out on a hay heap chewing a straw and curling her vulvalike lips as she awaited her off-camera lover, kept appearing everywhere.

His stars remained his prisoners, on tiny salaries, unable to work for anyone else. When Darryl F. Zanuck, caliph of 20th Century–Fox, asked for Russell to play Doña Sol, the Spanish beauty and man-eating bullfight fan of *Blood and Sand*, Hughes refused, thus costing Russell the chance of a lifetime. The part was taken by Rita Hayworth, whom he would eventually bed, as he would her costars in the picture, Tyrone Power and Linda Darnell.

There is no evidence that Hughes cared for any of these su-premely attractive sex partners as people; he was as casual in mak-ing love to them and leaving them as most people in Hollywood. In the flesh market of southern California, breasts and muscles were traded in a frivolous search for the perfect companion; few were unavailable. Hughes retained his sex appeal; he was handsome, slen-der, with hard muscles; he had a vulnerable, little-boy-lost quality and immense charm; but even if he had not been good-looking and desirable, his wealth and power would have acted as an aphrodisiac on the men and women he wanted.

Restless and tormented as ever, Hughes turned his attentions to aircraft building. He was as brash as always: he clashed directly with the Washington big brass. As early as 1939, he had refused to allow General H. H. (Hap) Arnold, General of the Army Air Corps, into his hangars to see his airplanes in progress; he outsmarted himself with the War Department and lost a valuable contract to Lockheed; he refused to allow any government office to dictate terms of manufacture.

Nor would he obtain Washington's advice on the structure of a multimillion-dollar plant he built at Culver City, on 1,200 acres of land obtained by Noah Dietrich. When Dietrich went to Washington to seek contracts to justify the enormous cost of this deluxe factory with over 300 employees, General Oliver P. Echols, chief procurement officer, screamed at him, "That son of a bitch will never get a dime's worth of contracts out of me as long as I'm in this office!" Only by going over Echols's head was Dietrich able to secure a contract for airplane parts and a tentative commitment to Hughes's latest brainchild: an all-wooden (later plastic) D-2 fighter plane.

Hughes had been working on the D-2 since 1939. Hap Arnold wasn't impressed with Hughes's plans; he was appalled when he discovered that the plane was flammable and that its glass nose was composed of breakable glass. Arnold's spies told him that the Culver City plant was a disaster. Hughes was seldom there, workers were slack and uncontrolled, inefficiency prevailed, each individual vice president criticized every other one, several went to Hughes behind each other's backs. In the industry, the factory was known as the Country Club, a contemptuous reference to its lazy, slack, and self-indulgent atmosphere.

Distracted by his private affairs, which were as hopelessly confused as ever, Hughes neglected the very plant that he purported to control. He was furious at the government's indifference to him and refused to realize that Lockheed (on which he was forced to rely for certain specifications) and Douglas were far ahead of him; that his plant was the bottom of anybody's list.

He was too proud to do what he should have done at the time of Pearl Harbor: flown to Washington, agreed to accept total governmental control, accepted any Air Corps or other military figure appointed at Culver City, and arranged an appointment with Arnold to apologize for his bad behavior. Instead, in 1942 he dispatched his high-powered press agent, Russell Birdwell, and a pimp, Johnny Meyer, whom he had just hired away from Warners, to supply women to any military men who might feel in the need of sexual release.

This sleazy, ill-advised, two-pronged attack impressed few in the nation's capital. But luckily for Hughes, he had one Houstonian ally in that city: Secretary of Commerce Jesse H. Jones, who had known him when he was a boy. Birdwell told Jones about the six-million-dollar twin-motored bomber D-2, cheerfully ignoring the fact that Arnold had declared it useless, emphasizing the fact that the craft was redeveloped from the H-2, with which Hughes had won the transcontinental speed record.

The president was notably indifferent to the idea. In fact, when Jones suggested to him that he should make a public announcement affirming the value of the plane, he declined irritably. His secretaries, Stephen Early and Marvin H. McIntyre, made sure he wasn't troubled in the matter again. "I happen to know Russell Birdwell," Early wrote McIntyre with contempt for Hughes in an interoffice White House memorandum dated July 14, 1942. "He is a high-powered Hollywood press agent."

Three days later, Birdwell had somehow managed to talk Hap Arnold into a more considerate position.

One of the reasons that Arnold was feeling better about Hughes was that Hughes had managed to secure the support, indeed the partnership, of multimillionaire shipping tycoon Henry J. Kaiser, creator of the Liberty Ships. In San Francisco for some mysterious assignation, Hughes was stricken with pneumonia and at first Kaiser was unable to track him down for a meeting. But when the two men met they had a powerful rapport. Kaiser was concerned about building a massive Constellation transport plane that could fly 4,000 miles and carry fifty-seven crew members; Hughes promised him $10 million to assist the construction and an across-the-board deal with Lockheed to carry out the orders. In the end, Hughes unwisely told Kaiser he would supply no less than 500 of these sturdy aircraft. Russell Birdwell announced deliriously to the press, "This will be the most ambitious aviation program the world has ever known."

During a series of tense, charged conversations that went on for weeks, Hughes and Kaiser conceived a more remarkable construct than the original plane. It would be a huge transport ship with wings, designed to fly troops to the war zones and circumvent the sinking of so many seagoing vessels at the time. It would be an eight-engine amphibian, to be made of wood, and two hundred tons in weight; when Kaiser went to see Jesse Jones to discuss it on September 16, Jones told Kaiser, "You are safe in proceeding with Howard Hughes. I have known him since he was a boy—and I have known his able father before him—and I know of no more capable and reliable a man . . . He is thorough and he is a genius and do not interfere with him."

The agreement finally called for three planes to be finished in two years. But no sooner had Hughes agreed with Kaiser to complete the job in that time than he began to panic. On September 27, at midnight, Hughes appeared without warning at the Los Angeles hotel suite of Merrill C. Meigs, deputy director of the aviation division of the War Production Board, and for two hours poured out his agonizing doubts. Meigs did his best to reassure him. On November 16, 1942, Hughes signed the formal contracts. All three planes would be built at the Hughes Aircraft factory at Culver City.

He was right to have expressed doubts to Meigs, in point of fact, since his understaffed and inefficient plant was incapable of carrying out the orders. Hughes was in an unusually neurotic and testy state throughout the winter of 1942. He sold his house on Muirfield Road after almost twenty years of occupancy and moved to 619 Sarbonne Road in Bel Air. He absented himself from important government meetings in order to revamp the soundtrack of *The Outlaw* and to make some final cuts that at last would allow it to be shown.

He opened *The Outlaw* for its first public screening in San Francisco. He had put together a stage act in which Jane Russell and Jack Buetel wrestled in a forest glade. The first night the curtain stuck half-way up, showing comically only the stars' legs; the second, police arrived and closed the theater. Once again, Hughes petulantly locked the picture away in a vault.

Worse was to come. In May, he resurrected his old Sikorsky S-43, which had been in mothballs for years. He was forced to sell the beloved plane to the Army Corps of Engineers for use in Reykjavik, Iceland. He was uneasy that it might fail on a transport flight and cause loss of life so he decided to test its landing gears at Lake Mead, Nevada. With three other men, including government aeronautics inspector Charles W. Von Rosenberg, he set out on the major test flight in ideal weather conditions on May 16.

He came in for a good touchdown, but then he lost control of the plane and the S-43 took off on the water in a sudden, porpoise-like series of wild jumps, hurtling skywards and then plunging into the depths. The plane was torn to pieces with terrifying speed; Hughes sat stunned as Rosenberg managed to drag him to safety. They struggled onto the life raft as the plane sank.

He was rushed to Boulder City by ambulance. His trusted Dr. Lawrence Chaffin flew up there, cleaned the scalp wound, trimmed the hair around it, washed it with soap and water, and closed it with skin clips. Hughes walked out of the hospital without spending much time there as a patient.

Von Rosenberg's spine was shattered; he was in pain for the rest of his life. Government inspector Bill Cline died, trapped in his seat; his body was never recovered. Hughes's mechanic, Dick Felt, passed away from his injuries in the hospital. It was found later that Hughes's old problem of loading had done him in; the excessive number of cameras, cargo items, and gadgets had thrown the plane hopelessly off balance. Had Hughes landed on soil instead of water, he also would have been killed.

His lack of preplanning, which he had just gotten away with on his transcontinental and world flights, had cost two lives. He had no less appalling problems at his plant.

Hughes became increasingly irrational after the crash of the Sikorsky. Although his injuries appeared to be superficial, his concussion and shock may have included some brain damage. Certainly, in 1943, he embarked on a totally ill-advised, even crazy attempt to secure preferences from the still coldly indifferent president by financially seducing Roosevelt's son.

Hearing that Air Corps Colonel Elliott Roosevelt, a handsome and dashing man about town who was just back from Africa, was under orders to obtain a satisfactory reconnaissance plane, Hughes invited him to Los Angeles and made sure that his favorite pimp, Johnny Meyer, met Roosevelt off the plane. He instructed Meyer to make sure that the long-delayed and still quite inoperable, even dangerous D-2, which still had not secured a government contract, would be on the table for discussion with Roosevelt, along with the availability of various starlets or female dress extras.

Meyer knew an actress who would be an ideal ally for him in his negotiations: the coolly intelligent Warner Bros. player, Faye Emerson. After bedding her several times to check out her sexual performance, he found her expert at fellatio and introduced her to Roosevelt, who was looking for a wife, and, as he and Hughes planned, she proved to be exactly what Roosevelt wanted. She had the looks, the poise, the presence, and the elegance to entertain his wealthy and important friends in Washington. Meyer offered Roosevelt a house to live in, one of Hughes's several properties in Beverly

Hills. But Roosevelt felt that would be too obvious and instead, rashly, allowed Hughes to pick up his hotel bills—a dangerously corrupt move. Hughes also set about bribing high-level military officials.

Meyer never paid the various dignitaries in cash, but instead arranged for their bills at the Town House in Los Angeles to be met through a fictitious organization called Howard Hughes Productions. He arranged for gifts of hard-to-obtain black market nylon stockings, or handbags, to be given to the wives; Meyer obtained the stockings through a network of hotel bellhops who would trade the stockings for liquor. He made gifts to Major General Bennett E. Meyers, who was a crucial figure in Air Corps procurements. Hughes entertained Meyers lavishly at Hollywood restaurants, including the currently popular Romanoff's, and gave him a $40 a day suite at the Town House.

More funds were expended on a trip to Catalina in which Hughes acted as a host to Faye Emerson and others, including some very high-ranking military officers in the procurements division in Washington, D.C. Hughes basically controlled the War Department. The list went on and on. Hughes even had Meyer deduct the cost of certain available girls he was supplying to individual Army Air Corps figures on his taxes.

On August 11, 1943, Hughes did the unthinkable: he personally took Elliott Roosevelt around his plant, then flew him to the D-2 testing ground at Lake Harper. Roosevelt, as Hughes expected, went back to Washington glowing with praise, and Meyer followed him, with a gift of a parcel of TWA shares. By now, Roosevelt was Hughes's property: Hughes told Meyer to spare no expense in paying for Roosevelt's and Emerson's nightly jaunts in Washington and New York. The glamorous pair were seen in all the glitter spots: the Stork Club, El Morocco, the Copacabana. Hughes kept in touch with Meyer every day, making sure they were comfortable. He even paid for their Manhattan hotel suites.

The bribes paid off. On August 20, Roosevelt officially urged the ever-skeptical Hap Arnold to pick up a contract with Hughes for mass production of the D-2. Arnold agreed, provided that Hughes changed the structure from wood to metal. Hughes's old enemy, Major General Echols, opposed Arnold, knowing that the D-2 was hazardous to men and materials; in short, a disaster. Arnold overruled him; the plane was redesignated the XF-11.

General after general opposed the decision. Many smelled a rat: that Hughes had obtained the procurement by improper means, using the president's son to upset Roosevelt's implacable mistrust of Hughes. Hughes cried all the way to the bank: because of his matching of Elliott to Faye Emerson (and they married), he now had a $43 million contract to build 100 XF-11s.

Having bought seemingly the entire Air Corps brass in one go, Hughes had the ball to run with all the way to the finish line. But he stumbled badly on the way. He made a hash of the orders; distracted by his sexual affairs, he hired the able Chuck Perelle to run the Culver City plant and then made Perelle's life a misery by sheer interference and contradictory demands. He kept switching the XF-11 from metal to wood and back to metal again; he maddened Perelle with shifts and changes on the giant flying boat, now nicknamed *Hercules*.

Perelle pointed out to Hughes that to launch the flying boat he would have to build a launching dock, probably at Long Beach, as San Pedro was commissioned by the Navy. Hughes refused to submit any such plans to the government, even though the government was going to pay for it. Perelle screamed at him, "I'm not going to Washington, for Christ's sake, and negotiate these things, waste my time and the other people's, and then have you come along and wash out what I have done. . . . !"

When Perelle fired Johnny Meyer because he was occupying office space at Culver City as a mere pimp, that was the last straw. On December 6, 1945, Hughes fired Perelle. Perelle refused to be a slave; Hughes wanted wimps and servants.

He continued to enslave General Meyers. He even considered giving Meyers Perelle's job, which would probably have been reason enough for Meyers to face a court-martial. But Meyers overplayed his hand: he fatally asked the tight-fisted Hughes for a $50,000 loan in the form of Liberty Bonds. Hughes refused. Now that the war was over, he didn't need Meyers anyway.

## CHAPTER EIGHT

# Of Sex and Corruption

By 1940, Howard Hughes was, to all appearances, among the most fortunate of men. Though he had long avoided any exercise more vigorous than golfing, he enjoyed excellent health, in part because of his sparse diet and refusal to drink or smoke; he was thin, wiry, and still handsome; he was earning, from the Hughes Tool Company, close to two million a *month;* he enjoyed all the sex he needed and probably more; he had a majority of shares in the airline that would later be known as TWA; he had a standing invitation to the best parties; he had flocks of servants, several houses, and a permanent suite at the elegant Town House. Only his deafness, and a certain insecurity in his sexual performance, were blights on his existence. For him, every dream was instantly fulfilled; every element in his Jekyll-and-Hyde nature, alternately gentle and considerate, terrifying and controlling, could have free reign.

Yet he was impatient, restless, because there were people even he couldn't buy, and the president (if not the president's son) and the moguls of Hollywood were stubbornly resistant to his charms. He was tortured by paranoia that was by no means unfounded, holding his business meetings in his beaten-up Chevrolet, on public telephones (people had to call him back from other telephones), or in obscure motels; he sensed, without knowing it, the truth: that J.

Edgar Hoover had him on the watch list for buying Elliott Roosevelt, senators, congressmen, and Air Force and Army bigwigs. The truth is that his political activities were dangerous, criminal, and subversive.

In the early years of the decade, Hughes again crossed, with more confident self-indulgence, into another area: the then criminally punishable, dark, and stimulatingly dangerous world of homosexual life. Rumors spread that he was involved in scenes of punishment: of torture and bondage in dungeon rooms in which he was the dominant figure. The late actor and decorator William Haines told the author of numerous incidents of this.

It would certainly fit with Hughes's personality that he was the dominant partner, anonymously male and powerful, submitting men to ropes, handcuffs, gags, and chains; in that murky world, in the near-darkness, it was not necessary to be a great cocksman; relief was often obtained by mutual or individual masturbation. He may have sought out the underground, with its constant atmosphere of tension and terror—there were police raids, with naked men rounded up with nightsticks, paradoxically a gay fantasy fulfilled— yet he also is said to have found more concrete sexual situations. And it was always safer to enjoy movie stars, who would have much to lose if they informed on him, rather than hotel bellhops, swimming pool attendants, or lifeguards who might easily blackmail him.

Information about Hughes's individual sexual affairs was, of course, guiltily hidden, and could not have been mentioned even in the most scandalous publications of the time. But Hughes did confess the truth to his uncle Rupert, with whom he had become much closer over the years, in secret meetings at Rupert's magnificent Moroccan mansion on Los Feliz Boulevard. He swore Rupert to secrecy, but Rupert passed the information on to *Photoplay* magazine publisher James Quirk, who, in turn, again passed along these confidences to his nephew, Lawrence, who gave them to this author.

In the early 1940s, Quirk states, Hughes had relationships with two handsome actors, one famous and the other little-known and struggling. Richard Cromwell was about thirty, a blond, corn-fed, strapping Californian. He began as an interior decorator, working for William Haines; he made mask portraits of some of the best-looking male stars. He was shy, soft-spoken, and passive: Hughes's requirements. He looked sharp in eighteenth-century British regimental uniform in *The Lives of a Bengal Lancer,* was a knockout in Navy whites in *Annapolis Farewell* and *Our Fighting Navy,* and some- how survived Bette Davis in *Jezebel.*

Hughes was his lover on and off for years; but Cromwell had many others. His vulnerable good looks and gentle good manners in 1945 eventually attracted the unwitting young Angela Lansbury, who was usually the model of shrewd intelligence; she was married to him for eight months before she divorced him. The actor died of cancer at fifty.

Hughes's other lover was equally ill-fated. Russel Gleason was the wayward son of the popular character actor James Gleason. According to Quirk, Russel fell under Hughes's magic spell. Unlike Richard Cromwell, who was lazily narcissistic and self-indulgent, Russel Gleason was tortured and miserable for all of his fine looks and figure and high intelligence; apparently, Hughes gave him no more emotional support or security than he did anybody else, and Gleason—after a spell as a photographer in the armed services— threw himself out of a New York hotel window on Christmas Day, 1945. Like Cromwell, he had asserted his manhood in a marriage, but, according to Lawrence Quirk, could not overcome his conflicts any more than Hughes could.

But some male Hollywood stars failed to respond to Hughes's charm. Robert Taylor refused Hughes, as he didn't find him appeal- ing, and Errol Flynn, lured to a joking nocturnal assignation with Hughes by the inescapable Johnny Meyer, turned him down as a "deaf haddock." Not even Hughes could win everybody, all the time.

There is solid evidence, in FBI-bugged telephone conversations, that Hughes became seriously involved with the rising star Linda Darnell. Born in Dallas, Texas, like another of his sex objects, Jack Buetel, she was as voluptuously warm and fleshy as a Rubens nude. A postal clerk's daughter, just nineteen in 1940, she had been driven by her show biz mother into tap dancing and beauty contests, win- ning most of them. With little struggle, she quickly made her mark: her dark, lustrous hair, ruminant liquid eyes, big, creamy shoulders and breasts, and lushly contoured body more than made up for a meager acting ability and a rather thin voice. She was sweet, pliant, as readily and sensually available as her fellow 20th Century–Fox contractee Tyrone Power.

Hughes found her fascinating and pursued her for six years with very few breaks, following her career and watching her pictures on his private screen with as much avid interest as he watched Tyrone

Power or his other star lovers. Seeing her with Power in *Blood and Sand* must have been a voyeur's treat: Power, half naked in tight matador's pants; Darnell, in revealing Spanish dresses. Even as the Virgin Mary in *The Song of Bernadette,* perched like a plaster figure in a grotto's rocky niche, she was something to lose sleep over.

Darnell's marriage to cameraman Peverell Marley in 1943 failed to dampen Hughes's continuing lust for her, and, with a remarkable degree of courage (since Marley was feisty and furious, a rugged craftsman of the old school who knew how to use his fists), Hughes risked secret meetings with her until at least 1946. She died in a fire at forty-three after watching one of her old movies on television; for years she had been terrified of fire, telling everyone close to her that she hated the scenes when she was in flames in pictures, including *Anna and the King of Siam* and *Forever Amber.*

By contrast with these affairs, Hughes embarked on, of all things, a platonic relationship with the dazzling but sluttish and coarse-grained Ava Gardner, who had risen from a Tobacco Road slum in the South to become the hotshot Mrs. Mickey Rooney and a slinky MGM contractee brunette. She was trained to give an imitation of acting; few males cared that she wasn't exactly Sarah Bernhardt. Everything about her—her movements, her fluttering eyelashes, her half-open lips—was calculated to excite high temperatures, and succeeded.

It may seem incredible that these two high-powered human beings, Ava committedly lustful, Hughes insecure and inadequate as a lover, but consistently adventurous and experimental, never actually copulated. Why? It must have been because Gardner wasn't at all submissive; she was as dominant as Hughes. And, unlike Gene Tierney and Linda Darnell, she was challenging, witty, sharp, and nobody's fool. She didn't find Hughes appealing sexually; although she was careful to dodge the matter in her memoirs, she more than implied in them that she knew he was bisexual.

Ambitious and self-indulgent, a lazy cat who waited for men to proposition her, she first met Hughes just before he crashed the Sikorsky on Lake Mead. He enjoyed being with her because, like the very different Katharine Hepburn, she was interested in politics, airplanes, and cars: she could be a brother, a mate. She, in turn, liked to be in the company of money and power: she had only to turn up with Hughes at a fully booked restaurant or nightclub without a reservation for the maitre d' to whip out a table; when Hughes walked with her onto a dance floor, the band would play "Deep in the Heart of Texas"; and when she traveled by TWA, planes would miraculously materialize to take her wherever she wanted to go—as the only passenger.

What she didn't like was Hughes's cheapness with automobiles—he refused to drive her around in a Rolls or a Daimler, but instead took her on dates in a beaten-up Chevrolet. One trip she took with him, in 1943, to San Francisco by train when he met with Henry Kaiser, told her much she hadn't known about him.

Chastely housed in a separate compartment, he invited her to the dining car for dinner. She sat down at a table and waited for him. Everyone stared at her. Suddenly Hughes appeared, not in his usual unpressed shirt, baggy pants, and sneakers, but in a feminine ice-cream pleated suit, belted at the back, cut like the famous cross-dressing costume worn by Marlene Dietrich in *Morocco*. It was much too small for him, suggesting that it must have been a woman's.

Hughes began to pirouette, like a girl, showing off the absurd garment, as Ava blushed, embarrassed, and the passengers, many of whom must have seen photographs of Hughes, sat aghast at the sight of America's hero acting like a fairy. Here was the man who flew round the world behaving like a sassy schoolgirl!

They checked into separate suites at the Fairmont Hotel. After his bout of pneumonia, Hughes took Ava out for the evening. She expected to be taken to Chinatown or one of the various fashionable restaurants of the time. Instead, he whisked her off to a gay night-club, where men dressed as women, in spangles and paste jewelry, danced on the stage and swapped campy insults with the homosexual audience. This normally cautious and private man felt no such need for caution in a wide-open gay city like San Francisco, which may explain why he spent so much time in it; later, he had an affair with one of the dancers at Finocchio's, another transvestite night-club.

Back at the Fairmont, Hughes showed his ugly, controlling side. He decided, presumably stimulated by the sight of pretty boys at the club, to make love to Ava. She only wanted to enjoy a glass of champagne and read the funnies. He snatched the comic section from her hand and made it clear he wanted her undivided attention. She got up, furiously, ran into her bedroom, and locked the door. Hughes lost his temper. He telephoned Ava's sister Bappie in Los Angeles and told her to fly up at once in one of his private planes and take Ava home. When Bappie arrived, Hughes showed her a cheap cardboard box full of diamonds, emeralds, and rubies—a sultan's treasure. He said Ava could have the lot if she married him. Bappie begged Ava to accept the jewels. Not known for her ladylike language, Ava replied, "Tell him to stick them up his ass!" And she cleared out.

On one occasion, Mickey Rooney arrived home on army furlough to find a battered Chevrolet outside Ava's door. Not realizing it was Hughes's, he grabbed the occupant and swung him around. Slightly startled that the man was America's hero, he hesitated, then threw a punch. Hughes, not as daunted as he was by Oleg Cassini when confronted by a five-foot pygmy, bent over and struck back. The pair landed up on the sidewalk with wildly flying fists.

On another occasion, at Ava's house (he was paying her rent), Hughes found her naked in her bedroom, engaged with a Mexican matador. She flung on a robe; the matador fled down the back stairs. Hughes chased her to the living room where she threw down a drink at the wet bar. He struck her across the face and bruised her badly. She picked up a chair and hit him on the head. He blacked out. When he came to, several teeth were loose or missing and he had to wear partial dentures for the rest of his life.

Even though he didn't lust strongly for Ava, he couldn't stand the idea of a muscular Mexican embracing her, possessing her. He hired Mormon bodyguards, whom he favored because they didn't drink or smoke and didn't expose secrets (though he must have been made nervous by their traditional homophobia), to follow her everywhere. When she resumed her sexual relationship with Mickey Rooney he became enraged and threatened her life. But even he was quelled when she told him she wasn't frightened of him. He had to admit it: he had met his power-driven match.

He also met a match in the Canadian actress Yvonne De Carlo, and she *did* find him sexually attractive. She was bright, dark, quick, busty; he was obsessed with her. Born plain Peggy Middleton in Vancouver, Canada, she was twenty-three when they met in 1945—a little old for him. But when he saw her over and over again, in his private projection room, dancing voluptuously in Walter Wanger's movie *Salome—Where She Danced,* he knew he had to have her.

As an exotic Viennese spy, she was crazily miscast; her part was based on the international adventuress Lola Montez. But she gave the picture charm, humor, and a tongue-in-cheek feel that he found very appealing.

Her background was no more impressive than Darnell's or Gardner's. First runner-up as Miss Venice (California), she groaned away in nightclubs without much of a singing voice but with a degree of sex appeal that worked on tired businessmen. She had been on occasional dates with both musician/band leader Artie Shaw and stringbean hotshot James Stewart and had been friendly with the virile and hard-boiled Austrian writer-director Billy Wilder.

Hughes ran into her in Vancouver over the 1945 Labor Day weekend; Johnny Meyer introduced them and he took her for a vacation flight over the city in his TWA Douglas DC-3, and thence to Lake Tahoe and Reno, where they went boating (she swam; Hughes didn't). They made love in Las Vegas and gambled; he became excited, like his friend Bugsy Siegel, with the possibilities in that city.

This strong and independent woman was as desirous of a singular partnership as Hughes was of just another affair. She didn't like the fact that in his permanent suite at the Town House in Los Angeles he had pictures of Jane Russell strewn on the floor of his rooms, taking up the space like a carpet of breasts, or that he constantly told her, even in bed, that his only true love was Ginger Rogers. He talked too much after intercourse, comparing male and female orgasms in a way that seemed too clinical and detached. She was finding out as all other women and men did that for Hughes sex was no more than relief (or proof of potency), that he wasn't inventive, tender, or considerate, that he was using human orifices for his satisfaction, and that men and women were merely entrances for his pleasure.

He wasn't, of course, faithful to her; she didn't know about his affairs with men, but she needed only to have picked up a newspaper to learn that he was sleeping with Gail Russell, a dusky, sloe-eyed beauty of exotic appearance and a pliant, weak, tormented person who would die prematurely—at thirty-six, from drink and drugs. He had seen her in the ghost movie *The Uninvited,* in which she touchingly played a delicate, haunted girl. He saw her frequently for two years. He also had under personal contract, still another sultry girl, Faith Domergue, whom he signed at fifteen and didn't use in pictures for six years.

Hughes revived his earlier sexual interest in Gene Tierney. She was married by now to designer Count Oleg Cassini, and in 1943 had a daughter who turned out to be retarded. Hughes used an alleged sympathy with the little girl to ease his way back into Tierney's favor and put Cassini off guard. At a party at Jack Benny's, he had the nerve to proposition Gene in front of her macho husband.

Cassini called his bluff. Instead of having Hughes step outside and put up his fists, Cassini drew him into a corner and told him that if he seriously intended to marry Gene, and she wanted to marry him, he would not stand in their way. But Hughes must *really* marry her, and announce that he would to the press and radio, or he would personally beat him to a pulp.

Hughes ignored the threat, and when Cassini was out at a boxing match took Gene to Las Vegas in his plane to make love to her. Cassini found out and waited for them to return, crouched in the dark garage. He jumped up and, rather oddly, instead of decking him, struck Hughes on the behind with a plank. Hughes fled. Cassini despised him for being a weakling and not fighting back. Later, Cassini chased Hughes up a staircase at a party and Hughes, instead of punching him, hid in a bedroom and locked the door like a nervous virgin. Was this America's hero?

Through all of those sexually consumed years, Hughes kept buying Air Corps, Army, and presidential contacts who could give him preferments for his airplanes. His actions were almost comically corrupt.

In 1945, the venomous columnist Westbrook Pegler, who delighted in taking on enemies as Hughes delighted in taking on lovers, came up with staggering proof, "stolen" from FBI files (with the surreptitious aid of J. Edgar Hoover), of Hughes's influence-buying schemes that were securing Hughes millions in government orders at Culver City.

Pegler wrote of parties for nine at the Stork Club; $132 for pairs of nylons for Faye Emerson; weeks in which Elliott Roosevelt stayed at the Beverly Hills Hotel at Hughes's expense, the bills marked "Mail to Hughes Aircraft," and signed by Elliott Roosevelt with the word "OK"; huge accounts at the Waldorf-Astoria, with CODs signed by Meyer for Hughes Aircraft; costs for the Roosevelts' wedding party in December, 1944; a weekend Roosevelt trip to Palm Springs, including a maid's transportation, housing, and tips; payment of Faye Emerson's bets at the race track at Caliente; and two expensive handbags.

Hughes was plagued by visits from the investigative committee of the U.S. Senate, which was conducting hearings about his ability to produce airplanes that would justify the $40 million invested in his company. The committee found that Hughes had just paid Elliott Roosevelt a staggering $75,000 for his support. Hoover was convinced that the matter might result in both Hughes's and Roosevelt's indictments. Hughes accused Senator Owen Brewster, who was in charge of the investigation, of being a pawn of rival aircraft tycoon Juan Trippe, of Pan American, and trying to blackmail him by offering to drop the inquiry if Hughes gave him a parcel of TWA shares and cash. He hired the Schindler Detective Agency and a former Washington cop to bug Brewster's phones.

Later, Westbrook Pegler claimed that Hughes had given parties for Elliott Roosevelt in which "semi-nude lovelies swam in a mirrored pool" at one of Hughes's houses.

In early 1945, J. Edgar Hoover opened a major file on Hughes. Hughes and Meyer had hosted a party for visiting Russians; he was hoping, via Elliott Roosevelt, to make an across-the-board deal with Russia for his flying boat without the authorization of Henry Kaiser or General Hap Arnold. And he was busy using Bugsy Siegel as a contact in Las Vegas.

During the war years, Hughes ran TWA like his own private airline; when his ex-lover Bette Davis's second husband Arthur Farnsworth fell ill in Minneapolis, he had her flown solo to the stricken man's side; he made sure that rival Hollywood columnists Hedda Hopper and Louella Parsons never went on the same plane, always traveled free of charge, and were supplied block-length limousines—to ensure their support of him. Bribed, they played ball.

Every time one of his Constellations took off, several seats were reserved in case his friends should decide to travel. TWA staff resented this arrangement, but he wouldn't budge.

If any celebrity grumbled to Hughes about the plane service or baggage handling, heads fell, and their fares were refunded. Employees Walt Menke and Johnny Meyer were instructed to take care of anybody who appeared in *Who's Who* or the Blue Book. Hughes pimped handsome pilots to aging stars but they had to make love to them without overtime. The reward was a free night with a beautiful starlet or call girl.

His eccentricities fascinated or annoyed his TWA employees; he would borrow cars, coats, hats, and money and seldom return them. He would snitch cash from the lowliest to pay a cab driver. He was tight as ever with his own money. One actress he often flew on TWA as a mascot was turned on sexually by taking money for a night of pleasure. He handed her two fifty-dollar bills before climbing into bed. She left them in her purse. When she was sleeping, he handed one of them to Johnny Meyer, who had clambered up a drainpipe and through the window in the dark.

In the summer of 1945, Hughes decided to take *The Outlaw* off the shelf and release it, with all of the publicity hoopla that Russell Birdwell could manage. There was a rumor in the film industry that he made a nude version of it for masturbatory use. The rumor persists among veterans today.

The FBI was alerted to the fact that Hughes had so infuriated the film industry that the five and a half million feet of raw film he needed to make prints of the picture were denied him, and he had run out of his own supply, presumably because of his obsession for printing hundreds of takes of his half-naked stars. The War Production Board proved reluctant to help.

He enlisted the help of a handful of movie executives favorable to him, including Sol Lesser, producer of Tarzan pictures, and director Leo McCarey, whom he had had under contract in 1930. He engaged the popular Harry Gold, United Artists' sales manager, as general manager of *The Outlaw*'s worldwide distribution.

One of Hughes's favorite restaurants was The Players on Sunset Strip, an elegant nightclub owned by the writer-director Preston Sturges, who was a close friend of Rupert Hughes. The heavy-drinking, self-destructive, brilliant Sturges was fascinated by Howard and shared his love of aircraft and beautiful women—Sturges was strictly heterosexual. They would sit, very late at night, in some murky corner banquette, talking while their dates fell asleep, Sturges pitching his voice very high so the deaf Hughes could hear him.

In March, 1944, Hughes formed a partnership with Sturges to make a picture. They moved into the California Studios opposite Paramount, which had let Sturges go. Almost at once, Hughes tried to control Sturges: a serious mistake. He daringly offered him a salary; Sturges wanted, and got, a partnership. Among the partners in the deal—Hughes Tool owned 37 percent of the stock—were Frank Orsatti, a glorified pimp/agent with a criminal record, who helped find Hughes sexual companions when Meyer ran out of them, and Jules Furthman, author of *The Outlaw.*

Hughes heard Sturges's ideas, which included a film version of the Lizzie Borden story, with Lillian Gish, to be directed by D. W. Griffith, and finally agreed to a sequel to comedian Harold Lloyd's silent comedy, *The Freshman.* It was called *The Sin of Hilda* (later *Harold) Diddlebock.* United Artists would release it as *Mad Wednesday.*

Hughes insisted on checking every detail of Sturges's script and the production, which began on September 12, 1945. Because Hughes still had little skill at producing and kept the budget too low, and Sturges was in decline from alcohol, the picture turned out to be a dud; it was fifty-two days over schedule and $600,000 over budget. No sooner was it finished than Hughes let Sturges make *Colomba,* the title changed to *Vendetta;* in it, Hughes at last gave a break to Faith Domergue, whom he had had under contract, idle, for six years. Then Sturges yielded the direction to Max Ophüls, a prominent director who had become a cult figure in Hollywood.

Hughes approved Preston Sturges's script in June, 1946. Designed to show off Faith Domergue's Jane Russell–like beauty, her lustrous eyes, sensual mouth, and large breasts, the heavy-breathing melodrama was the story of a Corsican girl who seeks, with multiple heavings and gaspings, to revenge her father's murder. Hughes costarred Domergue with the drop-dead George Dolenz. They made a notably wooden pair, their acting styles resembling two bedposts rather than two people in bed.

By early 1946, Hughes launched a new advertising campaign for *The Outlaw,* with pictures of Jane Russell, breasts aggressively busy, and with such new slogans as "The girl with the summer hot lips—and the winter cold heart," and "Who wouldn't fight for a woman like this?" Hughes engineered a long list of prominent people who complained to the papers . . . the giveway of the phoniness of this was that Jules Furthman was among the complainants.

When the picture opened, all over the nation and abroad, Russell Birdwell's sexy campaign succeeded magnificently. In London, the lines were around the block, as long as they had been at the same theater, the London Pavilion, for *Hell's Angels.* The angry or mocking reviews, the gales of laughter greeting Russell's mountainous breasts, the shoals of complaints aimed at the censors, all ensured a colossal success, as Hughes had hoped. The billboards of Russell, mean, moody, and magnificent as ever, made her a byword in Britain. There was scarcely a heterosexual male in Britain who didn't lust for her, even though they might laugh at her image as well.

When Maryland banned the picture outright, Hughes threw his lucky brown hat in the air. But at the same time, he had other preoccupations.

During those years, Hughes neglected his family; but he was shocked when, on March 23, 1945, Rupert Hughes's wife, the former actress Elizabeth Patterson Dial, died of an overdose of pills, probably a suicide. She had suffered from severe depressions for months. Had she found out about Rupert's affairs with men? Hughes had grown close to Rupert after their initial disagreements over his father's estate; he had never blamed him for initiating him into gay sex; and now he could pour his heart out to Rupert over his secret, guilty homosexual affairs. Rupert Hughes must surely have promised complete secrecy; Rupert knew that gay activities were criminal offenses then, but he didn't keep the secrets: as we know, he relayed them all to his close friend, James Quirk of *Photoplay*, whose nephew Lawrence has only now revealed them.

On February 14, 1946, Valentine's Day, Hughes personally piloted a large crowd of stars chosen by Johnny Meyer, and Lana Turner, in whom he had resumed his earlier interest, aboard his newfangled TWA "Connie," or Constellation aircraft, for an inaugural flight to New York. The top brass of Hollywood, hating Hughes as much as ever, disgusted by the fact that he was working on a rerelease of *The Outlaw*, refused to come. Louis B. Mayer and Harry Cohn, in particular, remained repelled by his anti-Semitism. He invited Bugsy Siegel, who continued to interest him in possible investments in Las Vegas, his intermittent lover Cary Grant, Alfred Hitchcock, Paulette Goddard, who attracted him strongly, and Edward G. Robinson. Cary Grant was the only passenger allowed to sit next to him at the controls.

The guests arrived at the Sherry-Netherland Hotel, where they stayed at Hughes's expense. The FBI was alerted to the trip and followed Hughes throughout, with an agent on the plane and local agency boss Richard Hood in charge.

Hughes was bugged by the FBI, including his visits to Lana Turner's suite and his evenings with her at El Morocco. While he was trying to consummate their relationship in sex, he was, FBI records show, treacherously calling Linda Darnell in Hollywood for hours at a time, insisting she marry him, declaring his love. She must have known that he had no more intention of marrying her than she had of marrying him. He was a wife-stealer, after all: a Casanova with as much substance as a knave on a playing card.

Hughes returned to Los Angeles with Swedish Count Bernadotte, who was connected to Hughes's shipping interests in Sweden following Axel Wenner-Gren's blacklisting as a Nazi sympathizer, and with ex-Governor Paul Laxalt of Nevada. On March 30, he was at an eyebrow-raising bachelor party with Cary Grant at the popular Clover Club, a plush gambling joint on Sunset Strip. Bugsy Siegel was among the guests.

Early in April, Hughes arranged another assignation with Lana Turner at the Sherry-Netherland. Johnny Meyer made her reservations. She arrived on April 17, and Hughes left twelve days later.

Hughes flew to Louisville, to see the Kentucky Derby. In New York, he filed a five-million-dollar lawsuit against the Motion Picture Producers and Distributors of America for interference with trade in their opposition to *The Outlaw*. He withdrew from the MPPDA again the same day. In San Francisco, a trial of Hughes by the city for indecency over that picture collapsed when the judge informed the jury that there was nothing disgusting about breasts.

Hughes was beginning to feel more optimistic when he made a mistake which might have cost him his life.

## CHAPTER NINE

# Crash!

Hughes vanished from Culver City, and from his home in Beverly Hills, for over eight months. He set out on a strange, seemingly meaningless journey, abandoning the all-important work on the XF-11 reconnaissance plane and the *Hercules* seaplane; he was exhausted, worn out by his struggles with the authorities and the efforts to subordinate Washington to his will. It was as though, having made a supreme effort to obtain favors for his beloved aircraft, he ceased for a while to care for them.

With a small group of trusted mechanics, a navigator, and copilots, he took off in his favorite, and now aging, Sikorsky S-43 Amphibian for a nostalgic trip to Shreveport, Louisiana, where he had spent so much of his infancy with his long-dead parents. One night, in drenching rain, he walked off, leaving his team at the local hotel, and apparently went looking for the various places he can scarcely have remembered, including the Caddo Hotel. Instead of taking a cab or a rented car, or even an umbrella, he walked off in the downpour in his battered hat, which miraculously had survived the years, filthy white shirt, ragged trousers hitched up above his ankles, and battered sneakers, looking like a hopeless tramp.

Soaked, he paused for a few minutes in the shelter of a gas station, eating sodden cupcakes from a bag and drinking milk from a dripping glass bottle.

A policeman drew up beside him in a patrol car and asked him for his ID. He was unable to produce it; what was more, he had no money on him, not even a dime. Bundled into the car, he protested that he was Howard Hughes. The cop ignored him. When he reached the precinct, he stood, with a puddle forming round his feet, looking like the bedraggled Scarecrow in *The Wizard of Oz*. Chief of Detectives Jim Davis said to him, "Who the hell are you?" "Howard Hughes," the wretch replied. "If you're Howard Hughes, I'm Shirley Temple," Davis said, with a laugh.

Hughes, protesting loudly, was put into a cell along with various riffraff. Detesting blacks, he was especially furious when two of his cellmates turned out to be Negroes. He shook the bars and yelled that he was who he was. The others laughed at him.

Later that night, he whispered to the jailer that there would be $5,000 if he would give him another hearing with Davis. Something about the way he said it was convincing. Davis went irritably to the cell. Hughes began to give details of his career in a manner no tramp could have managed. Next morning, Davis called the Hughes Tool Company's local Caddo subsidiary. At first, the manager thought it was a hoax. But Hughes talked to him on the telephone and he was convinced.

Hughes joined his companions and they flew on to Orlando. He ran from the plane and grabbed an airport bus. He wasn't heard of for three months. He turned up in Miami after riding the rails. He drove up to his team's hotel in a battered Chevrolet with several white boxes crammed into the back. One of these, a very long one, like an outside flower box, looked mysterious. Hughes would not allow it to be touched. His men spent weeks conjecturing what it might contain until at last they gingerly opened it. Hidden under piles of comic books and folded newspapers were . . . a dentist's drill and two douche bags.

Hughes vanished again, only to turn up at the Plaza Hotel in New York in a tuxedo and sneakers; he spent the night at the Stork Club in that garb. When his team packed up for him they found amazing things in his closet he hadn't bothered to hide: both men's and women's clothing and half a dozen more douche bags.

By the time he returned, Hughes's engineers had been working for five years on the revamped XF-11. Even more than the *Hercules* flying boat, whose vast, ghostly-white, birdlike form was being hatched in the secret nest at Culver City and would soon be shipped to Long Beach, the XF-11 was Hughes's dream. Ted Carpentier, friend of Hughes and aircraft engineer, told me, "It was, for all of us at Hughes Aircraft, a sleek masterpiece, a silver beauty." Hughes was so tickled by his creation, which carried with it his friend Sherman Fairchild's personally invented aerial cameras and for use of which he had, of course, bought the Air Corps brass, that he insisted on testing it himself.

That was a reasonable decision, although he was in a bad state of nerves at the time, and, again, on the verge of a nervous breakdown. Carpentier thought this was due to Hughes's basic conflict in his sexuality, and increasing anxiety that his bribery and corruption would be exposed and he would be ruined. But from the moment he planned the first test flight he acted with such recklessness, such near-suicidal folly, as to beg description.

In his arrogant defiance of the authorities he had so skillfully manipulated and corrupted, he ignored each and every one of the instructions given to him and every warning of mechanical faults given him by Odekirk, Carpentier, and all other members of his team.

It was mandatory, when a controversial airplane was being tried out, that it be flown over an unpopulated area such as the army test flight base in the Mojave Desert, where, if it crashed, only a few jackrabbits or snakes would be killed. Sometimes Nevada was used for the same reason.

But Hughes was determined to test the plane over heavily-populated Culver City and MGM studios, where Katharine Hepburn and other friends would be able to see him, and where, always the anti-Semite, he told Carpentier, "That kike Louis B. Mayer might have to shut down for the day because of the noise."

Suicidally, he decided to fly for an hour and a half when the maximum fuel allowed, 600 gallons, would permit only forty-five minutes in the air. Insane as this was, he felt he could beat the law of gravity. He loaded up 1,200 gallons, which as in the past, provided the deadly threat of too much weight per square foot. He had forgotten the lessons learned when he had overburdened his previous planes; he had forgotten that he had almost crashed in front of the world when he took off from Floyd Bennett Field, New York, because he had crammed the L-14 too heavily with cargo.

And he wasn't only risking his life, but other people's as well. In addition, he declined the use of the Army Air Corps authorized radio channel to be used in an emergency, alerting ground rescue crews, and swept aside the requirement that he check the still-experimental Hamilton propellers; he ignored the fact that, in the initial tests, they were not showing sufficient pickup of oil pressure.

He failed to check the all-important seals behind the propellers that prevented the oil from leaking. And there is a disturbing mystery here: one of those seals was found to have been loose. Why? Was this sabotage? If the seal had been properly affixed there would not have been a loss of oil. Had someone deliberately loosened it?

Certainly, enough people were out to get him; enough people in high places would be exposed if he were to testify against them on a witness stand.

All things considered, he was woefully careless in almost every respect, and incomprehensibly so; after all, the XF-11 was his baby.

On the morning of the test flight, Sunday, July 7, 1946, he ate an uncharacteristic breakfast of banana cream pie à la mode. He tinkered with the plane for hours, then had the excessive number of fuel gallons deliberately siphoned in. He arranged for Johnny Meyer to accompany Glenn Odekirk, who was flying his B-23 bomber, to observe him; with Johnny in the plane were James Cagney's brother William, with whom he was working on a Culver City real estate deal, war hero and actor Audie Murphy, and, most importantly, Murphy's friend, Jean Peters, a young actress from Ohio he had only just met at one of Bill Cagney's parties.

He took off in clear, sunny weather conditions at 5:20 P.M. Almost at once, as he circled over Culver City and MGM, and then out over the ocean, he noticed a red light indicating that there was something wrong with the landing gear. He retracted the gear repeatedly. But then he felt a powerful drag on his right wing like, as he said later, "a giant hand pulling me down."

Although he didn't know it then, the right rear propeller blade was reversing badly; the seal had ripped off the tank. He unfastened his seat belt; he looked to see if the wings, tail, or gear door had been damaged. They were intact. Again, he raised and lowered the landing gear. Again, the red light refused to go off.

The XF-11's inadequate instrument panel, whose design he had so sadly neglected in his absence in his tramp guise, failed to tell him exactly what he needed to know. But the oil gauge must surely have indicated to him that oil was leaking at the propeller seals. He acted with incredible incompetence for so experienced a pilot. He lost his head, and instead of landing at once at Culver City Airport, began banking steeply inland, as far as Beverly Hills, looking for a golf course on which to land. But it wasn't 1936 and he wasn't flying the H-1 or H-2. He careened; his right wing again pulled down sharply. Out of control, agonized and ashamed and even a little afraid, he began to plunge.

He saw the streets of Beverly Hills rushing up to him. It was too late to cut down the engines or to cut them out, advisable procedures in such an emergency; it was too late to bail out. All he could do was hang onto the wheel to try to avoid crashing nose-first. He pancaked through a roof on North Linden Drive, slicing it off like the top of a cake.

He ripped across the street at 200 miles an hour, his left wing slashing through the master bedroom of a second house, owned by actress Rosemary De Camp, covering it with debris and shattered glass. The right wing snapped off and the tip killed a neighbor's dog. Hughes, with a series of tearing, smashing sounds, crashed the XF-11 to rest in the tangled eucalyptus trees of Whittier Drive.

As the gas tanks threatened to explode, Hughes stood up like a blazing scarecrow, his hair and clothes on fire, hanging onto his hat. He forced open the Plexiglas cockpit cover, searing both hands to the bone. He staggered onto the right wing stub and into the arms of a marine, Sergeant Bill Durkin. Seconds later, as Durkin dragged him clear, the plane exploded. "Was anyone else in there?" Durkin asked. "No," Hughes replied through blackened lips. "I was alone."

He sat on the grass, holding his head and moaning. The pain was too intense to bear; it seemed his body had turned to charcoal. People stood around staring. Nobody so much as brought a glass of water. A fireman turned up and did nothing; he didn't even aim a hose at the stricken man.

Durkin thrust the spectators aside, burst into the house of actor Dennis O'Keefe, and called the paramedics. They managed to get Hughes into a stretcher, though every time they touched him he could not hold back the screams. The ride to the Beverly Hills Emergency Hospital was a horrifying ordeal. Every traffic stop or bump in the road had him crying out and clawing at the glass. He aged twenty years on the journey.

When he was carried into the hospital shouting his name, a

white-clad attendant appeared and told him he couldn't stay there. All doctors were off duty on a Sunday. The richest man in America had to be carted off to Cedars of Lebanon, on the eastern side of town, a time-consuming journey even on a Sunday.

When he got to Cedars someone asked him to fill in a form absolving the hospital of blame if he should die. Glenn Odekirk had managed to find him and almost killed the official who presented the form. For hours, neither Dr. Lawrence Chaffin nor Dr. Verne Mason, his personal physicians, could be located. At last, Chaffin turned up.

He found Hughes barely conscious by now and in a severe state of shock. Almost incoherently, Hughes murmured that he hoped nobody would blame him for the accident; that something infernal had happened to the plane. Chaffin acted promptly. He ordered a blood transfusion. But, first, Hughes's blood had to be tested. Only one sample of his blood type could be found for a transfusion.

Chaffin told the nurses to dress the burns on the left arm, left chest, and left leg. Nine of the left ribs were fractured, and three of the right. The area where the ribs attached to the breastbone was splintered like matchwood, as were the left clavicle and the sixth and seventh cervical vertebrae. The left side of his chest was filled with blood. He had such severe bleeding of the esophagus that he couldn't swallow for days. His heart shifted to the right, and the right heart wall was contused. He was bruised and lacerated from head to foot, and, it seemed, the bleeding would never stop.

He was given intravenous feeding and morphine and was told he might not survive. His burned hands could not even be guided over the signature space on a will. Indeed, he was in no condition to make one.

As soon as the news hit the radio, an extraordinary array of past and present lovers or friends besieged the hospital, which became a scene that very few fashionable parties could match. The all-star cast of visitors included Cary Grant, Tyrone Power, Linda Darnell, Gene Tierney, and Richard Cromwell; of these, Hughes admitted to his room only Cary Grant. Noah Dietrich was out of town; Glenn Odekirk moved into an adjoining room and was in devoted attendance for days. Johnny Meyer was not allowed in. When his aunt Annette and her husband, Dr. Frederick Lummis, flew in from Houston, Hughes hurt them by saying he didn't want to see them. He didn't intend to wound them: he just didn't want them to see him in that condition, and he may have felt, unjustly, that they were there to get money if he died. He was happy to hear that Jean Peters, Audie Murphy, and Bill Cagney were frequent visitors.

He had a team of engineers work around the clock to design a more comfortable bed for him in moving sections with an aperture and a pipe to conduct out urine and feces. He drank gallons of orange juice, which he said sustained him, but, in fact, caused hyperacidity.

His chronic constipation and hemorrhoids added to his misery. Remembering what had happened to his mother, he was terrified of the necessary surgery. He fought day and night for life, rallied, relapsed, and rallied again. He was sustained by plans for a lawsuit against Hamilton Propellers and by seeing pictures of a very young Marilyn Monroe in a magazine; he tried to sign her but lost her to Darryl F. Zanuck, a major blow.

Even in his painful condition, struggling against severe discomforts to walk again, Hughes acted controllingly. He decided he would sever Jean Peters from her companion, Audie Murphy, the most decorated of war veterans, whom millions worshiped as much as they worshiped Hughes himself. Heartlessly, cruelly, he urged Jean Peters to drop Murphy and this practical, decent girl weakened before his promise of limitless wealth and power. When she did tell Murphy he had no chance with her anymore, and it must have taken all of her courage to do so, the actor was hysterical, almost insane with rage. All of the bottled-up anger that had driven him to kill before as a soldier drove him to murder Hughes if it was the last thing he did.

He took a gun and sought Hughes out at the Town House; he claimed later that he succeeded in bribing all but one of the Mormons who protected Hughes, so that when Hughes made an appearance from the hotel, he would mow him down in the parking lot. But that remaining henchman refused to cooperate.

After six weeks at Cedars, Hughes went home to Beverly Hills. Jean Peters came to dinner almost every night.

In October, she went to Mexico to shoot *Captain from Castile* with his ex-lover, Tyrone Power. Hughes flew twice to Mexico City to see her—and Power. At the Hotel Reforma in Mexico City, he told her something that drew her to him very strongly; after he died, his fortune was to go to the Medical Institute he had envisaged when he made out his first will at the age of eighteen. He was concerned that she would be protected. She, with characteristic good humor and common sense, told him, "Don't worry about me. I can always work."

After his second trip to Mexico, in February, 1947, Hughes flew Cary Grant to Washington, D.C., to attend the Special Senate Committee hearing, headed by Senator Owen Brewster of Maine, that was set up prior to the U.S. Senate hearings on his malfeasances in the matter of wartime contracts. At lunch with Hughes at the Mayflower Hotel, Brewster, a close friend of Pan American Airways' Juan Trippe, offered to drop the investigation if Hughes would allow TWA to merge with Pan Am. Hughes refused. He knew Trippe had bought Brewster.

The Senate panel, which included the wretched Joe McCarthy of Wisconsin, was convened to take his secret testimony on February 11th. Hughes gave a clear-cut, precise account of himself.

He showed a sharp intelligence, as well as an insolent, cool detachment; what was a Senate committee when you had $300 million? He flew off to Los Angeles with Cary Grant in the S-43, but, at the last minute, the continuing lovers decided to make a detour to Mexico to see Jean Peters. They flew through a storm over Nogales; they deliberately didn't radio their whereabouts and were delighted to hear that they were reported missing. When they strolled into the lobby of the Hotel Reforma in Mexico City, the headlines greeted them at the newsstand: CARY GRANT AND HOWARD HUGHES KILLED IN PLANE CRASH. They called their friends, saying cheerfully, and in unison, misquoting Mark Twain, "Reports of our deaths have been greatly exaggerated."

March in Hollywood was a painful month. Threats of being held in contempt forced Hughes to open his complex ledgers; he was so overly confident that he hadn't bothered to make, as many dubious individuals did, a second set. Brewster Committee investigator Francis D. Flanagan found a gold mine in the books: evidence of influence buying on a hair-raising scale. The charges for the parties, the swimming pool scenes, the lavish dinners, and the pretty girls were all too clearly laid out. Meyer had spent over $170,000, or ten times that much in today's money, on these forms of bribery and corruption. He had even charged up to the Hughes Tool Company one of the limousines that brought President Roosevelt's family to the state funeral.

The hearings began on July 28, 1947, in the Senate Office Building, Room 318. Michigan Republican Senator Homer Ferguson was the high-strung, irritable chairman of the panel. Joe McCarthy was still on the committee; the rest were a mix of liberals and conservatives. Hughes, using Russell Birdwell as a ghost, published articles under his own name coast to coast in the Hearst press, reminding the public of his achievements, accusing the committee of witch-hunting, demanding that Brewster admit the trial was based on Pan Am's urgings. Hughes was still a national hero, and his attacks on his enemies in the press and on the radio pulled off the confidence trick that he was being martyred by a corrupt administration. At the hearing, Elliott Roosevelt and Johnny Meyer made an odd team as they delivered a dual witness stand performance; they had the audience rocking with laughter as though they were Abbott and Costello. A crowd of 1,500 cheered Hughes as he struggled through police, reporters, and photographers to the suffocating marble room.

Hughes was the last witness. Surprisingly (and cleverly) dressed for the occasion in the first suit in years that fitted him, white shirt, and dark tie, Hughes spoke in a subdued voice, but his eyes were very sharp as he took the oath. He was on the stand for two days, brilliantly turning the tables on the senators. He not only had the confidence of his wealth, but he also knew he had the public with him: his inept engineering, his clumsy running of the Hughes plant, his disastrous squandering of taxpayers' millions, his flying fiascos, his interminable work on the *Hercules,* none of this counted with the public, which would never forget his flight around the world. He was no more blamed by the masses of people than Charles Lindbergh had been blamed for Nazi sympathies in 1939 and 1940. If many suspected he may have run off with $50 million of government money, then why not? These senators were fools and fuddy-duddies anyway, as cranky as old maids in a sewing bee, running a kangaroo court.

Hughes forced Brewster to the wall again and again on the Pan Am matter; rudely, he told the world that Brewster had bummed free TWA plane rides off him. He stabbed at Ferguson, who bumbled hopelessly; instead of dredging up proof that Hughes had wasted $28 million and bought Washington, Ferguson went in on the wrong angle: that Hughes had profited by the deals. He hadn't, of course, any more than the nation had. Once he dropped the ball, Ferguson never picked it up again. Hughes ran away with it and the public was thrilled. Few seemed to care that much of his lost cash had come out of their pockets as taxpayers.

On August 11, the hearings, a disaster and further waste of public funds, were suspended. Hughes waved a victor's farewell to the great crowd that stormed the Senate Office Building, the Mayflower Hotel, and the airport when he left.

## CHAPTER TEN

# From *Hercules*
# to Hollywood

Hughes returned to Los Angeles in a buoyant mood. He had made a vigorous boast, at one of his numerous encounters with the press, that he would ensure that the *Hercules* would do what it was supposed to do: fly. He devoted much of his energy in the following weeks to making sure that it did.

And yet, behind the boast, there was a magician's art of deception. By 1947, the flying boat that would be nicknamed the Spruce Goose was of no more use than a plastic bird in a bathtub. It was the ultimate child's toy, the ultimate wealthy man's indulgence—again at the taxpayer's expense. It was, of course, a beautiful artifact, but it was already as obsolete as an Egyptian pyramid. Its purpose, to carry troops so high over the ocean that U-boats would not be able to intercept it, had never made sense to begin with: it was lumbering, could not be camouflaged, was highly flammable, and was a literal sitting duck for any self-respecting German or Japanese fighter pilot. Its miserable speed alone would have done it in, if the Zeros—those copies of Hughes's H-2s—or the Messerschmitts had intercepted it.

And it may be that, in a kind of jubilant despair, Hughes realized that truth. He cannot have entertained fantasies that the Hercules would be of use against the Russians. Although he shared his uncle Rupert's and millions of other conservatives' view that the Soviet Union was planning to invade the Western Hemisphere—despite the fact that no such plan was ever actually envisaged—he could scarcely have expected a fleet of giant *Hercules* craft to be of use in the Baltic for counterattacks. No; all that was needed now was to prove that the damned thing could somehow get off the ground. He knew that if his plan to fly it worked, he would effectively deactivate the Senate Committee's renewed hearings in November.

On November 1, he and Johnny Meyer invited reporters and photographers to a bang-up party at Long Beach to see the winged white elephant. Even the hardiest veterans could not restrain their gasps as they walked into the hangar and saw the monstrous but aesthetically pleasing Bird framed dramatically against the darkness. They rushed to the telephones with the statistics: a full-sized tank and 700 military personnel and crew could fit into the looming, classically formed cabin; from wingtip to wingtip, it was the length of a football field; the tail was as high as an eight-story building.

Later in the day, an immense crowd, alerted by a tornado of advance publicity, gathered on the edge of the inlet with hampers, rugs, and cameras. Hughes gingerly piloted the Bird into the wind-tossed waves but to groans and sporadic disappointed clapping had to retreat uncomfortably because of the stiff breeze. He promised the press that next day would be better. But on November 2, the wind had actually increased.

What was he to do? Risk disaster yet again on a maiden flight? Knowing in his heart that the Hercules was a paper giant, woefully underpowered for all its eight 3,000 horsepower Pratt and Whitney engines, he was petrified. Even in a light wind it might not make it off the water; the world would make a laughingstock of him. Or he might be killed along with his crew.

Once more, he had to summon up all of his courage and make the attempt. He took excited reporters on two trial runs, forty-five miles per hour on the first run, ninety on the second, and then, telling his crew to exert every effort, with radio reporter Jim McNamara as the only media representative aboard, he, in his lucky hat, took hold of the wheel and taxied sharply into the waves.

Perhaps even he, atheist though he was, prayed at that moment. The vast bulk trembled. He put the wing flaps down, and pulled up. As a thrill went through him (and probably the thought of "God-damn the senators!"), the *Hercules* at last showed muscle, and flew for about a mile.

With Hughes commenting to an army of listeners in his sharp, high-pitched, inimitable Texas deaf man's voice, the great bird soared. Because of the roar of the engines, which would have temporarily deafened anyone who wasn't deaf already, he may not have heard the screams and shouts of joy from the shore, or the whistles, sirens, and tooting horns of a flotilla of boats in the bay. He touched down smoothly. He was back on the world's front pages with promises that the Big Bird would fly for many more miles in the next spring of 1948.

It didn't. *Hercules* was impotent. It lay in the hangar for years, maintained for $1 million and more a year out of his own pocket.

Where would he go from there? His restless spirit couldn't find satisfaction in retiring at the age of forty-two. He had no desire to live the life of a rich playboy in the Mediterranean or at Palm Beach with the international set. He would have been out of place in London or Paris, and he was no longer young enough for his gaucheries to be found charming in Manhattan or on Long Island Sound. But there were always the movies. Suppose he were to buy a studio in order to fulfill his frustrated fantasies of power and voyeurism? Which one would be for sale?

While he was casting about, he began reorganizing his 7000 Romaine Street headquarters and hired, on his secretary Nadine Henley's advice, the twenty-seven-year-old Bill Gay, a Mormon, to run it. Gay had planned to be a college professor, but Hughes, who was impressed by the young man's subdued, academic manner and lanky good looks, hired him as an Administrative Equipment Assistant and told him to staff the headquarters with only Mormons. They would neither drink nor smoke; they traveled in pairs like nuns, and knew how to keep a secret. Like him, many also disapproved of blacks and Jews.

Gay had no experience of administrative work and needed none. Though capable, he was no more of an executive than a ventriloquist's dummy. Hughes instructed him in everything: in the meticulous neatness and order of the office files; in the operation of the twenty-four-hour switchboard; in the staff instruction manual ("Always tell the truth, remain on the job, and brief your successor on the shifts; check with Hughes or Miss Nadine Henley on every problem"). Teams of Mormon drivers, some of them handsome and homosexual, were hired. Ironically, Mormonism was very hard on gays. Almost all of Hughes's Mormons were like Disneyland employees in later years: clean-cut, slim, athletic, Aryan, crewcut, immaculately groomed. One reason for having them take his various starlets around for shopping was that they wouldn't go to bed with the girls; another reason was, that, in a few instances, Hughes could have sexual access to them.

Hughes, for months, had shopped for a studio. MGM remained an unshakable bastion under Louis B. Mayer and Nicholas Schenck. Warner Bros., under Jack and Harry Warner, Columbia, run by the pit bull Harry Cohn, and Universal, home of yashmak operas, were equally elusive and entrenched. But RKO Pictures was up for sale.

It was a small but spunky and vibrant studio under the banner of Hughes's old friend (and husband of Jacqueline Cochran) Floyd Odlum, chairman of the multimillion-dollar Atlas Corporation. It was the studio that had made Katharine Hepburn's pictures in the 1930s, and Ginger Rogers–Fred Astaire musicals, a fact that made it attractive in itself.

Cary Grant was under contract there; that fact would provide a discreet umbrella for their continuing relationship. And Hughes was delighted to find that a close, strictly heterosexual friend, John Wayne, was also at RKO. Wayne was his ideal American, both politically (he was to the right of Genghis Khan) and as a strapping outdoor hero.

There was just one problem with it: RKO housed certain directors and writers who had either been fellow travelers or had actually been (or were still) Communists. Rupert Hughes, working as an undercover agent, listed a number of RKO employees who had attended Cell meetings, and gave Howard the lists.

Hughes could take care of that: he would, five years later, cleanse the nest, and satisfy the ever-probing, ever-vigilant House Committee on Un-American Activities and J. Edgar Hoover, who might take the heat off him if he proved to be helpful in political witch-finding.

Hughes called his friend Jacqueline Cochran and told her of his interest in RKO. She passed the news on to her husband, who, in turn, invited Hughes to stay with them at their ranch near Indio, not far from Palm Springs. He flew down for the weekend. Odlum, a victim of arthritis, was in constant pain and had to talk when immersed in mud baths or in a heated pool.

The Odlums' housekeeper, Vi Strauss Pistell, recalled, "Mr. Hughes used to come for dinner and not eat anything. He'd sit at the dinner table and spread out his long legs and talk. . . . He used to open and close all the closet doors and make sure nobody was hiding." Sometimes he would have long conferences with Odlum under a palm tree, but with Mormon bodyguards on call, to make sure nobody was eavesdropping. He would often glance nervously at the sky as though Somebody Up There was listening.

He urged Odlum to retire early as chairman and continue to run RKO with him as a board member. Odlum should have known better than to do business with Howard Hughes. But Hughes charmed everyone at the ranch and the Odlums were like putty in his hands. They might as well have argued with a hurricane as argued with him.

Two survivors of RKO from that time, director Richard Fleischer and producer Stanley Rubin, both recall that everyone at the studio was disturbed by news of the negotiations. They knew Hughes was notorious for wanting excessive control; that he had a tendency to fire those who stood in his way. When the news came through in mid-May that he had sealed up the purchase for $8,500,000, a bargain price, Richard Fleischer, hearing the news in B-picture chief Sid Rogell's office, said, in a direct reference to the *Hercules,* "He'll never get the studio off the ground."

Hughes was determined that the purchase would make the front page of the Hollywood trade papers. Fearful that his bad reputation and position as a Jew-hating maverick would do him in, he tried to buy *The Hollywood Reporter* from its owner, who wouldn't sell without editorial control. He tried to shoehorn *Variety* into a major coverage of the deal.

William Feeder was a crack *Variety* writer at that time. Hughes startled Feeder by calling him personally; he asked Feeder to go to a pay telephone near the *Variety* building and call him from there so they wouldn't be overheard. Feeder complied; then Hughes called him back. Hughes didn't trust Feeder; he was afraid Feeder was calling him from an office. He summoned him to the Goldwyn building; he had taken his sneakers and socks off. Feeder saw the burns on his feet.

Hughes gave him the exclusive and then, leaning over, said sharply, "I hear Dore Schary is a Communist. Is he?" "I don't think so," Feeder replied. Hughes lied that he would make no changes at the studio; that everything would go ahead as planned. Satisfied with Feeder's article on the purchase, Hughes hired him as a publicist.

From the day he took over, Hughes once more showed a voyeur's obsessive interest in the performers. He was especially fascinated by *Out of the Past,* with the broad-shouldered, sleepy, 195-pound Robert Mitchum, and Jane Greer as the prototype of his favorite character: a murderous woman who enslaves a handsome mate.

Jane Greer had been under personal contract to him in the early 1940s. Hughes had her trained by a drama coach in "enunciation and poise." He had, according to Miss Greer, some twenty other girls, none of them emerging as famous, in the same stable. She annoyed him by dating singer Rudy Vallee against his orders; they were married on December 3, 1943. He dropped her, irritably, because of that, in 1944; now she was back under contract to him as an RKO star.

He asked Greer in his usual cool manner how she was. He expected the usual response of the average troubled individual, "Pretty good." Instead, she shocked and angered him by saying she was "very happy"—that she was married now, and had a child. Hughes revealed the torment he lived in when he told Greer she "couldn't" be happy. She insisted she was. He was upset and restless; happiness was foreign to him. He told her, in a threat he didn't fulfill, that she wouldn't work at RKO as long as he ran the studio. "That ought to get you," he added.

Jane Greer said later: "I asked him, 'Will that mean the end of my career?' He replied, 'Yes, I guess it will.' I told him, 'Well, I'll just keep having babies.' " He tied her to a contract that eventually forced her out of pictures and he paid her $2,500 a week to keep her out. She remained happy; he remained angry and miserable.

Hughes had several meetings with outgoing RKO president N. Peter Rathvon, who flew in from New York, and executive vice president Ned Depinet. He was determined to reverse a fall in the studio's profits from just over $12 million to just over $5 million, chiefly due to the escalating costs of production and distribution through the RKO theater chain. Many feared he would slash budgets and fire staff. They were right.

Hughes also had some meetings with Dore Schary, the tall, mild-mannered Jewish RKO production chief. The executive was a determined liberal middlebrow with rather dim intellectual aspirations who had set out on a policy of making well-written realistic pictures, on tight budgets and with lesser stars; writers, under his guidance, had considerable freedom and the quality of their work was high.

Hughes knew from the grapevine that Schary had badmouthed him from the moment he began meeting with Odlum, saying he would resign if Hughes took over. Anti-Semitic at the best of times, he hated this child of immigrants whose horn-rims and big, shambling figure were the opposite of what he found appealing in a man. When he first met Schary in the garden of N. Peter Rathvon's house, he said sharply, "I hear you want to quit."

Schary was as stunned as though he had been shot. He mustered up the courage to reply, "Well, you won't need me at my price to deliver your orders!"

Hughes forced Schary to repeat the words. Schary did; everyone present quailed. "Everything will stay the way it was," Hughes lied. He left as abruptly as he had arrived. Rathvon told Schary that if Hughes didn't keep his promise, "I'll be out of there before you grab your hat." He was.

Hughes summoned Schary to a further meeting at Cary Grant's house. He made it clear that whoever ran his studio would take orders with no questions asked. He asked Schary why he wouldn't take orders. "If I was in the airplane industry I'd be happy to," Schary replied. "I'd know you'd know more than I. But since I know more about making pictures than you do, I'd take a different view." Hughes asked Schary what he wanted in severance money. Schary said he would like the rights to a picture, *Battleground,* which he wanted to make, and which Hughes detested as a project. Certain the picture would be a flop, Hughes agreed. Schary took it to MGM, where it was a hit.

Schary left in July, 1947. Ned Depinet, whom Hughes reluctantly kept on in charge of the distribution arm, was appalled that Hughes had not consulted him in the firing. Hughes waited until Depinet was in Dallas attending a funeral before he announced the resignation. Even then, Depinet had to learn about it in the press.

Hughes met with Depinet and the other executives on July 12 and 13; instead of expressing bright visions of quality pictures, he wore everyone out by talking about cost cutting. He announced there would be no more big-budget pictures; Sid Rogell was upped to vice president and told to continue his cheapskate B-picture policies; Bicknell Lockhart, one of Hughes's engineers, was put in charge of many aspects of production; cost accountant C. J. Devlin was hired away from General Service Studios as the third of this ruling triumvirate. All three men knew that they would have no powers of decision. In terms of executive powers, they were the sultan's eunuchs. When one executive, Creighton Perlin, argued with Hughes about budgetary plans, Hughes threw him out. Then he fired four more bigwigs and scrapped thirty-six picture projects.

He began running rushes at Goldwyn of pictures recently completed. One of them bothered him: *The Boy with Green Hair,* which Dore Schary had put through as a pet project, with Stephen Ames as producer and Joseph Losey as director. The picture's cowriter, Al Levitt, remembers that Hughes was appalled by the movie, an antiwar story about an orphan whose hair turned green because of a chemical reaction to something that happened in the conflict; he is teased, mocked, ill-treated as something freakish. The movie was a passionate plea for tolerance.

To Hughes, it was a Commie picture. He found out that director Losey was decidedly left of center and may have been a Communist. He may have read into the picture an implied attack on mistreatment of minorities, blacks, and Jews who were denied admission to the sort of clubs of which Hughes was a member. Ironically, Hughes never realized that gays—himself included—suffered many of the same persecutions that he and his friends were guilty of.

He thought of scrapping the film, but Stephen Ames, a conservative of independent wealth, persuaded him to change his mind. *The Boy with Green Hair* went back to the cutting room and emerged as an innocuous fable, all of its powerful elements castrated by Hughes. He forced the unwitting twelve-year-old child star Dean Stockwell to speak anti-Communist lines he wrote himself.

He so greatly reduced the production schedule that the moment three pictures that were holdovers from the Schary regime, *Every Girl Should Be Married* with Cary Grant and Betsy Drake, *Adventure in Baltimore* with Robert Young, and *Easy Living* with Lucille Ball, were finished, he made only one movie at a time. The first two, *Follow Me Quietly* and *The Clay Pigeon,* were cheap, unimportant thrillers, B pictures directed by Richard Fleischer.

By August, Hughes was involved in a fight with Howard Hawks. He sued Hawks and producer Edward Small for plagiarism, stating that they had stolen a sequence from *The Outlaw* for the finale of their big John Wayne western, *Red River.* He held up release of the picture; he obtained an affidavit from writer Borden Chase which stated that Hawks had ordered Chase to include the offending sequence and that he had refused; Hawks, Chase said, had written it himself. On the 19th, Hawks showed a cut version to Hughes, who was furious. The sequence had barely been touched. Hawks left for Europe to make a movie, and Hughes demanded, and got hold of, a print from Edward Small and cut the episode himself. His rampant ego satisfied, he was faced with another hurdle.

In the early hours of September 1, 1948, he was wakened by a phone call. Robert Mitchum had been arrested on charges of being in possession of marijuana and was in the county jail. Hughes had Mitchum's picture *Rachel and the Stranger* ready for release.

According to Norman Foster, who directed the film, Hughes was delighted by the news and sent Mitchum a reassurance that not only would the picture be released, he would back him to the limit. Hughes was shrewd enough to realize that the public would support Mitchum in his plight.

Hughes rushed out *Rachel and the Stranger;* it was, of course, an immediate hit. There were lines around the block in every city in America. The Publicity Department, under Perry Lieber and Bill Feeder, worked overtime to extract every ounce from the campaign. Hughes insisted that Sid Rogell come up with a new movie for Mitchum, whose trial was postponed until January. A thriller script was pushed through. Since Mitchum was up on criminal charges, Hughes said to Rogell, "Why not call it *The Big Steal?*" Rogell was delighted. It began shooting in January.

Hughes hired security man Kemp Niver to keep a close eye on Mitchum. The star was found guilty and was sentenced to a year in the county jail. *The Big Steal* was suspended. Hughes tried to get the imprisonment postponed until the picture could be finished, using the spurious reason that 1,500 people would be thrown out of work if the judge refused to agree. The judge did not agree. Hughes then made sure that pictures were taken of Mitchum mopping the prison floor and pulled strings to have him switched to a minimum security prison farm at Castaic.

Hughes drove to Castaic and told Mitchum he admired him and would continue to help; what did Mitchum need? "Fifty grand," Mitchum replied, "For a home for my family." Hughes loaned him that sum at 5 percent interest, the amount to be deducted from Mitchum's salary of $3,500 a week. Mitchum was released for good behavior on March 30; Hughes had been shooting *The Big Steal* in Mexico with a double. By now, Mitchum was eight pounds lighter and had lost his beer gut, and Jane Greer was pregnant. It took all of director Don Siegel's skill to cover the problem. "They'd switched stomachs," Siegel told this author in 1971. "It was crazy!"

Hughes fired 200 more employees and forced N. Peter Rathvon and Floyd Odlum off the board.

The first picture other than the two Fleischer B-unit efforts that Hughes authorized was Schary-originated, *The Set-Up*, a boxing movie based on the poem by Joseph Moncure March, who had rewritten *Hell's Angels*. Hughes agreed to accept Robert Ryan as the boxer protagonist. Director Robert Wise wanted to cast the aging Joan Blondell, who had been very effective in *Nightmare Alley* as a carnival queen, as Ryan's wife. Hughes ran the picture and screamed at Sid Rogell, "Are you guys crazy? She looks as if she were shot out of the wrong end of a cannon!" "He had no interest in whether she could act the part or not," Wise says. "She didn't attract him; that was the issue."

He submitted a long list of models to Sid Rogell, including fashion models, and the other kind. None could act. He put Robert Wise on layoff while he waited for Rogell to respond. Rogell did not agree to such casting purely for Hughes's pleasure. Finally, Hughes sent a list of big-breasted actresses. One of these was Audrey Totter. She turned out to be excellent for the part, but Hughes had to pay through the nose to the hated Louis B. Mayer to obtain her services.

He altered the endings of so many pictures that director Richard Fleischer dubbed him an "anal neurotic." Disliking the run-down, shantytown look of RKO, which looked like a set for *Tobacco Road* or *The Grapes of Wrath*, Hughes did all of his editing at, and sent all of his instructions from, the better-looking Goldwyn lot; still embarrassed at being deaf, he preferred not to meet most of his executives face to face. When he did visit the sleazy studio one night to look around, he uttered only two words, "Paint it!" And went home.

While he was busy interfering on every aspect of production, Hughes was embroiled in further complexities in his personal life. He was involved with three women at once: Jean Peters, still; Rita Hayworth; and the eighteen-year-old Terry Moore, who was under contract to RKO.

His relationship with Jean Peters remained calm, measured, and comfortable. According to Jean Peters's maid, Macy Todd, Hughes kept a permanent master bedroom—with a king-sized bed—at Jean's house, commuting daily from Cary Grant's house, which she would sometimes visit. He would slip in and out, limping from the XF-11 accident, through the kitchen and the back service door, afraid of being spotted by photographers. Macy had orders to listen for his limping footstep, and until she heard it going down the stairs, she was on no account to enter the bedroom and clean it up. She changed the bed linen every day according to his instructions. He left at exactly two o'clock every afternoon.

The room was always dark, with heavy drapes lined in black crepe, to blot out even the slightest hint of light. Macy was told never to draw back the curtains, which Hughes had her dust every day; she must not lift the telephone receiver off the hook to clean it; she must hold the receiver down tight in its cradle as she dusted. She must have dozens of Kleenexes for him at all times; he even used them for turning doorknobs.

Macy and the cook, Margaret Morrissey, were sworn to secrecy about the relationship. They were never to listen when Jean's family were present. Hughes arranged for a duenna or chaperone, a young woman, to accompany Jean everywhere to make sure she had exactly what she wanted. Often, without Jean, the woman would try on a dress in a store, advise Hughes it was suitable, and only then tell Jean about it. The woman would bring it to the house and Jean would usually wear it.

Gradually, Macy Todd's duties were changed: she would work for Hughes four days a week at the Grant house and three days at Jean Peters's house. Hughes forbade Margaret Morrissey to enter the Grant house; he engaged cook Eddie Barry at that home. The first day Macy Todd went to the Grant house she was astonished to see dozens of white shirts stacked from floor to ceiling in the master bedroom; they were all exactly the same, and Hughes would wear one a day for months, working down the pile, and then they would all go to the laundry and be returned. And he would start the cycle all over again.

According to Macy, Jean had to put up with the fact that Eddie Barry, who cooked for her as well as Grant, was a very messy cook. Miss Todd said:

> He would make a stew and put a lot of vegetables in it in a big old colander. He would strain them through and use the juice for Mr. Hughes's steaks. And I don't know how as Mr. Hughes

could eat it at all; it would boil over onto the stove and make a mess and I had to clean it up.

Rita Hayworth was the opposite of Jean in temperament: she was emotionally fragile, insecure, and tended to drink to bolster her courage on and off camera; bold and striking in pictures, a fine dancer, she was a sad little mouse in private. She had just suffered the shipwreck of a marriage to Orson Welles, and instead of learning a lesson not to get involved with controlling egotists, she was now off and running with Howard Hughes.

Hayworth became pregnant from Hughes. When he found out, Hughes, who hated children, was hysterical; the affair ended as abruptly as it had begun. Hughes demanded an abortion, which, given her hypersensitive nature and thwarted longing for children, must have been agony for Hayworth. But her boss, Columbia Genghis Khan Harry Cohn, agreed; in those days, a woman who had a child out of wedlock could be destroyed by the women's clubs and the Legion of Decency, and her career could have ended.

She took a sea trip to Europe. In Paris, she became sick; the abortion had done damage to her health. She went to the American Hospital at Neuilly for a curettement. She never saw Hughes again after he refused to pay the bill.

Concurrently, Hughes had become fascinated by the pretty, sexy Mormon Terry Moore. Like Fay Wray before her, she had gained fame by being gripped in an outsize monkey's paw. In *Mighty Joe Young*, made by the *King Kong* team, she was the keeper of a giant ape who, in a scene of mammoth destruction, wrecks a nightclub but spares her from the melee.

Hughes arranged to waylay her via Johnny Meyer at the Beverly Wilshire Hotel when she arrived, in a tight sweater, with her current date, an antic young actor named Jerome ("Cojo") Courtland. Hughes's eyes burned into hers. He stripped her with his gaze. She mentioned her interest in airplanes; he was hooked. He shrewdly didn't take her for a joyride alone; he let her bring Cojo along. But later, he switched airports at the last minute and left Cojo stranded.

Just as he had followed Katharine Hepburn when she toured in the play *Jane Eyre*, so he followed Terry Moore when she promoted a comedy, *The Return of October*. He turned up in airport after airport, like an expensive ghost. He invited himself to her home, and met her family; at the end of meals, he washed the dishes while she dried. He called her late at night, keeping her up until dawn, obsessively asking her for details of her boyfriends and their dates, necking, and partying. Naive, she never guessed the voyeurism that inspired these questions. He screened rushes of RKO movies with her at Goldwyn, asking her opinion; he held off from making an advance. Terry Moore described what happened in her memoirs:

> That night, as we were driving home, he took my hand and kissed it. *Zing!* Fire seemed to spread through my body.

Cojo Courtland may not have been a heavyweight in the acting field, but he knew how to put up a fight. He told Terry Moore to forget this Texan creep; Hughes was having affairs with several other women. Cojo may have known that in addition to Jean Peters, Hughes was again making overtures to Joan Fontaine. He offered her second husband, producer William Dozier, the job of production chief of RKO if Dozier would sell Joan to him. Dozier refused; he eventually got the job on his merits.

Once again, Terry Moore followed her predecessors into the Venus flytrap of money and power. Hughes had his Mormons track her everywhere, spying on her and Cojo at the same time as a separate detail was following Hayworth to Paris, and tracking Joan Fontaine to Bill Dozier's house. When Terry Moore complained and said that Hughes was known to be in love with Jean Peters, he lied that Jean was only a friend; she believed him.

The affair continued. Inevitably, as he had done to very nearly every prominent female movie star, he cynically proposed marriage. In June, 1949, when it was essential that he be present to deal with the numerous problems that arose at the studio, as well as with the painful fact that he was compelled by government consent decree to separate the theater chain from the studio operation and with the very poor box office results on several movies he had authorized, he took a month off and spent it with Terry Moore at Harbor Island. And this, despite the fact that he was still living at Jean Peters's house three days a week when he took off with Moore (for a time, Moore had him sleep on the sofa in her parents' house).

He repeated the same ceremony he had performed with a dozen women, including Gene Tierney and Jean Peters. He took her to the top of Mulholland Drive, in the hills high above Hollywood, and proposed marriage to her, with the well-worn atheist's words, "Only God can marry us, in a marriage under heaven." The difference was that he didn't offer her his permanently half-finished house to live in. They knelt together, he put a ring on her finger; he embraced her. But she wouldn't make love to him or agree to announce the "wedding" to her parents. She was a Mormon; rules were rules. And she refused intercourse when he invited her to the Beverly Hills Hotel. According to her, just before Thanksgiving, Hughes flew her to San Diego, where his prewar vessel the *Hilda,* captained by Captain Carl Flynn, was waiting at anchor. The yacht was covered in decorations of white gardenias and Terry Moore was drunk on champagne. According to Nadine Henley, Hughes claimed that he had Flynn sail the vessel outside the five-mile limit, "so the marriage wouldn't be legal."

Hughes had flown in hot dogs from Coney Island for the occasion; as Flynn performed the ceremony, Hughes put around Terry Moore's neck what he claimed to be his mother's pearls. The wedding cake was a replica of the scene in *Mighty Joe Young* in which the ape picked up Moore while she was playing the piano. She cut it, and everyone laughed.

She was still a virgin. That night, Hughes massaged her clitoris, using a Japanese technique of arousal that overcame her inhibitions. Apparently, Hughes had picked up some technique in the wake of his coolly impersonal possession of other Hollywood beauties. Miss Moore stretches credulity considerably when she adds, "I didn't know what was happening or had happened." Had nobody told her about the birds and the bees—even in Los Angeles?

That Hughes managed to sustain this marriage, or form of marriage, while still seeing Jean Peters seems incredible. But Jean Peters never suspected what was going on.

Meanwhile, RKO production continued at a crawl. The studio was mainly a releasing organization for Walt Disney and Samuel Goldwyn pictures of varying merit. An addict of thrillers, Hughes churned out low-budget action pictures such as *The Threat* and *A Dangerous Profession,* or humdrum westerns such as *Riders on the Range.* But one picture did engage Hughes's attention: *The Woman on Pier 13,* originally called *I Married a Communist,* which was made and released in April and May, 1949.

It provided proof of Hughes's naive, simple-minded political thinking and became an instant laughingstock with both the critics and the public, despite the starring performance of Hughes's favorite, Robert Ryan. It had overtones of the San Francisco waterfront activities of Australian union leader Harry Bridges: a shipping magnate, who has rejected his left-wing past, nearly becomes involved in a subversive plot to tie up shipping in the Bay Area. This fling at pleasing the infamous House Committee on Un-American Activities cost Hughes $650,000.

In a desperate effort to bail out a sinking company, Hughes made a coproduction deal with the still-potent box office star Claudette Colbert, as partner in the independent Loring Theater Corporation. But the pictures he made in partnership with Loring—*Bride for Sale* and *The Secret Heart*—were very poor. He also bought a wretched thriller, *Destination Murder,* from the obscure (and misnamed) Prominent Pictures. A better deal was made with Argosy to release John Ford's *She Wore a Yellow Ribbon,* which did fairly well; and *Wagonmaster,* which appropriately enough was a saga of the early Mormon settlers. Though vigorous and exciting, the second western was a flop. Early in 1950, production chief Sid Rogell walked out, leaving Hughes to carry the ailing, half-dead baby. It took him months of anguished and futile effort, foolishly playing one potential buyer against another, before he sold the RKO theater chain months after the government deadline had expired.

In October, 1949, Hughes embarked on the most disastrous venture of his career so far: *Jet Pilot,* another anti-Communist propaganda picture, in which Janet Leigh would appear as a Soviet spy, posing as a defector, who flies to Alaska, in an exact copy of Hughes's flight from Yakutsk to Fairbanks in 1938. Her control, Colonel John Wayne, like the hero of *Ninotchka,* introduces her to the pleasures of capitalism, this time not in Paris but, of all places, Palm Springs. They get married and take off to Russia, with Wayne as spy; he manages to get some information before they are pursued by Red airplanes from Moscow back to America. The script by Jules Furthman and Hughes matched the screenplay for *The Outlaw* in absurdity.

Hughes hired the British Peter Godfrey from Warner Bros. to direct. But after only a few days, he was fired. Hughes directed some scenes. Then Hughes, on Furthman's advice, lured the failed director Josef von Sternberg from "retirement" in New England to take over the reins. Von Sternberg was noted for his exotic movies starring Marlene Dietrich, his erstwhile mistress, including *Morocco* and

*Shanghai Express.* He was the worst possible choice for the picture, which called for an action director like John Ford or Raoul Walsh. Hughes had him squander almost two months on photographic tests of the principals; then, at last, the picture began shooting on December 8. Hughes, as was his custom, fretted and fussed interminably over hairstyles and clothes so that Wayne's rugged, rangy physique and Janet Leigh's exquisitely proportioned figure would be fully emphasized.

He called Jules Furthman into his office and asked him to make sure that Janet Leigh would "marry Mr. Hughes" at the earliest possible opportunity. Knowing that Hughes was already "married" to Terry Moore, if only by a captain at sea, Furthman didn't ask the question. Furthermore, she was already in another relationship. Surprisingly, Hughes gave von Sternberg a free hand; the director, a small, commanding martinet, was as brutally controlling as Hughes was, but without his smooth bedside manner. He infuriated both Wayne and Leigh with his rudeness; at one stage, Wayne told Leigh he would like "to kill the son of a bitch," and if he ever got started on him, he would.

In mid-February, Hughes tired of the director and fired him. Production closed down for five days; Don Siegel took over; Hughes rehired von Sternberg and sent him to shoot in Las Vegas. Meanwhile, another director, Paul Cochrane, handled the aerial scenes on location at March Field, Muroo, and Denver; for weeks, the crew was left idle because Hughes didn't like the cloud formations in the daily rushes; at vast expense, he shifted the one-hundred-strong unit, including numerous Air Force personnel, to Fargo, North Dakota, where he was told the huge, breastlike cumulus clouds with which he was obsessed were present. They were not. Cold winds and slush hampered shooting there in early March; Hughes switched the men back to Denver; there were no clouds there at all. He ordered the team to Great Falls, Montana, where they ran into a snowstorm and had to go back; the same thing happened at Rapid City, South Dakota. When they returned to Great Falls, all the work was scrapped because, Hughes said, conditions did not meet those in Fargo. He went crazy, now dispatching second and third camera crews in zigzags across thousands of miles, looking for fuckable clouds. More and more planes were rented or bought and rushed into Lowry, Great Falls, Reno, Las Vegas, Oakland, Burbank, Rapid City, with Cochrane fired and director Byron Haskin taking over. Snow and rain hampered the work continually; Haskin was almost burned to death when a B-25 caught fire; further locations were at Toulonne Meadows, Mount Shasta, Mount Lassen, Sacramento . . . Back in Los Angeles, there was a fog that hampered shooting still more.

Month after month, the insanity went on. Hughes fired Haskin in June; pilot Chuck Yeager was almost killed when an F-86 bomber lost power and he had to make a crash landing. By December, after almost a year, the crews were still scattered, leaving Hughes dissatisfied and the studio on the edge of ruin.

On the local front, Hughes relieved von Sternberg again and had Jules Furthman take over as director, as he had done on *The Outlaw.* The shooting dragged on until May, 1951, a total of seventeen months of shooting, the longest schedule in RKO's history.

Hughes was still unhappy, and hung onto the film for several years more until all of the early jet technology in it was out of date. He cut the wretched picture, which ran many hours long, to a releasable length, and, in 1957, threw it into the jaws of the critics and the wet blanket of a notably bored public. It lost millions.

Later in 1949, Hughes surpassed himself in exploitation and sexual overtness. He decided to capitalize on scandalous stories surrounding the making of Roberto Rosselini's Italian film, *Stromboli,* starring Ingrid Bergman, which he would distribute in the U.S. He discovered via the international grapevine that, while married to another man, she was soon to have Rosselini's baby. The moment he got confirmation of this, and it was told to him in confidence at the Beverly Hills Hotel, he called Hearst columnist Louella Parsons and, viciously, gave her the scoop.

A puritanical America flared up, as Hughes hoped it would. Virtually every public figure who supported morality and propriety condemned her out of hand. Hughes injured Bergman, whom he had once dated, as surely as if he had kicked her in the womb. Not only that, he took the picture away from Rosselini and recut it to emphasize the sexual angles. On March 14, 1950, Hughes's greatest dream for the picture was fulfilled: Senator Edwin C. Johnson of Colorado spoke up in the Senate chamber and denounced the erring couple, and called the sweet-natured Bergman an "influence for evil."

By that stage, *Stromboli* was in the theaters. Hughes had let his fantasies go completely in the advertising, showing a phallic volcano spouting lava like semen, compelling millions of women to watch a symbol of a male climax. Of course, nobody guessed the homosexual wish fulfillment the advertisement indicated. Hughes, under pressure from the Legion of Decency, was forced to withdraw it. But it hung in his office for months. And the entire *Stromboli* campaign, so fiendishly engineered to exploit a hapless female star, backfired. The volcano became impotent; the fire and brimstone had no effect; *Stromboli* failed. Hughes had overlooked one fact: it was a bad picture and was even worse after he got through with it. Would "his" RKO soon become an extinct volcano as well?

Since he owned RKO outright, Hughes had nobody to argue with. He careened on, destructively, reckless as ever with human lives, careless in the matter of starting and finishing pictures, seldom producing anything worthwhile. And, as usual, his personal life was completely off the rails.

Somehow deceiving Terry Moore and Jean Peters as to his purpose, he took off to San Francisco for clandestine nights with a male lover. Judge Harry Shafer, of the Superior Court of Los Angeles, recalls that when he was a young lawyer in early 1950 an early case was that of a woman who was suing her husband for divorce. She claimed that her husband had betrayed her with a man; that man, Shafer was astounded to learn, was Howard Hughes. Shafer looked into the matter and found that Hughes's lover, a businessman in the daytime, was at night a dancer at Finocchio's, the drag nightclub. Hughes would go to San Francisco to make love to him after the show, and then would return to Moore or Peters as though nothing had happened.

Shafer was obliged to tell the young man's lawyer that Hughes would be named in the suit; such a revelation would have created a sensation. Hughes was appalled; he offered anything to have the woman charge cruelty instead. Decent, she took a small amount. Soon after that, Hughes was walking on the edge of disaster again.

According to Ted Carpentier, police on Santa Monica Boulevard arrested Hughes for picking up a boy prostitute and compelling the boy to give him fellatio in his Chevrolet. He was taken to the precinct, fingerprinted, and asked for his identity. Instead of responding, he wrote out a check for one million dollars and signed it Howard Hughes.

After his ID was checked, he was released with no further questions asked. Carpentier said that Hughes, now forty-five, was finding it harder to find men who were attracted to him physically (though he retained the thinness that was mandatory in most gay circles, he looked older than his age, and was gaunt). So he would pay, and extravagantly, for the services of call boys, supplied by a well-known male madam.

That madam specialized in a number of services. He catered parties for the rich, and the men were handpicked from the countless beautiful youths who flocked into Hollywood looking for work as actors; they would serve drinks in shorts, deeply tanned, their muscles gleaming with carefully-applied oil. For a sum of money thrust into their clothing, they would disappear into a bedroom with their buyer; unlike most prostitutes of either sex, they were trained to give prolonged pleasure, not just to rush their patrons into a quick release. They learned massage; and if paid sufficiently well, and that could be a hundred dollars and up, they even condescended to climax.

Hughes reveled in the Hollywood brothels, which MGM and other studios sponsored, most of them tucked away in equally obscure canyon locations. Here the most beautiful girls often specialized in being look-alikes of Lana Turner, Ava Gardner, Betty Grable, or other beauties. This was the real Hollywood, a sordid jungle of sexual intrigue, where bodies were sold as readily as goods in an Istanbul bazaar.

Whether at Hank Valdez's pool parties, where gang bangs were arranged at a price of several thousand in advance, or at prominent bordellos such as that of Lee Francis, who would supply raspberry jam if that was an element of kink, Hughes was in his element. And there was the advantage, in seeing prostitutes, that his sexual performance was a matter of indifference to them. It is doubtful if those romantically besotted ladies most frequently linked with him in the gossip columns suspected that this fastidious man, who used Kleenexes to open doors with, was risking syphilis and that they might catch it from him.

Somehow Hughes found time to interfere with as many RKO pictures as he could. He had a fierce, angry working relationship with one of the few directors who could put up with him, the brutal Australian John Farrow, father of Mia Farrow, a sadist and high-level Catholic with strong pro-Fascist leanings. Farrow refused to put up with Hughes's prima donna behavior; yet he succumbed when Hughes insisted on lingering, erotically charged shots of the inescapable Faith Domergue parting her lips steamily as she vamped a hapless Robert Mitchum in his thriller *Where Danger Lives*. With poster artist Mario Zamparelli, Hughes spent hours brooding over the positioning of Domergue's sensual lips, measuring them to the exact inch.

*Where Danger Lives* was an example of Hughes's favorite misogynist theme: the steamy, evil *femme fatale* who lures men to their doom. Breathing heavily in deep shadows that reflect her disturbed psyche, a rich man's wife lures a doctor who has saved her from suicide and frames him with her husband's murder. But then, foolishly, improbably, she runs away with him, spending all her money, trying to cross the border into Mexico, as he becomes progressively paralyzed from a blow to the head. The picture was an excuse for luscious close-ups of Domergue and Mitchum seemingly lit by a match.

Another picture in which Hughes took a sexual interest was *His Kind of Woman,* with Robert Mitchum entangled with Jane Russell, also directed by Farrow, a melange of sex and violence that was typical of Hughes's fantasy movies. Violence turned him on as much as sex, and he fired Farrow and hired Richard Fleischer to pep up the scenes of Mitchum being beaten by gangsters and taking revenge. For months in a bungalow at the Beverly Hills, he rewrote the picture with Fleischer; that improbably mild-mannered craftsman seems not to have suspected Hughes's dark motives. A heavyweight villain was added to the story; then, after the whole movie was reshot, Hughes scrapped the villain and replaced him with Raymond Burr, whom he had seen on a TV show.

Announcing through the advertisements that Mitchum and Russell were "the hottest combination ever to hit the screen," Hughes had a huge electric sign erected on an empty lot on Wilshire Boulevard with the stars locked in an erotic embrace.

Mario Zamparelli designed it. The most sexual painting ever exhibited publicly in Hollywood, it was framed in gilt, and was a hundred times larger than life. Hughes drove over many times, stared at it, and thought of an additional sexual touch: gas jets would leap up, like spurting semen and the flames of desire, from every part of the stars' bodies, thirty feet into the night sky. As he watched, workers crawled over Mitchum's muscular shoulders and Russell's luscious breasts, fixing the jets in place.

Once everything was finished, Hughes had his metaphoric climax. He became bored by the idea of the painting; the orgasmic moment was over; the whole vast likeness of the lusty stars was pulled down. "Gotta roll with the punches," he told an understandably distressed Zamparelli.

He was equally obsessive in his narcissism. He hired Zamparelli to do his official portrait. Not some great painter, or even a photographer like Karsh of Ottawa, but a poster artist. He insisted the likeness be done in an insane two days; once more he wanted instant gratification. Zamparelli promised it in three and worked for seventy-two hours almost without a break.

He brought it to Hughes's office. Mounting a chair with his legs spread wide, the back pushed against his chest, Hughes sat silent for a very long time. At last, he spoke. He said he liked the picture. Zamparelli, exhausted, relaxed. Then Hughes said that something must be done to it: a thirty-second of an inch must be taken off one ear, and similarly tiny amounts of other features changed. He gave the instructions over and over again; Zamparelli did as he asked.

Hughes began renting apartments in which he stashed numerous actresses. He seldom visited them, but wanted to be sure that, if he felt aroused at, say, three A.M., and in the unlikely event he was alone, or too lazy to call a service, he could drive to that young woman's home, ring the doorbell, enter—no other man was ever allowed to share their beds—strip, penetrate, climax, dress, and go home.

## CHAPTER ELEVEN

# More Misadventures

T hrough much of 1950, Hughes lived with Terry Moore in Bungalow 19 of the Beverly Hills Hotel. He gave her a major role in *Gambling House,* with Victor Mature; he fussed endlessly over her hair and wardrobe. But, at the same time, he had befriended the actress Mala Powers, who was appearing in *Outrage,* directed by Hughes's former flame, Ida Lupino. Terry Moore was in a constant state of jealous anger and tears, telling her mother of rumors that Hughes was seen with practically every woman he had under contract.

She began spending nights at her parents' house in Glendale. He had her followed everywhere, bugged phones, called her in restaurants and at parties; he did this to all women who were not available to him day and night. He pushed her through drama lessons, singing lessons, constantly switching coaches, in a manic, ill-fated desire to mold her into a musical star. He flew her on trips to Catalina, Palm Springs, Las Vegas, and the Grand Canyon. When she went to Florida to shoot *The Barefoot Mailman,* he became hysterical that she was costarring in it with Cojo Courtland. When he heard that she would be swimming in an alligator-infested river, he called countless times in one day, insisting she be protected. She learned the alligator mating call; in her memoirs she wrote, "To this day, I can let out the mating call, and alligators will miraculously appear." From then on, they used the call to each other. She took a boa constrictor back with her on the TWA plane to Hughes in Los Angeles. "You should have flown it Pan American," he said.

Angry after catching Hughes with a starlet in Las Vegas, Moore began a romance with Los Angeles Rams football star Glenn Davis, who had once been engaged to Elizabeth Taylor. Hughes, learning of this, was determined to break the relationship. He called day and night, wherever she was, demanding she come back to him, reminding her of their marriage. He insisted she have one last drink with him at the Beverly Hills Hotel. She agreed; still unable to resist his hypnotic appeal, she even wore the same dress she had on the night of the shipboard wedding—and she was wearing Glenn Davis's engagement ring.

Hughes was upset to read of her marriage to Glenn Davis on February 9, 1951. But he lured her; Davis wanted to make a business deal involving some lead pipe contracts with Hughes Tool and, Moore claims, almost threw her back into Hughes's bed. Hughes asked her to play in the picture *High Heels,* had Michael Woulfe design skin-tight dresses for her, ogled her tests in the soundproof projection room, and finally got her to his office. He made love to her against his desk. The picture was never made.

In his headlong rush into the affair with Terry Moore, Hughes had overridden her conventional, humdrum middle-American Mormon father, who hated Hughes and also Glenn Davis. After much urgent beseeching, Hughes allowed himself to be lured to a family meeting in Glendale. Davis took a clumsy swing at Hughes, and Hughes fell over. Terry Moore's mother threw herself on his body to protect him from the footballer's flying fists. The scene continued with recriminations on both sides until Hughes, showing as little ability at the manly art of self-defense as he had with Oleg Cassini, fled into the night.

In late 1950, Hughes became fascinated by the British actress Jean Simmons; he ran all of her movies and brooded over her stills. She was very much his type: beautiful, dark, and far more talented than Faith Domergue, Ava Gardner, or any of his other women. She was engaged at the time to the handsome star Stewart Granger. Hughes dared not provoke Granger, who was hard-bitten, fierce-tempered, and much handier with his fists than Glenn Davis. So in order to ingratiate himself with her, he arranged for an out-of-Hollywood wedding for the couple, which would take place where the press would not be able to find them.

It was one of his most ingenious game plans. He would make Simmons grateful to him and would simultaneously disarm Granger. He contacted MGM publicist Howard Strickling (Granger was under contract to that studio), and placed a private Convair airplane at their disposal to fly them to Tucson, Arizona. He had them picked up by a Cadillac and driven to the Arizona Inn. He even flew in a close friend of theirs, actor Michael Wilding, to be best man.

He arranged for a lawyer in his employ to entertain them while they were in Arizona, picked out the church and the preacher, and even the bridesmaids, all the time calling everyone they met, insisting hungrily on obtaining every detail of their movements. To make sure that they weren't lonely, he talked his former mistress Barbara Hutton into taking her son, Lance Reventlow, to Tucson for his asthma and gave her a Convair to fly in as well.

A few weeks later, Hughes met for the first time the woman he had gone to such extraordinary lengths to please. He took her and her husband to the Grand Canyon with Cary Grant on a double date: all four booked into a local hotel.

Hughes and Grant were standing side by side at a urinal when Granger was in the toilet. As Granger reported the conversation:

"What do you think of Jean?" Grant asked.

"He's a goddamned lucky son of a bitch," Hughes replied. "I'd like to sink my teeth into *that.*" Then he added, "My cock is caught in my zipper."

Grant had to dislodge it.

Granger was furious. He tried to get up and beat Hughes to a pulp, but by the time he had pulled up his trousers, the two men had left.

Apart from *Jet Pilot,* Hughes's most plagued production was *The Big Sky,* which began shooting, under Howard Hawks's direction, in Lewiston, Wyoming, in July, 1951. The filming became an ordeal of adverse weather conditions: days were lost because of rain, snow, sleet, and bad light. So confused was the production manager that reports that wound up on Hughes's desk mentioned boats sinking in the river, while others announced that the river was dry. Hughes shifted the company, over Hawks's objections, to Yellowstone National Park; he borrowed the 20th Century–Fox lot from his friend

Darryl F. Zanuck to finish the picture, a month behind schedule. Weather also plagued the second unit, shooting under assistant director Christian Nyby in Wyola, Montana. Hughes was appalled to learn that a buffalo hunt sequence was ruined when the beasts panicked before the cameras and lights and stampeded in every direction; the crew was snowed in; only a ranger's Jeep could get in and out of the area. Hughes had to send a rescue party in and fly the unit back to Hollywood on September 24th.

The heavy cost of *The Big Sky* further affected RKO's failing finances.

Three Hughes-RKO pictures that did well in 1951 were *The Blue Veil,* made by the semi-independent team of Jerry Wald and Norman Krasna, a protracted but well-made weepie about a children's nurse that Hughes found nauseating (he detested children); a remake of his 1927 silent *The Racket,* spuriously tied into Senator Estes Kafauver's racket-busting Senate Crime Investigation Committee; and the Wald-Krasna *Payment on Demand,* in which Bette Davis, Hughes's old flame, played a vicious divorcée. The studio also made Howard Hawks's *The Thing,* about a human carrot who menaces aviators at the North Pole, and *Tarzan's Peril,* which offered Hughes the guilty pleasure of seeing Lex Barker in a loincloth. It also had the advantage over previous Tarzan pictures of being shot in Africa, a surprising extravagance for Hughes.

He embarked on his most ambitious aviation picture since *Hell's Angels: Flying Leathernecks,* the story of a World War II fighter squadron at Guadalcanal, starring his favorites, John Wayne and Robert Ryan. Something of the level of his team's approach to promotion may be judged by a memo from promoter Lincoln Quarberg, rehired from the old days, to chief publicist Perry Lieber, dated March 8, 1951, suggesting a launch of the picture in the Orient:

> [Columnists] Jimmy Starr and Harrison Carroll could go along for the ride [to Tokyo]. Jimmy and Harrison, in the 25 years I have known them, have never had any of that Japanese nookie, and it isn't to be sneezed at, especially after you have mastered the technique of the mount.

It was a notation of which Hughes himself would have been proud.

Hughes had many conflicts with the German director Fritz

Lang, who made the picture *Chuck-a-Luck,* later called *Rancho Notorious,* at the studio. Hughes himself spent a few token nights with Marlene Dietrich (who was Lang's mistress at the time) even though she was too old, and not his type. He wanted to upset her relationship with Lang; when Lang objected, he blacklisted him. Columbia boss Harry Cohn hired Lang at once. Cohn hated Hughes.

In another picture Hughes put in motion, *My Forbidden Past,* the central figure was, again, a woman who destroys men: an heiress, she wants to emasculate Robert Mitchum as surely as Faith Domergue had done in *Where Danger Lives.* To play this symbol of female evil, Hughes, with typical black humor, borrowed Ava Gardner from MGM.

Despite the fact that Terry Moore was hoping to divorce Glenn Davis and Hughes was married to her at sea, Hughes asked Ava to be his bride. The problem was that she was having an affair with Frank Sinatra. Sinatra hated Hughes, not only because he was sure Ava was lying when she said she hadn't been to bed with him, but because Hughes pushed him down to third billing in the picture *Double Dynamite.*

Hughes barred Sinatra from the lot. He had Mormon spies working overtime checking on Ava's every movement; the quarrels she had with Sinatra; the nights she spent with him. He took her to long dinners to lecture her on Sinatra's promiscuity. When Sinatra, insane with jealousy of Hughes, tried to kill himself in New York, Hughes called Ava to say that she should have heeded his warnings. He sent her a gold bracelet and necklace, which she threw out of a window to show Sinatra she wasn't emotionally involved. Sinatra still didn't believe her.

Hughes's men brought him word of more fights, of slammed doors, departures at night, frantic telephone calls, and heroic bedtime reunions: a tragicomic opera, mindless and melodramatic. He was pleased by these reports but was unable to part Gardner from Sinatra.

A blow fell in October. Nancy and Frank Sinatra were divorced, in Nevada, on Halloween. Next day, Ava agreed to marry Frank. The nuptials took place on November 7, in Philadelphia. Hughes begged Ava to get a quick divorce and marry him. He was still involved with Terry Moore and Jean Peters. Ava turned him down.

Because Moore was still married, Hughes was more fanatical than ever about keeping their affair a secret. He hid her in a succession of sleazy motels; he rushed her to a desert ranch, flying in to visit her for the night, romantically dipping the plane wings as she ran out to greet him, just as he had done with Katharine Hepburn.

He took her up in his Constellation, let her fly it, put the plane on automatic pilot, and (she claims) made love to her in the cabin on a pile of mink.

He installed her in a house on Sunset Boulevard; he bought out the Beverly Hills Hotel restaurant so they could eat there undisturbed.

He at last got Glenn Davis to discuss a divorce. At the first meeting with lawyers, Davis, according to Terry Moore, delivered the immortal line, "All I want is money." When Hughes refused to pay Davis the cash, Moore had to borrow $7,000 from him, with interest, to pay her husband off. No sooner had she handed over the check, leaving her broke, than Hughes left her for Jean Peters.

He tried to make it up to her by flying her and her family to Palm Springs for Thanksgiving. She found out he had had two Thanksgiving dinners with beautiful young women before he joined her. She disappeared with Elizabeth Taylor's ex-husband, Nicky Hilton.

According to Moore, even after receiving the $7,000, Glenn went on fighting the divorce. Hughes settled on a ploy. Knowing Davis wanted a movie career, he dangled in front of him the chance of becoming a movie star. He pointed out that to become a sex idol, Davis must be single. Davis fell for the idea. The divorce went through, but Hughes double-crossed him. Davis did not appear in a film.

He still could not be faithful to Terry Moore. He saw Elizabeth Taylor, gorgeously in her youth in *A Place in the Sun,* with Montgomery Clift; he decided he had to make love to her. He didn't approach her directly; he asked his lawyer, Greg Bautzer, to make the suggestion. Bautzer said, "Have you asked her?" Hughes said, "No. I want *you* to ask her." Bauzer replied, "I wouldn't know how to do that."

Hughes said, "I want you to take a proposal to her mother." "That you want to screw her daughter?" Bautzer asked. "No. Not in so many words. You're to say to her mother that I am prepared to pay a million dollars for Elizabeth to be my bride."

"That isn't the way it's done," Bautzer said. "It's the way I'd like to do it," Hughes replied. The astonished Bautzer valued Hughes as a high-paying client and went to see Mrs. Taylor. He said to her, "I have a very unusual proposal to make. Howard Hughes wants to marry your daughter." Sara Taylor answered, "But she doesn't *know* Hughes." Bautzer said, "There's an inducement attached. He's prepared to pay a million dollars for her." Mrs. Taylor thought for a minute and said, "Tax free?" They burst into laughter and Bautzer went home empty-handed. Later, Taylor was asked if she would have accepted if Hughes had asked her directly. "No way," she replied. "His socks stank!"

While Hughes's administration at RKO limped along—his dismissal of Sid Rogell, the crude but able vice president in charge of production, was a serious mistake—TWA was flourishing and his aircraft factory, a loser since its inception, with millions of taxpayers' money down the drain by 1949, at long last began to show a profit. Preoccupied with his sexual adventures and his voyeuristic self-indulgence in buying a studio, disillusioned and embittered by the attacks on him by the Brewster Committee, he had abandoned Culver City to other hands. For once, he sat still long enough to take advice, and took note when Noah Dietrich, whom he still trusted more than anyone else, recommended that he take the bold step of hiring as chief executives two of the high-ranking Air Force figures who had criticized him savagely in 1946 and 1947.

They were retired Lieutenant Generals Ira C. Eaker and Harold L. George. Not only were they capable administrators, shuttling between Culver City and Houston with a remarkable degree of autonomy, but they were invaluable in maintaining a respectable and profitable liaison with the Air Force procurements division in Washington, D.C.

Given carte blanche by Hughes, Eaker and George poured his millions into the then comparatively unsophisticated field of electronics. With the Cold War under way, and with definite plans afoot to attack the Soviet Union, thus beginning World War III, they plunged into an elaborate program in Washington.

Hughes, by devoting his efforts to expunging Communists from his studio, was only supporting ideologically a policy that would assist in providing more money for Hughes Aircraft: a policy of confrontation with the Soviet Union. He would also, by cleaning the RKO nest, appeal to Washington. He was delighted that his factories, of aeronautics equipment, planes, and films, were firmly in harness in the cause of politics.

Of the Hughes Aircraft's instruments of death, the most formidable was the Falcon, a guided missile that Hughes Aircraft's launchers would make sure hit its Russian targets. It was a more sophisticated version of the German V-2 rocket bomb that assailed London in World War II. Eaker and George had the inside track on the F-102 supersonic interceptor, a warplane for which they supplied a powerful antiaircraft electronics system.

When the Korean War began in June, 1950, Eaker's and George's friends and colleagues in Washington signed an across-the-board agreement giving Hughes a monopoly in interceptors for the U.S. Air Force, an arrangement excused, despite the fact that it was in breach of the Sherman antimonopolies act, because of wartime emergency arrangements. By the end of 1950, the war had made Hughes even richer than before. He once again became synonymous with heroism: the destroyer of Communist-backed airplanes and human beings, the winner in a conflict, the leading maker of weaponry. His profits from fighting a "hot" war were as high as $5.3 million by 1952, and, by the end of 1950, Hughes Aircraft had on its payroll 15,000 employees and 1,000 scientists, some of them Germans who had worked for Hitler in World War II.

By the late summer of 1950, Hughes could no longer resist interfering in the Culver City operation.

He reneged on promises to Eaker and George and canceled plans to use available tracts of land at Culver City to extend the vast plant; he refused to allow a new laboratory, with the latest research equipment, to be built within the same extension. Instead, he decided to build a new factory near Las Vegas, a city he still loved for its available sex, unlimited building opportunities, and freedom from state tax.

Through string pulling and finagling in Washington, he overcame the laws that restrained the use of U.S. government land for profit. He had his eye on 25,000 acres of federal desert property, but, since America was at war, it was definitely not kosher to make land deals with the government. Hughes managed to find a loophole. Noah Dietrich dug up the Taylor Grazing Act, an obscure law that allowed a direct exchange, not a transfer of funds, between government and individuals. Hughes handed the Department of the Interior 730,000 acres of northern Nevada, itself obtained in exchange for other properties, and, in return, was allowed to acquire the Las Vegas land for nothing. Despite opposition from the Department of the Interior, and despite the fact that the deal was no more than an ingenious tax dodge, it went through—because the War Department needed Hughes, and he knew it.

He took the bold step of hiring the prominent attorney Clark M. Clifford, former aide to President Truman, as his counsel to act for him in Washington; Clifford pointed out to him that no special influence could be exercised by the law firm on the president or anyone else. Hughes coolly pointed out that he needed no help where personal influence was concerned; he was sufficiently close to Truman already. That influence, of course, in part came from his Air Force leader employees.

Despite his continuing relationship with Terry Moore, Hughes was as promiscuous as ever. Late in 1950, he became involved with the beautiful actress Barbara Payton, who was twenty-three at the time; she was far removed from the dusky, lazy, voluptuous women who normally appealed to him; she was a blonde, blue-eyed Minnesotan of Norwegian ancestry, famous for her skills in the bedroom; she had risen quickly in Hollywood, up a ladder of beds. She had recently appeared with James Cagney (to whom she was under personal contract) in *Kiss Tomorrow Goodbye,* and with Gregory Peck in *Only the Valiant.*

Her spectacularly sleazy private life repeatedly figured in the headlines. She was busy, when Hughes was sleeping with her, abstracting the handsome but aging star Franchot Tone from his neurotic actress wife, Jean Wallace, who stabbed herself almost to death in an outbreak of fury and jealousy. Payton dumped her husband, an automobile salesman, and took up with a gangster; she appeared tearfully at the gangster's trial, providing an alibi. She was a central figure in a statewide, multimillion-dollar dope ring.

Hughes continued the affair with Payton as Tone fought a custody battle with his wife over their two children. Tone's wife was handicapped by the presentation in court of sordid love letters, too steamy to be reproduced in a family newspaper, from her stud, George Michael. Her lawyer asked Franchot Tone during the hearing, "How often have you seen Miss Payton naked? A hundred times?" "I don't know," Tone snapped back. "Frequently."

According to Noah Dietrich, Hughes paid several hundred thousand dollars to Barbara Payton to prevent her from telling the press about their affair during the trial. He was afraid of Tone, who, although almost forty-six years old, was as lean as a whip and as quick with his fists as Oleg Cassini. But Payton did tell Tone of her affair with Hughes, and Tone then made threats on Hughes's life; Hughes had to double his Mormon bodyguard.

Hughes's entanglement with Payton continued. After shooting *Bride of the Gorilla*—Payton was Hughes's third girlfriend to be the movie companion of an ape—Payton announced, to Hughes's fury, that she would marry bodybuilder-boxer-actor Tom Neal. Tone, who wanted Payton back, had a fist fight with Neal that left him badly battered and hospitalized; and Payton, who tried to intervene, got a black eye. With a bandaged face, Tone gave interviews in the hospital, while Payton, with dark glasses to hide her bruise, fought off a swarm of reporters outside. Hughes had had enough. Payton moved from Neal's bed to Hughes's and back again before she finally married Tone. One month later, she returned to Tom Neal, who, in later life, went to prison for killing his wife.

Yet Hughes was still preoccupied with Terry Moore. He was planning, in keeping with his hatred of taxes and the move of his factory operation, to settle in Nevada. One evening, they dined in Las Vegas with Maxwell House coffee heir Robert Neil and with Debbie Reynolds. Hughes disappeared with Reynolds from the table. Terry Moore threatened to go back to Los Angeles; Hughes insisted his walkout with Reynolds was innocent. Moore records that she flirted with singer Johnnie Ray in front of Hughes to provoke Hughes's fury; can Hughes not have known that Ray was homosexual? Moore continued to be convinced that Debbie Reynolds and Hughes were involved—but there was no basis for such a belief.

During all of these goings-on, Hughes resumed his earlier hunger for Jean Simmons. He saw her British picture *So Long at the Fair* and lusted for her. He decided to buy her, like a piece of cattle, from the British movie tycoon, J. Arthur Rank, for both his bed and his studio—despite the fact that she was still married to Stewart Granger.

Rank made a handsome profit on the deal. He didn't tell her; her agent, Bert Allenberg (who acted also for Stewart Granger) was forced to break the news to her. Allenberg made clear that if she refused to sign a Jane Russell–like, seven-year contract, Hughes would destroy her by putting her into bad pictures. The Grangers asked him to dinner to discuss the matter; present were Michael Wilding and his fiancée, Elizabeth Taylor. Hughes spent most of the dinner ogling the women's breasts.

Hughes with his mother, Dallas heiress Allene Gano. (Dietrich/Sygma)

His first wife, Ella Rice.
(Dietrich/Sygma)

With his trophy-winning Boeing, in the 1930s. (Sygma)

Hughes with his mother, Dallas heiress Allene Gano. (Dietrich/Sygma)

His first wife, Ella Rice.
(Dietrich/Sygma)

With his trophy-winning Boeing, in the 1930s. (Sygma)

With Errol Flynn.
(Bettmann)

Randolph Scott.
(AP/Wide World)

Hughes's second wife, Jean Peters. (AP/Wide World)

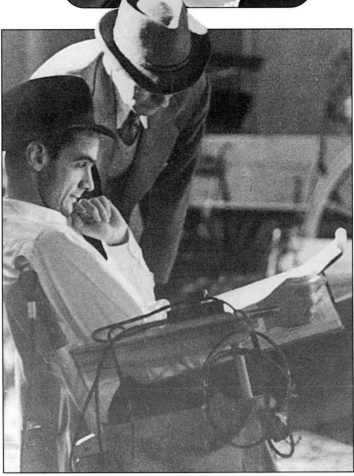

During the filming of his notorious picture *The Outlaw*. (Sygma)

Airman and hero.
(Bettmann)

World famous after
flying around the
world, July, 1938.
(AP/Wide World)

After another pioneer
flight, 1936. (Bettmann)

After a continental record-breaker, 1935. (Sygma)

In his H-2
racer.
(Bettmann)

With leading lady Marian Marsh. (Bettmann)

With Jean Harlow. (Bettmann)

With Ginger Rogers, a 1930s
romantic interest, at a Manhattan
premiere. (Bettman)

With actress Ida Lupino in
Hollywood. (Bettmann)

In Manhattan with one of his unrequited loves, Ava Gardner. (Bettmann)

With his lover, Cary Grant, at a reception in Mexico City in the 1940s. (AP/Wide World)

During flight tests for his flying boat *Hercules* (Spruce Goose),late 1940s.
(AP/Wide World)

Inside the fuselage of *Hercules*. (Gamma Liaison)

The "Spruce Goose." (AP/Wide World)

Flight of the *Hercules*. (Sygma)

Before a test flight in his XF-11, Culver City, 1940s. (Bettmann)

Battling the Senate to victory, 1947. (Sygma)

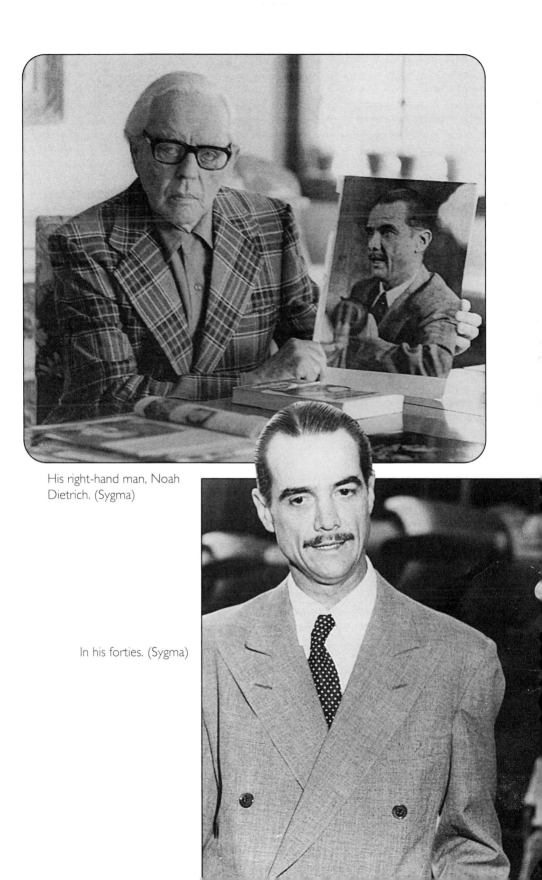

His right-hand man, Noah Dietrich. (Sygma)

In his forties. (Sygma)

Actress Terry Moore. Their child died shortly after birth. (Sygma)

Hughes Air West. His takeover was hugely controversial. (Sygma)

James McCord. (Sygma)

E. Howard Hunt. (Bettmann)

G. Gordon Liddy. (AP/Wide World)

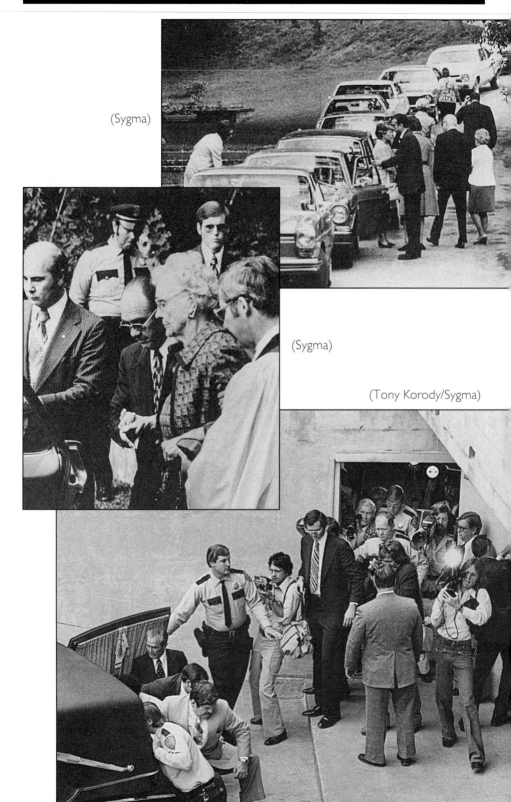

(Sygma)

(Sygma)

(Tony Korody/Sygma)

Granger asked Hughes as the meal ended, "Which of these girls would you like?" He replied that he couldn't decide. "You're not going to get either of them," Granger snapped. "So up yours!"

Hughes's revenge was to prevent Simmons from making the picture she had set her heart on—*Roman Holiday,* which later became a triumph for Audrey Hepburn. He was determined to make Simmons a prisoner. Somehow, some way, he would get to bed with her.

He embarked on a devilish campaign. First, he invited Granger, Elizabeth Taylor and her fiancé, Michael Wilding, and Simmons to Lake Tahoe for a vacation at his expense. He took them on a joyride in a flying boat that, he promised, would later take them to Acapulco. Knowing Granger had a cold, he deliberately nosedived the plane several times, causing Granger to injure his eardrum.

Pretending anxiety, he flew the couple to Las Vegas so that Granger could get treatment. He told Granger it would be dangerous for him to fly to Los Angeles; leaving him in bed, he took off with Simmons to the various shows. Simmons brushed him off.

When she was safely back at her hotel, Hughes, at 3:00 A.M., flew his plane to Los Angeles, switched to a car, and met Bert Allenberg at a secret location to discuss Simmons's contract. Without Simmons to support him in his arguments, Allenberg crumbled before Hughes's persuasions and set up a deal for her that allowed her no choice of vehicles and handcuffed her to Hughes for three years.

Hughes acted again. He was still determined to get Elizabeth Taylor into bed. He called up his old friend, columnist Hedda Hopper, and told her that Michael Wilding was a "faggot" and that she should use her influence and her column to break up the couple's engagement. Hopper summoned Wilding and Taylor to her home and berated Taylor, saying, in front of Wilding, "How can you think of marrying a homosexual?" Weakly, Wilding failed to deny the charge (he had been one of Noel Coward's boys in the 1930s but had forsworn gay sex for years). Taylor refused to believe Hedda and soon after married Wilding in London.

She had escaped Hughes; Simmons had not. He summoned her to secret meetings with her in his car; she enjoyed the intrigue, but remained faithful to Granger. Hughes cast her in a version of George Bernard Shaw's *Androcles and the Lion;* he tricked Shaw into granting the rights by accepting the condition that Shaw's favorite,

Gabriel Pascal, directed; then he fired Pascal. He destroyed Pascal's career; he effectively killed him. Pascal died in 1954 of what Stewart Granger described as "a broken heart." Meanwhile, Terry Moore infuriated Hughes by again dating, and being photographed with, Nicky Hilton, who had recently divorced Elizabeth Taylor. The merry-go-round of sex and bed-swapping continued. Moore went a step further: she began to date Greg Bautzer, who was still Hughes's lawyer.

CHAPTER TWELVE

# Troubled Years

**W**hile his personal affairs remained as complex and turbulent as ever, Hughes had no happier a situation at RKO. His arguments with producers Jerry Wald and Norman Krasna were not lessened by the fact that he had given them autonomy to make pictures, and at the same time kept nibbling away at that autonomy. They complained loudly and bitterly, in numerous interviews in the press, that here they were, Hughes's most important and successful producers, and they couldn't meet the boss. Finally, they succeeded in irritating Hughes so much with their public complaints that he was pricked into calling Greg Bautzer to have them come to his Beverly Hills Hotel bungalow. They arrived at 1:00 A.M., the only time he would see them; the room was almost completely dark, lit by one naked electric light bulb. Hughes was wearing nothing but a pair of expensive, two-toned shoes.

"Very nice shoes!" Jerry Wald said, embarrassed.

"They're OK," Hughes replied. "And now, if you'll excuse me, gentlemen, I have some work to do."

They left, and never saw him again.

By 1951, the studio had lost $5,832,000 due to a succession of bad pictures and Hughes's maddening disruptions of schedules and overspending on *Jet Pilot*. In addition, he had interfered with, and held up, several good movies, including the excellent *The Narrow*

*Margin,* thus depriving the RKO theater chain, of which he was now forced to divest himself, of important product. On his release slate for the following year, the most important entries were not his own but independents': Samuel Goldwyn's *Hans Christian Andersen* and Walt Disney's *Alice in Wonderland.*

He had to deal with a nervous Louis B. Mayer, whose partner, multimillionaire San Francisco businessman Louis R. Lurie, wanted to buy Hughes out. Hughes proved as skittish as ever in the negotiations, telling *The Wall Street Journal,* "I'd rather toss my stock in the ocean than take a loss on it." By the end of May, he had decided not to go ahead.

He was irritated by a proxy fight for control of the company, led by a disaffected shareholder, Wall Street banker David J. Greene. Greene complained to the press about Hughes's mismanagement, authorization of dud pictures, and absurd releasing pattern. Greene fought to secure proxies to outmatch Hughes, and by early summer, the gloves were off with a vengeance. But Greene failed.

Hughes's behavior at work was more eccentric than ever. He still refused to come to the studio. A stream of complaining memoranda in the Jerry Wald files show that Wald was unable to get Hughes to make decisions on anything. Even when Hughes agreed to make the Wald-Krasna *Casanova's Big Night* and *The Eddie Cantor Story,* he suddenly reneged on his promises and sold the scripts to other studios. He fussed over retakes on Josef von Sternberg's Russell-Mitchum vehicle, *Macao;* he yet again tried to force Wald to make *High Heels,* the musical starring Terry Moore, and when Wald refused, screamed with fury; he failed to make *High Heels* with another producer. Only a handful of pictures got made at RKO in those years; the lot was like a ghost town. Hughes was treading water, taking little or no interest in his pictures except, of course, when they exhibited half-naked bodies. Not even making movies could release him from the boredom and aridity in which he lived.

In 1951 and 1952, Hughes's crusade against Communism, still exacerbated by his desire to have Hughes Aircraft profit from the Korean and any future anti-Soviet wars, intensified. He focused his attention on Paul Jarrico, a writer who had cowritten the pro-Soviet propaganda picture *Song of Russia* at MGM at a time, during World War II, when the United States was the USSR's ally against Hitler. Jarrico had written *The Las Vegas Story,* designed to attract the public to Hughes's investments in that city, for Jane Russell and

Victor Mature. In April, 1951, Jarrico refused to admit he was a Communist to the House Committee on Un-American Activities, and Hughes dismissed him and removed his name from the film's credits.

The Screen Writers' Guild had strict rules that no writer should be denied credit who had contributed 30 percent or more of a given work. When members threatened a strike if Jarrico should be denied credit, Hughes issued a statement saying, "They might as well get on with it." He railed at his staff that anyone who joined or supported the strike would be fired at once.

The Guild sought arbitration with Hughes, but he refused to countenance even the briefest meeting, and would not take phone calls. Hughes railroaded through a superior court–issued declaratory judgment which gave him the right to remove a writer from screen credits if he, as majority shareholder, so chose.

Jarrico sued Hughes and RKO for $350,000 for wrongful dismissal. The complaint was dismissed; Hughes had acted within the boundaries of his contract.

Mary McCall, Jr., a writer *(Keep Your Powder Dry, The Maisie Series)* and president of the Writers' Guild, stated, "Mr. Hughes has thrown a mantle of Americanism over his own ragged production record."

According to his chef, Robert Poussin, Hughes fell in love at the time with the attractive and gifted French star Zizi Jeanmaire of the Roland Petit Ballet Troupe of Paris, who had been in Hollywood under contract to Goldwyn for *Hans Christian Andersen.* Captivated by her athletic body and dark hair, Hughes brought her back to California with Petit and the troupe to make a movie version of her stage success, *Carmen;* he engaged his chef Poussin as interpreter. According to Poussin (who made the statement under oath during trial preparations over the Hughes's will case in 1977):

> For him, sex [by then] was mostly to dance with his head on [a star's] shoulder. He tried to have sex with Zizi Jeanmaire. She told me he was impotent with her.

Later, Zizi married Roland Petit; their joyous professional and romantic partnership continues to this day.

According to Poussin, Hughes was impotent with others by 1953. But Poussin had no evidence of this, only hearsay, and the available facts deny it. Wasn't it simply that he was, as always, successful with some women and not with others? Poussin pointed out in his testimony that a certain kind of makeup, or perfume, could switch off Hughes's desire—that reaction, after all, was not uncommon in delicately balanced men. And his injuries and unhealthy life-style, as well as his age, would slow him down anyway.

And, despite his attempt with Zizi Jeanmaire, Hughes was still, according to her, sleeping with Terry Moore, who late in the summer of 1952 was offered, and accepted, an important role opposite Fredric March in Elia Kazan's *Man on a Tightrope,* a thriller to be shot in Germany.

Shortly before she left Hollywood, Moore missed two periods. Hughes sent her to his doctor, Verne Mason, for a checkup; Mason gave her the rabbit test and told Hughes she was going to have a child. It gives some indication of Hughes's power over his doctor that Mason advised him and never advised Moore. Hughes told her himself.

She said later: "[Howard] wasn't surprised. I don't think he was particularly pleased, but he wasn't displeased."

She added that he was worried she wouldn't be able to finish the picture, which was puzzling. If he didn't want her to make the movie in the first place, why didn't he use her pregnancy as an excuse to have her break her contract? Obviously, because he didn't want her to have the child. If she gave birth, she might force another, unquestionably legitimate marriage, which would tie him down for life. If it got out that he had an illegitimate child, it could play havoc with his image (those were moralistic times) and he still detested children.

Once she left, he called her in Germany obsessively, by day and by night, making the sounds of his alligator love call, their standard form of amorous communication from the days when she had been in Florida with Cojo Courtland. Hearing that she was unable to buy fresh fruit in the war-ravaged country, he air-freighted her a crate of California oranges.

She told Hughes she was suffering from bleeding and bearing down pains; the news cannot have sat well with him; it is clear from his behavior at the time that he wanted her to abort the baby. While in her bathtub at the hotel, she had a sudden issue of blood from her womb; she had unwisely been doing several dangerous scenes, including swimming in a river, that a pregnant woman should never have undertaken.

Hughes dispatched Dr. Verne Mason to take care of the delivery—the trip involved a desperate, sleepless, twenty-four-hour flight from Los Angeles. At the Munich Hospital, Mason cruelly told her that Hughes didn't want her to have the baby; that it would be an inconvenience to him. Moore became hysterical; the birth was even more than usually agonizing, and after twelve hours of life, the little girl was dead of septicemia. She was several months premature; Hughes made no secret of his relief. Moore charged him with making sure the baby was killed. For years, she was certain he had had the child murdered. Whatever the truth, if murder can take place in the heart, it was certainly in Hughes's.

He showed no concern during her slow, painful, and miserable recovery; he didn't fly to Germany to offer her any relief; instead, he plagued Darryl F. Zanuck, head of 20th Century–Fox, which had made the film, to keep the whole matter a secret. Zanuck needed no prompting from him. If the Legion of Decency and the women's clubs had found out, it could have wrecked the picture, Moore's career, and the studio itself.

Even more viciously, Hughes tried to have Zanuck pull Moore from her remaining scenes and reshoot the picture with another actress, offering to put up the cost himself; he feared that, when she was interviewed, she might let the truth slip out. Zanuck pretended to agree, took some money from Hughes, and then finished the picture with Moore. Hughes was apoplectic with rage.

After the horrifying episode, Moore eventually forgave him. She is unable to explain why—just that she was still, in spite of everything, in love with him.

She resumed her affair with him that winter; he flew to New York to be with her for the premiere of *Come Back, Little Sheba,* in which, as a high-powered, sexy bobbysoxer, she was nominated for an Academy Award, and he spent Christmas with her astonishingly forgiving family in Glendale. Once again, she was seduced by private planes, American beauty roses, promises. He was pleased to note that she was still in love with him.

But this insatiable user could not be faithful to the woman who so unwisely came back to him. He was, according to chef Robert Poussin, constantly dating other women.

He set up an apartment with a skylight at 8484 Sunset Boulevard over a photographer's studio, which he had bought. His aide Walter Kane, who replaced the overworked Johnny Meyer, lured young girls to the studio on the pretext of wanting to make photographic tests to see if they would look good in movies. Kane promised them stardom if they would do what Hughes wanted.

Hughes took pictures of them himself. Then they climbed the stairs to his apartment, where Poussin prepared a gourmet dinner. Champagne cooled in a bucket. Candles burned in silver sticks. Kinkily, Hughes made love to some of them in the larger Kane's clothes, even down to the loose, hanging undershorts.

Moreover, he insisted on cleanliness. The girls had to have a medical examination before he would even touch them. Before they set foot in the apartment, he dusted every inch with Kleenex, along with the silver and crockery. He was so nervous about Kane and Poussin that they had to wash their hands with soap before he arrived and show their fingers to him so he could see the nails were manicured.

His eating habits were growing increasingly bizarre. He would consume a pound of cookies and a half gallon of milk at a sitting, followed by two cups of vanilla ice cream with chocolate syrup. One night, he ordered dinner for six, a large roast, and ate the roast when the other five people failed to appear. He would go three days without eating anything and make his way to the toilet where he would sit for six or seven hours at a stretch, turn on the bathroom TV, watch it, and make dozens of phone calls.

He engaged a hypnotist to put him under because he couldn't sleep more than ten minutes at a time. A girl Hughes was dating and threatened to drop tried to kill herself by slashing her wrists. The police were howling; Poussin tried to wake Hughes up to tell him. Hughes was stretched out on the bed, naked under a sheet, his face white and his eyes bulging and fluttering open. He was hypnotized.

Poussin tried to drag him off the bed. Hughes was unable to respond, and Poussin left him lying nude on the floor. Walter Kane fixed things with the police, and Poussin talked the girl into wanting to live. Hughes never thanked him.

Meanwhile, he continued to crave Jean Simmons. When she remained indifferent to him, he gave her a terrible picture, *Angel Face,* in which she played a psychotic girl who murders her parents, and told the director, Otto Preminger, to treat her as badly as he wanted. A sadist, Preminger bullied her for the entire length of production, reducing her frequently to tears.

She managed, after weeks of trying, to arrange a meeting with Hughes. She shouted at him that she wanted no part of him; that she intended getting out of her contract; that she wouldn't make a third picture she had agreed to do; that she would fight him in the courts if necessary. Hughes was horrified. He announced through the studio grapevine that she had agreed verbally to a seven-year contract with him and that if any Hollywood bosses hired her, he would sue them. Simmons took a risk in a company town and went to court to declare, based on the existing contract, that Hughes had no rights to her after the third picture.

He was furious. Bautzer tried to intimidate Simmons at the deposition meetings; meanwhile, everyone warned her that to go on fighting Hughes might destroy her career. Hughes sent spies to England to try to expose some dirt in the Grangers' past. The spies failed.

He tried another ploy. He messengered a check for $187,000 to the Grangers' house with a receipt. They returned it. If they had accepted it, Simmons would have been tied down for seven years. It was the exact amount Simmons had agreed to if the longer contract had been made.

Stewart Granger decided he would kill Hughes. His method would be clear-cut: he would leave town; Hughes's spies, who were staked around his house, would follow him when he drove to the airport. He would immediately, having given them the slip, return by car or train. Simmons would call Hughes and ask if she could see him alone; she would take him out onto the terrace of their house, which was on a high cliff. At a prearranged moment, she would scream as though Hughes were raping her—loudly enough for the neighbors to hear.

At that moment, Granger would rush out of the house and hurl Hughes over the balcony to his death onto the rocks below. He would call the police and say that Hughes had tried to rape Simmons. And, in the struggle, he had accidentally fallen. Next day, Granger thought better of the plan; Hughes wasn't worth going to the gas chamber for.

Simmons walked through her third picture for Hughes, *Affair with a Stranger,* while Granger made *Salome* with Hughes's former mistress, Rita Hayworth, who told him of her shared hatred of Hughes. The Simmons case came to court, and she won. She asked no damages; only lawyer's fees.

Distracted, angry, Hughes sold RKO in September, 1952, to a Chicago syndicate headed by mail-order millionaire Ralph E. Stolkin, for the sum of $7,345,940. Within six weeks of his signing the contract, *The Wall Street Journal* denounced Stolkin and his partners as having questionable financial histories. They had to back out of the deal and Hughes was left holding the baby.

At the same time, Hughes had an emergency meeting with Eaker and his other Hughes Aircraft executives at the Beverly Hills Hotel. They complained of Noah Dietrich's interference with their operation, and Hughes's neglect of it. He responded by threatening to sell Culver City from under them, then failed to carry out the threat. The next year, 1953, two of his top executives resigned; Harold E. Talbott, former secretary of the Air Force, told Hughes he had made a mess of the operation and his government contracts would be canceled unless Hughes improved the company's management.

Other executives backed out. But it was a storm in a teacup: Hughes was supplying crucial weaponry to the government, and internal executive squabbles were scarcely enough to justify canceling a lucrative source of revenue for both the Air Force and Hughes, not to mention a chief source of destruction should the Cold War against the Soviet Union become hot.

Back in charge of RKO, Hughes took a more personal hand in production than he had done for years. He launched a 3-D production, *Second Chance,* and borrowed for it Linda Darnell, for whom he still entertained strong feelings, in a part that Jane Russell could easily have played. Wearing special glasses at screenings, he could see Darnell's breasts seemingly thrust in his face. Made with sadistic relish, the picture tortured the audience's nerves with a protracted sequence aboard a cable car marooned high up in the Andes.

Hughes launched, with his name on the credits, the most personal picture of his career since *The Outlaw: The French Line,* again shot in 3-D. It was based on the chestnut about the wealthy heiress who switches places with a parvenu friend to make sure that the man chasing her is interested in her alone. The production was once more an excuse for Hughes to sit in a projection room using 3-D glasses and watch as the female cast members' breasts—Jane Russell's, Mary McCarthy's, and Joyce MacKenzie's—shot out like footballs.

Standing naked in front of a mirror (hidden from the audience by a towel on her back), Russell's millionairess Texas oil tycoon (a more or less female version of Howard Hughes) sings about the heaven she is about to experience on her wedding night; she describes herself "as ornery as bull mink in the mating season." A Latin lover looks at her breasts and refers to her "peculiar riches." She forces a bride and groom apart on their honeymoon trip; much of the story is taken up with the groom's frantic efforts to enjoy his wedding night. The farce reaches its nadir as Russell engages in a bump and grind, throwing her crotch into the audience in one 3-D close shot after another—the roughest entertainment outside of a stag show in Hollywood's history to that date.

The film ran into censorship problems. In its report, the Legion of Decency stated:

[It] contains grossly obscene, suggestive and indecent action, costuming and dialogue . . . is capable of grave, evil influence.

Many lines Hughes wrote himself troubled the Breen office and were cut. At one stage, Russell-Hughes said:

All I need is a man! . . . Short, tall or elongated, thin, muscular, obese . . . seventeen or seventy will do! Stand back and watch my private chemical reaction.

Breen made Hughes remove scores of girls in underwear, a French "Professor of Love" teaching his pupils the skills of the bedroom, announcing, "I've never had any complaints" (as a love-maker), and discussing the Kinsey report. Cut also were lewd references to "the lay of the land," and that an unspecified object might not be "hard on the honeymoon." A reference to a man as "a pansy" was deleted. Despite these deletions, the Production Code Administration denied the picture a seal in December, 1953. Hughes defied the P.C.A. and showed it, starting in St. Louis, Missouri. He had to pay a $25,000 fine as a result. In January, 1954, *The French Line* was again denied a seal, and was declared finally by Breen to be "indecent and obscene."

On February 17, Noah Dietrich, prompted by Hughes, went to Breen's office and tried to make him change his mind. Dietrich failed. The picture never was granted a Seal. Soon, the lines were around the block. But it was banned in New York, Pennsylvania,

Kansas, and British Columbia. Then the theater chains refused it. Hughes lost a fortune on *The French Line.*

Jane Russell was mortified. She was disgusted by her "Looking for Trouble" number that Breen wanted to cut to ribbons. Asked how she, a decent Christian, could exhibit her breasts while a character ogled them and talked of her "big, brown . . . eyes," she snapped back, "Christians have breasts, too!" But she was very unhappy.

Another voyeuristic picture in which Hughes became involved was *Underwater!,* which the overworked Jane Russell began within a few weeks of recovering from an illness on *The French Line.* Not only did Hughes salivate over the thought of Russell in skin-tight bathing costumes, being pawed over by the lean, dark Mexican actor Gilbert Roland (a substitute for himself), but he flew in and out of Honolulu during the shooting and designed some underwater equipment.

With typical eccentricity, even foolhardiness, Hughes chose to shoot *Underwater!* at the worst time of year, November, when there was the constant peril of konas, or tidal waves, one of which struck the coast not far from the location. Heavy seas and winds of forty-five miles per hour handicapped the production. The men could barely load and unload the equipment-laden bags because of the heavy seas; one skiff was swamped and a crewman almost drowned.

In even worse conditions, shooting dragged on through December. Hughes tore his hair out as the unit, with very little in the can, flew home for the Christmas holidays. *Underwater!* continued, with Newport Beach standing in for Honolulu, in January and February; by March, the interminable picture was still in production. On March 10, a badly timed explosion injured two special effects men; Hughes's insistence on using live sharks in one scene almost cost an extra his leg.

Suddenly, he closed the picture; it was two and a half months before he found enough patience to start it again. At great expense, scenes were shot in Nassau, the Bahamas, where Hughes flew to set up gambling connections with the local crime bosses. It was not until July 2, 1954, that the eight-month movie, millions over budget, was completed.

He never ceased to keep his spies on track, following his present and former loves. When Linda Darnell crushed a finger in a hotel door in Mexico City during *Second Chance,* he found out before the press did and he flew to her and fussed over her like a duenna. When she flew to Rome for an assignation with producer Giuseppe Amato, he fretted and fumed. Yvonne De Carlo's involvement with leading man Carlos Thompson irritated him, but when she was robbed of $10,000 in jewels and traveler's checks in London, he was the first to hire detectives to solve the crime. Terry Moore and Ava Gardner were dogged day and night by his men.

He had a new sexual interest. He had for years known Susan Hayward as a casual friend and dinner date; insecure, nervous, often on edge, and noted for her temper, a chainsmoker (he hated that), Hayward seemed, in pictures, to be cool, aggressive, and a picture of athletic health. He had been taken with her acting as the evil Empress Messalina in *Demetrius and the Gladiators,* and once again began to lust after her.

She had been suffering from a wretched marriage to a classically constructed Hollywood jock, Jess Barker, and they had had two boys. The couple fought for years. Hughes had borrowed her for *The Lusty Men.* When he became involved with her, once again cheating on Terry Moore, she was drugged out, exhausted, and on the edge of a breakdown.

While Hughes dated her, Hayward had her worst fight with Barker, who asked her for $3,000 to invest in an oil well. Out of work, just another Hollywood pretty face, the unhappy hunk was desperate to make something of himself. She screamed at him to get a job; she accused him (falsely) of being "queer." He struck her hard; she hit back; they beat each other all over the house.

Finally, he tossed her in the swimming pool, almost drowning her by holding her head under water. Fleeing to Hawaii, Hayward met Hughes, who was there for *Underwater!* When she returned to Hollywood, after trying to stub a burning cigarette in Jess Barker's eyes, she arranged a divorce and Hughes helped her put it through.

Hughes decided to build a major vehicle around her and John Wayne—his most expensive production to date. It was an act of insanity, since he decided Wayne, the epitome of rugged Americanism, should play Genghis Khan in *The Conqueror,* a movie since regarded as one of the worst to come out of Hollywood. Susan Hayward would play a fiery Tartar princess—typecasting at least. Hughes worked on the script with one of his favorites, Oscar Millard, who, with others, had churned out the screenplays for *Angel Face* and *Second Chance.* With equal perversity, he hired Dick Powell, who had been the only director used by the gangster purchasers of RKO, to direct. It would become a Mongolian western, and worse, it would prove fatal to several of the cast and crew, as well as the director.

At first, Susan Hayward refused to appear in *The Conqueror.* The script appalled her, but Hughes wouldn't hear "No" for an answer. How could she, an Oscar-winning star, respond meaningfully to such lines as "I shall keep you, Bortai, in response to my passion. Your hatred will kindle into love"? Hughes offered Darryl F. Zanuck one million dollars under the table if Zanuck would lend him Hayward. Zanuck told Hayward if she didn't go to Hughes, he would suspend her. Overwhelmed by the costs of her divorce suit, she was forced to accept.

Hughes's misuse of Hayward undermined whatever feelings she may have had for him. She hated the clothes Hughes had Michael Woulfe create for her; she screamed with anger at the sketches. Dick Powell coerced Hayward into accepting the clothes; Hughes told Powell to lie that if she didn't wear them, Hughes would fire Woulfe.

Hughes sent the unit, at the beginning of 1954, to the area around St. George, Utah, to shoot the movie. Sensitive as always to the pollution of the environment, he chose to overlook the fact that his stars (and six million dollars, or $60 million in 1993 money) would be plunged into the most dangerous area of the United States.

On May 19, 1953, at the time Hughes was planning the picture, the government set off a nuclear explosion at Yucca Flat, Nevada; the radioactive ash fell over a wide, inhabited region, including St. George, which was about 145 miles distant. It was the latest of over 100 devices exploded in the region since 1951, an atrocious act by the Atomic Energy Commission since there was no call for evacuation or rehousing of anybody within the explosives' radius.

It cannot be used as an excuse that Hughes had no knowledge of the possible danger of radiation. He had put through the script, filmed under the Stolkin regime, for *Split Second,* also directed by Dick Powell, which dealt directly with the danger of radiation in Nevada. As a manufacturer in touch with the Pentagon and the Air Force, he was well aware of the nuclear testing sites; his prolonged delay in building his factories in Nevada was based on his unease over the tests. He could easily have shot *The Conqueror* in the Mojave Desert or in Mexico; he failed to obtain from his important contacts in Washington the truth of the danger inherent in using the site; and he pressed recklessly ahead. The result was an act of what could generously be described as involuntary manslaughter; it is the worst of all the countless stains on his record. His Mormon aides may have had a hand in the decision. St. George was a Mormon town.

The statistics were appropriate for a giant epic: two hundred men were engaged to turn 100 square miles of virgin country into something allegedly resembling the Gobi desert; 1,000 horses and 5,000 extras were shipped in; twelfth-century Mongol and Tartar villages were built from ancient drawings and trucked into the location; two houses and twenty-two hotels were commandeered.

In temperatures of 120 degrees, Wayne and Hayward sweltered and swore; actor Pedro Armendariz's horse stumbled and threw him, breaking his jaw; Susan Hayward's pet panther tried to take a bite out of her as she played the Tartar princess, and had to be replaced by a hand-painted mountain lion; John Wayne's falcon took ill and another had to be flown in, delaying the picture for days.

Hughes, cravenly, never went to St. George. Instead, he began rounding up slave girls, via his various pimps, and casting them in the inevitable harem dancing scenes. Michael Woulfe's costumes gave the illusion they were almost naked—and resulted in another brush with the Breen office.

For all its absurdity, and the dreadful script, the finished picture's action scenes were rousing, exciting in CinemaScope; and the reviews were surprisingly mild. Nobody in those days noted the typical Hughes blend of keyhole peeping and sexism; it is possible he himself wrote (he must certainly have approved such lines, sure to bring boos today), "Should her perfidy be less than any other woman's?" A typical exchange went:

GENGHIS:  I shall keep you, Bortai, in response to my passion. Your hatred will kindle into love.
BORTAI:  Before that day dawns, Mongol, the vultures will have feasted on your heart.

The outcome of the picture's shooting was horrifying. Susan Hayward contracted lung, and then brain, cancer, and died; John Wayne also died of cancer; the brilliant actress Agnes Moorehead was yet another victim. When Pedro Armendariz found he had the deadly disease, he shot himself through the heart. Dick Powell succumbed as well.

More than half the crew perished. And another fact, suppressed at the time, surfaced years later: Hughes ordered sixty tons of radioactive dust shipped to Hollywood to allow for a continuance of the Gobi Desert scenes.

He was obsessed by *The Conqueror,* which fulfilled his ultimate voyeur's fantasy: no doubt in his mind he was Genghis Khan himself, able to chose and bed any woman in the world, barbaric and ruthlessly virile in his impulses; in his fantasy he was able to make love to Susan Hayward mindlessly, vigorously, in a manner she never allowed in real life. He himself, flawed in his manhood, of questionable orientation, succeeding with some women, failing with others, could imagine he was a barbarian; and he could easily fancy that his skinny physique had swelled up into the magnificence of Wayne's, whose powerful arms were on show in almost every shot. So complete was his consuming identification that after the picture's first runs—a year and a half after it was made—he withdrew it from circulation so that he alone could see it, and he ran it over and over, hundreds of times, no doubt to the tune of hundreds of attempted or actual sexual climaxes; nobody was admitted to the screening room when he was watching it, and eventually he projected it himself.

None of Hughes's other 1954 pictures were noteworthy. Nostalgically, he cast his old flame Yvonne De Carlo in *Passion,* with one of his favorite male beauties, Cornel Wilde; he tried for a lip-smacking erotic musical, *Susan Slept Here*—and the audience slept; he relished the muscles, bosoms, orgies, and killings of *Sins of Rome,* which he distributed; he squandered Robert Ryan and Barbara Stanwyck on *Escape to Burma.*

He indulged in one final, personal creation: *Son of Sinbad.* Even the sober Richard D. Jewell and the late RKO executive Vernon Harbin, coauthors of *The RKO Story,* called it a "voyeur's delight." It contains an astonishing number of phallic symbols, spears and swords thrusting into the frame, spikes, muscled men stripped half-bare; and a unique number of shots, even for Hughes, of women with their breasts almost exposed and midriffs heaving. The film almost matched *The French Line* as a thinly disguised stag movie, on the very edge of being soft porn.

Vincent Price, one of the stars, told this author that the whole purpose of making the picture was to pay off former beauty contest winners Hughes had "sponsored" by promising them a part in a movie but had left in mothballs for years; and to pay off, also, the numerous girls he had under contract meaninglessly. Thus, he conceived of a story in which instead of the tale of *Ali Baba and the Forty Thieves,* he would have *Ali Baba and the Daughters of Forty Thieves.*

Hughes managed a feat of cross-casting: he turned the forty thieves' daughters into harem girls, slim enough to fit into jars. When Cornel Wilde was unavailable, Hughes turned to another Hollywood hunk, Dale Robertson, whom he borrowed from Darryl F. Zanuck, to gambol with the slave girls with muscles flexed and bare. He had an eye-rolling, lip-smacking Vincent Price wander through the movie's gilded halls as Omar the Tentmaker, reciting verses while he ogled the harem.

Hughes ran headlong into the Breen office. When he submitted the screenplay in February, 1953, Breen warned him that several scenes, particularly a harem dance, offered dangers of censorship; "breasts," Breen warned, "must be fully covered at all times." Sequences in baths must not suggest nudity; the line "All these hours she's been bathing—waiting to be surprised," must be cut. So must the line, "He has harem privileges on Saturday nights." Kisses must not be open-mouthed, as indicated in the writing; there must be no bumps and grinds as in *The French Line.*

Hughes cut the offending lines in the script, then restored them stubbornly in the movie itself; he kept in scene after scene of semi-nudity, bumping and grinding, legs parted and raised; and all suggestions of sexual combat. It was implied that Sinbad was making love to every woman he met; and Hughes allowed a shot in which, during a lineup of the forty female thieves, one girl actually had her left breast exposed.

New York State, Ohio, and Massachusetts made cut after cut, and Breen refused the picture the Production Code seal. He only yielded after many trims and excisions, but then the Legion of Decency issued a statement on May 19, 1955:

[The film is] a serious affront to Christian and traditional
values . . . it contains grossly salacious dances and indecent
costuming . . . [it is an] incitement to juvenile delinquency.

He had begun to weary of these efforts by Joe Breen to stifle his wet dreams, and decided once more to sell the studio. He had recently revived a tax dodger's dream: the Howard Hughes Medical

Institute. It would be cynically dedicated to the memory of his late parents, and in view of their deaths from cardiac failure, would focus largely on the treatment and cure of heart disease.

He settled on Miami as the location for the Institute, and traveled there to talk with the authorities. To support it, he would need state tax-free status, which Florida could supply. He would hand over the stock of Hughes Aircraft to the Institute; it would earn millions in tax-free interest each year.

Despite exaggerated statements by Hughes and his publicity staff, who began telling the press lies that there would be lavish facilities, with large buildings, swimming pools for staff and patients, and tennis and racquetball courts, the Institute was not conceived as a luxury hospital; indeed, there was insufficient money set aside for such a project. It was to be a cheaply-run bunch of specialists who would travel the country to seek new information, disseminate advice, and supply the latest research. For such a freewheeling operation, only limited space was needed; the focus was a penthouse floor, and part of another, at the University of Miami.

Hughes's folly in permitting extravagant announcements of the Institute would prove disastrous. The IRS correctly saw the venture as no more than a dodge for Hughes Aircraft and Hughes's enemies in armed forces procurement saw it as a way of saving Hughes Aircraft from having its contracts canceled. Hughes scarcely helped the cause by being slow in supplying adequate funds for the Institute; of more than three million dollars in profits from Hughes Aircraft in the first year, he supplied less than one percent to the hard-pressed staff of the HHMI. In the meantime, he was so irritable with the IRS that he talked of selling his entire empire in one go—to Laurance Rockefeller. Characteristically, he met his supremely wealthy visitor in a flophouse. He was dressed in filthy rags, and his chin was covered in stubble. Rockefeller and his associate, real estate multimillionaire Bill Zeckendorf, jointly offered him $350 million. Hughes said, "No." They upped the offer to $450 million. He held out for $500 million. Foolishly, they walked out. The empire was worth ten times that much. The circumstances of the flophouse meeting, Hughes's appearance, and his notorious unreliability, made his visitors feel he would never go ahead; that he would pull out finally. Hughes went back to his Romaine Street headquarters in his beaten-up jalopy to a kingdom that was earning an estimated $350 million a year.

While he pursued a stop-start-stop policy on his Institute, and seemed incapable of controlling the disruptions at Hughes Aircraft, Hughes managed to squeeze in many hours a week actually running, on a personal basis, TWA. After years of losses, Hughes hired an expert president, Ralph Damon, to head up the operation. The majority shareholder, Hughes used TWA to ferry his prominent friends and mistresses all over the world. Just about anyone, from heads of state to lowly movie harem girls, would find themselves alone on his Constellations, flying to his bidding or to some assignation on his behalf. TWA became chief sponsor of Walter Winchell, the nation's most influential broadcaster and columnist.

He dreamed of introducing jet travel to America; he wanted to break the competition from the British de Havilland Company, whose Comets, to his annoyance, had beaten everyone. He made a deal with Convair to design two jet aircraft; but once again, his fatal indecisions and confused state of mind cost him the lead in the race. By 1955, Boeing and Douglas had evolved the pioneer 707 and the DC-8. Hughes failed to place orders with these rivals, who had publicly stripped him. His enemy, Juan Trippe, head of Pan American (who, he still was sure, was behind Senator Brewster's 1947 investigation into his business), swept him off the table by ordering 707s and DC-8s in quantity. Hughes was left standing at the post—still running propeller aircraft that were as obsolete as horse-driven coaches.

Ralph Damon died of a heart attack, probably because of Hughes's changeability and inability to act. It was not until 1956 that Hughes forced himself to make a deal with Boeing. He embarked on plans to build his own jet planes—which he should have done in the first place. Mindful again of Florida's state tax–free status and the necessity to be close to his beloved Institute, he decided to set up a factory near Miami. But once again, and after meetings with the Florida governor LeRoy Collins, the plans collapsed. Instead, he went back to Convair and ordered sixty-three jetliners, which would cost close to $200 million.

Most of his assets, which yielded him almost twice that much in annual income, were tied up in property and resources; he didn't have $200 million in liquid capital. He was afraid to raise a bank loan, using his properties as collateral, because he had always bragged that he was self-supporting. By the end of 1956, the situation was unresolved; Hughes was committed to orders he couldn't pay for. Finally, and in humiliation, he was forced to borrow.

## CHAPTER THIRTEEN

# Withdrawals

H ughes's inability to sustain relationships with his numerous women remained as serious as ever. Yet their fascination with his wealth and power remained unabated.

Terry Moore continued, at least in her own mind, to lead the field; but there is no evidence that he took her more seriously, or cared for her any more deeply, than any other human being.

In 1954, she went on a publicity tour to Korea to promote her latest CinemaScope pictures *Beneath the Twelve-Mile Reef* and *King of the Khyber Rifles*. Hughes risked attracting attention by driving her and her mother to the Los Angeles Airport; nobody recognized the seedy, unkempt driver who deposited them and took off at record speed. He telephoned her, with his usual obsessiveness, with the alligator love call, wherever he could reach her. She made headlines when she pulled off her trench coat on a Korean stage and showed the 10,000 troops her figure in an ermine bathing suit.

Hughes was furious when he heard she was being shipped home in disgrace by the Army. In hypocritical Hollywood, the only disgrace was to be publicly disgraced. She was slaughtered in the press. The Casanova of his generation had the nerve to tell her she had made a big mistake, then told an aide, with Hollywood running in his veins, "Terry Moore's a household word. We should be able to capitalize on her somehow." Most of her Californian friends deserted her. The troops demanded she be allowed to stay. Faced with a choice between mutiny and morality, the authorities gave in.

Hughes was maddened by photographs of her riding on a Waikiki beachboy's shoulders on the way home. He humored her by agreeing to adopt a Korean orphan, but, luckily for the child, he found it another home. He met her at the plane; he drove directly onto the tarmac, speeding past the reporters as she and her mother hid in the back.

He annoyed her by telling her that he had dated Susan Hayward during her absence; according to Noah Dietrich, on New Year's Eve, 1953, he promised three women he would join them at the Beverly Hills Hotel for the celebrations: Hayward, Jean Peters, and actress Merry Anderson. He had Hayward meet him in the Polo Lounge, Peters in the main restaurant, and Anderson in the coffee shop. He commuted between the three. Susan Hayward followed him to the restaurant and caught him with Peters. She stormed out; Peters laughed the whole thing off.

Yet again, he promised all three he would marry them. Jean Peters rebelled and, in 1954, married CIA contact Stuart Cramer III. But she was still in love with Hughes and the marriage didn't last.

Hughes decided he would turn Moore into a nightclub star in Las Vegas, despite the fact that she still couldn't sing or dance. He forced her to cancel an Argentinean tour and pushed her through five months of lessons. For her Flamingo Hotel opening, he had Michael Woulfe design a costume from his own specifications: a black and gray soufflé of sequins that gave the audience the illusion they were seeing Moore's naked breasts. Then, with typical cruelty, Hughes sent her a $15,000 bill for her clothes. She paid it, spending all the money she had. Even after this, she went on seeing him.

Soon afterward, Hughes met Ava Gardner at the plane from Madrid, where she had been filming *The Barefoot Contessa* and was having a much-publicized affair with celebrity bullfighter Luis Miguel Dominguin. He drove onto the tarmac and whisked her off the gangway before the cameras started popping. Then he flew her to Lake Tahoe, where he had bought her a house.

He tried, once more, to go to bed with her. When they were out boating on the lake, she mentioned the sapphire color of the lake water. Soon after, he gave her a sapphire ring to match the tint. It was, he lied, a Kashmir stone of finest quality; though he had had it flown in from Tiffany's, he said he had had a team searching the world for it. Late at night, in her suite, no more than a day after he had last proposed to Terry Moore, he asked her to marry him. She refused; she only began to warm up when he said he would buy her a yacht. She didn't invite him to her bedroom.

When Dominguin arrived from Madrid, Hughes paid members of Gardner's staff to spy on her. They were to report the couple's first major quarrel; both Gardner and Dominguin were as heroic in their arguments as they were in their sheet-tossing sexual acrobatics. Gardner invited Duke Ellington and his orchestra to the house. She flirted with Ellington. Dominguin, who had expected to go to bed with her, struck her so hard (she wrote later) she fell down the stairs. Johnny Meyer, who knew Dominguin, called him the next day and told him he should teach Gardner a lesson by leaving town. Hughes supplied the means; a TWA aircraft was waiting in Los Angeles to whisk the bullfighter off to Madrid.

Gardner forgave Hughes's tactic; he sent her to Miami so that she would be close to him when he was in meetings over the Medical Institute. While she was on the way to join him, he flew to Philadelphia to pick up Moore, who was on tour in a play, and took her to Fall River, Massachusetts. He assured her there was nothing in stories that he was pursuing Gardner. But the moment he got to Miami, he rented Gardner a villa.

He again had Gardner watched. He dangled a promise in front of her even she couldn't refuse: the gift of a pearl and diamond necklace that he lied had belonged to Catherine the Great of Russia. It was just another bauble from Tiffany's. She decided to get out for good. His spies called to tell him she was packing; he intercepted her. During the subsequent quarrel, she threw the "Kashmir" sapphire ring at him. It was just as well; he had only leased it.

She went to the airport and flew to Havana. Hughes followed her. She hid from him in Ernest Hemingway's house. He returned to Jean Peters, whom he had brought to Miami.

When both Moore and Gardner insisted that Hughes was really interested in marrying Jean Peters, Hughes fooled them. He had Stuart Cramer III flown to Miami to be with Jean. But he never stopped propositioning her.

In July, 1955, Hughes sold RKO to General Teleradio, Inc., a subsidiary of General Tire and Rubber. GTR president Tom O'Neil needed the studio's backlog of pictures to fill the program slots of six TV stations. Within a year, production had stopped. O'Neil sold the studio to Lucille Ball, who was appalled at its condition. She turned it over to making the *I Love Lucy* series. And this was the RKO that had made *Citizen Kane*.

Hughes wasn't out of the picture business. He resurrected his earlier idea of making *Carmen*—he had never forgiven Harry Cohn for stealing his idea of filming the story (with his ex-lover Rita Hayworth) and he was still smarting over his failure with Zizi Jean-maire when he had planned to present her ballet version of Bizet's opera. In collusion with Darryl F. Zanuck, he offered Ava Gardner the picture; he flew to her home in Palm Springs with a cardboard box containing $250,000 in thousand-dollar bills. As he opened the box in her garden to show her the money, bills blew away in the wind. She turned him down; she knew he didn't really want her to play in *Carmen*. He was still hoping to buy her for sex.

She signed a contract with MGM to make *Bhowani Junction* in Pakistan. She seldom saw him after that. And then Terry Moore became pregnant by him again.

Once more, Dr. Verne Mason tested her, and once more told Hughes, not her, the result of the test. The news was as much of a shock to her as a pleasure. She was afraid that she might be treated as savagely by the press at having a baby out of wedlock as Ingrid Bergman had been, despite the shipboard "wedding." To appease her hysteria, Hughes said, with icy, callous cynicism, that he would remarry her. He had only a few days before proposed marriage for the umpteenth time to Susan Hayward.

He had her picked up and flown to Las Vegas; thence they were to continue to a ranch near Tucson, Arizona, to be married at the home of two friends, Jack and Helen Fry. The delirious Moore rushed off to Beverly Hills to snap up an expensive trousseau. That evening, she broke off her romance with Nicky Hilton.

Once she was in Las Vegas, Hughes tried to bribe, scream, and argue his way to getting clearance to fly Moore to Arizona through a violent dust storm; he would not have survived the journey, nor would Moore and her parents. Denied permission, he drove them back to the Desert Inn. Suddenly, Nicky Hilton turned up; Hilton had learned that she was in Las Vegas and was determined to win her back.

Hilton had an edge. He had had his detectives check up on Hughes and found that Hughes had several women he was dating in

Las Vegas. Hilton and Hughes clashed in a violent scene in the lobby. Hilton struck Hughes; and Hughes, once again, instead of hitting him back, threw his hands in front of his face like a woman. Moore's mother protected Hughes with her body. Why she wanted to save this man who had twice made Moore pregnant out of wedlock and betrayed her with countless women is a mystery.

Pregnant by Hughes or not, Moore could not resist Hilton's pleas to come with him and leave the son of a bitch to his own devices. Hughes screamed that if she walked out on him now, her career would be over.

Despite the fact that she was three months with child, Moore rashly embarked on extensive ballet training for the musical *Daddy Long Legs;* she miscarried a malformed baby. Hughes turned up in the hospital and managed to make sympathetic remarks and shed a few crocodile tears. Soon after, she was back in bed with him, at the Beverly Hills Hotel:

> Slowly and ever so gently [she wrote in her memoirs] he
> undressed me and melted into my body. We made love with a
> renewed passion.

She didn't bring up the subject of marriage again. Hughes had her followed during an extensive publicity trip to Europe; he was jealous when she continued to see Nicky Hilton and when she was seen in public with producer Mike Todd. He was furious when Panama City insurance executive Gene McGrath pursued her, and her visit to the theater with future Paramount chief Robert Evans cost him sleep. McGrath proposed marriage to her, and she accepted. It isn't clear why she, even though Hughes had kept his threat and slowed down her career, was prepared to give up Hollywood to live in the sweltering heat of Panama City, but apparently the handsome McGrath's bedroom performance gave her a sufficiently good reason:

> Every fibre of my being wanted this stranger. I wanted all of
> him. . . . he had expertise in each and every part of the female
> body.

Hughes had his spies search McGrath's bungalow at the Beverly Hills Hotel (a foolish choice of address) for anything he could pin on him to destroy his marriage to Moore. He failed. All he found out was that McGrath was a CIA agent. On January 1, 1956, she married McGrath. The night before, Hughes telephoned her, viciously smearing McGrath's reputation. But she wouldn't listen. By 1958, she was divorced; later she married Jean Peters's ex-husband, CIA man Stuart Cramer III. The merry-go-round of beds continued. She never saw Hughes again. But she tried to unsuccessfully, on several occasions.

Jean Peters was nobody's fool; she knew that Hughes was involved with Terry Moore and Susan Hayward, and was still obsessed with Ava Gardner; yet, divorced now from Stuart Cramer III, Peters agreed to marry him, at the end of 1956. Why? Knowing how often he had asked women to stand before a minister or justice of the peace, perhaps even knowing that he had been married by a yacht captain, she actually took him seriously when he proposed to her at New Year's.

In her sensible, down-to-earth heart, this decent woman was no more able to resist Hughes than anybody else. In a lengthy court deposition in 1977, Peters made clear that his strongest attraction for her was his devotion to the Hughes Medical Institute. She fell for his lie that he would give everything he had to helping the sick.

And, of course, the vulnerable, little-boy-lost Hughes act worked its charm on her; here was this powerful, commanding public figure and captain of industry, this former head of a movie studio, who needed her to find fulfillment for his miserable, lost soul. As with every other woman he met, he could pull out of his limited bag of tricks the plea that he was lonely, incomplete, and felt ill. Maternal instincts were strong in Jean Peters. It is a misfortune that Hughes had made sure, with cold callousness, she would never bear his child. Since his early mumps had, as we know, not entirely removed his live sperm (though the count was probably very low), he had had a vasectomy in 1955. Wickedly, he hid this from her. She can only have dreamed of having a child with him, which might have been another motive for marrying Hughes after her failed marriage to Stuart Cramer III.

Hughes chose, as the site of his wedding on January 12, 1957, a town in Nevada, Tonopah, almost identical to that which was featured in his RKO movie *Split Second,* and subject to radiation fallout which could have affected his and his wife's health. One of the advantages of marrying there was that they could wed under assumed names (G. A. Johnson and Marian Evans), and that press and public would never find them; not only was Hughes famous, but so, to a lesser extent, after starring in a number of CinemaScope hits, was Jean Peters.

Another advantage was silver. Hughes had been tipped off that when the turn-of-the-century Nevada silver boom ended, after over $170 million of the precious metal had been mined, and flourishing Tonopah had become shabby and deserted, the mining interests had failed to note the continuing existence of several lodes.

It is possible that he had heard that his late father, in his restless wanderings as prospector, had spent some time in Tonopah. Hughes began, even as he was in town for the wedding, snapping up old claims; during the next several years, he would absorb as many as 100 in the region, and would spread out to obtain more than 600 others, engaging a battery of researchers to find the ancient records. He didn't even tell Jean Peters the reason for selecting the location, or why the richest man in America entertained her, not at a splendiferous Hilton, but at the overgrown shack known as the Mizpah Hotel.

It is sad to note that Jean had none of her friends or family present.

At this time, Hughes's everpresent hypochondria and paranoia suddenly surged to a peak; it was as though all of his mother's terror of germs was recurring in him so many years later. It was as though fears that he was in the grip of an immunosuppressive illness, somehow related to his airplane accident in Beverly Hills, had now taken hold. References to this fear surface in the numerous depositions in his estate files in Texas. And this happened just at the moment when he was a married man for the second (and happier) time; when he should have moved on, in the company of a sensible young woman, who loved him for himself, not his money and power, to the most stable and comfortable part of his life. Instead, he plunged into an abyss of misery and suffering relieved only by Jean Peters's compassionate and down-to-earth presence.

Back at Bungalow 4 of the Beverly Hills Hotel, with his wife in another bungalow, Hughes became manic over flies. He hired three strapping Mormons to work in eight-hour shifts at the bungalow, not just to make sure he wasn't killed, but to intercept the insects.

The winged creatures terrified him. He fantasized them grown large, their multifaceted black eyes staring at him with the impersonal coldness of insects, their plump, hairy bodies sticking all over him like burrs, their feces-covered feet, the explorers of a thousand turd piles, pattering across his bony chest and limbs, crawling into his mouth . . . Noah Dietrich, whose intimate knowledge of Hughes was about to result in his dismissal, told this author of Hughes's flyblown nightmares; even a speck on a bulb could remind him of his nightly horrors.

Hughes would sit for long periods of time in his bungalow, naked, except, very occasionally, for a Kleenex diaper, staring into the light in case some fly should buzz around it. Even clothes made him uneasy; perhaps cotton or wool carried some contagion, cotton from cotton plants (he perhaps had not forgotten a foolish rumor in Shreveport that cotton boats carried yellow fever germs), wool from sheep, who were, he thought, repulsive, and polyester, which was surely a toxic chemical. As for silk, was there anything more disgusting than a silkworm, wriggling in its little box, eating gnats or whatever it was fed with, spinning the silk from its own ugly little gut?

The guards were forbidden to use flyswatters, because they might stir the air and recycle germs lying dormant in the air conditioning system. They must not use a chemical spray, as it might be cancer-causing (he may have had a point there). Sticky flypaper surely emanated poison—hadn't women killed their husbands by soaking the arsenic off it in water and putting the deadly stuff in drinks? Furthermore, these athletic bodyguards must pursue flies as cumbersomely as elephants. If they moved fast, they could send dust clouds spinning from the layers of filth that Hughes paradoxically allowed in the room.

One of these guards, Ron Kistler, recalled that Hughes insisted on inspecting a fly when Kistler managed to catch it in Kleenex; according to Dietrich and Ted Carpentier, Hughes would put a pin in the fly (a long woman's hat pin believed to have belonged to his mother) to make sure it had no reflexes.

In the midst of this squalid existence, Hughes made questionable forays into political influence-buying. He arranged for playboy Pat DiCicco, along with Los Angeles accountant Phillip Reiner, to "oversee" the business affairs of Donald Nixon, brother of Vice President Richard Nixon, on behalf of the Hughes Tool Company.

The Hughes-Nixon loan affair, which was to cast a lasting shadow over Richard Nixon's reputation, began in the fall, when Noah Dietrich received a call from Washington lobbyist Frank A.

Waters, who said that Vice President Nixon wanted a $205,000 loan for his brother. Hughes personally approved the money. Dietrich claimed in his memoirs that he warned Nixon not to allow the loan as it would wreck his career; this is, to say the least, unlikely, since if Hughes had found out, he would have wrecked Dietrich's career.

One favor Hughes wanted in return was to have his medical institute, the recipient of millions from Hughes Aircraft, granted tax-exempt status. Nixon's mother, Hannah, received $40,000 to settle a debt, and Donald received the cash for his failing chain of Nixonburger-selling restaurants. The "security," which was insecure, was Hannah Nixon's $13,000 block of real estate in Whittier.

Donald Nixon went broke in 1957. James McInerney, in charge of special investigations for John F. Kennedy, spaded up the dirt just when it was needed, in 1960, when Kennedy was to run for President against Nixon. He gave it to Nixon's enemy, columnist Drew Pearson. (Hughes's lawyer, Edward P. Morgan, also represented Drew Pearson.) The matter leaked to Nixon, who tried to bury the story by issuing, on October 24, a lying statement through campaign manager Robert Finch that Frank Waters had made the loan, and that the land used as collateral was worth between $200,000 and $300,000. On October 26, the columnist Jack Anderson printed the truth, which is said to have been a major factor costing Nixon the election. However, neither Drew Pearson, nor Jack Anderson in his memoirs, *Confessions of a Muckraker*, could produce evidence that Vice President Nixon used the money to secure preferences for Howard Hughes for TWA, Hughes Aircraft, or the Medical Institute. The truth is that, like so many of Hughes's ventures, the expedition into influence buying was a waste of money. The cash went down the toilet in Whittier, and the lack of security flung around the deal resulted in Hughes's having a Kennedy presidency on his hands when what he needed was a Nixon.

The list of Hughes's eccentricities lengthened. When he felt overheated—understandably, since he had had the air conditioning turned off in his bungalow—he would take a quart bottle of Poland Water and remove the cap. Then he would pour water over his head until the water flooded the carpet.

He had strict rules over the delivery of magazines. His aides, Johnny Holmes, Jack Egger, and Ron Kistler, would carry three copies of current magazines into his room on a service cart, finding him naked as usual—though sometimes he placed a Kleenex over his genitals. They would have to stand before him for as much as twenty minutes, in silence, while he repeated, as many as twenty times, instructions for pushing the cart at him, inch by inch, without breathing on him, so the air and the dust would not be stirred.

Then he would stare at them, and they would stare back, until at last he gave the signal they were waiting for. When the cart came within reach of his fingers, he would reach out, his hands and arms swathed in paper like an Egyptian mummy's, and delicately, with infinite slowness, remove the middle magazine from its companions. He would repeat, over and over again, instructions for the other magazines to be burned. He would push the cart back for the men and they would remove it, but only after another protracted interval of his staring at them.

To married men, he accorded the task of bringing in *Time, Newsweek,* and *Life.* Only bachelors could bring in the magazines with naked women in them.

The only male visitor Hughes would allow in was Cary Grant, whose fastidious taste must have been offended by Hughes's body odor (which has been described as resembling that of a dead goat), the piles of rubbish, the filthy bed, and the slow movement of big men catching flies. But his love for Hughes didn't fade.

During the months at Bungalow 4, Hughes only changed his bed sheets three times; on one of the three occasions, he made sure that they were burned. Despite his increasing mania over hygiene, and sleeping in a nest of Kleenex, there were stains of urine, feces, and semen.

He took off with Jean to Palm Springs, to a rambling ranch-type bungalow of seven rooms in a small clump of tamarisk trees situated between the Racquet Club and the stables.

Hughes made sure the house was cleaned from top to bottom. His bodyguard, Jerry Bell, was told to remove every flower, plant, and rubber tree from the rooms and burn them in a pile in the backyard. Every window had to be taped and the air conditioning cleaned.

He would allow no meat or fish to be supplied. Bell ensured a flow of chocolate, fruit, and fruit juice for Hughes and the same for Jean Peters—who must have longed for more substantial fare. Hughes wanted no prints of movies in the house. Nobody was allowed in except the guards—not even a poolman. As a result, the pool bred bacteria—paradoxically, those things which filled Hughes with dread.

When a duck died in the pool, Hughes smelled the decaying flesh and allowed a poolman in. But he was appalled to find that the poolman had six fingers on each hand. He fired him; the pool continued to stink.

Hughes devoted those weeks to Jean's body and mind; he cut out the world in order to pleasure her as best he could. At times, early in the morning, the guards, who were kept beyond the chained gate, would see the couple walking hand in hand under the fragile shade of the tamarisk trees.

An incident forced him to quit the house. A local security service, popular in the desert, had a determined owner who wanted to prove he could provide a better protective service than the Mormons did. He studied the property, hoping to find a loophole. Finally, in the early hours of one morning, he found the gate chain undone. He drove up to the house, his car's headlights blazing through the curtains; Hughes became hysterical, fearing a burglar or a killer, but before he could grab a gun, the car was gone. Surprisingly, Hughes didn't dismiss his guards as a result; he returned to the Beverly Hills Hotel.

Jean Peters had moved into a separate bungalow. She hated living there now, and longed for a proper house. Hughes took leases on homes, promised her he would move with her into them, and then failed to do so. Uncared for, they fell into disrepair.

He continued to use the Goldwyn studios projection room. He would allow nobody but the projectionist to be present, except on the rare occasions in which Jean Peters was with him. She wearied of the screenings and backed off. He began seeing pictures alone in stretches of as many as seventy-two hours, old, new, anything; it didn't seem to matter. He saw some movies in full; others would make him impatient and he would have them stopped after a reel or two. His chief motive in seeing these films was to find new girls to add to his harem.

Then, suddenly, his use of the screening room came to an end. Sam Goldwyn and director Otto Preminger used it to run a rough cut of their film *Porgy and Bess*. Disgusted by the idea of an all-black picture, Hughes announced he would never set foot in the room again. He began showing pictures at Max Nosseck's on Sunset Boulevard.

He would spend hours at Nosseck's making small, neat piles of Kleenex boxes, then taking the piles apart and reconstructing them, like a child with a Meccano set. When he was busy rearranging the boxes, he would allow no films to be shown. He had his food delivered in paper bags; the bags had remained untouched in a sealed cupboard for two years. The drivers had to wear white cotton hospital gloves when they carried the bags in. Hughes extracted the food—mostly Hershey bars and milk—with Kleenex wrapped around his hand.

He didn't risk turning the doorknob, even with gloves. He would kick the door as a signal and the drivers would open it. He was obsessed with the toilet. He urinated on the floor; then he covered it with Kleenexes to sop up the fluid. He refused to let his men use the toilet; instead they had to use empty ice buckets.

The stench of urine in the screening room was disgusting but Hughes refused to allow the buckets to be emptied. Finally, the guards rebelled and poured the urine down a storm drain.

Hughes resumed his habit of sitting on the toilet seat, now for twenty-six hours at a stretch, straining at stools. When he dressed again, his clothes were soon covered in filth. It was only when they turned into rags that he stripped naked in front of guard Ron Kistler and allowed Kistler to burn them. He succumbed to wearing first a shirt only, and then a shirt and trousers. His flesh began hanging where what was left of his body fat had gone. He had no muscle tone; his skin was gray and flabby.

He lied to Jean Peters that he was in the hospital but refused to say which one. He returned to the Beverly Hills Hotel, declining to tell her of the nature of his (imaginary) illness. His manic desire to control his drivers recurred. They were ordered never to speak to him, only to communicate in notes; they were not allowed to order food unless he authorized it. Even the food itself he must approve. They must not, for example, eat pork, garlic, or onions.

For long periods he forbade his team to drink when on duty. Cruelly, he would drink Poland Water in front of the parched men. Ron Kistler described the experience as the equivalent of being trapped in an unswept monkey cage at the zoo, but at least a monkey keeper could drink. When Kistler literally begged Hughes for water one day, Hughes yielded, but with vicious, cruel sarcasm at Kistler's show of weakness.

He talked for hours to Jean Peters in her bungalow while refusing to let her into his. He was as full of promises as ever: world cruises, a magnificent house they would share together, years away from everyone in the South Seas. At the same time, he still kept her in her luxurious jail; she wasn't allowed to go out—not even for shopping. He had his detectives watch her constantly. Her career over, she filled her days embroidering and making metal sculptures. Her worst ordeal was not being able to go to the Dodgers baseball games.

And she had another cross to bear: Hughes maintained his old stable of starlets, but now, platonically.

His rules for the underage girls were rigid. The appropriate actress would be given the use of an elegant house in Beverly Hills or Bel Air, with a maid. At exactly seven A.M., she must rise and take a shower and make up. At seven-thirty, the maid would serve her breakfast. At eight, a driver would take her to acting, dancing, and singing lessons. In the afternoon, she must rest or watch TV. Shopping was permitted once a week. In the evening, she would go to one of six restaurants Hughes specified. She was forbidden to date. A driver would be her companion for dinner. Her food was selected by the office; the table must never be in a draft. Families were given occasional visiting rights—by request and by appointment only.

Not one of the girls developed as a performer or obtained a studio contract. The drivers had to zigzag around the city trying to coordinate movements so that the starlets would be able to keep to their rigid, unalterable schedules. Sometimes, a driver had to have two dinners with two different girls to fulfill Hughes's prescriptions.

If a starlet rebelled, the drivers had orders to discipline her; sometimes, a girl would run headlong from a car in a desperate effort to escape and the driver would chase after her and pull her back into the seat.

On one occasion, an actress took a ride by herself; accused of being a thief, she was rounded up by police. Another girl upset Hughes by marrying her driver; Hughes dismissed him at once. No starlet was allowed to ride horseback, motorcycle, or bicycle.

They almost never met Hughes. When they did, they had to be medically examined, strip and bathe three times with antiseptic soap, and wear white gloves to shake hands with him. He never went to bed with them.

Control, not sex, was the meaning of his relationship with these women.

The drivers were told never to negotiate bumps in a road at more than two miles an hour as the jolt to the automobile might cause the girls' breasts to sag. Hughes sent detectives to make sure that the men who were not homosexual would not go to bed with the girls. If a driver visited anyone in a hospital with a contagious disease, Hughes fired him at once.

When he sacked Noah Dietrich over a trivial matter in 1957, he didn't even see the man who had been his loyal servant for thirty years.

Only once in mid-1957 is he known to have gone out. He sneaked out of his bungalow early on a Sunday morning and slipped into his car. In a fit of nostalgia, he made his way to Lockheed and test-flew a brand-new Electra for several minutes before making a neat landing. He was delighted, animated, a boy again. Then he returned to the hotel.

Another moment of joy is described by Ron Kistler. Hughes was thrilled to learn that there was a brushfire in Benedict Canyon: Noah Dietrich's house was in that area. He was disappointed it didn't burn.

He didn't entertain destructive feelings for a new right-hand man, Robert Maheu. Gentlemanly, intelligent, subdued, the stocky, soft-spoken Maheu was his most trusted telephone companion apart from Jean Peters. "I was fond of him," Maheu says today. "He was the poorest man, as well as the richest, in the world."

A former FBI agent, Maheu had joined the CIA; he was involved with Stavros Niarchos, the Greek shipping magnate, in a CIA-backed scheme to break up Aristotle Onassis's oil monopolies in the Arab empire. Hughes had him investigate Jean Peters's (and later Terry Moore's) husband, Stuart Cramer, to see if he was a CIA agent. Maheu was able to report that Cramer was not a full-time operative. Later, Maheu was involved in Hughes's abortive spying operation on Ava Gardner. He handled the assignment clumsily—Frank Sinatra even spied one of his operatives on a boat in Lake Tahoe and chased the man off—but Hughes kept him on.

As head of Robert M. Maheu Associates, he had a special contract with Hughes that allowed him a Cadillac and an office and staff in association with Hughes associate Bill Gay. Maheu's next assignment was to silence a blackmailing minister of the church who had found out about one of Hughes's affairs with a young girl. Maheu determined that the minister had homosexual secrets. If the preacher stayed silent, so would Maheu. The technique worked. When another blackmailer threatened to expose Hughes, Maheu secretly recorded the conversation. Evidence of blackmail would have destroyed the man, and Maheu successfully trumped his ace.

At the time of the 1956 election, Hughes found a better use for Maheu. He was determined that Richard Nixon should continue as vice president.

Hughes paid Maheu to back Nixon with cash against Minnesotan Harold Stassen, who wanted Governor of Massachusetts Christian A. Herter to be vice president. He had Maheu arrange a burglary of Stassen's headquarters in Washington to see if the poll Stassen had conducted showing that Nixon was unpopular had any validity. It did.

Meanwhile, Hughes had Maheu whip up an opposing poll. The results of both were read at the San Francisco Republican Convention; the pro-Nixon poll had a larger count. It helped that Maheu knew what the anti-Nixon count was. The action led directly to Nixon's remaining vice president.

Hughes had Maheu investigate potential or actual Communists in the Culver City council, which, he felt, was interfering with his factory. Maheu did better. He formed a pressure group for Hughes—the Better Business Association, which could pull strings if the council should interfere with Hughes's activities. Hughes was pleased; he made Maheu his second in command.

In the summer of 1957, Hughes emerged from his self-imposed jail and took off to Montreal, Canada, where he wanted to buy several British Britannias and Vickers Viscounts, owned by Air Trans Canada, to bolster his lagging TWA fleet. He pulled himself together sufficiently to dress properly and he piloted his Constellation 1649 for the journey. With him went Pat DiCicco, John Holmes, Bill Gay, and several bodyguards.

On the first night at the Ritz-Carlton Hotel he acted as weirdly as ever. He had a rule that all ice cream served to him must be vanilla. He was upset when the room service waiter arrived with an ice cream that had a hint of strawberry in it. From that moment on, the ice cream had to be brought in from outside.

He complained that grease ran from the trolley casters to the carpet as it was wheeled in with the grill the hotel installed in his room. He would not allow his steaks to be cooked in the kitchen; the grill had to be cleaned and he had to inspect it before he would allow his team to cook the meat. His bed had to be pulled apart sheet by sheet, blanket by blanket, down to the mattress, and then, when remade, covered with Kleenexes before he would lie on it.

His only joy in those weeks was in test-flying the British aircraft—but he never bought one. He flew on to Nassau, in the Bahamas, for telephone discussions over buying property in that tax-free colony. He paid one of the Emerald Beach Hotel chefs to work for him personally. He disliked the local pastries and was pleased that Holmes had packed some in Montreal. But when he opened one of the wrapped cakes, he was horrified to find it was mildewed. He urged the chef to check all his food even more thoroughly and he engaged a pastry chef to bake each cake and cookie individually. He insisted the local baker remove the sugar from a canvas sack in which it was kept and moved to sealed tins where cockroaches wouldn't intrude.

When the pastries came to him, he again had the chefs check the trolley wheels to make sure no oil was dripping from the wheels. He was afraid also that some insect might be clinging to the metal. When he saw a cockroach on the wall, he screamed like a child.

He brought Jean Peters to Nassau for a few weeks. He also summoned Robert Maheu and told him to buy the local radio station, houses and hotels, anything that was for sale.

Maheu was worried that Hughes would be stranded in the Bahamas; that his dream of owning Nassau might collapse in a bloody strike or riot. The civil unrest in the black community was considerable. Hughes refused to listen, but finally the very poor Nassau telephone service infuriated him so much that he and Jean took off to Los Angeles—he again flew the Constellation himself. Probably unbeknownst to Jean or Maheu, he carried with him, and would continue to carry, in ever-increasing amounts, Mason jars of his own urine, preserved for years like the finest champagne.

## CHAPTER FOURTEEN

# Sealed Rooms

Returning to the Beverly Hills Hotel, Hughes moved into Bungalow 4, with Jean Peters in Bungalow 15. He was renting at least four bungalows in any given week. At one time, he moved to a suite in the Crescent Wing of the main building. He seldom went out. On one occasion, he was caught damaging hotel property: he was trying to cut down a fly-harboring bougainvillea bush with a pair of paper scissors. Even he could not get away with that, and no matter what he offered, the management would not let him have the beautiful bush dug up.

The nightmare continued. By mid-1958, Hughes was addicted to codeine (which he injected into his arm), Valium, and Demerol; he had fits of temper and emitted streams of meaningless words; he spurted his urine onto the bathroom door so that it trickled into his room; he extended his Kleenex obsession to Jean Peters. When she went to a theater or a movie, audience members would see her escort going through the astonishing ritual of cleaning the seat she sat on. Hughes began writing immense, complicated memoranda, in a surprisingly neat, schoolboyish hand, which, in essence, treated his employees like actors in a play of his composition, a play of such meaninglessness that even on the written evidence it is hard to believe.

One memo, dated October 13, 1958, was written to executive

Kay Glenn, in a delirium of paranoia; accessible in the Hughes estate files in Houston, Texas, it shows, also, an obsession with controlling everything, every detail of his life, as though he were the God of a tiny world.

He forbade his aides to go into any area of his bungalow to which his man Johnny Holmes had exclusive access, no matter what circumstances might arise (presumably, that included earthquake—this was Los Angeles—or fire). It is extremely doubtful whether anybody on his staff obeyed these crazed instructions, at least on the rare occasions when he was neither vigilant, his eyes flickering rapidly round the room, nor sleeping. Hughes also insisted they not even fetch magazines, Kleenexes, or food; this meant that when he wanted any of these, or all three at once, only Holmes could get them—and Holmes was, of course, liable to want to sleep himself, or go out. No door to the storeroom could be opened even the tiniest fraction or for the very smallest amount of time. To confuse his addressee, Glenn, even more, he added at the end of the immense and hysterical document a requirement that the *waiters* (who were, after all, from the dangerous and contaminated outside world) be allowed to enter the sacred closets—an afterthought that made nonsense of everything that went before it. But, despite the character of the memo, which on the face of it seemed the work of a man out of his mind, it does not, on analysis, display insanity; rather, it resembles the words of the head teacher of a Victorian girls' school, delivering instructions to the domestic staff. It is a profoundly effeminant document.

Rising at 3:00 P.M. each day, Hughes was on the Kleenex-wrapped Bungalow 4 telephone for hours at a stretch talking to his executives about the problems at TWA. The airline's president, the able Carter Burgess, weary of not being able to see Hughes in person and of the long, rambling, meaningless phone conversations, resigned in December, 1957. Hughes had ordered Burgess to buy a series of jet planes from Boeing but he had no cash to pay for them. When former Navy Secretary Charles S. Thomas, whom Hughes hired, following his custom of wanting government preferments, took over from Burgess, Thomas was stymied. When the First Boston Corporation seemed to be about to supply financing, with Hughes Tool assets as collateral, FBC chairman George Woods was refused a meeting with Hughes, and backed out of the deal.

William Forrester, Jr., of Merrill Lynch began protracted

negotiations with Hughes, but he insisted on selling Hughes Aircraft and Hughes refused to allow the money to be pulled out from his Medical Institute—according to his enemies, because he feared a colossal tax bill; according to his friends, because he would not let the Institute die. He contacted Fred Brandi, of the conservative and influential bankers Dillon, Read, to raise a total of $165 million, with further debentures of $100 million.

Hughes Aircraft for years had been misnamed: it was, in fact, still a defense contractee of, and an adjunct of, the American government. It monopolistically supplied electronic armament control systems for all-weather interceptor airplanes of the U.S. and Canadian air forces, the first line of defense against potential Soviet use of the H-bomb. In addition, Hughes Aircraft provided almost all air-to-air missiles of the Falcon series. They were, since 1956, the chief armament of the Air Defense Command. Hughes Aircraft was the main supplier of ground radar systems, employing revolutionary inventions and techniques. One armament control system alone contained 100,000 individual parts. Hundreds of millions of dollars poured into small industries which supplied specific tiny components of this vast, top-secret arsenal. In addition, Hughes Aircraft utilized some $19 million in government-owned equipment. In 1957, Hughes Aircraft won the Industry Defense Teamwork Award. Thus, the Hughes Medical Institute was paid for by government agreements—reason enough for its tax-free status.

Because Hughes had positioned his companies in the heart of the Cold War effort, he was assured a prestigious position when it came to his lawyers' negotiating for him, despite his continuing unavailability for face-to-face discussion and despite his reckless mismanagement of TWA.

He managed to scrape up sufficient millions for TWA to buy Boeings, then panicked and sold six of them to the hated Juan Trippe of Pan American. He also panicked when it came to orders of Convair 880 jets. He had the effrontery, not to say the gangsterish toughness, to send men with rifles to the Convair plant, aim the guns at the workers, and order the planes off the assembly line. After hijacking them, he had them towed out to lie useless and rusting in the sea air. Convair's bosses were infuriated and at once disassembled every other Hughes 880. But they didn't sue him for the millions they should have; perhaps they thought they could profit from him later?

During the delicate negotiations with major financial institu-
tions, it was essential that Hughes, shuffling around half-naked in
pajama tops or bottoms and addicted to Hershey bars, apples, and
Poland Water, should display at least a nominal solidarity with the
executives at the top of his companies. But he infuriated and alienated his new TWA boss Charles S. Thomas, even refusing to speak
to him at all between April and July, 1960. He had the nerve to ask
Thomas to leave his post and become an employee of the Tool
Company. He refused to up Thomas's meager salary of $60,000 a
year or grant him stock options. Thomas walked out. Within twenty-
four hours, the consortium that Dillon, Read had at last pulled
together for the $265 million desperately needed to meet Hughes's
jet plane orders backed off, outraged.

On September 1, 1960, Hughes was expected to come up with
$54 million in cash to pay back previous loans. He didn't have the
money. Insomniac at best, he went sixty hours without sleep. Not
even morphine helped. He was so hysterical that even a light tap
on his bedroom door made him scream like a wounded animal. At
any minute, he could lose everything; the banks could foreclose on
him.

Like a spider struggling to escape pouring water, he twisted and
turned, ran up and down his room, rolled himself into a ball—and
searched and searched for a way to save his empire. He couldn't save
TWA; by late 1960, it was obvious he had no alternative but to
surrender control in return for the $265 million raised from new
sources.

The condition was that Hughes, who had signed no legal documents in years, would have to put his signature to the papers himself,
surrendering voting rights on his 78 percent share. Hughes refused;
Bautzer told him he had to sign them. How could Bautzer make him
do so?

Bautzer called the Beverly Hills Hotel bell captain and told the
captain to take the papers to Hughes's bungalow. The captain was
not to leave the room until Hughes signed them. Somehow, the
captain managed to get permission to go into the locked room. He
told Hughes he must sign. Hughes opened the envelope and read the
documents. "I'm not going to sign," he said.

"You *have* to," the bell captain told him.

"Why?" Hughes asked, whining like a plaintive, spoiled child.

"Because if you don't, I'll get fired," the bell captain replied.

Hughes looked at him very intently, saw that he was telling the truth, and signed the papers that cost him his beloved airline.

The deal was completed on December 15, 1960. To assuage his bitterness, Hughes moved out of Bungalow 4, and, in an act of rare consideration for Jean Peters, took off on his alleged birthday, December 24 (he knew how to humor her with falsely sentimental gestures), to Rancho Santa Fe, a luxurious retreat south of Los Angeles, a favorite of the wealthy retired, where he had rented a comfortable but not opulent cottage.

Oddly, in Rancho Santa Fe, he allowed Jean Peters to sleep with him again and to control the housekeeping. But he wouldn't let her vacuum the five-inch-thick shag carpet. Finally, she overcame his objection, but he refused to see the ugly fat bag of the cleaner. Aide Johnny Holmes had to stand outside the room with the bag while Jean Peters used the hose. But she couldn't get under the bed or into the corners of the darkened room without bringing the bag in, and therefore she was unable to keep up the task. It was difficult anyway because Hughes would not allow her to draw the curtains to let light in; Holmes had to aim a flashlight through the door crack to assist her. She finally gave up the unequal struggle and let the dust collect.

She tried to move around with dusters, but he wouldn't let her touch certain objects, such as the television set.

Later on, Hughes and Jean moved to an imitation French chateau, 1001 Bel Air Road, Bel Air. Once again, she tried to vacuum. But Hughes had complicated wires all over the floor that tripped her and made it hard for her to do her work. When she ducktailed the wires against the wall, he deliberately strung them out again. When at last she talked him into washing off the encrustations on his body in a shower, he splashed around and flooded the carpet. When he was asleep, Jean cut out the damaged carpet and installed tiling. She could not get him to brush his teeth and his breath was foul.

He forbade her to touch his girlie and Air Force magazines and newspapers in their huge stacked piles. He would not let her sleep in his room—as she had courageously done at Rancho Santa Fe. As at Rancho Sante Fe, he placed his hospital bed, the specially made one he had used after his 1947 accident, in the center of the bedroom. Exactly two feet from his face was the TV. Next to it, always, was a sack containing torn up messages and crumpled Kleenexes. An aide, Oran Deal, was in charge of the sacks. By 1961, Peters's visits to his room were down to twice a day: fifteen minutes in the morning to tell him her plans for that evening, and thirty minutes in the evening before she went to bed alone.

He added something new: a tape that attached the door to the wall, a tape which must only be removed by his team. One day, he was shocked when a five-year-old boy, son of Jean Peters's foster sister, walked in—the tape had worn thin and he had broken it off. After that—somehow he restrained himself from screaming at the child—Johnny Holmes had to double the tapes. He insisted on Holmes's giving him a full, written explanation on how the tape had broken; Holmes provided one. It was ten pages long.

By late 1961, Hughes had stopped, under pressure from Jean, going around naked. He sometimes wore his pajama tops, sometimes the bottoms, never both. He wore brown shoes, dating back to the 1930s, to go to the bathroom.

He began, after a long interval, "celebrating" December 24 as his birthday. But he celebrated in the most depressing manner; he watched television for hours and asked Johnny Holmes to invite Jean in for a brief visit. Christmas was equally lifeless. He always sent her flowers instead of giving them to her in person, because he hated and feared them and was sure there must be insects in them. They had to be washed in Poland Water before Holmes gave them to her—with white-gloved hands.

In the late summer of 1960, Hughes made occasional and futile efforts to disrupt TWA's activities, even after surrendering his voting rights. This was unwise, since he was in every instance dismissed humiliatingly by the new boss, Ernest R. Breech. Hughes's name was a byword for stupidity in the boardroom now that he had brought TWA down to a miserable 20 percent share of the market. Then he made an even more reckless decision. As a CIA associate, he approved a plot by that agency and Robert Maheu to assassinate Fidel Castro.

At the same time, he leased an island named Cay Sal in the Bahamas. This island was used as a base of secret operations against Cuba, as well as a place where troops were trained. It was only one of countless Hughes connections to the CIA, of which he may said to have been (in his own eyes) a patriotic as well as profit-making instrument, with colossal contracts awarded to his companies, from scrambler devices for phones, bugs and intercepts, and lasers made by his wholly owned Hughes Tool, to satellites made by Hughes Aircraft (he had to sign approvals for eleven contracts), which he had given a degree of across-the-board autonomy.

Maheu decided he would hire an old friend of his FBI and CIA days, the gangster Johnny Rosselli, whom Hughes had been close to in the 1930s and who had powerful Las Vegas connections. "Uncle Johnny," as Rosselli was known to Maheu's sons, had married Hughes's girlfriend June Lang, been behind the craft union, IATSE, that had been active in smashing up other movie unions when Hughes was at RKO, and had been involved in Cuban gambling interests. According to Maheu, Rosselli took on the assassination out of patriotism; but surely Maheu was deceived. Rosselli's real motive must have been that he would be able, with Castro out of the way, to take over the Havana casinos; not only that, the CIA and FBI (which operated in the Caribbean) would go easy on him in return for his efforts—yet Maheu did not, at first, inform J. Edgar Hoover of the hit.

In August, 1960, Maheu met Rosselli at the Brown Derby restaurant in Beverly Hills, an amazingly public place—but in corrupt Hollywood meetings between gangsters and "legitimate" executives, studio or otherwise, were commonplace. They even discussed the plan over lunch. Rosselli in turn contacted Sam Giancana, the Mafia kingpin. Greedy for Havana, filled with patriotic burblings, Giancana came in on the deal. He knew the president would protect him. He had something on Kennedy: they amicably shared the same mistress, the nubile Judith Campbell. He wanted to be rid of the Communist leader who not only had seized his concessions, but might invade Florida and grab some more of his properties.

In Miami, at the Kenilworth Hotel, Maheu met with Rosselli, Giancana, and Santo Trafficante, who had once run the Havana mob and also was smarting at being tossed out in 1959. They hired Rafael ("Macho") Gener, a Cuban contact, who was planning an anti-Castro *coup d'état,* to undertake the mission. In October, Maheu, James O'Connell of the CIA, Sam Giancana, Johnny Rosselli and Santo Trafficante met in a suite at the Hotel Fontainebleau to discuss the plot. O'Connell, to keep the Agency's hand spotless, wanted an armed bandit raid on Castro's stronghold. ("Let's make it nice and clean.")

Rosselli and Giancana demurred. They knew it would be impossible to ambush a dictator who was surrounded day and night by armed guards. If the mission failed, some injured would-be assassin might blab. How about poison? O'Connell told the CIA laboratory to come up with something. They did: a pill. But it was useless, because the pill they used it wouldn't dissolve in water. CIA operative Sheffield Edward's idea was instead to kill Castro with botulism germs.

The method of murder was chancy. Certain mushroom poisons are extractable and undetectable; one of these should have been used. Instead, the CIA laboratory settled on the clostridium botulin germ, obtained from contaminated food. The problem was that living germs in a new, soluble pill form would die on contact with hot water or be severely weakened by alcohol; but to use dead germs would be a problem since the symptoms—vomiting, acute pain, collapse—would occur at once, allowing Castro's men to arrest anyone and everyone present at the scene. Live germs would not act until some fifteen to eighteen hours later, permitting the killer to get away.

The solution was to use botulin toxin, one tiny speck of which would be sufficient to kill 2,000 mice, and would not act until the same, later period; and this might survive dissolution in hot liquid, alcohol, or food. The problem with it was that in pill form it could not be guaranteed to dissolve in cold water, if that was the only drink Castro was imbibing. And how, with every movement watched, could even a trusted lieutenant risk being seen, and killed instantly?

Finally, and most importantly, in a hot, humid climate like Havana's, botulism from badly refrigerated food was common and could be easily recognized, and antitoxins would be available at a moment's notice; the antitoxin would be applied the moment Castro was stricken. Why did nobody at the CIA think of this?

At a further meeting in March, 1961, it was agreed that Maheu would pay $10,000 to Rosselli for "Macho" Gener, who was one of Castro's trusted officials, to make the hit. Though Maheu doesn't recall it, later hearings on the matter included statements under oath that he handed Rosselli the money in bills that he emptied out of a suitcase. But he does admit he handed over the saccharine-sized pills.

By now, Hughes was restless at Maheu's long absence in Miami. When Maheu told him what he was doing, he said, according to Maheu, that it seemed to be "a pretty good idea" to kill Castro. For years he had wanted to get his hands on Cuba, and to thrust into the lucrative gambling deals in Havana. Since the early 1930s, he had been in and out of the City of Sin several times, most recently when he chased Ava Gardner there and she hid with Ernest Hemingway. He had had, unbeknownst to Maheu, substantial land holdings under the protection of now-exiled president Batista and in league with sugar baron Julio Lobo, now in Mexico.

As it turned out, the effort against Castro misfired. "Macho" Gener fumbled and dropped the ball. His cook contact in Castro's favorite restaurant could do nothing with drinks because Castro stopped going there. Rosselli and Giancana contacted former Cuban senate president Manuel Antonio de Varona, who longed to see Castro dead and wanted to be back in power.

De Varona promised to deliver the poison to Castro's secretary, Juan Orta, for a bounty fee, if the plan came off, of $150,000. In return, Orta wanted to be given a secret cache of transmitters that would assist in the *coup d'état*. But Castro's secret police found out that Orta was planning a counterrevolution and put him in prison before he could do anything. An effort was made through a French secret agent and his girlfriend, to whom Castro was attracted. But Castro caught her—Leon Uris used the story in his novel *Topaz*, which became one of Hughes's favorite films. Only days later, Kennedy staged the disastrous Bay of Pigs invasion that led to the president's ignominious slip as a world leader. After that, Hughes lost patience and pulled Maheu back to Las Vegas. And to this day, many believe that Kennedy's assassination was caused by Castro, operating through Lee Harvey Oswald, in revenge for Maheu's attempt.

Hughes hired a new lawyer who would soon play a major role in his life. Chester C. Davis was a friend and representative of Floyd Odlum, who was still in touch with Hughes, along with his wife, Jacqueline Cochran, the 1930s aviatrix. Loud, aggressive, with a hefty physique and a booming voice, Davis was an expert Wall Street infighter, a stock market marine sergeant who could take on anyone with a verbal rifle butt. He drank hard and lived hard. Hughes needed him; TWA sued Hughes in July, 1961, for violation of antitrust laws and mismanagement. At first, he was prepared to settle. He would have put $150 million into the airline, but then he decided to fight. In doing so, he double-crossed Greg Bautzer by not telling him what he was going to do.

On February 13, 1962, he filed a countersuit against TWA. He averred that the airline bosses had conspired with Dillon, Read and insurance companies to divest him of the company illegally and that he should be allowed to reobtain a controlling interest. He should also be paid $366 million in damages. TWA had to serve Hughes a subpoena. A detective was hired to track him down. Hughes arranged with Maheu for an actor to be hired as a double. Incredibly, although the TWA executives must have known Hughes did not travel outside his home, they fell for the stunt. The actor moved to Reno, Lake Tahoe, San Francisco and San Diego, and Squaw Valley. When it was revealed he wasn't Hughes, the efforts to serve the subpoena were thwarted.

John Sonnett, TWA's unsparing attorney, was determined to flush Hughes out of his lair. Hughes recognized in him a single-minded and implacable enemy. Sonnett obtained a court order allowing him to interrogate Hughes's employees as the basis for building a case of contempt. He also filed—in Delaware—another suit against Hughes, this time for $35 million; under Delaware law, failure to answer or appear could, for a defendant, mean the loss of his stock and other assets. Sonnett included the Tool Company in the action.

One day after the deadline expired, Chester Davis presented a forged document to Sonnett—a so-called authorization to accept a subpoena, signed in an imitation of Hughes's handwriting. On September 6, Sonnett told the Superior Court of New York, Judge Charles M. Metzner, that the document was a forgery. Amazingly, Metzner agreed but did not act against Hughes on charges of contempt.

Chester Davis tried using delay tactics to prevent Hughes from appearing in court, although he did, at last, accept a subpoena in Hughes's name. Hughes was petrified that if he did not appear he would lose millions. But his fear of being seen in public was worse. When, on February 11, 1963, he failed to turn up at the Los Angeles Superior Court Building as called for by subpoena and agreement, Sonnett bounced the case back to New York.

Hughes's countersuit was dismissed as worthless—lacking in any "cause of action." Hughes ordered Chester Davis to go to the Court of Appeals. On June 2, the court upheld Judge Metzner's decision, and furthermore, dealt harshly with Hughes's contempt of the law.

Spending so many hours on the telephone, in his pajama tops or bottoms, that he virtually sacrificed sleep, Hughes made one more

206 ◆ C H A R L E S   H I G H A M

effort to regain control of TWA. By selling off assets to the tune of $92.5 million, he would buy back his promissory notes to two of the main lenders in the original deal—Equitable and Metropolitan Life Insurance—and help to bail out a money-losing Trans World. Besieged by a high-powered battery of Hughes lawyers in Washington, D.C., the Civil Aeronautics Board could find no legitimate reason to deny him the opportunity, and on July 10, 1964, granted him permission. The TWA board was furious, but could do nothing. But if he was to be allowed to gain control of TWA, he must dump another ownership—Northeast Airlines, in which he had invested to help Floyd Odlum, who owned it.

TWA petitioned the Court of Appeals, seeking a review of the CAB decision. At the same time, Hughes hired the very powerful Washington, D.C., attorney Abe Fortas (later appointed to be a justice of the Supreme Court) to petition that Court for a full-scale review of the decision to strip him of his money and property because of the default judgment. On December 7, 1964, the appeals court overruled the CAB decision.

On March 3, 1965, Chief Justice Earl Warren presided over a judicial review of the appellate court finding. Chester Davis argued that a conspiracy had been set in motion by the banks and insurance companies to strip Hughes of his control of TWA. He pointed out that no violation of the antitrust laws had taken place. John Sonnett for TWA referred to the countless futile efforts to have Hughes respond to subpoenas. He delivered a deathblow: Hughes's refusal to attend to the law showed contempt and invalidated effectively every aspect of his behavior. Sonnett said, in his closing argument, "This is not the case where a man cannot testify. It is a case of a man who *would* not testify. It is that simple."

Earl Warren and his fellow justices were so impressed by Sonnett's point that all of the complicated legal arguments Davis dragged out next day were straws in the wind. Warren, in what must have been a very rare admission, said that his Court's decision even to review the lower court's findings was "improvident"—that is to say, a mistake. Referring to the evasion of summonses, he pointed out that Hughes had slapped the law in the face by refusing to adhere to its commands. Thus, he must be punished to the limit possible: his countersuit was again dismissed and the default judgment against him was sustained.

It is paradoxical that Hughes actually gained in the long run: he won on the roundabout what he lost on the swings. On May 3, 1966, Hughes sold just over six and a half million shares of TWA, receiving $546,549,171. Ruth Ellen Taylor of Hughes's staff will never forget seeing the small, not executive-sized, check arrive in the Romaine Street office, like a payment for groceries.

Throughout the early 1960s, Hughes's hearing deteriorated still further. He had to have a special telephone system installed with a ring that was as shattering as an ambulance siren and used to wake up everybody in the house at all hours of the night. Meetings between him and his aides were more strained than ever because he would scream at them, as though they themselves were deaf, or, alternately, mutter, because he had no sense of the timbre of his own voice.

Dr. Howard House, the leading Los Angeles ear specialist, was always available to help. But for years, Dr. Verne Mason's and Dr. Lawrence Chaffin's pleas to Hughes to see Dr. House went unheeded. At last, Hughes, exasperated by his condition and irritated by his hearing aids, most of which he left around the room, or even hid, agreed that Chaffin could call House and promised that he would come to House's consulting rooms in downtown Los Angeles for an appointment.

That appointment, he thoughtlessly specified, must be in the dead of night, at 11:00 P.M. This was unheard of for any physician, even in those days, but House, like seemingly everybody else in the world, was unable to refuse Howard Hughes anything. House paid his staff overtime and took them to dinner and the theater as well. He returned to his office and made all the necessary preparations for an exhaustive test.

Then, as 11:00 P.M. struck, Nadine Henley, dragged out of bed, called to say that Hughes had changed his mind. Chaffin called the irritated physician right after that and said he should charge Hughes $500 (about $5,000 in present-day money) but House, a man of rare integrity, said that he wouldn't charge Hughes as he hadn't done anything for him.

About a month later, Chaffin called House again and said that Hughes was ready for a test. "Could we make the appointment a little earlier, at 10:00 P.M.?" House asked. Chaffin agreed. And, once again, with total lack of concern for a doctor and staff who had turned out in the night, Hughes had Henley cancel. Again, House didn't charge him.

Years later, Hughes was in the Bahamas when Chaffin called House again. Alerted by Hughes's previous behavior, even the generous House would not leave his many patients to fly there. He sent Dr. Chaffin instead—with instructions and five hearing aids and a tuning fork. If Hughes could hear the tuning fork without an aid outside the ear, or pressed behind it, then full hearing could be restored by an operation. The stapes bone, which had been altered by hereditary otosclerosis, could be removed by Dr. House and Hughes's long and painful isolation because of his deafness would be ended.

Chaffin had an aide hold Hughes's head while, with hands in rubber gloves, the instruments sterilized in front of Hughes, he tapped the tuning fork outside the ear and against the mastoid bone. Hughes exploded with the words, "What's all this bullshit? Any engineer worth his salt could make a better hearing aid than that!" He could, in fact, hear the tuning fork—and it irritated him. This was proof that he could be saved by surgery, but he ignored Chaffin's statement to that effect and sent him home.

Still later, Hughes was in London. He read in the paper of a new form of surgery to remove deafness. He summoned Chaffin, and this time submitted to the tuning fork test. Hughes agreed to have the operation. But no British surgeon must do it; nor would he, perhaps remembering his mother's death under chloroform, agree to go to a hospital. The operation must be done in the hotel suite.

House flew to London with his surgical team, including his anesthesiologist and his nurses. Hughes canceled again. Even for House, that was the end (Robert Maheu claims that certain people of Hughes's inner circle convinced him not to risk the operation; they wanted him to remain deaf so they could control him better and say things behind his back).

Because of the technical nature of his deafness, Hughes was able to hear better in crowded rooms or in the din of airplane motors. But by now, he would never set foot in a room with more than two or three people in it, and he seldom flew.

Burned out, his previously overworked penis useless for pleasure or procreation, his face and physique beyond the accepted range of attractiveness, Hughes, by 1964, had become a government-fighting, tax-fighting machine, a disembodied brain in a skull-like head attached to a poorly articulated, toneless, and unmuscled bag of bones.

In his miserable state, it might have been hoped that Hughes would obtain some pleasure and relief from the performance of his aircraft company in the service of space exploration. But the record was as lamentable there as in any of his other enterprises.

Interviewed in 1992, Bernard Barker, chief burglar of Watergate, said that in 1964 Hughes was personally involved with the activities of E. Howard Hunt, the peripatetic CIA spy and middleman, in the secret war against Castro. This completely fits with his obsession with the Communist threat in his Hollywood years and goes back to his uncle Rupert's connections to secret operations before and during World War II.

"Hughes worked with Eduardo [nickname for Hunt] in lasers," Barker told this author. To confirm this, I contacted John Prados, an authority on Operations Pluto and Mongoose, the CIA's successive anti-Castro operations of those years. What laser deals would have been made through Hughes Aircraft, which was already deep into advanced spy technology?

Among these were ship-to-shore communications techniques—useful because at that time intercepts were not available. There were such absurdities on the drawing board as a submarine that would surface off the port of Havana and supply a laser sound and light show accompanied by a voice in Spanish that would state, to undermine Castro, that Christ was about to stage a second coming there.

In Operation Pluto, Hughes was involved in many activities. One laser use was in the Air Force, in directional bombing; another in air-to-air contacts. Unlike radio communications, light communications were not interceptable. In many of these operations, Hughes's Sal Cay island in the Bahamas was often used.

Under contract to NASA, Hughes Aircraft built the all-important Surveyors, soft-lander spacecraft designed to settle on the surface of the moon. Hughes had made a sharp, even brutal deal with NASA whereby he would be fully reimbursed and would even be given a profit even if Surveyor failed in its purpose. As usual in his empire, acting rudderless without Hughes's own leadership, the Hughes Aircraft management procrastinated, spending so little time on the project that it threatened to be a public scandal until NASA forced their hands.

But that was after four years of NASA's failure to push Hughes's and Hughes's executives' gross delays. An estimated $50 million cost rose to $190 million in Hughes's pocket with nothing much achieved. When the Jet Propulsion Laboratory investigators looked into the Hughes work, they were appalled. Staffing was shockingly poor, there was no centralized design activity, Hughes refused to supply any explanation of costs. There were any number of engineering and design problems. The result was a hopelessly inefficient spacecraft which, if adapted to use with human cargo, could destroy lives. Two thousand people were toiling to little effect and Hughes himself did nothing about it.

Matters grew worse. One Surveyor crashed and burned; another was damaged beyond repair. Motors were scrapped, redesigned, and scrapped again. The final costs escalated to a staggering $469 million of taxpayers' money, more than four times the price of the rival Mariner spacecraft. On top of this vast profit on a wretched craft, Hughes got $20 million in fees on top of the profits, which amounted to no less than $345 million.

Hughes was excited when his first Surveyor landed on the moon on June 2, 1966. His publicity machine and a friendly press buried the fact that the landing was three years late and had stripped NASA of much of its budget. He won glory in the face of the truth, like so many popular figures. When Surveyor III provided the first pictures of Earth from the moon, and of an eclipse of the sun by Earth, followed by over 30,000 photos obtained by Surveyor VI, soil samples, details of the moon as planet, not meteorite—Hughes was in heaven. And all of the squandering of time and effort and his own complete failure to take any interest in the operations of Hughes Aircraft were forgotten as he wallowed in the glory. Irony could go no further—even in Hughes's life. It was like his round-the-world flight in an overweighted aircraft, and all the other poorly prepared ventures that ended, at last, in triumph. He had ripped off the government, and he loved it.

Not only did Hughes profit vastly from these operations, he wasn't taxed on them because of the arrangement whereby Hughes Aircraft's profits went to the Hughes Medical Institute, in which, at the time, he only invested about half of one percent. The rest was stashed in secret bank accounts or siphoned, under the table, into Hughes Tool.

But the Medical Institute served one purpose: it was the ideal front for Cay Sal, which Hughes owned in the Institute's name, the Bahamanian island thirty miles north of Cuba where he planned to launch an attack on Castro before and after the Kennedy assassination.

During 1963's first six months, a dozen exiled Cuban anti-Castro armed units were trained on the island by CIA operatives, while Castro's Russian MiG-21s and Komar torpedo boats kept vigil and checked on their activities. There were frequent bursts of armed combat as ship-to-shore raiding parties tried to seize the island. Refugees swarmed ashore under cover of night, starving and in rags, given shelter and food under the Hughes/CIA aegis. Coast Guard cutters sailed in regularly to take the exiles to Key West, where many were trained for a prospective future war. Sometimes Castro's boats intercepted the escapees, and, after an exchange of shots, returned them under armed guard to Havana.

Three Americans vanished at sea in August, probably killed by Castro's men. Off Cay Sal's northern shore, two American vessels, the *Floridian* and the *Ala,* were strafed by Communist bullets. Even after President Kennedy, and Lyndon B. Johnson after him, forbade raids on the Cuban mainland, the CIA continued to use Hughes's island, and allowed him to pretend that it was a focus for the Medical Institute. Don Bonafede wrote in *The Miami Herald* (August 25, 1963): "Cay Sal has served a dual purpose, as a rendezvous and arms storehouse, for exile raiders, and, for anti-Castro refugees, the first stop to freedom, a gateway similar to the Berlin Wall to anti-Communist East Germans."

Throughout 1965 and 1966, Hughes did everything to suppress efforts to write books about him. Even the idea of an article upset Hughes; he had Davis read every word of them for any possible hint of libel. But a book—Hughes dreaded the thought of that even more than he dreaded being photographed.

There was talk of journalist Leonard Slater's writing a biography, but nothing came of this. Former bodyguard Robert Hall announced a memoir, but that, too, wasn't heard of again. Davis cajoled and threatened, and the projects were dropped.

Veteran writer Leo Guild embarked on a projected life story. Chester Davis, acting on Hughes's behalf, paid him a substantial sum to abandon the idea. Ezra Goodman, another hard-working Hollywood writer, was under contract to publisher Lyle Stuart for a biography. Greg Bautzer summoned Stuart to Faye Emerson's town house in New York and suggested that he should desist. Stuart refused to be bought. Bautzer offered a deal: if Goodman would delay the book, and eliminate certain elements from it, including Hughes's sex life, then Hughes would sit down for some questions and would answer them in writing. Hughes would, of course, not be available for a direct interview.

Stuart promised to discuss the matter with Goodman. Bautzer further tried to exercise his power by flying Goodman, at Hughes's expense and with Hughes's approval, to New York, where he put him up at the St. Regis. Goodman was tempted to sell out, but Lyle Stuart wouldn't hear of it.

Hughes ordered an artificial company named Rosemont Enterprises (the name of Hughes Tool executive M. E. Montrose in reverse) set up, with offices in Encino, California. Three Hughes associates, including Davis, were put in as directors, and Davis's New York headquarters was also Rosemont's. The fabricated corporation was designed for one purpose: to hold the exclusive rights to Hughes's life story.

Davis, through Rosemont, paid Ezra Goodman an indirect bribe to desist, by hiring him to write an imaginary biography, of no commercial promise, on the pioneer filmmaker D. W. Griffith, paying him $38,250 for it, a staggering sum for those days, and a fee, the reason for which was unexplained, of $4,250, for his lawyer's expenses. Lyle Stuart was furious when he found out. He sued Ezra Goodman for recovery of the $10,000 advance and won the repayment, plus costs. He successfully sued Hughes, Bautzer, Chester C. Davis, and Rosemont, as well as Hughes's publicity man, Perry Lieber, for half a million dollars for breach of contract, and the same sum for loss of potential profits on the biography. Hughes unsuccessfully sued Goodman for recovery of the $38,500 after Goodman delivered what he regarded as an unsatisfactory manuscript on "D. W. Griffith"—actually an authorized book on Hughes. Yet another writer who embarked on a Hughes book was Tommy Thompson, later famous as the author of *Blood and Money* and *Serpentine*. Robert Loomis of Random House signed him up. But when the manuscript came in, Loomis was unhappy with it and hired a writer, with Thompson's consent, with the impertinent name of John Keats, to redo the biography.

Greg Bautzer called Loomis's boss, Bennett A. Cerf, and went to see him. When he found that Cerf could not be bought, Bautzer said there would be "litigation" if the book came out. When Cerf refused to listen, Hughes had Chester Davis fire off a letter to Cerf. The letter stated, absurdly, that nobody could write a book on Hughes without

Hughes's permission. Cerf filed the letter, Hughes was hysterical, and Bautzer turned up at Random House a second time.

This time Bautzer said that if Cerf would cancel the Keats contract, then Hughes would agree to Cerf's appointing an approved writer to do an authorized biography. Cerf didn't trust Bautzer, or, more importantly, Hughes, and declined. Hughes received the bad news and was depressed and fretful.

Keats felt he must seek the impossible: he must try to talk to Hughes. Loomis was opposed to this, feeling that Hughes might delay the interview, and then not grant it, thus holding the book up indefinitely.

Hughes hatched a plan. He had somebody at Random House steal the typescript and smuggle it to him. Chester Davis found that Keats had drawn much of the information from a biographical series in *Look* magazine. Hughes bought the copyright of the *Look* series in order to charge Keats with plagiarism when the Keats book came out. Rosemont, for Hughes, sued Random House and Keats for infringement of Hughes's exclusive rights to his own life and plagiarism of *Look;* Judge Frederick Bryan of the federal district court in New York allowed Rosemont an injunction on the plagiarism issue, not on the infringement. The book, barely published, was withdrawn on the grounds it was too close to the *Look* series, not only in content but in wording.

Random House appealed. The appellate court reversed the lower court's decision and the book was released for publication. Chief Judge Lumbard made the point in a separate written opinion that Hughes had acted improperly in a "nefarious" scheme to set up Rosemont to suppress the book. He charged that Rosemont was Hughes's "instrument of interference." Hughes tried one last effort to stop the book by having a writ issued. This failed. And after all that, the book was merely bland.

After a toilet overflowed at 1001 Bel Air Road, Hughes decided to quit the house. Then, in July, 1966, he decided he would defy the various attempts to have him pay state taxes in California. Although he had lived in the state almost continuously for years, he maintained that he was a resident of Texas. He had, from the late 1920s, tried to avoid taxes in Texas as well, and was in a constant state of stress as to where he should be a resident; he would do anything, even risk being seen by press and public, to avoid giving any percentage of his vast profits back to the local (much less the federal) government.

He would slip out of town to Boston, Massachusetts (a very bad choice, when he could have gone to state-tax-free Nevada or Florida), but not by air, because the press had the airports staked out. Because it was unthinkable he would travel in any of his hated rivals' aircraft, he went by train. Even in the 1930s, he had almost never taken a train journey.

Without telling Robert Maheu the reason (he seems never to have told him the reason for anything), he had Maheu obtain two private Pullman cars, which would be coupled together and used at the end of the Santa Fe Chief. With great difficulty, Maheu made the arrangements; but at the last minute, Hughes panicked, presumably at the thought of being seen, and backed out. For ten successive days, while Maheu called the railroad president at home, Hughes procrastinated. When Hughes finally agreed to go, it was too late. The train had gone.

Maheu commandeered a special train to travel, with its own engine and the two cars, ahead of the Chief. It was scheduled to leave at night. While Hughes shilly-shallied at the last minute, the Pomona stationmaster called the Bel Air house. Because Hughes hadn't arrived, the Chief could not depart on time—and punctuality was the trademark of the famous train.

At last, Hughes yielded. Driven to Pomona by Johnny Holmes in Jean Peters's limousine, he at first refused to leave it—fear of the air, of germs, of seeds, of insects, of people staring, froze him. The station authorities were becoming hysterical. At last, he yielded to his men's and Robert Maheu's son Peter's entreaties and agreed to board the train. But first, Hughes's men had to clean every speck of dust in the compartment and wipe down the walls, then open the door for him, as he—a ghostly figure in his lucky hat, in gray—climbed in.

He urged Holmes, who had told him he could not, for family reasons, make the trip to Boston, to stay with him and his other team for the whole journey. But Holmes again declined. "Do you have a piece of paper in your pocket?" Hughes asked.

Holmes took out a notepad. "I want to dictate a message to you," Hughes said.

Hughes dictated nothing—instead, he assigned his staff different bedrooms. After a long wait with pencil poised, Holmes asked, "What about the message?" "We have plenty of time," Hughes replied. The train started to move. Holmes had promised to go home to his family.

The time ticked along. Now the train began to slow. "Where are we?" Hughes asked. "We're coming into San Berdoo," Holmes said.

Hughes told Holmes to hold the train. To the stationmaster's annoyance, the train lingered on, holding up the Chief intolerably while Hughes decided what to dictate. At last, he relented. He dictated a message to Jean. It read, "I love you dearly. I will be back. I welcome the day when you will come and visit me in Boston." Holmes left the train with the message and drove Jean's limo, which another aide had driven to San Bernardino, back to her in Bel Air. There can be no doubt she was touched by the note. The fact that this aging, sick, and terminally eccentric man could find time, thought, and energy to write to a woman he had seen only twice a day for five years shows the depth of his affection for her; she was the one decent, clean, and honest thing in his life. That he had the clearsightedness, in his condition, to recognize that says much for him.

He got to Boston. He had left instructions with Maheu: that he must stay at the Ritz-Carlton Hotel, that he must occupy the "penthouse" (actually, the sixth or top floor was being redecorated and reconstructed so he had to go one floor below). Restless on the train, he had to have a grill put into the private cars, with ten fillet steaks, cans of peas and beans, bananas, cans of fruit, vanilla cake, and pastries. Somehow, Maheu managed this through a contact in Cleveland.

The press got wind of Hughes's presence at the Ritz-Carlton. One pressman set off a fire alarm to drive him out, but he didn't hear it. The fifth floor was blocked off; now the hotel could only accommodate three floors of guests. Every day, armies of maids under Hughes's supervision had to clean every inch of the rooms. The windows were not merely closed, but sealed.

Then, an extraordinary event took place in Los Angeles. On October 30, Maheu's birthday, at a Santa Monica condominium owned by Maheu's party host and hostess, Mr. and Mrs. Keith Hanna, Bill Gay, still Hughes's highest-ranking aide, called Maheu to the kitchen and also summoned Dr. Robert Buckley, a psychiatrist. To Maheu's shock and astonishment, Gay announced that he wanted

Hughes declared incompetent. Both Maheu and Buckley were furi-ous and refused to discuss the matter any further. "I was stupefied and shocked," Maheu says. "And Gay had tried it before."

Gay had first sought the incompetency ruling that summer, at the Bel-Air Hotel, when he had said to Maheu, "We need to make immediate plans."

"For what?" Maheu asked, suspicious.

"In case Howard dies or collapses mentally," Gay replied.

Maheu had told him to go to hell. Now he told Gay the same again.

Maheu tried to warn Hughes, but Hughes wouldn't listen.

Although constantly on the verge of going to the local hospitals for a checkup, Hughes always backed out at the last minute, terrified of what the doctors might find. When physicians came to examine him, he either avoided them or allowed a minimum amount of test-ing—blood pressure, urine. Suffering from a painfully prolapsed rec-tum, piles, and a fissure, due to severe intestinal blockage and constant straining, he declined to have a cauterization. He wouldn't even let the doctors probe into his rectum—a reminder, perhaps, of old guilts.

It finally dawned on him that he would be paying state taxes in Massachusetts if he stayed any longer, and he decided to depart for Nevada—first Lake Tahoe, and later Las Vegas. But, in the mean-time, Jean Peters had arrived and was appalled to discover she wasn't allowed into his room. She remained in a separate suite, and, Maheu reports, was furious. Then Hughes did admit her, and they looked at maps of Boston, where, he lied, he planned to build a house for them. But he was already having his men prepare for his depar-ture. Jean went back to Bel Air and continued talking to Hughes about his plans.

He decided to make the journey, once more, by train. Once again, the hard-pressed Maheu had to commandeer two private cars, to be placed ahead of the other carriages on the 20th Century Limited and Union Pacific.

The actor used before to play Hughes was dressed in his clothes, taken out of a door at the Ritz-Carlton, and helped into a limousine. The press gave chase, allowing Hughes to exit the city unobserved. But in Utah, the train had a mechanical problem, which meant that it would not, as Hughes wanted, arrive in Las Vegas before dawn.

Maheu knew that Hughes would be hysterical if the train came in during daylight. He had to pay $18,000 for the exclusive use of another engine in Ogden, as the private cars were shunted off onto a siding and recoupled.

Meanwhile, reporters got wind that Hughes was coming to Las Vegas; someone had seen Maheu check in under an alias at the Desert Inn. Maheu managed to have the train stopped five miles outside the city; Hughes was carried out on a stretcher. The stretcher was accommodated in a van, and Hughes was brought in through a back door. He was taken by a service elevator to the top floor, which had been exclusively reserved for him.

The security was very tight in the hotel. The stairway to the penthouse floor was blocked—a direct contravention of the fire regulations. The ninth-floor elevator button was removed and replaced with a key-operated lock. The curtains were always drawn, and the air conditioning system ducts checked and rechecked. Despite the fact that it would have been impossible for the FBI to bug the suites, every inch of the walls and floors was examined every day for any intrusive monitor. Closed circuit television provided information on any individual standing at the front door.

In his womblike, comfortable darkness, Hughes saw nothing of the corrupt, sun-drenched city, whose featureless buildings, flanking an ugly, neon-lit stretch of concrete streets, had mushroomed during the years since he had first visited it in the 1940s. His consuming need was, in order to avoid crippling capital gains taxes on the money paid him for the sale of TWA, to turn the liquid assets over to buy as much of the tax-free city as he could. He appointed Maheu in charge of the operation; Maheu had the right contacts, was loyal and trustworthy, and knew, because of his FBI background, the criminal networks that spiderwebbed the metropolis.

By moving into the Desert Inn, he had walked into a scorpion's lair. For years, one of the owners of the hotel operations (the actual hotel was owned by Harry Helmsley, later married to Leona in New York) was the Bugsy Siegel associate Morris (Moe) Dalitz, who, after years of running gambling rackets, had snapped up the Inn in 1950. Hughes was furious when he found out. He detested the idea of the mob's running the city, and when Dalitz, after raising the suite and room rates again and again, tried to evict him to accommodate his high-roller gangster friends, Hughes took action. Like Mae West, who in 1932 had bought a Hollywood apartment building when an old woman in an elevator accused her of being a prostitute, Hughes decided to buy the rights to run the Desert Inn.

"The mob was wearying of Las Vegas and was talking of selling out its operations," Robert Maheu told this author in 1992. Maheu contacted lawyer and former FBI man Ed Morgan and gangster Johnny Rosselli, who had, of course, been involved with him in the attempt on Castro's life, to oil the wheels towards the purchase.

Co-owner of the Desert Inn was Ruby Kolod, a gang member associate of Dalitz, who had recently been indicted for extortion. Kolod knew his days in the gambling business were numbered; the Nevada gaming control board wanted him run out of town. He was anxious to sell, but he was afraid, like almost everybody else in the business world, that Hughes would renege on the deal. He felt that Hughes was pretending to buy the concessions, but actually was buying more time. Maheu called Jimmy Hoffa, who, as teamster boss, affected every aspect of labor in Las Vegas: Hoffa had his boyhood friend Dalitz, much to Kolod's fury, give an extension of Hughes's stay past New Year's—New Year's Eve was always reserved for high rollers.

Kolod found out that Hughes had never relinquished his suite at the Ritz-Carlton in Boston, and took this as further evidence that Hughes was stalling. But Maheu, via Rosselli, Hoffa, and Morgan, as well as other persuasive characters, finally convinced Kolod that Hughes meant business.

Negotiations took place in January. Hughes was not, as Bill Gay kept saying, incompetent and insane. In his curtained lair, this mangy, skin-and-bone old lion was by no means crazed or toothless. In fact, he swung the deal with all of his own skill and manipulativeness, inspired by anger that the mob should have the effrontery to try to push him out of his stronghold.

He organized it that the sale would be in the name of Hughes Tool; when Maheu expressed some unease, lest there be complaints from the board, Hughes reminded him that he owned Hughes Tool outright. He kept having Maheu alter the terms of the deal, nibbling away at the price, relishing the delaying tactics and the fact that he was still ensconced. He dragged in lawyers from all over the map, including Las Vegas hotel honcho Del Webb and Houston legalist J. Richard Gray, to help in the transaction, piling up his usual mountain of attorney bills. Gray, unlike the others in the protracted boardroom wranglings, actually insisted on seeing Hughes. After countless requests, he succeeded in fulfilling that improbable fantasy. Hughes appeared for a moment in pajamas, a robe flung over his emaciated frame, his eyes blazing with anger. "I exist, dammit!" he snarled at the astonished lawyer. "Are you satisfied?" Gray wasn't, but he took the brief appearance as evidence of goodwill, and, on Hughes's uniquely granted power of attorney, prepared the necessary documents for the operations purchase. Neither Helmsley nor his partner would agree to sell the hotel outright.

Gray had to apply to the gambling control board to secure the license to run the casino. The board had a rule that any applicant must provide a detailed statement revealing all of the facts of his personal and commercial life. Hughes refused to supply these. In desperation, seeing the deal fall apart in his hands and his imminent eviction into the street, he made a typical move. He went direct to the governor, Paul D. Laxalt. Laxalt was anxious to run the mob out of town. He knew, from his sources at the FBI (a fact confirmed to the author through an FBI Deep Throat in 1992), that Hughes was clean of any criminal associations, that Maheu's links to Rosselli were merely opportunistic. He saw Hughes as a new broom in a filthy city. Millions were being siphoned off, untaxed, into the mob's pockets. Maybe Hughes could stop all that? To bolster Laxalt's case with the control board, which was essentially beholden to Laxalt, Hughes delivered a trump card which also served a purpose he held dear. He lied that he would finance a medical school—a symbol of his desire to improve Las Vegas's image.

The medical school would be attached to the University of Nevada, and would receive a total of some six million dollars in a period of twenty years. The proposal was rapturously received at a meeting of the Nevada Assembly. On March 30, the state gaming control board convened; despite the fact that Hughes had still not supplied sufficient information, the board granted the license the following day.

Inexperienced in running a gambling concession, Maheu took a bold step: he brought in Moe Dalitz, who had just stepped down as coowner of the hotel, as his consultant. The result was a highly successful operation.

Unfortunately, Hughes's so-called nest-cleaning activities, flushing out the Mafia from an evil Las Vegas, proved beneficial to the mobsters. Moe Dalitz benefited considerably from the sale of the

Desert Inn gambling concessions and made substantial inroads into another community, Rancho La Costa. The gangster John Rosselli, so useful in the Hughes-approved CIA murder plot against Castro, not only got a finder's fee for the sale, but retained a suite at the Inn, with Hughes's permission, and then obtained a concession on a gift shop at Hughes's Frontier. The questionable Carl Cohen and Jack Entratter, high on Attorney General Bobby Kennedy's special target list for investigation and prosecution, were in Hughes's pay even after they had supposedly been dislodged from the Sands Hotel, a later Hughes purchase. Hughes's Washington lawyer, Edward P. Morgan, handled the deals; Robert Maheu cannot be blamed for the outcome beneficial to the mob, since Hughes issued orders nobody could disobey, and it is probable he didn't know the finer points of taking away from the mob with one hand and giving with the other.

Hughes's deals brought together strange bedfellows: among those involved in the Desert Inn sale were, allegedly, Hank Greenspun of the *Las Vegas Sun*.

Maheu was in charge of the Desert Inn showroom. At the time he took over, a patriotic showroom musical extravaganza named *Good Morning, America* was in full swing, with girls in stars and stripes costumes waving flags. He replaced it with another show which failed to attract patrons. Hughes insisted on approving every show in the future, but soon lost interest. In fact, he never saw, on closed circuit television or in person, any of the shows from then on, nor did he make any attempt to lure one of the countless beautiful girls hired for the shows to his suite, or even insist on seeing their photographs. The fire in his loins was well and truly burned out.

But he did begin to feel a revived affection for the warm, spunky, and optimistic Jean Peters. He began snapping up property in Las Vegas that he thought might please her: the large Major A. Riddle estate, and the almost equally imposing ranch of Hitler's arms supplier Alfred Krupp's wife Vera. He urged Jean to take up residence in either one, and sent her brochures, floor plans, photographs by the bushel. But she was still in love with him; she wanted to live with him again. He wanted her to be close; she needed—with ill-founded and naive optimism—a restored marriage. He wouldn't agree to that; and he evidently feared that this well-scrubbed, impeccably clean human being might infect him with some deadly germ. They talked, wrangled, made up; it is sad to reflect that he still was deeply fond of her, but they could reach no conclusion. She stayed where she was; he made sure she lived in luxury still, but he continued to have her watched. Had she taken up with another man, he would undoubtedly have been hysterical. But that decent woman didn't.

Hughes hired the man who was to become the most faithful and devoted of his personal aides, Gordon Margulis. A tough, good-natured Cockney, born in London within the sound of Bow Bells, a former boxer who had graduated from flyweight to middleweight, he had emigrated to America and was a room service waiter at the Desert Inn, working his way around the country at the time. Hughes executive Kay Glenn took him on. He was assigned the job of preparing the food for Hughes's then-favored waiter, Fred Harvey. He was recommended by Don Borax, in charge of security at the hotel, and Joe Boc, who took care of catering when the mob ran the city.

He worked closely with aides John Holmes, Howard Eckersley, Roy Crawford, and George Francom to satisfy Hughes's dietary requirements. He and Holmes were the odd men out in a group of Mormons: like Maheu, they were Roman Catholics. Soon, Margulis assumed a new role: a bodybuilder, powerfully put together, he became a bodyguard and was assigned to blocking any stray curiosity seekers who might make their way up the back-stairs.

Hughes ordered medallion steaks, cut into very small pieces, with boiled potatoes and peas. He liked the steaks burned a little bit, charbroiled on the outside, served medium rare. He ate only vanilla ice cream, with a little syrup on occasion. Later, he would have Margulis chop up steaks—changing at last to chicken—and cook them into a soup with vegetables. This healthy, monotonous diet was far removed from the Robinson Crusoe cuisine of legend and supplied him with at least 2,000 calories a day.

He was fussy about his soup: he liked Campbell's chicken soup, which had pieces in it, but insisted that whatever can he received have no dark meat in it. This was an impossible matter to arrange, so he reverted to Margulis's homemade brew.

His memory regarding his cutlery and crockery was amazing; he never wanted them varied. Childlike as ever, he had a special spoon, which must never be replaced; he had it given to Gordon, wrapped up, and eighteen months later asked for it back. Prepared to drink only California orange juice, he had it flown in from the Beverly Hills Hotel each day.

He favored Baskin-Robbins ice cream. The flavor of the month at the time was Banana Nut. He liked it and decided he wanted more.

But when he got around to making the decision, it was no longer flavor of the month, and, in fact, had been discontinued. He asked Margulis to call Baskin-Robbins and see if they could make a couple of gallons.

They replied that they only made 300 gallons at a time. Hughes said, "Get it." Margulis ordered the gallons from Los Angeles. The Romaine Street staff told Margulis he was not to reveal that the huge consignment was for Hughes. The transaction was so surreptitious that Margulis had to have a space cleared in the hotel's receiving area without revealing what he wanted it for.

It was driven in, refrigerated, and every few miles the driver would call Margulis on his walkie-talkie to announce that the expedition was progressing—with as much dramatic emphasis as though it was Stanley going to see Livingston. When the van arrived and the back doors were open, Margulis was shocked to see HOWARD HUGHES PRODUCTIONS in enormous letters on the ice cream covers—that cover was already blown.

Margulis and the other aides moved the ice cream into the freezer. Everyone was watching; there was barely room for the vast store.

Finally, Margulis took some of the Banana Nut–flavored goo up to Hughes. Hughes tasted it, then told George Francom, "I don't want any more. I want to go back to vanilla." The ice cream was distributed to the hotel staff; it took days to get rid of the contents of the ten three-gallon drums.

All food, as usual, had to be handed to him with Kleenex-wrapped hands; his hands were also wrapped when he received it. Margulis took this requirement in his stride.

Hughes was, by now, in constant pain, and the drugs he took, codeine, Empirin, Tylenol, Valium, so often described as being the indulgences of a mere addict, or the applications of brainwashing aides, were to dull the gnawing agony that began the day of his life-threatening crash in Beverly Hills. Pain that would never leave him until death; the pain of rotting teeth, of jaw and gums, of headaches, of back and neck and shoulder pain, of limbs atrophying from disease.

Every nerve ending was exposed in his miserable suffering. His life had become a hell, relieved only by the constant nursemaiding of his little team, by the occasional phone calls from Cary Grant or other friends, and by the wheeling and dealing in which he indulged.

Worst of all was the pyorrhea and toothache, so bad that he had
to give up steak and concentrate only on soft boiled chicken and
cakes; he couldn't face a dentist, much less a periodontist or endo-
dontist, and he was in constant danger of blood poisoning from the
infected gums. He made curious requirements: the air conditioning
had to be icy cold in the penthouse, so much so that when doctors
came to see him, they had to wear overcoats. He hated anyone other
than his Mormons to know that he was seeing physicians: the aides
would tell Margulis that the visitor was an accountant—even though
he had a stethoscope around his neck.

## CHAPTER FIFTEEN

# Buying Las Vegas

Despite all of his unmatched wealth, Hughes could not escape the sense of despair, futility, and emptiness, of regret and promises unfulfilled, which afflicts many less fortunate men in their sixties. Jean's refusal to be near him, her disappointment at his broken promises and procrastinations that would soon lead to divorce proceedings, was profoundly painful to him, and he, loving her still, had the decency not to blame her. Even more agonizing in his nervous, highly-strung state must have been the thought that if he lived again in the same house with her, he would have to face his loss of virility. A man's failure with a prostitute may mean nothing; but with a loved one, it can be devastating. It takes no leap of the imagination to figure that he dared not take the risk.

And so his monotonous life continued in the sterile, gently whirring air conditioning of the Desert Inn, its ducts cleansed often, no hint of breeze or buzz of insects disturbing the flatness of the beige-furnished rooms that were about as inspiring as airplane cabins or diesel train drawing rooms. He seldom read now, fatigued as he was by the old process of plucking a middle magazine from its soon-to-be-burned companions; even the piles of girlie magazines failed to stimulate him. He didn't, so far as we know, even look outside the window at the admittedly uninspiring view of electric light signs, so dumb and forlorn in the daylight hours, the long spangled ugliness of the Strip, the desert, as depressingly featureless as a badly-ironed brown tablecloth, and the insignificant purple mountains.

Instead, he lived the life of the insomniac, sharing the traditional sleeplessness of the American rich and famous; tossing in his old hospital bed, pacing up and down, he didn't even have the quietude of spirit to play pinochle, stud poker, or gin rummy, or even, God help him, solitaire or honeymoon bridge. He might as well have been an underfed caged hamster, so monotonous his diet of chicken and napoleon cakes, so dismal his horizon of stark, off-white walls, hotel paintings done to order, brass or wooden lamps with pleated shades, and cottage-cheese ceilings.

Hughes didn't even establish a male-to-male relationship with his bodyguards. He never discussed football with them or baseball, or women, or exchanged locker room jokes. He summoned his men with the tap of a clawlike, unmanicured fingernail on a plastic bag stuffed with used Kleenexes, or rang a bedside crystal bell, then screamed at the aide. When he grew tired of his hearing aid, which irritated his ear, he wrote out instructions on long, ruled, yellow sheets of paper, hundreds of which were passed to Maheu. He used the telephone less often now, even after a minute check proved that the FBI was not bugging his line.

He remained as dependent on his team as ever, raging or petulantly sulking when he couldn't summon what—or who—he wanted at a moment's notice. He was still his mother's spoiled, rich little boy, complaining over the slightest criticism, praising and blaming according to the degree his wishes were carried out, his ego flourishing, like some creature in a science fiction movie, a living mushroom-with-eyes in a claustrophobic box.

He hated it if Robert Maheu behaved like a normal human being; when Maheu went off with his family for a weekend vacation, he besieged him with calls.

His habits changed, but were never less than weird. In the rare occasions when he wasn't seated on the toilet, he sat at the bathroom basin, rubbing alcohol on his hands and arms for hours at a stretch, over and over again. Aide Mell Stewart had to obtain exactly the kind of hospital alcohol he preferred to any other.

For days, he would eat no soup except chicken soup—it had to be Campbell's—and then the vegetable soup homemade in the Desert Inn's kitchen. A glimpse of a TV commercial for frozen turkey TV dinners converted him to that modest fare for weeks. Then he decided he didn't like the apple cobbler supplied with the dinner and wanted peach cobbler instead. When he found that the manufacturer, Swanson's, wouldn't make the change, he futilely tried to buy Swanson's. When he failed, he had a run on Arby's roast beef sandwiches. But when Arby's refused to supply a sterilized steel blade that would cut his beef exclusively, he went over to filet mignon.

As in his younger years, he wanted the steaks cut very thin and charbroiled on the outside, with peas that had to be small enough to be threaded through a fork.

He became obsessed with apple strudel. He didn't like the Desert Inn's variety, so he sent for the strudel made by the Sands. When he fretted about his guards leaving him to pick up the dessert, the Desert Inn's pastry chef had humiliatingly, on pain of instant dismissal, picked it up from the rival chef himself.

And now, all of Hughes's energy, interest, and sublimated sex drive went into one colossal and meaningless enterprise: to exercise that power which his loins had lost by snapping up the city in one go. Now that he owned the right to operate the Desert Inn (and how dearly he would have liked to have bought it from Harry Helmsley!), he set about his first outright hotel property purchase, the Sands.

He had another motive, other than mere acquisitiveness and liking its apple strudel, for buying the hotel. He still retained his hatred for Frank Sinatra, who at one time had had a nine percent ownership of that hotel, but, without Hughes's power, had been forced out by the gaming commission because of his links to one of Hughes's chief contacts, gangster Sam Giancana.

Sinatra loved the hotel, was fond of its part owner, entrepreneur Jack Entratter, and not only played there often to packed audiences in the showroom, but brought in the famous Rat Pack, including Peter Lawford, Sammy Davis, Jr., Dean Martin, and Joey Bishop, whose antics helped pep up reservations and caused countless headlines. On July 19, 1966, Sinatra had married Mia Farrow in Jack Entratter's living room. In November of that year, Sinatra made a sensational appearance at the Sands.

Sensation added to sensation when comedian Jackie Mason, who had made scathing cracks at Sinatra's and Farrow's expense in his act at the Aladdin, called police to say that a gunman had fired at him and there was a bullet in his bed. Later, a Sinatra thug smashed Mason in the face and crushed his nose and cheekbones.

Hughes detested Sinatra, blaming him for such episodes; he had never forgotten or forgiven the fact that Sinatra had bedded (and wed) Ava Gardner, one of the tiny handful of women who had refused to have sex with Hughes. He knew that when he bought the hotel, he would have the pleasure of seeing Sinatra kicked out of it.

In July, 1967, Hughes pushed Maheu on to get the best deal possible for the Sands. The price was $14.6 million, the cash arranged through the Texas Bank of Commerce and Hughes Tool, the deal concluded at the beginning of August. Among those who aided the transactions was Johnny Rosselli. Hughes worried that the *Las Vegas Sun* newspaper might be critical. He bought its owner, Hank Greenspun, with one million dollars in cash, half of it for advertising the shows at the Sands and Desert Inn in the papers, the other half as pocket money to buy Greenspun's support. To that he added a $4 million loan, unsecured, at three percent; Greenspun said he didn't think there should have been any percent.

Sinatra had an existing contract with the Sands and Jack Entratter to appear on the Labor Day weekend. With incredible chutzpah, he tried to wrest from Hughes a better deal, which would result in his selling Hughes his Cal-Neva Lodge at Lake Tahoe, but Hughes, remembering Sinatra's nights with Gardner there, and unwilling to put an extra nickel in Sinatra's pockets, refused.

Sinatra was furious. When the singer tried to invade the sacrosanct ninth-floor penthouse, Hughes's men rebuffed him. Nobody rebuffed Sinatra. To Hughes's delight, he canceled his first appearance, and when he returned for others, he began screaming at people in the casino. Maheu told Hughes that Sinatra drove a golf cart through a Sands plate glass window when drunk; he screamed at Hughes's vice president Carl Cohen, "I'm gonna break your fuckin' legs!" when Cohen refused him credit after he had dropped $50,000 at the tables. Hughes had Sinatra thrown out when he began screeching at the Sands croupiers that he had made the Sands rich from his appearances and he should have all the "fucking cash" he wanted.

Hughes tore up Sinatra's contract and Sinatra made a deal with Caesars Palace. Hughes was awakened from a restless sleep at 5:00 A.M. on September 12. His staff advised him that Sinatra was in the

228 • CHARLES HIGHAM

lobby, demanding Carl Cohen's room number. Refused the number, Sinatra screamed for Jack Entratter. He terrorized the switchboard, searched the hotel, found the operators' room, and shrieked at them to open the door. They didn't. Sinatra flushed Cohen out of his room, flung gambling chips in his face, and called him a "kike." Cohen struck Sinatra and broke his teeth. Frank threatened to kill Cohen. Hughes's men threw him out into the street.

After this episode, Hughes tightened casino operations at both the Sands and the Desert Inn. He would allow no skimming of profits; he had all dealers watched by his security force to see if they put money in their pockets. The rooms bristled with hidden cameras, which Maheu used as monitors. Before Hughes, the mob had skimmed off thousands in undeclared revenue. Now, the casinos were as tightly run as any banking institution.

Hughes stopped the traditional use of cocktail waitresses or showgirls as prostitutes. He forbade the girls to have sex with the high rollers. When he found that certain of his aides disregarded the rules, they were fired.

Running true to form, Hughes hired former U.S. Air Force Major General Edward H. Nigro as general manager of the Sands. Nigro, of course, wasn't a gambler and knew nothing about gambling. He started Hughes's private air service under chief pilot Bob Wearley.

To bolster Hughes's ironical image of a moral influence, a new broom in Las Vegas, Robert Maheu entertained the right people, and confirmed his position on the correct conservative committees: the YMCA, the Boy Scouts, the American Foundation for Ecumenical Studies, Nevada Southern University, and the District Attorney's Advisory Council. General Nigro played an important part on a succession of boards, including the Governor's Advisory Board on Tourism.

Hughes was gripped by another obsession. Irritated by the drawn-out process of projectionists's putting reels on a projector, he had become obsessed with seeing old movies on television. He hated the fact that whereas in Los Angeles he could see ancient pictures, including his own, in the wee hours, now he couldn't, because the beams didn't come in from Los Angeles and the local CBS outlet, KLAS, closed down shortly after midnight.

So he decided to buy the station. Again, he had the problem of obtaining a license—this time from the Federal Communications Commission—without the usual personal and commercial statements and appearances before a board. He told Maheu to fix the deal.

Maheu was able to do so; Hughes associate Raymond A. Holliday appeared in Hughes's place, and the TV station was assigned in his name—thus letting Hughes off the hook, and eliminating any awkward questions by the FCC. But the moment the sale was made, Hughes issued instructions to Holliday on the running of the station. He besieged CBS emperor William Paley in New York for requests for favorite old movies, and, some of his requests granted (CBS didn't hold the rights to all studio products), he greedily watched the old movies until dawn. This small indulgence cost him $3.6 million.

At the same time, Hughes bought the land under the Castaways and the Frontier, two airports, and the local Alamo Airways. He began to perk up; he was notably more animated; he was like a child, winning at a game of Monopoly. Soon he owned one-fifth of the city, and had spent, in one glorious free-for-all, $65 million—still only a fraction of the ready cash in his piggy bank following the TWA sale.

In addition, Hughes made a purchase he had thought about since he married Jean Peters. He bought most of Tonopah, Nevada, including 710 claims, over some 14,200 acres of Nye County and seven other counties, at a cost of $10.5 million.

Again and again, the gaming commission issued Hughes licenses to operate his succession of casinos. When any reluctance was shown, Hughes revived the idea of the medical school, but, one year after he had promised to build it, he had done nothing. The commission acted on his behalf; once again, Hughes failed to keep his side of the bargain. He embarked on a plan, drawn up with Governor Laxalt's approval, for NEEDS (Nevada Essential Developments Surveys), a multimillion-dollar improvement scheme, which would include aid for the aged and the needy. But this was another cynically inflated pipe dream, no more substantial than the fine, windblown dust outside Hughes's penthouse windows.

He would concoct, lie, deceive, anything in order to get the hotels he wanted. He talked of building a vast, superbly equipped airport; a new Sands Hotel with countless rooms and big swimming pools and gymnasiums—all fantasies, dreamed up for his own consuming purposes. He had become an emperor not only among neurotics, but among liars.

So overwhelming was his purple smokescreen of PR that he

even got away with it when he acted like the evil queen in a fairy tale by canceling the Las Vegas youngsters' free-for-all, the well-founded, institutionalized, and beloved annual Easter Egg Hunt at the Desert Inn. Much to the chagrin of hundreds of parents, the event was not restored for years. Hating children as much as ever, the mental murderer (if Terry Moore is to be believed) of his own offspring, forgetting his lost, innocent years at Camp Dan Beard, groaned to Robert Maheu in memos that the little kiddies would scream and disturb him in his lair.

He had a fantasy that the dreaded infants might wreck the casino and actually slither up stairs and through his guards, infecting him with a host of unknown viruses, killing him. He suggested moving the event to the Sunrise Hospital and donating from $25,000 to $50,000 to the hospital as an inducement. In a March, 1968, memorandum, written to Maheu on the customary yellow stationery, he went on and on with stabbing, relentless insistence, instead of simply asking Maheu to take care of the matter. Maheu did.

Hughes developed a dislike of a show he had never seen, the Desert Inn's *Pzazz*, which was about as sexy as a Rotary luncheon, because he feared it was a breasts-and-spangles affair that would offend and work against his image of purification of the city. He insisted to Maheu that all future shows be approved by him; but he never saw one, even at a private run-through, and soon forgot the matter and let Maheu, with uneven success, run the showrooms. He proved indifferent to such popular stars as Dinah Shore, Alan King, and Wayne Newton, whom Maheu hired; the only response he gave was to Sammy Davis, Jr., whom he called a "nigger—those people have set back civilization a thousand years."

He cast his net wider. He decided he wanted to own more of tax-free Nassau as well. He made a deal with the CIA, which owned Mary Carter Paints, an improbably named "front" company, to let him buy the operating rights to Mary Carter Paints' Paradise Island Casino, Hotel and Ocean Club. The founders, in 1958, of Mary Carter Paints were Thomas Dewey and Allen Dulles, at a time when Dulles was head of the CIA and shortly before Dulles obtained Maheu's assistance in attempting to kill Fidel Castro, with Hughes's tacit approval. That same year, in 1960, Mary Carter Paints supplied the money paid to the Cuban forces of deposed president Batista in Florida. In 1963, the CIA linked up with mob connections through Mary Carter to support fascist governments in South America. By

1964, Robert Kennedy, even after he left the post of Attorney General, was aggressively exploring the Hughes–Moe Dalitz–Sam Giancana–CIA–Mary Carter Paints–Nassau connections.

While he continued to negotiate with the CIA front organizations, Hughes was also up to his eyes in problems with the U.S. government. For years, he had used one of his vice presidents, the brisk Albert W. Bayer, to ensure, much as Johnny Meyer had done with Elliott Roosevelt and the Air Force procurement leaders in World War II, preferential treatment when it came to Hughes Tool's selling helicopters to the Army Air Force.

Bayer didn't risk supplying women to the right military brass: instead, he took them on barge trips and coyote hunts—childish expeditions that mysteriously proved to be appealing to men who surely had better things to do. Bayer managed to make friends with the right people without causing them embarrassment with their wives—a golf club weekend had to make do in place of a Meyer orgy. By forming a whole network of respectable friendships, with countless officials on the Hughes expense account (but never entered into any set of books), he succeeded in getting contracts—the first one for $6.5 million—that stacked high on Hughes's overcrowded desk.

Hughes had cleaned up a fortune in the Vietnam War, another reason for keeping up his anti-Communist tirades. Helicopter orders were filed in the hundreds, but he overstepped the mark: he began to overcharge, and he was slow in producing the necessary 'copters. His attempt to run Hughes Tool by remote control had resulted in pathetically inadequate production, along with a fairly obvious attempt to cheat the Pentagon.

As a result of his failure to deliver more than a handful of aircraft, he was in bad odor with Washington, and Hughes Tool lost $23.2 million in four years. His constant remote-control mismanagement finally led him, once again, into disaster. He finally lost over $100 million and saw, to his despair, his chief rival, Bell, outbid him with the government and walk off with $123 million in profits.

His reckless spending, his raids on companies and buying of silver claims, resulted in his squandering as much as $268 million in three years. Yet he still had over $330 million in liquid assets, Treasuries, money market funds, government bonds.

Endlessly dreaming up new schemes to make money, Hughes decided to try to sell the helicopter-making branch of Hughes Tool Aircraft Division to Carl Kotchian, president of Lockheed. He also told Kotchian he would sell him Hughes Aircraft itself—despite the fact that Hughes Aircraft's entire assets were tied up in the Medical Center and it would be illegal for him to bail out because of his deal with the IRS.

When Kotchian understandably proved unimpressed, Hughes offered to spend one billion dollars, which he didn't have in available funds, to buy 100 Lockheed L-1011 Rolls-Royce–motored TriStars. But the Lockheed executives knew, through a quick check of Dun and Bradstreet, that he didn't have the cash, and they remembered how he had left the Convairs rusting on the tarmac years before. Orders for L-1011s from the major airlines were lagging, and, with incredible stupidity, they went ahead and allowed Hughes to place the order and began negotiating with him to buy his companies.

He hired lawyer Raymond Cook to conduct the absurd negotiations, deluging him with the usual number of manic commands, exhortations, grumbles, and inspirational statements. But he made a serious mistake in revealing to Cook that he was lying to Kotchian when he said he would be using the aircraft himself. He intended taking Kotchian for a ride: he would resell the aircraft at a profit.

Cook leaked the truth to the Lockheed executives—an act of incredible foolishness. Hughes spent hours on the telephone lying that Cook had misrepresented him; that he really would use the Lockheed L-1011s.

Kotchian unwisely yielded, but increased the price, at the same time reducing the number of planes Hughes would buy to seventy-five.

Then, and typically, just as he was about to close the deal on a deposit, Hughes pulled out. He was being charged, in Washington, during long drawn-out hearings over TWA, of being in breach of the monopolies laws; he didn't have one billion dollars and feared that if he borrowed that sum from the banks, he would have to put up all of his companies and hotels as collateral and might lose the lot if he couldn't resell the L-1011s at a profit. Even in his egomaniac certainty, he feared that Kotchian would learn he had been duped. To his fury, Kotchian, like countless business leaders before him, found that he had been playing poker with a cheat. And this wasn't the Wild West: he couldn't settle the matter with a gun.

Hughes was further disturbed by news that ABC President Leonard Goldenson, who hated him, was planning to set up a Las Vegas station in opposition to his own, and was talking about a program exposing his career. Giving the excuse that he disliked the ABC news division and that ABC was lagging behind the other networks, he decided to buy ABC outright. He knew Goldenson would never yield to him, so he would instead raid the stocks by offering the holders a substantial profit, allowing him to obtain a majority shareholding.

Despite Hughes's disgust at ABC's popular *The Dating Game* (which once showed a fair-skinned black girl he thought was white dating a black man in Rome), he pressed ahead. He told Bautzer to make the arrangements. He would offer $74.25 a share, or more than 14 percent above their value. But in his headlong rush, he had overlooked the ever-vigilant Federal Communications Commission, which would have to grant him an operating license when he fired Goldenson and took over the network.

Goldenson had enough pull with the FCC to make sure the Commission sought out Hughes's Achilles heel; he would be forced to appear before them, and this time there would be no excuses. He would have to yield up all of his corporate and personal secrets. He panicked; when Goldenson obtained an injunction against him, blocking the proposed stock raid, he was relieved. But then, before Hughes could stop him, Chester Davis pulled the usual number of strings in Washington and had the injunction removed. Hughes was hysterical, but found an out: he couldn't afford to buy the necessary number of shares anyway. Goldenson had swatted him as surely as Hughes swatted flies.

Tortured by the battle with Goldenson, Hughes became obsessed by a profound fear. Susan Hayward, who had, ironically, starred as a cancer victim in the film *Stolen Hours* (1963), Agnes Moorehead, John Wayne, and numerous crew members of *The Conqueror* were ailing from the effects of radiation caused by the location shooting of that film. Actor Pedro Armendariz had shot himself when his cancer was diagnosed. Knowing of these tragedies, and recalling his own insane decision to have the picture made in an area that had been contaminated, he was appalled to find that in moving to Las Vegas he had overlooked a significant detail: the nuclear tests were being resumed, and, in his ninth-floor nest, he, too, might be stricken with cancer.

To Maheu and others of his circle, his fear seemed irrational. But fear turned to abject terror when, on television late one night in April, Hughes saw an announcement that the Atomic Energy Commission was going to explode "Boxcar," the most powerful nuclear weapon yet, at Palute Mesa, only 150 miles from his place of residence. First, Hughes tried to get Hank Greenspun, who was still heavily in his debt, to publish a front-page story denouncing the explosion. Greenspun didn't dare; the bombsite provided substantial employment, and if the plan were suspended, it could cost many of his readers their jobs. Hughes tried to argue with Greenspun that he would, through the Medical Center and new hotels, outmatch the Atomic Energy Commission in bringing money to Las Vegas. This spurious effort failed.

Hughes tried to stir up dissent at the bombsite, followed by a strike; he threatened to support the Ban-the-Bomb groups he had consistently labeled "pinko"; he would, Maheu warned the AEC, pour all of his millions into an anti-AEC campaign. This was supremely ironical, since it was he who had so vigorously promoted the Cold War which was the alleged *raison d'être* for the tests' being made in the first place. In memo after memo, he charged that the AEC's contention that cancelling the tests would weaken America's defenses were "99 proof, unadulterated shit," and that "They [the AEC] better get down off their damned aristocratic high horse and start talking a compromise with us."

He fired off an immensely long, ill-argued letter to President Lyndon B. Johnson at the White House, seeking a ninety-day postponement, and this time citing the health-of-citizens issue. Johnson set the letter aside, and the test proceeded on schedule on April 26, 1968. From that moment on, Hughes was certain that he and most of the citizens of Las Vegas would be cancer-stricken. He was a nervous wreck by the end of the week.

He was determined that there would be no further tests. The 1968 election would be coming up in the fall. Whom should he back financially for his purpose? He couldn't back Nixon for president because Nixon wanted more tests. Of the possible Democratic nominees, he, of course, despised and feared Bobby Kennedy, thought Eugene McCarthy a weakling, but felt that Vice President Hubert Humphrey, now that President Johnson was stepping down, would support his case. He had already hired Humphrey's son Robert to work for him. On May 9, Maheu, acting under Hughes's instructions, met with Hubert Humphrey in Denver. Humphrey promised to do what he could.

Maheu then told Humphrey he had $100,000 of Hughes's money to contribute to Humphrey's campaign. Humphrey pointed out that Hughes must not go on fighting the Atomic Energy Commission and the Department of Defense, that Humphrey would appoint a committee of scientists to study the effects of radiation.

Hughes was delighted and pledged $300,000 to that committee. Now an elated Hughes dreaded that Bobby Kennedy would defeat Humphrey, who, in every way, lacked the glamor, charisma, and ineffable name of his rival candidate. If only Bobby would die. Hughes waited.

On June 4, 1968, in the early hours of the Las Vegas morning, the air conditioners whirring away, the lonely scarecrow figure with his flitting bodyguards sat in his pajamas and robe staring at the images on the television screen. The regular program was interrupted by an astonishing announcement. Hughes saw Bobby Kennedy, handsome, young, and confident, the triumphant victor of the California campaign, stride into the kitchen of the Ambassador Hotel, Hughes's home during his innocent youth, when a gunshot rang out and Kennedy crumpled. Hughes was delighted.

Through the many hours as Kennedy lingered between life and death, Hughes peppered Maheu with phone calls and memoranda. He was ecstatic; not only would Humphrey have a chance, he would offer to snap up Kennedy's entire campaign team (since he was sure anybody could be bought) and put them in his pocket in case Edward Kennedy should step into the breach. He began fantasizing that his ally, Governor Paul Laxalt, would enter the presidential race; that he would plunge his millions into pushing Laxalt into the White House.

In one of his memos he wrote:

> After they come to, following a 48 hour effort to drink
> themselves into oblivion, they will feel awfully and terribly alone
> and frightened. Of course, they will try and make it again with
> Ted, but that is a long and uncertain road . . . I am sure this is a
> once-in-a-lifetime opportunity to acquire a ready-made political
> organization, all trained and ready to go.

He decided to start at the top: he would buy Kennedy's vigorous campaign manager, Larry O'Brien. As a Roman Catholic, Maheu could be relied on to get O'Brien's ear. Although O'Brien knew that Bobby hated Hughes, he was a politician like all the others: Hughes had contributed $25,000 to the hated Kennedy campaign.

Maheu met with O'Brien in Las Vegas on July 4, 1968. He was briefed to the limit by Hughes. By now, O'Brien wasn't in a position to sell the Bobby Kennedy team. It had dispersed; O'Brien, in fact, was out of a job. Hughes didn't hire O'Brien right away, but he knew O'Brien could be useful in the future and might well play a role in any future administration, and encouraged Maheu to pay him $25,000. Maheu did. Soon O'Brien was on the Hughes payroll at $15,000 a month.

Undaunted by his $100 million disaster over the Hughes Tool helicopters and his dismal failure to cheat Lockheed over the L-1011s, Hughes embarked on yet another buying venture: he would snap up Air West, known popularly as Air Worst. Nick Bez, the Yugoslavia-born rags-to-riches chairman, had done brilliantly in the formation of the spunky new airline from three failing companies in 1964, but he had dropped the ball in terms of clumsy management, overbooking, lateness, and money losses.

Hughes asked Maheu to make the deal with Bez, who was dying of cancer. Bez was a tough bargainer, even though he no longer had anything to gain by making a better deal; his directors were squabbling and haggling; after much discussion, Hughes sent Maheu to the bargaining table with an offer of $20 a share, the total purchase price of the company being $80 million. Bez pushed the price up to $22 a share, but his board wanted more. Vice-chairman Edmund Converse, knowing Hughes's record, and mistrusting him, threatened to collapse the deal entirely.

Hughes acted at once. He would draw public attention, especially that of the Air West shareholders, to the airline's miserable record. Publicity hotshot Jimmy the Greek (James Snyder) was hired to blast Air West's fragile reputation to pieces. Hughes's old friends in the Hearst newspaper organization helped. Snyder sent out a press release on Hughes's instructions that a shareholder group in Nevada had hired Snyder, as they wanted to accept the $22 a share offer. No such shareholder group existed.

More help came from Democratic Senator Alan Bible of Nevada, who received $30,000 from Hughes for his election, despite Hughes's involvement with Governor Laxalt. The next day, Bible attacked Air West in the *Las Vegas Sun* (September 28, 1968).

While Hughes's flacks kept hammering away at the public, Air West fell apart. The Bank of America threatened to pull the rug from under Bez's feet. Realizing that the other board members might stumble the deal, Hughes had Chester Davis and Maheu insist that Bez remain aboard, even in his grievous state of health, to make the arrangements to the bitter end. Hughes knew that the longer Bez stayed in office, the worse the condition of the company would become.

By late December, the shareholders were happy to accept the $22, but the board ruled thirteen to eleven against the sale. They would instead sell to Northwest Airlines. Hughes was furious; he had until midnight on New Year's Eve to quash the decision or be forced to back out of his offer.

First, he had every Air West stockholder he knew, including Hank Greenspun of the *Las Vegas Sun,* dump their shares, thus reducing the market price. Chester Davis cooked up the idea of a stockholders' suit against its elected board, backed by the dying Bez and based on the issue that they had been deprived of profits by the directors' refusing Hughes's offer.

Bez promised Chester Davis and Maheu his support. Working round the clock, with the aid of a Delaware law firm, the Hughes team drafted the complaint; disaffected Air West stockholders joining in the action were rounded up with amazing speed.

The dissentient board members were bombarded with notes, anonymous phone calls, threats; they were battered by newspapers friendly with Hughes. He gave up sleep as the New Year's Eve deadline approached. Once the stockholders' suit was filed in Delaware, and Hughes made sure it was announced in every paper, a directors' last-minute bid to sell to Northwest in Seattle over Bez's head failed. Northwest bosses wanted no part of an encumbered sale.

Dissenting director John Parker gave up the fight. Edmund Converse was forced against the wall. At last, the deal seemed set: Bez would be able to sign the contract of sale—but he had to do it before New Year's Day began at 12:01 A.M.

On New Year's Eve, with just nine hours left, Chester Davis and Maheu took the Hughes private de Havilland jet from Las Vegas to Seattle, where Bez lived, only to run into a snowstorm. In terrifying turbulence, they were told the airport had closed. Every effort to land failed. Would they lose the deal and be fired by Hughes?

Nothing, neither weather nor the Devil himself, could stop a Hughes plan. Hughes had sent aviation director Francis Fox ahead to clear a runway and obtain permission for an emergency landing. The pilot managed a bumpy touchdown, and Davis and Maheu rushed to a waiting car and ploughed through the Seattle streets full of merry-makers and blinding snow flurries, to Bez's apartment, where the sick executive was entertaining his friends. Bez signed the papers; everybody noisily toasted the purchase as the New Year was announced on television. Maheu called Hughes, who was ecstatic but, typically, refused to cheer up Bez, who had less than three months to live, by thanking him personally. Then, at 12:15, the demon relented. He called Bez and chatted with him for twenty minutes about old and new times in aviation. Bez was overjoyed.

The game wasn't over. Hughes still had to obtain the approval of the Civil Aeronautics Board. And he began to panic that he had made a mistake in buying Air West. By January 14, he was considering pulling out.

Although dissenting director Edmund Converse had been forced to yield to Hughes, he doubted if Hughes would ever buy the airline. Like those mistrustful executives before him, he insisted that Hughes not only yield up his personal and business details, but appear before the CAB. He wanted Hughes to reveal his plans for Air West; would Hughes run it properly? Hughes, with the Bez signature in his pocket, said he would reveal nothing. The CAB, like seemingly every other government agency program which gave employment to thousands, didn't press Hughes for anything. It was mindful of the fact that Hughes Aircraft, with CIA approval, was supplying the government with many of its strategic intelligence devices, including satellites, and was involved in the profitable space program, and that Hughes, for all his many tricks, was still a government instrument.

Edmund Converse's attempt to subpoena Hughes to appear at the hearings was denied by the Board. But the Board did want to know who would run the airline. Shrewdly, Hughes proposed the impeccable General Edward Nigro, whose Air Force background suited him somewhat better to his new role of airline executive than that of running the Desert Inn casino.

But, even as the feeble CAB mulled over everything he wanted, even suggesting to him he set up a special subsidiary company to avoid having Hughes Tool's ownership of Air West publicly revealed and thus open to audit, he panicked again. Air West's losses mounted continuously, so that even his announced purchase of the shares failed to buck up the assets. After a year of shilly-shallying, with Maheu urging him to bail out, he at last paid $89,398,091 for the airline. But he cheated the shareholders who had so loyally gone along with him. By a series of complicated maneuvers, he stripped them naked.

In an under-the-table deal with certain of the owners, Hughes received $48 million of that sum back from them to compensate for the decline in Air West's net worth during the negotiations—a decline he had insured by publicizing the company's failings in the press and on the radio. This was done without the outside shareholders' knowing about it. Contingency fees and other payments reduced the amount payable to the owners of common stock to a mere $33 million; exactly what those other payments were, what in fact happened to the rest of the $89 million plus, has never been revealed.

The shareholders in the end received not the already inadequate $22 a share they had been promised, but a pitiful $8.75. For years afterward, the Securities and Exchange Commission and the Department of Justice tried to determine the truth of alleged kickbacks, an investigation that would lead finally to the spectacular fake break-in of Hughes's office some six years later, when all appropriate documents disappeared for good.

At the same time he was preoccupied with the Air West matter, Hughes was further involved in buying up gold- and silver-yielding properties. As well as consuming Tonopah and its surroundings, he was up to his eyes in paperwork buying up territory in another abandoned area: the surroundings of Virginia City, scene of the famous Comstock Lode which had enriched many thousands in the period before the Civil War.

On August 6, 1968, Hughes bought eleven claims in Nevada, and then, on October 16, another six. Maheu had convinced him that $150 million worth of precious metals and strategic minerals could be dug up from the earth. By year's end, he had consumed well over 100 more claims, spending millions in a frantic and nostalgic replay of his father's minerals hunger. Hughes aide John Meier made many of the deals, raking off profits from those selling to Hughes—in the form of commissions—and a percentage from Hughes himself. Meier even received parcels of shares in one Arizona company. One of the mining owners who sold to Hughes was also, and conveniently, state mining inspector for Virginia City, and could provide useful tips. Meier, on Hughes's behalf, traveled to Washington and put a high official of the Department of the Interior in his pocket, receiving from him secret information on new mining possibilities.

Hughes found that a way to dodge federal taxes would be to simply open up the claims, then hang onto the gold, silver, and other ore until the taxes might drop.

And the best way to insure that taxes were reduced or waived in his case would be to exercise influence over the White House.

Meier had formed a friendship with Donald Nixon, the president's brother, the same Donald Nixon whom Hughes had improperly lent $205,000 in 1956. The newspapers were hinting heavily that Nixon had interests in Hughes-connected minerals deals and the president became understandably nervous of charges of being used for influence-buying. Donald's visits to Nevada became increasingly frequent—so much so that the president sent his friend Bebe Rebozo to Hughes's associate Richard G. Danner to provide a warning.

Hughes and Maheu told Meier to behave. Nixon told H. R. Haldeman, White House Chief of Staff, and John D. Ehrlichman, Assistant to the President in Domestic Affairs, to break up the partnership. Donald Nixon hung on: his latest deal with the Hughes empire was to secure food supplies for Hughes's fleets of planes and ground staff canteens. If he yielded to his brother's presidential pressure, he might lose a fortune.

Nixon tapped Donald's phone, providing conclusive proof of his connections. Hidden cameras recorded a meeting with Meier at Orange County Airport in California on July 8. Hughes hung onto Meier, despite Maheu's request he fire him before it was too late. For Hughes, the idea of having the president's brother in his pocket was too good to be true. He gave his blessing to Meier's leaving on trips to various parts of Europe and South America with Donald Nixon, out of the range of Richard Nixon and the FBI.

Hughes had long been interested in the Dominican Republic, from his first visits by yacht in the 1930s. He authorized Meier to obtain mining concessions there; Meier promised to see to it that the United States' Dominican sugar imports would be increased. A third partner on these expeditions was Salt Lake City promoter and mining speculator Anthony G. Hatsis.

Maheu strove against Hughes's wishes to break the partnership for good. He directly promised Nixon's watch team that he would take care of the matter. Meanwhile, Meier continued to buy millions of acres of land. When Maheu learned that Meier was about to plan another meeting with Donald Nixon, Maheu was left with no alternative but to get rid of him. On November 2, in a charged meeting at the Frontier Hotel, Maheu asked for, and received, Meier's resignation.

In the wake of Meier's departure, with questions still being asked about Donald Nixon in anti-Nixon circles, staggering facts emerged. It turned out that over $5 million in mining deals had never gotten into Hughes's pocket, but instead, had been siphoned through tax-free zones to Switzerland. Of a total of $20 million spent, little could be accounted for; there was scant documentation of land titles and grants; and in the end, it turned out that $18 million had gone down the drain. Most of the mines, including those in Tonopah, closed down when it was found that the ancient lodes were barren of silver or gold. In the 1970s, Meier was indicted and arrested for tax evasion, much of his income being traced to improper Hughes transactions. Meier fled the country; in 1978, the Hughes Tool empire sued Meier for $8 million for buying worthless mines and siphoning the cash abroad. Meier flew to Australia where he was arrested. He was let go because he had diplomatic immunity: he had made deals with the king of Tonga, a South Seas island, and his passport listed him as an ambassador. He disappeared again, this time to Vancouver, and for good.

## CHAPTER SIXTEEN

# Buying Nixon

During the scandalous events involving Donald Nixon, Hughes was unfazed. It wasn't enough to buy the president's brother. He was determined to buy the president, as well as Nixon's Democratic opponent, Hubert H. Humphrey.

Successive administrations had given him soft-soap treatment, at least in part because of his extensive campaign contributions and under-the-table support, and Hughes Aircraft's usefulness to the CIA, Army, and Air Force. But all of the compromises in his favor, the endless waiving of rules by the Civil Aeronautics Board and other official bodies in favor of his retaining his privacy were not enough for him.

Hughes had several matters in 1968–70 that required wholesale bribery. One was his contemplated purchase of the Dunes Hotel in Las Vegas, which would give him a full quarter of Las Vegas even though it breached monopolies laws. Another was his need to avoid paying a gigantic bond sum in his continuing legal struggle with TWA. A third was his desire to be given Civil Aeronautics Board approval to take over Air West.

In taking care of these matters, he risked prosecution on any number of counts: payment of over $5,000 to a presidential candidate, which was then illegal and punishable by a fine of $5,000, or ten years in prison, or both; bribery; conspiracy to defraud the

United States; willful subscription to a false tax return; perjury; false statements. By March 5, 1974, U.S. Special Prosecutor Leon Jaworski would be seriously weighing these charges against him.

While he contemplated how best he might bribe the president to ensure favorable treatment, Hughes decided to take care of Hubert Humphrey. He instructed Robert Maheu to withdraw $50,000 for Humphrey from the cashier's cage at the Frontier Hotel, which he had recently bought; it was money used in the buying and selling of gambling chips. Since the cash would not easily be traced, that seemed a sensible method. Further, he earmarked one of his Washington contact attorneys, Richard C. Danner, who had many friends from his days in the FBI and had been a honcho in Miami as city manager, to take over the management of the Frontier. Danner would be a cover if questions were asked later on.

Maheu found a willing ear in Humphrey. When he suggested that the presidential candidate might welcome an "item"—i.e., a contribution of $50,000, or $45,000 above the legal limit—Humphrey was understandably interested. Thus reassured, Maheu took $25,000 in an attaché case by plane to Los Angeles and an associate brought the remaining $25,000, both lots in $100 bills.

On Hughes's instructions, Maheu checked into a suite at the Century Plaza Hotel in Century City on July 31, where Maheu was scheduled to attend a $5,000 a plate dinner in Humphrey's honor. Humphrey's associate, Lloyd Hand, made the arrangements. Maheu packed the remaining $25,000 into his attaché case after dinner and carried the $50,000 to Humphrey's limousine at the front entrance. He stepped into the vehicle, sat down, and handed over the case. Soon afterward, Humphrey sent a thank you note. Later, Humphrey stated, under oath, that he could not remember the incident. Presumably, he was afflicted with amnesia, since the transaction took place only months before his denial. A second $50,000 was in his pocket on October 17, this time in smaller amounts.

In the meantime, Hughes had set his sights on Nixon. As it turned out, while he was figuring how to go about it, Nixon's best friend in Miami, the handsome and dashing real estate millionaire Charles G. (Bebe) Rebozo, took the first step.

Rebozo contacted Richard G. Danner and said that he was jealous that Hughes had given money to Humphrey and why couldn't he supply an equal sum to him for the Nixon campaign? He followed the call with a written request on August 28, 1968. Maheu told

Hughes, who burst out laughing. He had been saved the trouble of making the first move.

Over the next two years, Hughes withdrew as much as $425,000 for political contributions, of which a sum described as $100,000, but possibly $150,000, went to Bebe Rebozo. Most of these sums were drawn from Hughes's account at the Texas National Bank of Commerce, the checks signed by his long-term associate Lee Murrin. As we have seen, $25,000 went into Larry O'Brien's pocket. Fifty thousand went (Maheu says) to Senator Alan Bible of Nevada. Fifty thousand was returned to the Frontier cage. The remaining payments are undocumented.

Hughes decreed that Danner, who knew both Nixon and Bebe Rebozo, should pay Nixon $50,000 directly, and he insisted Nixon sign a receipt. He wanted Donald Nixon and John Meier involved. Nixon was opposed to their involvement, and decided to postpone the matter until after the election. The payments could then be applied to the 1972 campaign. Maheu stored the cash. Nixon was elected.

On November 22, 1968, a member of Nixon's staff called Maheu and said it was time to make the payment. Hughes agreed. With typical boldness, Hughes said that he wanted no less than Paul Laxalt, who was still governor of Nevada, to make the delivery to the new president in person. Laxalt agreed.

Danner was in Las Vegas that week. Hughes rewarded him for his continuing bribery by giving him the long-promised job of manager of the Frontier.

Danner had been talking with Rebozo at length all week about money Nixon needed for his house in Key Biscayne, Rebozo's territory. Nixon was buying it from him.

On December 6, Paul Laxalt and Robert Maheu arrived in Palm Springs with $50,000 for Nixon. Laxalt was there to attend the Republican Governors' Convention Association Conference. On Hughes's instructions, the two men drove to Walter Annenberg's house. The governor got out and rang the doorbell.

At that moment, the other governors, some of whom might have thought it odd that one of their number was carrying a substantial sum to the president as a contribution, were standing on the terrace talking to the Chief Executive. Understandably, when informed that the governor of Nevada was on the doorstep with a person holding a significant briefcase, Nixon announced that he was too busy to see him, despite the fact that the other governors were being suitably entertained. The money was again held by Maheu in reserve.

In September, Maheu and Danner delivered $50,000 to Bebe Rebozo in Key Biscayne.

At the outset of 1970, Hughes instructed Maheu to buy the Dunes Hotel. Maheu stated later (January 21, 1974) that Hughes told him to send Richard Danner to Attorney General John Mitchell to obtain Justice Department approval of the purchase. Saying he was frustrated by the Justice Department in trying to buy the Stardust Hotel, he said he would no longer deal with the assistant attorney general, but only with Mitchell himself.

Danner met with Mitchell several times, starting on January 23. When he returned, Mitchell said Maheu told him, acting for Hughes, that "certain financial obligations would have to be met as a result of the trip." They were. The obliging attorney general overrode his reluctant Antitrust Division and allowed Hughes to buy the Dunes on March 19. When Hughes's lawyer, Edward P. Morgan, presented the necessary figures to document the Dunes's assets, Mitchell didn't even bother to discuss them with Antitrust. Danner told Maheu, "The case is taken care of in Washington and there will be no interference beyond that." The Watergate Committee later on decided that Mitchell's approval was based directly on cash gifts to Rebozo.

Another gift was forthcoming. Hughes had Maheu instruct Nadine Henley to withdraw another $50,000, and Richard Danner delivered it to Bebe Rebozo while both were staying at San Clemente, the western White House, for Nixon. The payment was made on the patriotic date of July 3, the eve of Independence Day.

A long-buried document found in the National Archives shows a sum larger than $100,000 paid to Rebozo. Stephen A. Haberfeld, assistant special prosecutor, advised Leon Jaworski, Watergate Special Prosecutor, on March 5, 1974, that "$150,000 could have been delivered by Danner to Rebozo on three of five occasions during 1970." If this is the case, and the complex document supporting the charge is available, then there was $50,000 unaccounted for and unmentioned in any press report on this case.

In the end, Maheu found that financial statements supplied to him on the Dunes were full of misstatements and irregularities; he told Hughes the price was too high, and Hughes didn't buy the hotel. As for the bond that the court required Hughes to lodge in the TWA case, despite numerous phone calls from Mitchell to the White House and many interested parties, Hughes still had to post $75 million. It could have been as high as $400 million without the influence he brought to bear.

In the Air West case, Hughes, as we know, did succeed in taking over the airline, but there is no evidence that Mitchell helped him in the matter, and Hughes had to make major concessions before the Civil Aeronautics Board approved. Like so much else in his life, his complex maneuverings wound up leaving him with handfuls of dust.

One hundred thousand dollars, plus an extra $100, was returned to Hughes; but the serial numbers on the first $50,000 in hundred-dollar bills showed that they were dated after December, 1968, when Maheu obtained them. Thirty-five of the hundred-dollar bills that allegedly constituted the San Clemente delivery were dated after July 3, 1970, when they were supposed to have been delivered. Later, Hughes supplied $150,000: $50,000 to Rose Mary Woods, and $100,000 to the Committee to Re-Elect the President, when the law regarding contributions changed in 1972. Fifty thousand of the CRP fund went to an individual named Gordon Liddy, who confirmed this in his book *Will*.

In its final report on the Watergate affair in June 1974, the Watergate Committee stated: "The circumstances surrounding the Hughes efforts to buy the Dunes Hotel show questionable conduct at high levels of the executive branch."

While Danner pressed ahead with negotiations at the very top of government, Hughes had another reason to encourage him. He was again seized by increasing nervous attacks about remaining in the city he was consuming.

The reason was the continuing underground nuclear testing, which not even his wealth and power could stop. While he was busy engineering the Dunes purchase, he had Richard Danner talk to Bebe Rebozo and have Nixon delay the blasts, which were scheduled for Easter, 1970. Nixon agreed to discuss the matter with Hughes in person, provided that Hughes came to some still unspecified location, possibly Camp David. For almost anybody alive, an offer to see the president would be irresistible. But Hughes, with a two-year growth of beard, his fingernails and toenails long and unmanicured, wouldn't consider such a trip. He wouldn't agree to speak to Nixon on the telephone; he was afraid that the president would talk him into accepting the tests by making technical arguments about safety precautions to which Hughes would not have an adequate answer.

He began talking about returning to the Bahamas, where he had stayed with Jean Peters years before. But his fear and hatred of blacks and concern over the political situation weighed against his love of the tax-free status of the islands.

Early in 1970, Hughes called Maheu, telling him that he expected him to "wrap up that government [of the Bahamas] . . . in every way," a statement quoted in many newspapers and on television and which was very damaging to him when it surfaced later.

He delayed his planned trip again and again.

In the midst of all his influence buying, Hughes's exhausting, round-the-clock telephone schedules, wretched diet, drug addiction, and failure to exercise had left him in a very poor state of health. Jean Peters had made clear, from her home in Bel Air, that she would be divorcing him (at any time, she would have been willing to visit him and take care of him; but even that strong woman couldn't deal with his procrastinations and failure to respond to her or see her). That depressed him deeply; he had failed as a husband and as a man.

His fondness for Empirin and mainlining codeine had affected his kidneys; and his fear of anyone's seeing his urine still compelled him to bottle it in Mason jars. His doctor, Dr. Harold L. Feikes, reported that he was a victim of internal and external hemorrhoids, which caused an agonizing prolapse every time he went to the toilet; the degree of gum and jawbone recession in a man over sixty was more advanced than normal, and he still had bleeding and ulceration of the gums. A peptic ulcer and a tumorous cyst on top of his head added to his misery. His bones were as brittle as those of a man of eighty. If he were to fall and break a hip, it might be the end of him. And he was only sixty-five.

Top executive Bill Gay was fretful at being phased out of Hughes's intimate circle and was determined to remove Maheu, who, he felt, was far too individually powerful, was drawing vast sums from Hughes for his own profit, and was an unfortunate influence on him. That the earlier attempt to declare Hughes mentally incompetent, vigorously rejected by the loyal Maheu, had been thwarted, had annoyed him; Hughes's continual refusal to take him seriously made him want to dislodge Maheu once and for all.

According to Maheu, Gay began his campaign against him by

blocking many of his messages to Hughes, with the support of certain of Hughes's limited circle of bodyguards. This Gay has denied. By contrast, Gay and Chester Davis charged that Maheu had gotten into a substantial investment in Los Angeles Airways for helicopter supplies without Hughes's authorization. This, in turn, Maheu denied; he, to this day, asserts that he had Hughes's approval. Davis also charged that Maheu had made an arrangement to loan $4 million to a bookmaker, Sidney Wyman, part owner of the Dunes, to oil the wheels for the purchase. Maheu says that he acted with Hughes's authorization; Gay and Davis denied it.

On June 13, 1970, Raymond M. Holliday, vice president and chief financial officer of the Hughes Tool Company in Houston, who joined the anti-Maheu faction, wrote a blistering memorandum to Hughes, reminding him that the Nevada properties, from mineral leases to hotels, were losing millions. What Gay, Holliday, Davis, and all the other honchos of Hughes's empire chose to ignore was the fact that Maheu wasn't the operative influence in Hughes's vast acquisitions, but the servant of Hughes's megalomaniac greed and obsession; his efforts to subdue Hughes's mindless driving need for control in hotel purchases had met with constant rebuffs.

Bill Gay decided to spy on Maheu, in order to support his case to Hughes with "evidence" of impropriety when there was none. He and Chester Davis knew of a CIA-connected security firm named International Intelligence (Intertel).

Intertel originated in Nassau, and was set up by Resorts International, a spinoff of the pseudonymous Mary Carter Paints, which ran the gambling concessions on Paradise Island, which Hughes was interested in buying. It was cofounded by William Hundley, a former special assistant to Robert Kennedy, and Robert Peloquin, another Kennedy man who had been senior attorney in the Department of Justice's Organized Crime and Racketeering Section. Others in Intertel were a former Nixon aide, James Golden, security director of the 1968 Republican Convention, an odd man out among diehard Democrats; David Belisle, former director of investigations for the National Security Agency; and various former CIA, FBI, British MI-5 and MI-6, and Royal Canadian Mounted Police operatives.

Robert Peloquin came to Las Vegas in July, 1970, following Bill Gay's visit to his office in Washington. A deal was discussed whereby Intertel would take over from Robert Maheu and his son Peter their surveillance and security operations in the Las Vegas casinos. Peloquin urged Hughes to revive his idea of going to the Bahamas, where he would be more tightly linked to Intertel's headquarters and would be out of Nevada when Intertel assumed control. Hughes listened, but then something happened to weaken his resolve.

He learned from his television station that the Pentagon was going to dump sixty-six tons of stockpiled nerve gas into the Caribbean, and only 150 miles from Nassau, the exact distance Las Vegas was from the nuclear blasts. He panicked.

He summoned his aides, and demanded, in a hastily scribbled memorandum, that they alert powerful publicity firms to arouse public sentiment against the dumping, as well as the British Bahamian government; Gay approached his friend Robert Foster Bennett, of the Department of Transportation, who could do nothing. Within weeks of authorizing Nixon's bribe, Hughes blamed the president for the decision, calling for Nixon's hatred of blacks to be used as the motive for the dumping—despite the fact that Hughes hated blacks himself and was a Nixon supporter and financier. He envisaged a cartoon, run through the Hearst newspapers, showing Nixon pounding on a black youth with a poison gas cylinder.

Maheu advised against that, but said he would approach the president in a friendly spirit instead. He was too late. The nerve gas was already being sent by train to be loaded onto an oceangoing vessel.

Maheu pleaded with the president to have the nerve gas sent elsewhere. Nixon responded by saying that the choice of the dumping site was for Hughes's benefit. The president had no idea Hughes was set for residence in the Bahamas, and the dump site had originally been planned for Nevada. Hughes, through Maheu, suggested the Arctic Circle as an alternative.

Bill Gay and Chester Davis pleased Hughes by taking up the cudgels in Nassau. Once there, they pointed out that Hughes would be bringing great wealth to the Bahamas. As a result, the Bahamian government protested the dumping. Hughes even had Chester Davis sue the government in Miami—backed by Claude Kirk, a Florida governor who was mindful of Hughes's investments in that state.

A Miami judge blocked the gas shipment, then reversed the decision, recommending, for some spurious reason, that the dump site would be better "in shallow water." When Hughes heard of this, he became hysterical. The shallowest water within 150 miles of the site was in the Bahamian Out Islands, of which he owned, of course, the CIA center, Cay Sal.

In a last, desperate effort, Hughes begged Maheu to see Nixon in person. Instead, Maheu offered to fly to San Clemente, where he would be able to convey a message to the president that would avoid the long air trip to Washington. But he was too late; on August 18, 1970, the beaten-up World War II liberty ship, *LeBaron Russell,* was sunk with its deadly cargo of gas 150 miles off Nassau.

The CIA files on its deals with Hughes are likely to be classified permanently, in the interests of "national security"—even now, after the end of the Cold War. We can only deduce how many millions of dollars worth of equipment Hughes was supplying the agency with by the time he was planning to leave Las Vegas in 1970.

High resolution cameras mounted on Hughes satellites were photographing secret installations in the Soviet Union, Vietnam, and China; his team developed sophisticated intercept devices in interoffice and interembassy computer links, scramblers and bugs, and laser weaponry components of SR-71 spy planes. And not only for the CIA, but for the national Reconnaissance Office of Air Force Intelligence and for the Pentagon.

Through the use of Hughes's sensory methodology, the U.S. government was able to determine details of Communist radars, missiles, and the movements of troops, all achieved with the aid of coagents in countries bordering (or inside) the Iron Curtain.

Hughes and Hughes Tool would soon make their biggest deal ever: in October, 1970, Hughes signed papers that made it possible for Operation Jennifer to begin.

Operation Jennifer was one of the costliest and most elaborate enterprises in the history of the CIA and Naval Intelligence. First, the Hughes Tool Company, operating with Hughes's authorization and CIA Director Richard Helms's personal direction, would send out *Glomar II,* a chartered Hughes vessel, to a point several hundred miles to the southwest of the Hawaiian Islands, where, so the Hughes publicity machine would announce, it would seek to survey the ocean floor for deposits of precious metals. The *Glomar* was equipped with drills using the Hughes bit, and would probe into the ocean floor.

Actually, the *Glomar*'s purpose was to make soundings on the site of an exploded Russian nuclear submarine, fresh from Cuban waters, which would be raised to the surface by another, far larger *Glomar Explorer,* to be built by Hughes Tool through subcontracts. The *Explorer* would be the length of two football fields and would be equipped with a giant claw which, in one fell swoop, would pick up the submarine, house it in the vast cargo hold, and ship it back to Honolulu or San Diego for inspection.

The cost of the venture would be *one quarter of a billion dollars* of government money. But why—just to bring up a submarine?

According to former CIA operative and author Victor Marchetti, the reason for the salvage operation was to obtain cipher machines which were believed to be aboard.

These machines, and the accompanying documents, would tell the CIA how to interpret/translate previous intercepted messages, of which a vast boxcarred stockpile existed in the intelligence rooms at Fort Meade, Maryland; through understanding what the messages contained, it would be possible to track and intercept Russian nuclear subs, especially off Cuba, and to determine how Castro was served by Soviet nuclear power.

Hughes was delighted to cooperate with this venture; again, his motive was carrying out the policies and intelligence schemes of the Nixon government. He would see hundreds of millions pouring into Hughes Aircraft, all of it tax-sheltered inside the Medical Institute.

At the same time Hughes authorized *Glomar,* via Hughes Tool, he was happy to see successive business deals with the CIA for Hughes Aircraft. Hughes Aircraft hired as chief executive no less than the brilliant young Albert (Bud) Wheelon; Wheelon had been the CIA's Deputy Director for Science and Technology, starting with the Agency under Director Allen Dulles as early as 1961. Trained under Dulles's successor, John McCone, and working later under Admiral William Raborn and Richard Helms, Wheelon had used many of the Hughes Aircraft satellite devices on Russia and China in carrying out his technical investigations. In 1966, the Senate Subcommittee on Appropriations for Technical Espionage questioned Wheelon, who appeared before the panel with a number of secret Hughes surveillance devices of James Bond triviality, including, Marchetti reports, a radio transmitter hidden in false teeth, a camera in a tobacco pouch, a tape recorder in a gold cigarette case.

He managed, with great dexterity, to sidestep questions about Hughes, Lockheed, and the other CIA contractees, and the questions evaporated.

Swinging the *Glomar Explorer* deal, through links with the CIA that tightened every day, Bill Gay, Chester Davis, and the other enemies of Maheu strengthened their hand in the fall of 1970. Had Richard Helms given Maheu the *Explorer* deal to handle, Maheu would have consolidated his power forever, but he had antagonized the others, and in particular, Raymond Holliday, who ran Hughes Tool and whom the CIA needed to make the arrangements.

Yet another Hughes operation with CIA support and financial backing, and with Hughes's personal involvement, was a further development of the earlier ship-to-shore lasers for use against the installations and the government of Cuba. This commitment and interest of Hughes allied him, once again, with the omnipresent spy E. Howard Hunt, who was continuing with the CIA. Asked to comment on Hughes, Hunt reacted angrily on September 21, 1992, saying that this was "deep background" and he would say nothing; i.e., it was still top secret. He thus gave his own game away—and not for the first time.

An exchange of memoranda that October sealed Robert Maheu's fate; Maheu made the mistake of asserting himself as a man. He decided he would make a trip to Europe. He wrote to Hughes that he had planned the journey for ten years; that he had promised it to his wife; that since it might be months before he heard from Hughes on various pressing matters, this seemed to be the propitious time for the trip. Hughes was furious. He told Maheu in a responding note that he had been ill lately; he had been distracted by trouble involving his wife (he meant their impending divorce), he couldn't keep abreast of the constant flow of memoranda, that he was trying to carry the load of twenty-five normal men.

Hughes added petulantly that Maheu, by going away, would be throwing away a true and most reliable friend, himself; that the friendship was in fact over by virtue of Maheu's decision.

Maheu was hurt and wrote of that hurt; he weakened before Hughes's childish, egotistical manipulation of him. Hughes replied angrily; Maheu urged him to consider whether the time hadn't arrived that he should try to face up to reality; that if he didn't he would finally be very lonely indeed.

Telling Hughes what to do was another miscalculation. It was like telling an eight-year-old boy to go buy groceries or walk the dog.

Hughes had other islands in mind. As Hughes stepped up plans to move to the Bahamas, he failed to mention his restored idea to Maheu, who had set plans in motion before, only to see them canceled. Hughes began to grumble about Maheu. If the man had been well paid at $10,000 a week, if his expense account had been lavish and unlimited, if his house was a palace, surely that was appropriate: he "was" Howard Hughes; Hughes could scarcely entertain people himself, and an enormous number of very important people had to be entertained. And often.

"Howard Hughes" (i.e., Maheu) could not be expected to travel coach or in commercial (and rival) aircraft; could not expect to have to take state governors and Air Force generals, retired or not, or presidential aides to McDonald's for a hamburger. Yet Bill Gay and the other enemies harangued Hughes on the telephone and in memoranda that Maheu was extravagant, that his son Peter had built a doghouse and a wet bar at Hughes's expense—an endless stream of unfounded complaints that made Hughes, ever the tightwad, nervous.

If the casino and drink sales in the hotels were losing money, the Gay-Davis cabal did not blame that on a periodic slump, but on Maheu alone. When Hughes saw the sums draining away, he was convinced that Maheu wasn't earning his keep. He had forgotten that it was he who had pressed Maheu to buy hotel after hotel, and that Maheu had urged him to be more cautious. When Raymond Holliday, head of Hughes Tool Company, told Hughes that losses on the casinos had risen from $700,000 in 1967 to $7 million in 1970, Hughes was convinced that Maheu would have to go.

Maheu persuasively puts down the Las Vegas losses to Hughes's procrastinations, indecisions, stinginess, and lack of power of planning—certainly borne out in any examination of his record, at least back to the buying of RKO.

In order to keep up the hotel showrooms and casinos in competition with others, such as Kirk Kerkorian's, Hughes had to approve thousand of dollars at a time for improvements. But he resented every effort of Maheu to spend money, including hard cash for the performers.

Thus, the losses on the hotels were attributable to Hughes and Hughes alone—but, like most people of power and celebrity, he

254 ♦ CHARLES HIGHAM

would always blame his underlings for his failures. And Maheu, dogged, loyal Maheu, was the fall guy.

Maheu's enemies made a number of new accusations, none of them well-based. Chester Davis charged that Maheu gave excessive amounts of credits to high rollers—actually Caesars Palace, the Flamingo, and the International gave more. He accused Maheu of sailing his yacht, the *Alouette II*, off Baja California when he should have been working; Maheu had sailed the vessel only four times in two and a half years and was on the telephone to Hughes from the bridge or his cabin during most of the sailings.

Davis talked of Maheu's and security chief Jack Hooper's hunting lodge, a British fish and chips operation, and a wholly imaginary import-export company. When Peter Maheu's wife gave birth to a child in Mexico City (to help Hughes obtain property in his name through the Banco Internacional), Davis stated that a company jet was used.

Whenever Maheu called the penthouse, the aide told him Hughes was unavailable. Only Hughes could have given such an order. It has been claimed that the reason Hughes behaved so viciously is that his aides were threatening him; if he did not, they would deprive him of drugs. Nobody threatened Howard Hughes. He would only have had to press a button or pick up a telephone for that aide to be ejected by Bob Maheu's security people. The final decision to get rid of Maheu was his.

He was ill at the time, with a mild form of pneumonia that led him to obtain unnecessary blood transfusions. His memoranda at the time, and his cunning in evading Maheu, show that his mind was as sharp as ever.

Maheu might have wooed him back by invading the suite, seeking a confrontation, and presenting Hughes with an explanation of the losses and of the true character of Davis and Gay. Above all, he could have told Hughes of Gay's effort to take over his empire by declaring him incompetent. He could, in short, háve warned him. But he didn't; today he wishes he had. He lost his head and fired Chester Davis off the TWA case without consulting Hughes—an act calculated to infuriate Hughes forever; if anyone did the firing, that person would be Hughes himself.

The reason for Davis's dismissal was his alleged mishandling of the long-drawn-out case of *TWA vs. Hughes* in which the airline was still trying to take a bite out of Hughes for his earlier stock raids and other supposed malfeasances. Davis rejected the dismissal.

The other miscalculation Maheu made was in underestimating the power of Intertel. That organization, some members of which had feet in both Hughes and Mafia camps, wanted to take over the running not only of the Bahamian Paradise Island security systems but also of those in the Las Vegas casinos, supplanting Bob and Peter Maheu.

On November 14, 1970, Hughes set about signing a proxy which would give Davis, Holliday, and Gay power of attorney to exercise all rights in Hughes's Nevada holdings. He wanted Maheu out for good.

Maheu was deprived of his power, and soon would be stripped of his property; for this, he and his son Peter blame Intertel. With him went Larry O'Brien, now Democratic Committee National Chairman, who was in Hughes's pocket to the tune of $15,000 a month at the same time Hughes was backing Nixon.

Hughes hired former Transportation Department legalist turned CIA front man/publicist, Mormon Robert Foster Bennett, in O'Brien's place. Bennett was the son of the senator for Utah. Charles Colson, of the White House, had Bennett buy up Robert R. Mullen and Company, a Washington, D.C., public relations firm, and also a CIA front. It soon became a Hughes front; Bennett hired E. Howard Hunt as a staff member.

Hughes made up his mind, after eleven months of procrastination, to leave the United States for good. His dread of further nuclear explosions and his lust to snap up the gambling concessions in tax-free Nassau pressed on his mind.

He was in danger of his bribes' being exposed. He was terrified of the Internal Revenue Service in the matter of the Hughes Medical Institute. The Institute's foundation was revealed at last as a tax evasion scam: Hughes now allowed a mere 0.2 percent of the vast assets earned from Hughes Aircraft on secret government projects to be spent on medical research; at least 4.0 percent of assets had to be spent to qualify it for tax-free status. In effect, Hughes had stockpiled a fortune that was tax-exempt and gathering interest in banks. Some $25.6 million of the money had gone into Hughes Tool—allegedly for interest on loans and payments on property leases.

Would his outrageous rip-off of the government be exposed,

along with his influence buying? He had to get out of town, out of the U.S., at once.

He made the move on November 25, 1970. In the icy night air, as wind was blowing sand from the desert, the sixty-five-year-old man, shivering and pale, wrapped himself in a threadbare robe, over the pajamas hanging on his scrawny, wasted frame. A copy of his old, lucky hat was perched on his head, his hair and beard were long and Christlike, as his aides edged him on his stretcher, step by metal step, down the nine floors of the outside fire escape. One slip, and he would have fallen, perhaps to his death. At the foot of the staircase, he managed to struggle weakly to his feet.

He was sick from a recurrence, in recent days, of a depressing condition, hemolytic anemia, which caused skin discoloration, too much iron retention, and extreme allergy to direct sunlight. He also had a cardiac condition and persistent pneumonia, due to recur several times in the next few years.

On a diet of some 2,000 calories a day, why was he, at six feet three, only about 103 pounds? Why had he lost forty pounds that summer after blood transfusions? Why was his immune system so weakened that he could not tolerate the danger of germs? Why did his eyes look bright and frightened, sunken as they were into their bony sockets? Why was he restless, irritable, intolerant? What was his inexplicable disease?

In order to determine his condition, this author contacted Dr. Joseph Choi, retired Los Angeles chief forensic surgeon. "Could Hughes have had AIDS?" He instantly said, "Yes."

Later drawings of Hughes, and his entire symptomatology, were indicative. His case file included recurring low-level pneumonia, constant emaciation despite a diet rich in calories, and loss of muscle tone, plus developing tumors and kidney failure. His devoted aide, Gordon Margulis, does not contradict the probability of his having AIDS.

The HIV virus was not isolated until the 1980s, when it was traced back to infections in the African green monkey, but Dr. Choi confirms that numerous deceased homosexuals whose bodies came to him and who had died of pneumonia, cancer, and kidney failure had case histories identical to Hughes's. Fearful as he was, Hughes must have, in his endless obtaining of reports on others, learned of similar infections and emaciation occurring in men he had slept with. He was fiercely, guiltily protective of his rectum, which he refused his doctors permission to examine. Did he guess that it was the route of his infection? Did he suspect it was the blood transfusions he had been getting?

The term AIDS was, of course, unknown in the 1960s and 1970s, although the recent reopening of case files of deceased patients with histories of symptoms similar to Hughes's resulted in the testing of frozen blood samples. The most disturbing sero-positive case in the United States has been that of a black male prostitute who died in St. Louis in 1968 of what is now defined as AIDS. In Britain, a sailor's blood, from as early as 1959, has been found, after being unfrozen from laboratory storage, to be HIV-positive. All the doctors could do following Hughes's shocking weight loss to a little over 100 pounds, the emaciation, and the fevers that wracked him, with a temperature seriously elevated for weeks and an accompanying increased terror of infection, was speculate on the cause. His hemoglobin count was a very low four—another indication. Normal counts are around fifteen. Later, he refused all blood tests, and, at the end of his life, went through AIDS-characteristic alternating periods of delirium and brilliant clarity.

If he did sense he had something strange, that alone could have shocked him into so deep a fear of sex with Jean Peters that he could have been rendered impotent; or, at the least, his concern for her would have led him to refuse intercourse. His agony continued.

Propped up between his men, Hughes stumbled through the wind toward a cluster of cars surrounded by armed guards wearing white identification buttons. They shooed off every other individual who tried to enter or leave the parking lot. He climbed into a van. He was driven to Nellis Air Force Base to meet a Lockheed TriStar airplane; apart from the nostalgic element in this, Lockheed was the one aircraft company with which Hughes felt comfortable.

With him in the van was a huge metal filing cabinet containing confidential papers, so big it proved difficult to load and unload; the aides had a hard time getting it through the plane passenger door but Hughes refused to allow it to be placed in cargo.

The plane left at 9:24 P.M. The pilot, copilot, and flight engineer were told not to enter the cabin; no steward or stewardess was called for. The TriStar reloaded in Atlanta, according to journalist Benjamin F. Schemmer, who managed to interview the aides, Hughes enjoyed the flight very much, exchanged jokes with the crew, and munched away at sandwiches.

On the way to Nassau, Hughes suddenly began talking to his aide, Gordon Margulis, about his first wife, Ella Rice. He told Margulis of remembered trips to the Bahamas with Ella.

He had confused Ella Rice with Billie Dove, his girlfriend of the early 1930s. He had never been to Nassau with Ella Rice.

In Nassau, two panel trucks arrived to pick him up, supplied by the Britannia Beach Hotel on Paradise Island, and driven by Intertel guards and Intertel deputy chief Jim Golden. Hughes was taken up in a service elevator to the ninth floor. Next day, a second TriStar arrived with records of the Las Vegas hotels that Intertel had raided.

Hughes settled into the Britannia Beach. The suite had to be watched for insects, since the humid Bahamian climate bred roaches, spiders and scorpions. He fretted endlessly. In view of the corrupt nature of Paradise Island, he was fearful of a mob hit; but Intertel, with its various assigns on both sides of the law, could take care of that.

On December 3, Hughes opened the *Las Vegas Sun*, which had been flown to him at his command. The headline read:

HOWARD HUGHES VANISHES! MYSTERY BAFFLES CLOSE ASSOCIATES

The article said that Hughes had disappeared after five years, that he was "spirited away"—Maheu charged Bill Gay and Intertel with kidnapping him. Hughes was furious. He sent a long, rambling memo to Chester Davis on December 3, dismissing Maheu's allegations that he had been taken to the Bahamas against his will and referring to the fact that the trip had been scheduled for much of a year and that Maheu had been involved in the planning. He accused Maheu of lying not only about this but about many other matters as well.

The memorandum, in style, form, and content identical to hundreds of its predecessors going back some forty years, cannot have been written under pressure from aides, nor would Chester Davis have dictated a memorandum to himself. It was pure Hughes from first word to last; and it was not insane. It was the expression of an irritated dictator, the master of his fate whose lieutenant has refused to be his puppet.

All Hughes had to do was inform Maheu through his guards that he was leaving for Nassau; but he did not. All he had to do was put down Maheu's reaction in charging kidnap and control to a natural loyalty, and be touched by it; that was not his nature. All he had to do was be man enough to tell Maheu in a memorandum why he was getting rid of him, how he objected to his charges against Davis and Gay, and give him a chance to speak for himself. That he was not man enough to do. He was at his worst in the memorandum; and Maheu loyally omitted any mention of it when he came to write his memoirs.

The truth is that Hughes betrayed his best friend; the man who had stood faithfully beside him against a dozen betrayers.

## CHAPTER SEVENTEEN

# From Nassau to Watergate

By now, it was merely a technicality that Hughes would fire Maheu; but Hughes was disturbed by news that reached him from his Las Vegas associates. He had wanted Davis and Gay to fly to Nassau at once, but instead they were locked in a battle with Maheu, who wouldn't give up. They again sent, with Intertel armed guards, a bunch of auditors to the casino cashiers' cages in a second, ill-fated effort to seize records that would "prove" Maheu's imaginary wrongdoings. Maheu had a restraining court order issued preventing them from doing anything of the kind.

Governor Paul Laxalt supported Maheu. He mistrusted the Mormons and wanted to get authorization from Hughes before he would recognize the Davis-Gay takeover. At 5:00 A.M. on December 1, Hughes called Laxalt long distance, dragging him from a meeting at the Sands Hotel, and lied to him that he had merely gone on a vacation and meant to spend the rest of his life in Las Vegas. He confirmed Maheu's dismissal and said that Chester Davis and Bill Gay were in charge from now on. There was nothing in his tone of voice or specific, clear-cut statements to indicate that he was being told if he didn't speak, his bodyguards would deprive him of drugs—as Maheu feared. Hughes was again acting of his own free will, treacherously, and with a rare degree of decisiveness.

Maheu wouldn't give in. Unable to believe (he still can't) that Hughes personally executed him, he was sure Hughes had been coerced into everything. Davis had Maheu prevented by court order from any dealings with Hughes properties. This Hughes approved.

Despite the fact that he had planned Hughes's departure for Nassau for months during the year before, Maheu was still convinced Hughes had been kidnapped. He put his son Peter in charge of investigating the matter. Peter hired Investigators Inc., of Miami, to invade the Britannia Beach Hotel and find out if Hughes was being held against his will. To monitor the team, Peter Maheu flew to Florida; with him went Doug Priest, skipper of Maheu's yacht *Alouette II.* If Hughes were indeed a kidnap victim, Priest would effect a James Bondish sea rescue, carrying Hughes by charter boat to Florida.

Intertel's Robert D. Peloquin was determined to stop this. He got wind of it and alerted the FBI. He asserted that the use of bugging devices in the Bahamas was illegal. Peter Maheu had been told that it wasn't: Intertel itself was busy with monitors there. Peloquin was going on the shaky ground that exporting bugs from American to British territory was against the law. Actually, the spy team could pick up devices in the islands.

As it turned out, the operation was abortive and more than a touch ill-advised. After unsuccessfully trying to monitor Hughes's suite from the rooms below, they had a transistorized transmitter hidden in a chafing dish on Hughes's (afternoon) breakfast tray. The transmitter failed to pick up anything except munching. Not a word of anyone's conversation was recorded.

Robert Maheu began talking of Hughes's signature on the power of attorney to Gay and Davis being forged, even though Hughes had told Laxalt it was not. Nevada District Court Judge Howard Babcock ruled against Maheu. Gay proceeded against him, surgically removing every person in the Hughes empire's top echelons who might support him.

Chester Davis pulled a string with President Nixon and an IRS agent arrived at Maheu's house with an announcement of an audit. ("Nixon had instructed the IRS people to sink their teeth in my hide," Maheu says today.) The IRS charged that Maheu's liability was $3.5 million, despite the fact that he had paid his taxes and that he hadn't earned a million a year, in fact, just $500,000. It took him fifteen years of struggle before he was in the clear.

On New Year's Eve, Maheu filed a $50 million suit against Hughes Tool for breach of contract.

That same evening, just as he was preparing to celebrate the holiday, Bill Gay sent Intertel agents to his door to evict him from his house; the land had been bought by Hughes from gangster Moe Dalitz. Within a week, Maheu was out on the street. Luckily, he was able to scrape up enough cash to buy another house.

Gay continued his campaign. He seized Maheu's Balboa Bay Club penthouse, his yacht, the *Alouette II,* everything he owned except the clothes he wore. The private de Havilland airplane he customarily used was locked up in its hangar by chief pilot Bob Wearley.

Hughes became irritable at the continuing fuss over Maheu. In a memorandum to Davis and Gay, he said he could not understand why the Maheu problem had not been put to rest and why there was still so much negative publicity. After all, Hughes had called Nevada's governor and district attorney to enlist their help to end the problem. And the duly constituted board of directors of Hughes Tool Company had arrived at the decision to terminate Maheu for reasons they thought were fair.

Written in immaculate handwriting on his usual ruled yellow stationery, the note was not that of a madman under drug control. When *Life* magazine asked handwriting expert Alfred Kanfer to analyze it, he observed that the writing showed not one superfluous stroke; that the writer had an imaginative mind which worked fast and was capable of swift changes and improvisations; that he was anxious not to waste any time; that his was a lively and sane personality.

Even Hughes could be capable of twinges of memory and regret. On January 19, 1971, he sent a telegram to his beloved Aunt Annette, whom he had for so many years ignored, or even shunned, never responding to her letters, wishing her very warm eightieth-birthday greetings.

If further proof were needed that Hughes was not mentally disturbed at the time, this telegram provides it.

The Gay-Davis faction had their hands full those first few months of 1971. They were grappling with the continuing matter of Hughes's tax evasion in the CIA–Hughes Aircraft–Medical Institute scam. Robert Foster Bennett, Hughes's Washington-CIA front man, used as an argument to the White House's legal adviser, John Dean, that Hughes Aircraft, as a supplier of strategic materials, including surveillance devices against Russia and Cuba, would be in trouble if it had to drain off cash to pay taxes on the Medical Institute. Bennett suggested that the newly onerous tax laws should not be too firmly exercised in the matter of the Institute. Bearing in mind Hughes's support of Nixon and the CIA deals, Hughes's cause was pressed with the IRS. As a result, Hughes was left off the hook; the scam continued. Throughout the years until Hughes's death, the Medical Institute still paid no taxes, and of the thousands of millions earned by Hughes Aircraft in government contracts, less than 0.4 percent a year now flowed into the Institute operations, just 0.2 percent more than before. By 1970, the CIA contracts were earning Hughes half a billion dollars a year.

Hughes was no more comfortable in the Britannia Beach suite than he had been in Las Vegas. For several years, he had been using a Barcalounger, a reclining chair with a retractable back that gave him some relief from the pain of body sores and an uncomfortably twisted spine; but when he got to Nassau, the Barcalounger no longer felt bearable. Instead, he had his old, self-designed hospital bed flown in, not used since he left the house in Bel Air, and he gained some small satisfaction from being able to raise and lower it, and from using the complicated piping he had once designed for it to allow his urine to trickle into a bowl without his getting up.

Small comfort indeed; not only was he still constipated from codeine mainlining, but his kidneys were so affected by misuse now that they couldn't function properly, and for hours, plagued by prostate problems, he would try unsuccessfully to urinate. When he did, the urine was preserved in yet another series of Mason jars. Still afraid that the sinking of the poison gas–laden Liberty ship 150 miles off the Bahamian shore might have affected the local water supply, which, in fact, was not desalinated from seawater but drawn from plentiful seasonal rain, he had a store of Poland Water flown in daily from Maine; he was so suspicious that it might be interfered with that, on more than one occasion, he hobbled over to inspect the quart-sized bottles, which were the only size he would tolerate, and examined the caps to make sure they were firmly sealed.

The presence of a population of blacks made him excessively nervous: could the milk be poisoned; were the cows dangerous? He had fresh milk flown in every day from Miami until at last a Nassau market was found that provided sealed American milk bottles. He would not have any black messenger deliver bottles to the suite, nor would he accept milk from the kitchen in a glass or in a carafe.

He was still obsessed with seeing movies; he would awaken at unpredictable times of night and the aides would lift him from his bed into a chair, where he would watch any one of dozens of pictures that had been rented from American exchanges and flown in. He would occasionally break off a movie to nibble some chicken and then nod off, wake up, and continue the same picture; if he liked it, he would run it many times.

He dreamed of getting out of the room and finding a new home on a yacht, where he would be tax-free; he might even sail up and down the Mediterranean. But Howard Eckersley and the other aides warned him that he might be vulnerable to possible danger in such a vessel. He sighed and gave up the idea.

Much of his activity was having his aides count his drug pills and measure his injections, move his pillows around, and make sure he had the correct kind of chicken and napoleon cakes he ate all day long.

In August, the recently appointed Governor Mike O'Callaghan, who had taken over Paul Laxalt's office in Las Vegas, was equally skeptical of Bill Gay's control of Hughes's operation of seven casinos and 8,000 employees, the largest gambling operation in the state, and questioned whether Hughes had authorized the appointment. Until he received a signed and fingerprinted, notarized document from Hughes, neither he nor the gaming commission would authorize Gay or Chester Davis to continue.

A letter was quickly forthcoming, typewritten, and taken to O'Callaghan in person by two of Hughes's doctors and Intertel's Jim Golden. O'Callaghan rejected it as not being fingerprinted. A second, properly fingerprinted letter in longhand arrived on September 9, and was delivered to Jack Diehl, gaming commission head, who said he still wasn't satisfied that it was not coerced. Like the first, it was on Hughes's yellow ruled stationery. An irritable footnote, scribbled by Hughes, read, "In this machine age, it seems a little odd to be asked [to write] a letter of this length in longhand." This was absurd; Hughes always wrote in longhand and the letter was only five paragraphs long.

The new letter, Diehl said, "might be genuine," but declared he would have to meet with Hughes to confirm that it was.

Exactly how Hughes heard about this next extraordinary matter, which was to vex him for several months, is unclear from the log kept by his aides. The log, which has deceived many chroniclers, was never complete; no word of it, except on very rare occasions, dealt with Hughes's telephone calls, as many as fifteen to twenty a day, to Chester Davis, Bill Gay, or Nadine Henley, or other officers of the Romaine Street headquarters in Hollywood. One of his worst nightmares had come true: a book purporting to be of his authorship, and telling the complete story of his life, was about to be published. And not by some fly-by-night publisher, but by the distinguished firm of McGraw-Hill, whose textbook list was among the most important in the nation. The book had, appropriately enough, been put together by a novelist, Clifford Irving, and contained lengthy transcribed "interviews" with Hughes; an "authorization" to publish had been "signed" by Hughes; the book contained his own "personally written" preface.

Since neither Davis nor Gay had actually met Hughes, they may have had qualms about his having talked to Irving without their knowledge. Hughes, at once, disabused them of that idea.

While Hughes pondered what action to take to quash the hoax autobiography, he suffered from new shocks. Author R. B. Eaton, who also claimed to have spoken to him, would soon bring out a second memoir by him. It would be serialized in the February issue of *Ladies' Home Journal* and published by Best Books. Yet a third book was threatened: Noah Dietrich had put together, with the journalist Jim Phelan (later to be replaced by Bob Thomas), a memoir that Hughes feared might be damaging to him. How could he suppress these volumes?

Hughes had no alternative: he would have to break fourteen years of silence and speak to a reporter. Richard Hannah, long his trusted public relations man at Carl Byoir Associates in Manhattan, cast around for a writer of whom Hughes might approve. He settled on Frank McCulloch, widely admired *Time* New York bureau chief, who had followed Hughes's adventures and misadventures for years. *Time-Life* owned the serialization rights to the Clifford Irving book. Hughes agreed to speak with him.

The telephone interview took place on December 16. Hughes

said he had never met Irving; that checks made out in his name were being cashed at a Swiss bank; that he would prosecute Irving for fraud to "the fullest extent of the law." McCulloch was impressed; but he knew how mercurial and capricious Hughes could be, and he had to bear in mind the fortune his employers at *Time-Life* had invested in the book. After questioning Irving on points of detail in the memoir, McCulloch decided Irving was telling the truth and Hughes was lying. Hughes was furious.

Hughes called Chester Davis every day, determined to track down through Intertel the hundreds of thousands of dollars that had been deposited in the Zurich bank in the name "H. R. Hughes" and on which the Internal Revenue Service was already threatening to tax him. It was his worst thought: he would be paying tax on money he had never received. At the same time, he, through Davis and Richard Hannah, kept up a further battery of denials of the book's authenticity, which only provoked McGraw-Hill to stand firmer behind their author. Best Books, the small firm which was to publish the Eaton book, and *Ladies' Home Journal* refused to be shaken by his threats, and so did Dietrich's publishers.

By the first week of 1972, Intertel had come up with no more than circumstantial evidence of Irving's fraud. Hughes would have to make a further denial in no less than a full-scale press conference. Richard Hannah set up a telephone conversation on January 7, exactly one month after the scandal broke, with seven journalists who had spoken to Hughes in the past. With NBC's Roy Neal as moderator, the seven men, who included Gladwin Hill of the *The New York Times,* Wayne Thomas of the *Chicago Tribune,* and Marvin Miles of the *Los Angeles Times,* assembled at the Universal-Sheraton Hotel in North Hollywood. Hughes chatted with them for almost three hours. From the moment they heard this high-pitched, hectoring, challenging, and plaintive Texan's voice, they knew it was him, but they pressed ahead anyway.

He began by discussing Nassau in guidebook detail; in a nostalgic reference to the days when he was partner of Swedish Axel Wenner-Gren, he mentioned that Paradise Island had once been called Hog Island.

He gave details of the Lockheed Constellation, claiming contributions to its design which had, in fact, been made by others. He discussed his second plane, the H-2, giving scant credit to his co-designers. Instead of being asked about some of those associates he would have remembered, for example, Glenn Odekirk, Lincoln Quarberg, Howard Hawks, or RKO sound expert Gordon Sawyer, he was questioned about obscure figures like "a pilot whose last name was Martin," and an "Avco executive" who had helped him with the FAA when he planned his pioneer flights in 1937. Why would he remember either one? He could not. Or why would he necessarily recall (he didn't) that Mrs. Wiley Post put a stick of chewing gum on the tail of the Lockheed when he was about to fly from Floyd Bennett Field, New York, to Paris? Wouldn't it have been better to have asked him what the name Wiley Post meant to him? Or of all the generals and other brass he had put on his payroll, why would he recall a General H. L. George?

He told lie after lie: that he was in fairly good shape; that his nails were not long; that he had no fear of contagion; that he intended meeting the press face-to-face; that Maheu was "a dishonest son of a bitch who stole me blind"; and, the biggest whopper of all, that he had poured untold millions into the Medical Institute for the benefit of humanity.

The interview made broadcasting history and became an international sensation. So Hughes had proven the Irving book was a fake! The richest man on earth had broken his oath of silence, as complete as a Trappist monk's, to denounce an obscure writer. Then questions were asked: Why hadn't he denounced R. B. Eaton? Or Noah Dietrich?

McGraw-Hill, *Time-Life,* and Clifford Irving stuck to their guns and accused Hughes of lying in his telephone press conference. For once, Hughes stumbled; he should have filed suit against all three for libel. Instead, Robert Maheu sued him for slander. The turmoil continued.

Now Irving dropped a new bombshell: he announced that the "autobiography" would have Hughes discussing the $205,000 bribe to Donald Nixon. How had he found out about this? Chester Davis began to wonder if Irving hadn't talked to Hughes, after all. He called Hughes, who furiously berated him.

The explanation was simple: Irving had obtained the story from files at *Time* and its associate, *Fortune* magazine—material which neither magazine had dared to publish. On January 15, McGraw-Hill president A. P. Leventhal reasserted the Irving manuscript's value and charged that Hughes had pretended Irving was lying because he revealed much in his memoir that would damage

Hughes's business interests. Leventhal stated he had a "signed indemnification" from Hughes, clearing his firm of any possible dangers of a libel suit.

On January 16, Irving went on Mike Wallace's CBS program *60 Minutes* and made the libelous statement that Clark Clifford, the most important of Hughes's Washington attorneys, had arranged the cash loan to Nixon. Irving told Wallace that he and his associate Richard Susskind had met with Hughes "in several places, including Mexico."

Next day, the Swiss Credit Bank in Zurich revealed that the "H. R. Hughes" who had opened an account there with McGraw-Hill money was a good-looking blonde using a forged Swiss passport. She was Mrs. Clifford Irving. The Zurich canton police issued a warrant for her arrest. The Irvings fled to New York. Even as they did so, R. A. Graves of *Life* magazine published a story reaffirming the editors' belief that the Irving book was "authentic." Then suddenly *Time-Life* weakened, saying that "disgruntled" Hughes employees "had passed on information to Irving and that he might have been duped."

Warrants were issued in Switzerland for the Irvings' arrest; the IRS filed tax liens against them; they refused to testify, invoking the Fifth Amendment, before the New York grand jury. A. P. Leventhal of McGraw-Hill flew to Nassau to attempt to reach Hughes, but failed.

Hughes and his aides were so distracted by these events that they forgot to renew his eight-month visitors' permit in Nassau. In view of his wealth, power, and investments in the region, that would not have been important, nor would the fact that those aides, none of whom worked for anyone except him, had no permits. In fact, for the more than a year that Hughes had been in Paradise Island, nobody had raised so much as a whisper over the permits.

Now, suddenly, the government began to make noises over Hughes's stay, making him seem unwelcome. Why? The truth is that the Black Nationalist opposition party had begun to turn the matter into a scandal; that they threatened to topple the prime minister, Lynden O. Pindling, at the next election, because he was harboring an illegal group of immigrants working for a boss who wouldn't hire blacks. Furthermore, certain government representatives were demanding, and getting, bribes to allow Hughes to remain, and he cut off the bribes. There was more to it; the left-wing liberal elements in

Nassau had picked up on the grapevine that Hughes was about to link up in a commercial and political partnership with the Nicaraguan dictator, Anastasio Somoza.

Somoza had played a crucial role in the continuing secret war against Cuba that followed the agreements after the Missile Crisis, agreements breached by both sides. Through the Banco Internacional in Mexico City and the Hughes account there, he had strong connections, via laundered money, to the CIA, and to the Hughes empire. His late brother, Luis, and his brother's family had linked up with Hughes associate E. Howard Hunt in "business deals" that were covers for anti-Castro activities. During the Eisenhower administration, he had become a direct instrument of American policy in Central America, and had given unlimited help to John F. Kennedy for the Bay of Pigs invasion as well as arresting Cuban guerrillas sent to Nicaragua by fishing boat.

He built an airport at Puerto Cabezas, code-named Happy Valley, and assembled men, aircraft, and ships. He flew to New York to meet with the president's father, Joseph Kennedy, and to Washington, D.C., for the inauguration, where he met with Allen Dulles, CIA director. As a result of the meeting, 1,300 trained Cuban exile troops arrived by plane at Happy Valley, as well as seventeen B-26s, bombs, and rockets. The cumbersome invasion force was notoriously wrecked because the U.S. supplied insufficient jet fighter cover. By Christmas, a defeated and humiliated President Kennedy had had to pay $2,925,000 and $28 million worth of Caterpillar tractors for the 1,100 Cuban and American prisoners, who had been tortured.

Now, in 1972, Somoza, with Hughes's specific approval, was dreaming of another attack. He was involved with Hughes Aircraft in intercepting Cuban-Russian efforts to retrieve photo cassettes parachuted to the earth from Hughes spy satellites. These cassettes, with vital information on Cuban installations, were often caught by Cuban agents in disguise as fishermen off the Nicaraguan Atlantic coast; one dropping place was the Corn Islands, in which Hughes had a special interest, envisaging them (Somoza's friends confirm today) as CIA posts similar to Sal Cay in the Bahamas.

Aware of the buildup of Russian arms in Cuba, some of this information obtained by Hughes's spy satellites, the U.S. State Department decided it would be a good idea to have Somoza invite Hughes to come to Nicaragua, make colossal deals with him, offer him sanctuary from the constant flow of subpoenas and threats and invasive reporters that plagued him, give him lifelong freedom from income tax, and make him, in return for the sums he would pour into Somoza's pocket, joint owner of Nicaragua.

There was another connection—U.S. ambassador to Nicaragua Turner Shelton. Shelton had met Howard Hughes before, in Hollywood, in the early 1950s, when he had been an executive at Eagle-Lion, which Hughes had discussed buying. Just before Hughes arrived in Nassau, Shelton had been U.S. consul general in the Bahamas; he had extended the invitation to Hughes to go there as early as December, 1969. Shelton was associated with Bebe Rebozo, E. Howard Hunt, and the Cubans in exile, and Intertel—hence a contact with Jim Golden. His appointment to Managua was a result of his friendship with Nixon and of his importance to the CIA. He was not only concerned to maintain anti-Castro activities in Nicaragua but needed Hughes to become involved in a massive project: nothing less than a revival of the old pipe dream of a trans-isthmus Nicaraguan Canal, which would provide a rival for the Panama Canal.

Hughes began discussions in Nassau on the matter of building the Canal; in partnership with him would be the Bahamian resident and friend of Shelton, the enormously wealthy Daniel K. Ludwig, and (despite Hughes's anti-Semitism) the banking family of the Rothschilds.

In addition, Somoza wanted to augment his personally-owned Lanica Airlines with two Convair 880 jets which Hughes had at an Arizona airfield, and which Jack Real, an important executive at Lockheed and an old friend of both Hughes and Somoza, had told the Nicaraguan dictator about.

Somoza finally put pressure on Real: he would buy the Convairs, hand Hughes a substantial, even a 30 percent, share in Lanica in return, if Real could deliver Hughes to him as his widely publicized guest as well as his future partner. Somoza, under local and international criticism for what was widely understood to be a mercilessly repressive dictatorship, needed a trump card to deliver against his enemies. Hughes, the great American hero and round-the-world flyer, would be that trump card. But Hughes kept dragging his feet, procrastinating endlessly. Real needed to seduce him to a final and irrevocable decision. He pulled a woman out of his sleeve.

He went to lunch with Chester Davis in New York and told him that there was a regular habitué of the Cave nightclub in Managua, Nicaragua, who was not only available but had a forty-four-inch bosom. Davis exclaimed, with his customary vulgarity, startling the diners at the next tables, "But Miss Chile is a forty-six!" Miss Chile wasn't available; the Cave girl was. That settled it: Davis called Hughes and told him what awaited him. Long since devoid of sex drive for anyone, Hughes apparently felt a need to at least seem to be a man. He announced he would go to Managua.

Hughes decided he would make the move as soon as possible. Managua was tax-free. Reckless as ever, he never considered that the region was as dangerous as explosion-threatened Las Vegas or poison gas–threatened Nassau. In 1931, Managua had been destroyed by an earthquake; it could be destroyed again. It was presently ravaged by a polio epidemic—and there was leprosy in the city. Cholera, typhoid, yellow fever—all were present.

Yet greed, the Cave girl, and the thought that he would be serving CIA anti-Communist activities in Central America drove Hughes to accept Somoza's invitation in February.

He had already, as early as 1969, cofinanced with Somoza the first Hughes Intertel satellite used in Nicaragua, which supplied excellent communications and was obtained through the communications company Telumundo. He backed the CIA's military activities in Managua coordinated by E. Howard Hunt, with whom, as we know, he had been associated in lasers, and he funneled money through the Managua banks for the CIA, a fact criticized severely in the pages of the Nicaraguan liberal newspaper, *La Prensa,* by its vigorous editor and publisher, Pedro Joaquin Chamorro.

Nicaragua was, thanks to being a dictatorship, one of the handful of Latin American countries with almost no Communists—no more than sixty men could be counted as such, all Sandinistas. Its currency, the cordoba, was sturdy; Somoza, who owned the country, ploughed his money back into the economy.

Hughes fancied buying, with Daniel Ludwig, a share in Somoza's shipping company, the Mamenic Line, and in the Managua hotel, the Intercontinental. He ordered Nadine Henley to fashion for Somoza a solid gold copy of the 1969 Nicaraguan satellite and the sixty-seven-foot transmitter that went with it.

In an undated memorandum to Chester Davis, written from Nassau, Hughes worried that Somoza would withdraw his support because of the bad publicity. Hughes thought that giving Somoza a fancy car would be a good way to express appreciation.

Soon after he penned the memorandum on February 15, 1972,

immigration and U.S. postal officers (the latter armed with several subpoenas relating to several lawsuits) marched out of the elevator at the Britannia Beach Hotel and banged on the door of Hughes's penthouse, demanding admission. Johnny Holmes and three other aides stalled the officials while Jim Golden of Intertel arranged a sixth-floor room for Hughes. They flew into Managua to make the arrangements for Hughes's immediate flight there.

Hughes aide Gordon Margulis will never forget the following hours. It was three in the afternoon when, with the immigration people blocking the elevator doors and inside exits, Golden had Margulis and two other aides carry Hughes by stretcher down the outside metal fire escape.

Margulis settled Hughes into the room where the maids kept their trolleys and went out to case the corridor outside. He ran into a friend from New York; he managed to edge the friend back into his suite, then began clowning with the maids, putting up a bed sheet he found and dancing with it as a shield while the other attendant wheeled Hughes in. Fretful, childish, Hughes was no sooner in the room than he asked to see a movie. Knowing the noise would attract attention from the neighbors, not to mention having to carry a film print downstairs, Margulis told his petulant boss that wasn't possible. Instead, Margulis unscrewed the brass bedknob and held it in his fist in case some official should walk in. Then he could knock the man out.

When darkness fell, they returned to the penthouse unobserved. Margulis produced a print of *Topaz*, of all things, a Hitchcock picture about an attempted murder of Castro that mirrored Maheu's Hughes-authorized attempted killing of several years earlier. Meanwhile, Jim Golden led the immigration and post-office people on a wild goose chase to the Emerald Beach Hotel.

Hughes left the hotel at 5:50 A.M., again by fire escape. Golden had decided it would be too risky for him to go to the airport where officials were likely to intercept him; any appearance of a private aircraft would instantly alert the government. Instead, Golden chartered a yacht, the *Cygnus*, captained by skipper Bob Rehak, to sail to Florida. Hughes was carried into the pilot house, where Golden and Margulis straightened him up. He stood, his robe falling open, showing his feeble naked body.

He boarded the *Cygnus* unsteadily at 6:45 P.M. He slept fitfully on his bunk for just over three hours until he woke in a heavy swell.

Feeling sick, he asked for Dramamine; Margulis lay on the cabin floor groaning and Hughes said, "It's dirty there. Get up!" Margulis did. Taking more Dramamine, then sleeping again, Hughes arrived, at one of his houses, in Miami, at 4:00 A.M. He was taken by van to the Fort Lauderdale airfield, where Jim Golden had chartered, not one of his own planes, but an Eastern Airlines chairman's jet. He was at his most irritable as the aides drove him to the airfield. "Where the fuck is the goddamned plane?" he kept asking. "It can't be that far!" He was quite active on the plane, enjoying a turkey sandwich and a glass of milk.

Despite pleas to Ambassador Turner Shelton in two long-distance calls from Fort Lauderdale, Golden had been unable to persuade Shelton to delay Somoza's already scheduled private visit to Panama, which was under his control. As a result, when Hughes's plane arrived at the Las Mercedes airport in Managua, Somoza had already left.

Driven in a Mercedes with an official police escort to the Inca-pyramid–shaped Intercontinental Hotel in Managua at 10:45 P.M. on February 16, Hughes saw an extraordinary landscape. The horizon was disfigured by squat, ugly volcanoes. Cloaked in suffocating heat and the fumes of automobiles, lit by a yellow moon, the sprawling, jerry-built city of featureless adobe and plaster structures was situated on the south side of a volcanic lake, sulphurous and crammed with decades of filthy sewage, trembling constantly as three adjoining faults, forming a sinister T-formation, threatened at any moment to give way under it.

His arrival at the hotel caused a commotion. As his aides moved him through the sparsely populated lobby, a man jumped forward and took flash photographs. Hughes shrank back and Margulis grabbed the man, pulled the film from the camera, and flung it to the floor. Two national guardsmen seized the intruder, who was only a tourist. Hughes had to be carried into a passenger elevator through the lobby since the service lift was out of order. Once in the suite, he relaxed, less exhausted than his worn-out aides, briskly asking for a chicken sandwich and milk.

Cutting off the eighth floor from access, Hughes's aides and the Intertel team threw out the hotel's elevator system, so that guests arrived on the wrong floors. One group of women was stranded between the first and second floors of the hotel and was trapped for over an hour. A guest inadvertently wandered onto the eighth floor and was met by armed guards and told to leave at once. The hotel guests were in a hubbub for days over Hughes's presence; there was no way of suppressing local interest in it, or holding off people attempting to take photographs through his windows from outside.

Even before he left Nassau, Hughes had, according to Gordon Liddy of Watergate fame and Hank Greenspun, publisher of the *Las Vegas Sun,* approved a venture that was a rehearsal for Watergate. This was a burglary of Greenspun's office safe, which contained the memoranda in which Hughes instructed Maheu in the Bebe Rebozo affair. He would supply an escape JetStar airplane to Managua after the job was done.

Hughes used as his instrument Robert Foster Bennett, his continuing public relations–CIA employee in Washington, Ralph Winte, his security chief in Las Vegas, and E. Howard Hunt. Hunt was now on Bennett's staff at the Mullen Company in Washington, working secretly for Hughes.

In an interview in *The New York Times* with Tom Buckley, dated May 13, 1973, Hank Greenspun said:

Hughes would give anything to get his hands on his own documents. That's why a Hughes plane was involved and . . . its destination was to be a Latin-American country. Hughes was in Nicaragua at the time of the attempted break-in.

He added:

If in fact the forces of the Federal Government were employed to serve the private enterprise of Howard Hughes then I am completely disillusioned by the thought that they may have turned over to a massive political contributor.

There was another reason for the proposed break-in of Greenspun's safe. Howard Hunt, his associate Gordon Liddy, and the White House "Plumbers" team, including spy Jim McCord, wanted to obtain information damaging to Democratic presidential candidate Edmund Muskie that was believed to be in the safe. What was it? The official view has been that the worst Greenspun had on Muskie was a record of a fish-poaching fine. But there were also rumors of a connection to an influential mill company in Maine, and, far more important, an unbased belief that Muskie was in receipt of funds from Castro. Greenspun had nothing of the kind in the safe; he had moved Hughes's papers to his house; even if the burglars had broken in, they would have found nothing more interesting than they were to find later at Watergate.

In his memoirs *A Piece of Tape*, Jim McCord, whom Hughes offered a job after the caper was done, wrote of his strong suspicion that Hughes was very much involved in the Las Vegas break-in; that he was protected from questioning by the Watergate grand jury later on by the fact that he was a billionaire.

There is no direct evidence that the CIA, any more than the president, was privy to plans for the burglary, though both gave their covert blessing to anything that would bring down the Democrats.

Mrs. Greenspun says that, despite statements to the contrary, the burglars did try to break into her husband's office and took down the doors, but the safe, though peeled, proved impregnable and the plans were terminated. According to Liddy, Hughes canceled the plane to Managua at the last minute, because he feared that the people he had hired would not be loyal to him and would leak the documents to the government.

On February 17, Hughes dictated a memorandum to Somoza; he had oddly forgotten that Somoza was in Panama—or it may be that Golden, nervous about the slip-up of arrangements due to Hughes's unannounced arrival, hadn't told him. He addressed the letter to the Casa Presidente, expressing his delight at Somoza's desire to have him as a guest.

Hughes was kept informed daily of progress in the Irving matter. The logs kept by his aides again omitted any mention of his countless phone conversations.

That week, he had Chester Davis issue an injunction stopping a firm named Flame Enterprises of New York from selling T-shirts and sweaters with his face on them, the buttons supplying, in tiny print, a comical account of the Irving fracas. People Pants and Bikini Boutique were prevented from selling underwear with his face on the crotches.

On February 22, Chester Davis, with Hughes's authorization, made an announcement. Hughes employees would prepare materials towards his authorized biography; Rosemont Enterprises, the organization set up exclusively to handle the matter of books Hughes might commission, would locate a suitable author.

Hughes's secretary, Nadine Henley, and one of his executives,

Kay Glenn, flew to Managua. Henley discussed with him this sancti-
fied, authorized book that would present an image to the world of a
dedicated, self-sacrificing philanthropist, whose Medical Institute
was the savior of the sick. Neither Henley or Glenn had seen him in
thirteen years.

They met in Hughes's suite. The bedroom was dimly lit; Hughes
was lying down on a bed, either asleep or playing possum, which he
often did. Without saying hello or greeting Hughes in a friendly
spirit, Miss Henley raised the matter of the book. Could she record
him for his memoirs? Hughes sleepily responded that she could not.

He must have known that a saintly chronicle would deceive
nobody, while an autobiography concentrating solely on technical
achievements would sell only to his employees. She pressed on with
the determination that marked her long career as a Hughes survi-
vor—would he allow her to use longhand? He most certainly would
not. She didn't return empty-handed. She made land deals for
Hughes in Nicaragua.

A Hughes-approved suit was filed that month in Delaware chan-
cery court against Fawcett Books, demanding all and any profits
from the Noah Dietrich book, charging that Dietrich had promised
in signed documents, starting in 1959, that he would not disclose
any information about Hughes. Dietrich and Ted Carpentier told this
author that Hughes called Davis in Washington to go ahead with the
case.

Dietrich responded that he never considered the agreement
binding, whatever that might mean. In fact, it was; Hughes would
have had it no other way. Dietrich's book was published. Hughes
ordered Rosemont to find a publisher for another book about the
perpetration of the Irving hoax. This didn't happen; meantime, nine
publishers began fighting for the right to publish Irving's own account of the affair—even before he had been found guilty by a court
of law. He held off. Random House tried to sign A. P. Leventhal,
president of McGraw-Hill, to write a memoir of the hoax, but this
was beaten by the London Sunday *Times* and Viking Press, which
commissioned the "Insight" team of Stephen Fay, Lewis Chester,
and Magnus Linklater to pull a book and serialization together in a
matter of weeks. A frail cry of "bad taste" from outstripped publishers convinced nobody.

On March 6, Irving finally appeared before the grand jury; four
days later Hughes received the news that the author was indicted on

criminal charges. The fraud had cost McGraw-Hill almost one million dollars in typesetting, advances, and legal fees.

Hughes was kept busy talking to Somoza on the phone, wiring or calling Davis; he hadn't been so stimulated in years.

In the short time he had been in Nicaragua, Hughes had grown to love it. He would soon have unlimited financial opportunities; the dictatorship ensured protection for his wealth; his aides were given secret police status and could use police cars. He called Chester Davis constantly in New York or Washington, by satellite, happy to be on top of things; Gordon Margulis had never seen him so contented. He hailed Turner Shelton and Somoza with memoranda, many of which have survived. But then he began to falter.

Hughes decided to leave Managua for, of all places, Vancouver, Canada. Why?

The reason was the continuing, blistering attacks on him by his enemy Pedro Joaquin Chamorro, in the pro-Castro newspaper, *La Prensa,* which he could read in Spanish. Chamorro had found out that he was going to stay permanently in Nicaragua; about his proposed share in Lanica Airlines, the Mamenic Line, and the tourist industry, in which, in fact, Hughes did intend to invest. He exposed the fact that Hughes was going to buy the Corn Islands on the Atlantic side of the Isthmus and turn them not into a CIA base but into a gambling paradise like Las Vegas or Paradise Island; several Sandinistas lived there, Indian-British by descent, and they would be brutally flushed out.

Hughes agreed with Somoza that it would be better to leave and come back at different times rather than stay permanently and risk being accused of being coowner of Nicaragua—which might have been true. He also had another purpose: to assist Air West, which he wanted to fly to Canada from Los Angeles and Las Vegas, and to find out where his former associate, John Meier, was hiding. He would return to Managua, he promised Somoza by phone, once he had made the necessary arrangements with the Canadian government.

He had Chester Davis fly in a handsome Grumman Gulfstream II from Miami to take him on his journey. He would have a last-minute meeting with Somoza and Turner Shelton aboard the plane.

The meeting took place on the Grumman at 10:45 P.M., on March 3, 1972. Somoza had returned the same day from a trip to Guatemala, but didn't hesitate to rush, with his armed motorcycle escort, to the plane to keep the appointment. In his pajamas and robe, hair and beard trimmed, Hughes sat with the plump, grinning Somoza and the polished Turner Shelton, showing no fear of contagion, and even shaking hands without a Kleenex.

At the beginning of the conversation, Gordon Margulis recalls, Somoza asked Hughes a question: Why was he such a recluse? Hughes replied that it was because he was tired of getting excessive numbers of phone calls and messages.

Somoza laughed.

Hughes talked with Somoza and Shelton about his knowledge of Nicaragua, gleaned from the maps; about the Canal project; about the investment possibilities he saw in the eastern seaboard, and especially the casinos he dreamed of in the Corn Islands. He flatteringly referred to Somoza's education at West Point; Somoza made equally flattering remarks about Hughes's flight around the world. He gave Hughes a vintage Balboa gold coin. Hughes said he would get out and see more people. He thanked his host for the extent of his hospitality, and the protectiveness of his privacy. The meeting ended a few minutes before midnight and Hughes had the door closed behind his visitors and told the pilot to head for Vancouver.

## CHAPTER EIGHTEEN

# The Cuban Connection

With Hughes on his new adventure were Jim Golden, Johnny Holmes, Gordon Margulis, and several others of his entourage. The plane touched down in Miami and Los Angeles; somehow Hughes evaded the writ servers and IRS men. Kay Glenn had flown to Vancouver to book the twentieth floor of the popular Bayshore Inn, overlooking the spectacular harbor.

Golden recalls that Hughes, for the first time in years, got out of the wheelchair on arrival and, braced by the cool, rainswept air, had enough energy and lack of shyness to walk through the tower lobby. While his entourage filled an elevator, petrified, watching him, he lingered, enjoying their discomfiture, to admire a display of flowers and to exchange greetings with a female guest. When he walked into the suite, instead of hiding in his dark bedroom, he strolled to the windows and gazed at the view of water and boats, a view he hadn't seen since 1942, when he was there with Yvonne De Carlo.

His aides told him he must come away from the window at once; that activists might be spying on him, about to film him with a telephoto lens or possibly kill him. This must have seemed sensible to him; underground groups knew of his twelve years of anti-Castro activities.

The day he settled into womblike darkness, mothered on his

child's diet of chicken and cake, the Nevada court was hearing arguments in Maheu's suit against him. On March 16, Nevada's Governor O'Callaghan and the state gaming board were again insisting that he should meet with them to confirm that Davis and Gay would sit in his place on the boards of the casinos he owned as the largest gambling operator in Nevada. He would have to approve in person Chester Davis's statement that Davis was entitled to a gaming license as Hughes Tool director and head of the gambling empire. The letters he had sent the previous summer were declared insufficient. He sent another. Despite the fact that Davis was unauthorized to do so, that busy lawyer was busy reorganizing the casinos without a license.

A small consolation for the situation in which Hughes might yet have to meet the Nevada governor he feared because he had replaced Laxalt was that the Clifford Irvings were indicted for their hoax. But there was alarming news that a new book, *The Nixon-Hughes Loan*, by N. North-Broome, was about to be published. One V. T. Schaub, whose interest in the matter was never disclosed, filed suit in Los Angeles superior court on May 6 to have it stopped. It wasn't; it contained an exhaustively documented account of Hughes's financial support of Donald Nixon. Four days later, twenty IRS investigators assembled in Las Vegas to investigate Hughes's employees for tax evasion and manipulation of funds.

In April, another embarrassing matter surfaced. Hughes's chief Mormon aide, Howard Eckersley, was charged with issuing a false prospectus in the matter of Pan American Mines, Ltd., of which he was president. It was listed on the Montreal Stock Exchange as having uranium and copper holdings in Arizona.

Howard Hughes's name appeared on the prospectus, and among the shareholders were listed associate aides George Francom and Levar Myler, as well as Kay Glenn of Hughes Tool. On the prospectus's appearance, thousands rushed to buy. The stock boomed from $5 to $12 a share. At the time, according to investigative journalist Jim Phelan, the company only had $15 in the till and Hughes knew nothing about it.

On April 20, following an inquiry, municipal judge Herman Primeau, in Montreal, issued a warrant for Eckersley's arrest. A lawyer, Mortimer Constantine, representing the aggrieved shareholders, stated that unless Eckersley, who had left Vancouver for

Salt Lake City, would return at once, he would be extradited from the United States.

When Royal Canadian Mounted Police arrived at Hughes's penthouse with the warrant, he exploded with rage. When he found other aides were involved, he was hysterical. Eckersley returned to Canada and the warrant was quashed on May 2 by a Montreal municipal court judge. The matter was buried, but Hughes demoted Eckersley and promoted Johnny Holmes to take his place. He was busy working with Holmes on building a hangar at a small airport, for use by his de Havilland private plane; Holmes confirmed in sworn depositions in 1977 that Hughes was very alert and busy at the time, and did succeed in getting approval for routes for his Air West planes to fly to Vancouver from Las Vegas as well as talking for half an hour to an unnamed international news correspondent. His security man, Jim Golden, confirms that Hughes kept in touch with absolutely everything.

When a salesman turned up at his suite dressed as Mickey Mouse, the man was ushered down the stairs at gunpoint. Hughes had a twenty-four-hour watch established through a local security service. He had reason to be worried.

A new Hughes link to E. Howard Hunt and Gordon Liddy emerged that spring. In late February, International Telephone and Telegraph, a CIA-Hughes connected instrument busy backing anti-Communist activities in Chile and other South American countries, paid $400,000 toward a Republican convention in San Diego, according to an ITT lobbyist named Dita Beard, to be let off the hook of an antitrust investigation. When Mrs. Beard's memorandum on the subject appeared in Jack Anderson's syndicated column, she fled to Denver and, suffering from chest pains, checked into a hospital.

Democratic National Chairman Larry O'Brien, who was no longer with Hughes, had much inside information on the bribe; in March, when Hughes was in Vancouver, either he, or Bill Gay on his own, began to panic about that fact. Why? Because of Hughes's dealings with ITT. Intertel, still working for Hughes, was instructed to find a way to disprove Beard's charges by declaring the memo a forgery. On March 13, Bill Gay called Robert Bennett, presumably with Hughes's authorization, and told him that the memorandum was a forgery.

Bennett advised Howard Hunt, who was not supposed to be working on Hughes matters as his employee at Mullen and Company, though, in fact, he was. Hunt reported to Charles Colson, in charge of him at the White House, what Gay had told him. Colson sent Hunt to see Dita Beard; disguised in glasses, a red wig, and a voice changer, Hunt pressed her to the point that the nervous woman said part of the memo—the part damaging to Nixon—was forged.

Based on Hunt's interview with the panic-stricken Mrs. Beard, Bennett took the statement alleging the forgery and published it, under orders from the Hughes executives. The public swallowed the story that it was a fake.

As in the Greenspun affair, Bill Gay, Robert Bennett, and Howard Hunt were working in unison with the White House and for the benefit of Howard Hughes and Nixon.

Soon afterward, Hunt made attempts on presidential candidate George McGovern's offices.

At the same time, according to Gordon Liddy (the most reliable of "inside" chroniclers of Watergate), Hughes personally authorized payment of $50,000 to CRP, the so-called Committee to Re-Elect the President, which Liddy was using to finance burglaries and harassments. The money was paid on his instructions out of Mullen and Company's treasury and made over to Liddy via Liddy's secretary, Sally Harmony. Other monies came from the Rockefellers and via the Mexico City Banco Internacional, used by Hughes and the CIA, Somoza, and Cubans in exile to back anti-Castro operations, and by such Texas backers of CRP as Pennzoil.

Hughes was always fanatical about knowing where his money was going, whether to bribe or coerce, and it is certain, as Liddy makes clear, that he knew Liddy would be using the money for raids on the Democrats. His $50,000 contribution provides strong evidence that Hughes was more than just a bystander of Liddy and Hunt.

By now, Hughes and Nixon had given their teams open and ill-fated agendas to obtain whatever dirt they could on O'Brien, as well as finding out what O'Brien had on them. So many matters needed to be dealt with: how much O'Brien knew about the aborted raid on Hank Greenspun; the Dita Beard/ITT affair; the Hughes-Nixon loans. Neither Hughes nor Nixon wanted to specify how the information would be obtained, and both, later on, were busy with the timeworn practice of asking their inferiors—Hughes, Chester

Davis, Nixon, John Mitchell, Charles Colson and others—what had happened. It was the old American story of heads of giant corporations and heads of state assuming complete ignorance when the policies they had set in motion, but hadn't executed in detail, fell apart.

It was no hardship for Hunt and Liddy to sell Mitchell—who gave a chortling, wave-of-the-hand approval without wanting to know the finer points—on a series of raids on Larry O'Brien's property. These irrepressible soldiers of fortune, in search of money and thrills, were given the run of Mullen and Company's offices, while Robert Bennett turned a blind eye to their activities. Since Hughes was still Bennett's principal client, Chester Davis and other Hughes honchos figured that this would be what he wanted, and they were right. Hunt and Liddy also operated out of the White House, and out of the CRP advertising office in New York known as the November Group.

By now, as documents reveal, Hunt and Liddy's Plumbers operation was an exact copy of Hughes's Intertel, modeled on it with Hughes's approval. "Above" the CIA and the FBI, it was operating on an across-the-board charter to do what it wanted. In the spring, two attempts were made to burgle O'Brien's apartment in Manhattan; doormen deactivated the efforts. A successful raid on his Sheraton Park suite in Washington produced unsatisfactory results. It was time to invade his offices at Watergate, and also the office of Spencer Oliver, son of Hughes's personal Mullen account executive and Washington lobbyist Robert Oliver; Spencer was believed to have a dislike for his father and might be in possession of dangerous information.

Hunt and Liddy were committed to Bernard Barker, a Cuban-American Miami real estate man and burglary specialist and his team of compatriots, who had recently tried to break into McGovern's offices and had raided the files of Daniel Ellsberg's psychiatrist. Hunt, with his long-term involvement in anti-Castro activities, was known to the Cubans in exile as their leader, code name "Eduardo," and indeed brought in the Cuban-American accounts to Mullen. He convinced Barker and his men that the Watergate offices would contain evidence of Castro-Soviet financing of McGovern and the Democrats, but he was also careful to say that since there would be no time to sort documents in the rush and sweat of a burglary, all documents showing contributions were to be stolen and photographed. A crude rogue burglary for Hughes's and Nixon's benefit had been turned into a patriotic mission.

"Hunt told me he was in touch with Hughes throughout the preparations for Watergate," Barker said to me in a 1992 taped interview, the first he had given in years. And he also told me Hunt said there would be a job for him with Hughes after the caper was over. Liddy said a Hughes aircraft would take the burglars by prior arrangement to Nicaragua after the burglary was over; Jack Real says it was one of the fleet of TriStars and others confirm this remarkable fact. Hughes had to authorize any such costly charters. Barker feels to this day that Hughes's involvement, as well as Hunt's, was, like his, strictly to expose Castro's financing of the Democrats.

At the House Committee on Security and Communist Infiltration in 1971, and later in 1973, Dr. Manolo Reyes, a Castro defector and broadcaster in Miami, testified, producing ample documentation, to the wholesale penetration of the United States by Castro-funded spies.

Reyes described agents' piercing American security through the Cuban office at the United Nations building; one spy was caught and deported as an undesirable alien in 1969. Cuban operatives were trained as professors, posing as Nicaraguans or Paraguayans, and were given jobs in colleges to stir up dissent in Hispanic groups, divide Cuban against Cuban, and infiltrate Castroesque ideas. In a nation whose youth had made a hero of Castro's murdered henchman Che Guevara, such efforts found rich soil.

It was an anguished knowledge of this, exacerbated by Cuban penetration into Chile via the Allende regime and by Hunt's lifelong commitment to counterintelligence in this political area, that provoked Barker and his followers.

And now another character entered the scene.

While the plans for Watergate continued, they were discussed not only in Washington, but in Manhattan, at the November Group, the CRP undercover organization in Manhattan. At the time, A. J. Woolstone-Smith, a British Secret Intelligence Service operative with an anti-Republican bias who carried a New Zealand passport and had his own security service in New York, began spying on Gordon Liddy and Howard Hunt at meetings of the November Group. He determined from these meetings not only the details of the proposed Watergate break-in but its purported purpose in finding evidence of Castro penetration of the Democrats. He learned of the attempts being made on the New York apartment of O'Brien and of the burglary of his offices at the Sheraton-Park Hotel in Washington.

He reported the Cuban-American/Hughes/Mitchell/Hunt/Liddy plan to William Haddad, a high-level Democrat and friend of O'Brien.

Haddad wrote to O'Brien, advising him of the matter. O'Brien asked the director of communications for the Democratic National Committee, John Stewart, to see if there was anything in it. Stewart left for New York and conferred at Haddad's office on April 26, 1972, with Haddad and Woolstone-Smith, who repeated his charges, and showed the bugging device he had used on the November Group. Stewart was skeptical; like seemingly everyone from that day to this, the idea of counterintelligence cooperation to investigate Castro funding of the Democrats seemed crazy. But Haddad believed it and began talking to pro-Democrats in the various secret agencies; he forwarded the scoop to columnist Jack Anderson, who dropped the ball.

After two unsuccessful attempts, Barker and his team got into Watergate on Labor Day. It appears that by this time, without Larry O'Brien's knowledge (he was apt to talk too much), certain Democrats in the CIA who hated Nixon (not at the top level) and other Democrats in the police and FBI removed the alarms; they helped members of O'Brien's staff to lay a trap. They shifted documents that might be damaging to Miami. They laid out neat little piles of documents on desks, and others in filing cabinets, for easy photographing by the intruders, who would use bulbs clamped to desks: these documents were mostly harmless interoffice memoranda, bills, schedules, minutes of staff meetings. As a gag, someone filled O'Brien's desk drawers with liquor bottles, which, Barker says, convinced him O'Brien was an alcoholic. Something of the cynicism of the mission's controllers can be shown by the fact that Barker wasn't even told there was a treasurer's office.

They had taken spy Jim McCord along as a "hitchhiker," to bug the telephones. He installed a bug on both O'Brien's and Spencer Oliver's phones; messages would be picked up by the Plumbers across the street.

The following can only be conjecture. But it seems that the anti-Plumber team of Democrats and security men put a small shag rug into an office and made sure that a plant in Barker's operation had the pictures taken against that rug. Later the rug was removed; it was seen in the pictures Barker processed in Miami, thus proving Barker's involvement. It is likely that, to protect O'Brien (Oliver's phone conversations would be largely of voyeuristic interest), the anti-Plumbers removed his McCord bug and replaced it with a faulty one. This maneuver provided a lure: the bug would have to be replaced, once it was found to be faulty, which would bring the burglars back in to be trapped.

The harmless documents served the same purpose: the White House would reject them, forcing the burglars to return.

How did the Democrats know when the second burglary would take place, to spring the trap once and for all? This has been a mystery, but it can now be resolved. An astonishing document, buried in the volumes of the Watergate hearings, has been overlooked. It is a note by Jim McCord to his lawyer, Gerald Alch, written just before he was due to be investigated by the grand jury the following year; he revealed that he knew that Democrat-associated spies had bugged the November Group on June 17, 1972.

So, on the eve of the break-in, the truth was known. And McCord knew it; did he turn double agent for the Democrats, once the truth was leaked to him?

He taped the locks on the doors to the Watergate offices to admit the Plumbers, only to find the tapes removed. He murmured meaninglessly about a mailman's being responsible—a mailman after midnight? Later, during the break-in, he told Barker he had removed the tapes himself. He retaped the locks horizontally so that a child could see the tapes.

The advantage of so obvious a giveaway was that the anti-Plumbers wouldn't have to be present, exposing the Democrat plot. Any guard who wasn't blind would see the horizontal tapes, and a guard did, and trapped the burglars.

Significantly, McCord, in his memoirs *A Piece of Tape*, expressed anger that Hughes's role was not exposed in the subsequent Watergate hearings; he railed that Hughes seemed to be above the law while others were crashing down. Asked for Hughes's role in Watergate, Hunt replied, once more, that it was "deep background" and he wouldn't speak, nor would Gordon Liddy, who failed to return five phone calls. Loyal former Hughes associates, like Robert Maheu, speak of Hughes's knowing of the matter only from television; the aides deny even that. But of the Nixon staff, Charles Colson,

John Dean, Jeb Magruder, and H. R. Haldeman all suspected or knew of Hughes's involvement and plausible denial, and it is obvious on examining "Deep Throat"'s and Robert Bennett's statements to Bob Woodward and Carl Bernstein, authors of *All the President's Men,* that the organization was protecting Hughes.

William Corson, intelligence wars veteran and author of *Widows* and *The Armies of Ignorance,* with manifold connections at high levels in the CIA, says:

> *Of course* Hughes was behind Watergate. In the United States, you tear away the Seventh Veil of Presidents, and there is Big Business.

In June, 1991, portions of the prosecutors' versions of the Nixon White House tapes were released. On these appear conversations between Nixon and Charles Colson, one of those who knew of Hughes's involvement in the Executive Office Building on January 8, 1973. Significantly, Nixon removed all mention of Hughes in his own version.

Nixon said to Colson, "We didn't get a goddamn thing from any of it [the office buggings] that I can see."

Colson replied, "Well, apparently we did, of course, at Watergate, mainly Hughes."

In other words, they retrieved some information from the buggings of Spencer Oliver's phone that illustrated Hughes's funding of Larry O'Brien: the president had caught his fellow conspirator in yet another trap.

Hughes's denial was even more plausible than Nixon's. To the world, he was mad, incommunicado, voiceless. Everyone has overlooked his $18,000 a month subscription to a secret telephone communication system, set up through his own satellites. Like Rudolph Hess in World War II, he was protected by the mirage of his supposed incompetence. He was the black widow—or one of two—who wove the spider web of Watergate.

There followed the operatic drama of cover-up, hearings, and presidential ruin. Nixon's tapes reveal his panic at Hunt's involvement in the burglary. Hunt knew about Nixon's involvement in the attempted killing of Castro by Maheu and his bosses; Hunt knew the texture of secret operations; Hunt was privy to the Cuban-American efforts of counterintelligence; worst of all, Hunt knew of the Hughes-

Nixon and the Hughes-CIA connections. CIA director Richard Helms was equally distressed; the CIA never authorized the break-in. The presidential tapes provide evidence Nixon didn't know of the plans for the burglary, and was horrified at the "rogue" nature of the operation. But he dared not fire Mitchell, Magruder, or anybody else; that would expose too much. And, at first, the media failed to pick up the importance of Watergate; they never picked up the Hughes connection.

When the story did break following arrests in September, and Hughes was in Nicaragua a second time, it was at last leaked that the burglars were after the Hughes-Maheu memoranda on the loans to Donald Nixon/Bebe Rebozo.

The matter of the loans so preoccupied the Watergate Committee that it absorbed much time and money; the purpose was to find something newsworthy to besmirch Nixon with, and in the process, Hunt's and Barker's statements under oath that the memos had nothing to do with the burglary were swept aside. A minority Senate investigation conclusively established the MI-6 leak on the Cuban purpose of the break-in.* But its findings were unpublished and ignored by the committee.

The end result of Watergate was to leave Mitchell, Magruder, Hunt, Liddy, Hughes, and everyone else involved with nothing. No evidence was found that Castro funded the Democrats or that O'Brien had the Nixon loan documents. Once more, Hughes wound up with a fistful of ashes.

Aside from Watergate and the Howard Eckersley affair, Hughes had much to preoccupy him during those months in Vancouver. On April 26, six men were convicted of plotting to conceal their illegal ownership of the Frontier Hotel, Las Vegas, and of being mob fronts and guilty of racketeering and spin-offs at the time the hotel was sold to Hughes. Early in May, a team of eight IRS investigators was in Vegas to investigate possible manipulation of funds and tax dodges by members of the Hughes organization. At the beginning of June, the Canadian immigration authorities became as harsh as the Bahamian: they began to insist that Hughes appear before them to extend his visitor's permit, which would expire in September. Irritated, he announced he might leave for Mexico.

---

*Minority Staff Report, *Investigation of Advance Knowledge of Illegal Political Espionage*, *Senate Select Committee on Presidential Campaign Activities*, 1973.

The IRS of the southwest region undertook a massive survey of the Hughes empire. No less than fifty agents were involved. An office was set up in Las Vegas with a chart that covered almost the entire wall of one room of the district director. John Mitchell, John Dean, and the president were advised of the investigation by the secretary of the treasury.

By August, the IRS had information that the Howard Hughes organization had paid substantial sums to Larry O'Brien and his associates; and the IRS was interested in finding out about these payments.

Hughes decided to sell the Oil Tool Division of the Hughes Tool Company. He was nervous that the final decision in the TWA case would go against him and he would have to find $170 million or more in cash; like that of most wealthy people, his money was tied up in investments that could not be liquidated easily.

He would offer five million shares of common stock of the Oil Tool Division, through a syndicate of investment bankers he had forgiven for opposing him in the past; his former enemy, Merrill Lynch, would handle the transaction as broker. He himself signed a detailed and skillfully worded prospectus of the OTD. He would retain the main Hughes Tool Company as a separate corporation; much against his better judgment, but to avoid confusion, Hughes agreed to Bill Gay's renaming Hughes Tool the Summa Corporation; he was still the sole stockholder and all transactions and activities had to be approved by him and by Chester Davis.

Hughes could obtain some bleak comfort from the fact that McGraw-Hill stock slipped badly as a result of the continuing negativity surrounding the Clifford Irving affair, as Irving, over a million dollars in debt, began to pen his account of his own hoax, *As It Really Happened.* On June 16, the eve of the Watergate break-in, Irving was sentenced to two and a half years in prison and a modest fine of $10,000. Then, on July 25, came some really bad news: Neil S. McCarthy, Hughes's lawyer for many years along with Chester Davis, died; Hughes contacted his lawyers to make sure that nothing dangerous to him would emerge from McCarthy's files. He personally sent the memorandum urging suppression of documents; it was described to this author in 1972.

During his stay in Vancouver, Hughes became interested in resuming his flying career. One of his favorite people still was Jack Real, who had played so crucial a role, with Jim Golden, in his

Nicaraguan connections. Real would often talk to him about flying; Hughes would respond with an enthusiasm he felt for few human beings. Delighted with the Grumman that had brought him to Vancouver from Managua, he talked of obtaining a Grumman flying boat, reminiscent of the aircraft he had flown in with Glenn Odekirk in the 1930s.

During the negotiations, Real got a shock. The lawyer acting as the Grumman go-between reminded Real that Hughes would have to pay Canadian taxes as an owner of aircraft or even just as a resident past six months' stay. Real knew of Hughes's horror of income taxes; he told Hughes of the situation, and Hughes canceled the arrangements for the amphibian.

He decided to leave Vancouver in September; the decision to move was based on the expiration date of his tax-free status, September 12. Another attempt, probably authorized by him, on Greenspun's safe occurred that week. Pilot Bob Wearley, an appointee of General Nigro, flew him and his men in the Hawker Siddeley de Havilland jet to Managua at the end of August. Reinstalled at the Intercontinental Hotel, the guests again shunted out of the eighth floor, Hughes made a deal to sell two Convairs to Somoza in return for 30 percent of Somoza's Lanica Airlines.

Hughes had become extremely irritated by the poor telephone service in Nicaragua. He still subscribed directly to his own Intelsat, the cooperative satellite communication service subscribed to by Somoza since 1969. He placed it in various countries after that, excepting the Bahamas, which did not have it; the cost of this was, as we know, a staggering $18,000 a month. He didn't have the patience to use the telephone system direct, and he used a Hughes Tool scrambler to prevent his conversations from being heard. Records were not detectable by federal agencies. When the switchboard lit up at his various headquarters, or at Chester Davis's office in New York, the staff knew he was on the line by satellite. According to expert Philip Klass, "He would have been better off using a ham radio."

During the next weeks, Wearley flew a shuttle of Hughes executives to Managua to discuss details of the Tool sale with him and to deal with the investments he was planning in offshore mining explorations and the Isthmus Canal. While the nursing logs continued to give the impression he was a movie-obsessed imbecile, and the

Hughes executives seemed anxious to support this impression, he was, in fact, as sharp, bright, and sassy as ever.

By September 26, Hughes had concluded the details of the Oil Tool Division sale. The company was flourishing; in 1971, its sales had increased by $17.5 million to close to $100 million. He was convinced that it was a good time to sell, at $30 a share, but he could not have foreseen the international energy crisis that followed and would double the price of the shares.

The OTD, his father's brainchild, was still manufacturing the drilling bits for which Bo Hughes had found his inspiration in Judge Hughes's kitchen in Keokuk. By now, the OTD was bringing out as many as 400 varieties of the bit; it fielded an army of 180 salesmen to every oil rig in America, as well as emissaries in the Arab countries and other petroleum-producing nations.

That Hughes was involved in the company's affairs is proven by statements by Raymond Holliday, his ToolCo boss man, that Hughes blocked diversification of his company. In an interview with *Fortune* magazine's Rush Loving, Jr., published in December, 1973, Holliday said, "Mr. Hughes felt it was his property and he was diversified enough. Hughes regarded it as his prerogative—and I agree that it was—to make acquisitions, but it worked a hardship on us." Were profits of $100 million a hardship? And what could be more sensible than restricting the operation to what the Hughes Tool people knew best, thus cutting down overhead? Hadn't many companies foundered *because* they had diversified? Holliday confirmed that many Hughes messages came from him through a Telecopier—another detail omitted in those wretched, misleading nursing logs.

On September 26, 1972, two Merrill Lynch executives, Julius Sedlmayr and Courtney Ivey, flew to Nicaragua to confer with him and obtain his signature of authorization for the sale. They had expected to see something of a zombie; instead, Mrs. Sedlmayr, Julius's widow, recalls, "Apart from being kept waiting for hours until around five A.M., my husband found nothing odd about the meeting."

She confirms that Hughes was alert, reasonable, and well-informed; gave a vivid account of the company history and of his father; insisted that $32 might have been a fairer price for the shares; made clear that only the original company was to be sold and not the assets of the presently reconstituted corporation known as

Summa; and was witty as he clearly and firmly signed the contract, saying, "If you have any doubt that this is my signature, check with the handwriting experts who confirmed Irving's documents as genuine! They ought to know!"

At the end of November, Hughes asked Howard Eckersley why Levar Myler and Chester Davis had not made for him further and major (now legal) contributions to Nixon in the 1972 election (despite Watergate, Nixon had been returned to office by a substantial majority). Eckersley sent him a written memorandum on December 1, saying that Hughes's contributions in New York and on the federal level had been extremely effective and timely; that when the polls showed a Republican landslide, contributions had dried up and many committees were out of cash until Hughes made his payments to Eckersley.

Eckersley also confirmed that "We gave as much as we could safely," a significant reassurance in view of the fact that Hughes had exceeded the Federal Campaign Act limit in earlier years. As for Nevada, Hughes had asked if the meeting with Governor O'Callaghan was really necessary? He had decided to meet the governor on the 4th or 5th of December.

Feeling ill, wanting to be at his best, Hughes delayed the meeting several times. O'Callaghan offered several alternative dates—up to December 22.

At thirty minutes past midnight on December 23, Hughes was lying on his bed when suddenly there was a loud, angry roar: the earth groaning. An amplifier, set up to relay the soundtracks of films when he set his hearing aid aside, toppled over and almost fell on him. The room shook alarmingly; all the lights went out. A lamp fell onto Hughes's stomach; he quietly removed it. Typically cool in a crisis, Hughes reassured his aides, as soon as the tremors stopped, that he was fine; he asked in a subdued voice what damage there was and said that the mess of fallen plaster and jumbled furniture should be cleaned up. He suggested staying in place for a few minutes—it would be safer. This was intelligent; his mental state was excellent. He had been through the 1933 earthquake in Los Angeles and remembered that; he had also been through an earthquake in Mexico, in the 1940s.

He dressed in trousers and shirt, had Mell Stewart pick up his drug box, and lay on a stretcher for his traditional exit. Once again, he used a stairwell; but the hotel management had, in contravention of the fire laws, put bundles of mattresses there. The aides had to clear floor after floor before they could reach the lobby and leave with their precious cargo.

They got him to the Mercedes, belonging to Somoza, that had brought him from the airport. As an aftershock rippled through the city, Hughes remained calm. Rickard drove Hughes and Jack Real, with Stewart, to a baseball field, one of the few areas not shattered or consumed by fire and burst water mains. It proved impossible to find a working telephone. But at last the aides were able to get through to Ambassador Turner Shelton's house, which was not heavily damaged, and to the embassy and the badly smashed presidential palace.

They got a message through to Romaine Street; it would take too long to dispatch the de Havilland or a Convair, so Jack Real had a Learjet flown in from Miami. It is incomprehensible that Hughes would not have had a plane on standby at the airport. He was compelled to wait at Somoza's country estate, in a *cabaña* whose windows were covered at his instruction not only by curtains but by blankets. Although this instruction has been described as eccentric, it was, in fact, sensible. Anyone who stayed on a Somoza estate, especially Hughes, could be killed by radical groups or crazed citizens wandering loose in the anarchic atmosphere created by the disaster.

Some sleight of hand was necessary when he arrived at Fort Lauderdale in order to avoid the IRS and Customs inspectors. He had his aides call Miami International Airport, announcing that they would be bringing him there and asking for the courtesies of the airport. As a result, IRS and Customs officials went to the wrong terminal. They got wind of the change of plan by intercepting the Hughes pilot's contacts to the Fort Lauderdale tower and drove helter-skelter to the spot. But when they tried to climb into the plane, the aides blocked them. Finally, a customs agent was allowed on to talk with Hughes, while an IRS agent was permitted to stare at him through the window. All of this appeared in a memorandum dated January 5, 1973, and signed by IRS intelligence agent John J. Olszewski.

Hughes was transferred to one of his rented houses, and fretted that he would be pursued by process servers there. Once in the house, Hughes told Jack Real he wanted to give help to Somoza for the earthquake victims, to set up a water desalination plant at record speed because the people would be without fresh water. Real was furious when certain Summa executives refused to go ahead with the deal.

Hughes had already decreed that he would go at once to London; he had been planning the trip for some time, to buy three airplanes to replenish the fleet of Hawker Siddeley private jets now that he was retiring the British de Havilland. He told George Francom, Mell Stewart, and Gordon Margulis to take Christmas leave. Once again, all normal rules were waived for Howard Hughes; he got into London without a passport. His cleverness is illustrated by his choice of hotel: The Inn on the Park. It had the best security in London; it was tucked away in an exclusive enclave near Hyde Park; it had an excellent fire escape; and it was not too large or overflowing with inquisitive people. It was owned by the Rothchilds, who could pull strings with the government. It was hard for the press to stake out the top floor, which (again) he cleared for action—except for one suite, occupied by a wealthy man, Barry Cowan.

Cowan, who was fond of shooting, indulged in the curious habit of hanging his game, that is to say, pheasants he had shot for a tasty dinner, on the balcony. One afternoon he was astonished to find the birds missing. Hughes had spied them and wondered if they contained bombs. An aide brought the birds back; they were very "high" (i.e., smelly) by now, and unfit for eating; Cowan had them stuffed.

In late January, a very awkward matter surfaced to trouble Hughes. R. L. Ash, a former Hughes Aircraft executive, had recently been appointed by Nixon as Director of Management and Budget; it was charged that Ash had, as Hughes's chief financial officer between 1949 and 1953, compelled accountants to make entries in the books that the accountants later admitted under oath were false; the effect of this was that the United States Air Force was overbilled for $43 million.

Ash conceded, following a $2.4 million out-of-court settlement, that he had ordered the accountants to make entries they were unhappy with, but claimed that those entries were not improper; he pointed out that certainly Hughes received $43 million more than he was entitled to, but that this did not violate the terms of the agreement (i.e., Hughes had a pay or play contract; deliver or not, win or lose, he still got the $43 million). What Ash was too loyal to say was that he had no will in these matters; Hughes had instructed him to rip off the government—and this was America's hero.

In London, Hughes watched television avidly; he took an interest in the excellent local newspapers, reading them with a magnifying glass; he even went (unnoted, of course, in the logs) for drives in a Rolls; writer Roy Moseley will never forget seeing the car drive out, with newspapers stuck on the windows, as Hughes took off for some unknown destination.

He heard tremendous news. The Supreme Court found that the other courts had erred in finding him guilty in the long-drawn-out TWA case. Exonerated, he found himself $170 million richer overnight. When the press rushed into the hotel, the aides appeared, saying that Hughes was ecstatic. That was an understatement. For years, he had watched every twist and turn of judgments and appeals. Now, at last, his worst ordeal was over. Though still weak and wasted from his AIDS-like illness, Hughes decided at last he would face the meeting with Governor O'Callaghan of Nevada.

Then, in the wake of the great TWA decision, Hughes fretted over the details. Would the long-standing letter of credit drawn up in TWA's favor, should he lose the case, be canceled now? Would TWA press another suit, filed in Delaware? How would TWA recompense him for costs? Would TWA exercise its right to have a rehearing, a right it would have to exercise in twenty-five days? Aides Eckersley and Waldron, under Hughes's rigorous instruction, began working round the clock obtaining complete lists of court charges. Documented to the last nickel, these were finally paid.

He set March 17, St. Patrick's Day, as the date of the appointment. He chose the date shrewdly because O'Callaghan was, of course, Irish. With O'Callaghan were Paul Hannafin, who was the chairman of the Nevada gaming commission, Chester Davis, and Bill Gay, to make sure that all the documentary authorizations were witnessed and in order. He had a haircut, a manicure, and a beard trim.

Despite fanciful accounts which described Hughes naked except for a blanket wrapped around him, his visitors saw him in shirt, trousers, and robe. He was again bright, quick, and sharp. He was visibly in charge, not a puppet of his aides; he didn't even include Gay and Davis in the discussion, ignoring them rudely as they sat in an adjoining room as he wittily confirmed that he was yielding up control of Las Vegas. When an aide interjected something, he verbally slapped him down. There was no evidence that the drugs, apart from killing pain and taking the edge off his anxieties, affected his reason in the slightest. He was still Howard Hughes, and he had the shrewdness to tell O'Callaghan what he wanted to hear: that he loved Nevada and would like to, indeed planned to, return. The visitors left satisfied.

Hughes had to invest his new mountain of cash from the drill bit sale as quickly as possible to avoid capital gains taxes. He had always been enamored of Lockheed airplanes since his round-the-world flight, and he imported Jack Real to London to make deals in which he would invest large sums in Rolls-Royce, which made the Lockheed L-1011 engines, and in Lockheed itself.

Bill Gay had worked diligently on a master plan for Gateway, a massive shopping complex to be attached to the Desert Inn. He had spent thousands of Summa's money on full-scale models, so massive that they had to be shipped in the airplane cargo hold in four sections. He set up the beautiful mock-up in a room next to Hughes and asked Hughes to come and look at it. Hughes, with his customary unpredictable ferocity, snarled to Jack Real, "I don't even want to see the fucking thing!" Gay was angry and hurt; Real, who had no love for Gay, was delighted. And Gay, who felt the same way about Real, was annoyed that Hughes was planning to divide his empire into East and West Coast segments, with Real in charge of the West Coast. Even Hughes's knot of aides were split in the Real-Gay conflict; Margulis and barber Mell Stewart were on Real's side, the others on Gay's—the mutual accusations were frequent and tension-provoking.

Hughes decided to buy a Hawker Siddeley 748, an airplane of a more recent vintage than the private DH 125, which would soon be replaced by Convairs in the United States and which Bob Wearley flew. To test the model, he made the nostalgic decision to fly an identical aircraft himself. Just as he needed no passport in Britain, so he dispensed with a pilot's license. Is it surprising that, as he told Chester Davis, he was pleased by the considerations of the British government?

This was the old Hughes reasserting himself: the young eagle who flew around the world, defying gravity in an overweighted airplane, who lifted the Spruce Goose over the water at San Diego for a few glorious minutes. It was not in the interests of his aides that he take off; suggestions that they were controlling him are not credible.

He had made no will naming them as beneficiaries; it would have been in their best interests to have drugged him, made him useless, anything to stop this headstrong adventure. Instead, they waited, helpless to control his will, while he made the arrangements with Hawker Siddeley's Tony Blackman, and with Jack Real.

Jack Real and aide Gordon Margulis went to Simpson's on his advice and bought him a nostalgic outfit of flying jacket, pants, and shoes, as well as a helmet, though to get his size at his height and weight wasn't easy. He was delighted and dressed up, cheerfully, like a kind of attenuated shadow of the hero he once had been.

To avoid both Gatwick and London Airport, Hughes settled on flying from Hatfield, north of London, where he could dodge passport control. Gordon Margulis had to arrange an elaborate decoy technique to get Hughes to the airport without being noticed. He hired a Rolls-Royce, and dressed to the teeth, ran out to it with with Jack Real, who was tall and almost as thin as Hughes, thus misleading the reporters. Then Hughes came out of the back of the hotel in a modest car (but its newspapered windows attracted fans looking for movie stars and they tried to peer in).

Hughes was driven out to the airfield, which was in the middle of rolling fields and low hills. He grumbled about the flush riveting (an old concern of his) but didn't bother with a germ inspection. Why? In fact, why, from his meetings with Somoza and Ambassador Shelton and Merrill Lynch executives on, had he become less and less worried about contagion?

The answer can be found in a deposition made by aide Clarence Waldron in 1977. By now, he felt he had only six, seven years to live. In his self-obsession and intense awareness of his own being, he knew he was dying. So why not live it up and forget about germs?

Throughout the flight, Hughes was a lively and intelligent companion, but his piloting was erratic and, in an odd repetition of the dangerous departure from Floyd Bennett Field in 1937, he miscalculated the length of the runway and Blackman had to compensate to save a crash. "You aren't the first man to criticize my landings," said Hughes with a laugh.

A second flight was arranged so that Hughes could renew the special visitor's visa granted him by the government illegally without a passport. He would go to Ostend in Belgium and reenter through immigration at Hatfield. Prior arrangements had been made with the passport office. Hughes settled on a date late in June. Once again, the Hawker Siddeley de Havilland 748 was commandeered for the flight.

Just before leaving, he suggested that he continue to Paris, where he remembered someone from his round-the-world flight thirty-four years earlier. "So complete was his self-centeredness it never occurred to him that the man hadn't been waiting ever since for him to turn up again," Gordon Margulis says.

In bad weather, through heavy rain and mist, Hughes took off with Blackman and another copilot; the conditions in the air were so severe that Hughes had to touch down at Stanstead Airfield, and made so clumsy a job of it that he was forced to go back into the cabin, furiously angry, while the copilot took the controls.

On July 17, Hughes took off for a third trip, this time in an exact copy of the de Havilland 125 that Bob Wearley flew in America. He would, he decided, buy two of these planes instead; this was a disappointment to Hawker Siddeley, which had wanted him to buy the more expensive craft. He was overjoyed, as he had always been, with the de Havilland; he made a series of takeoffs and landings at Stanstead, but did not venture across the Channel again. In a fourth flight still, also in July, he took off from Hatfield to Woodford, and was energetic and talkative during the trip.

Without any germ check or fuss, Hughes examined the model from end to end; his comments were sharp and explicit.

He was very impressed with the mock-up; he made suggestions for improvements in the landing gear that showed all his old flair and resulted in Hawker Siddeley's engineers' making the changes.

Once again, contrary to all the legends of his drug-ridden incompetence, he proved to be brilliant in negotiation. Jack Real was the chief go-between as he made a deal with Lockheed, where, of course, as a former executive, Real had many friends.

Lockheed needed Hughes's money desperately; the DC-10 had beaten them up in the market by outpacing them in 7,000 nautical mile flights; Lockheed needed to build an improved L-1011-2, and wanted $100 million from Hughes. From February 1973 to September, Hughes and Real met day after day to discuss the arrangements for the investment; Hughes seemed to revel in the constant discussions, and somehow Real's patience didn't wear away. He is too circumspect today to say that Hughes was procrastinating maddeningly, as always.

•

Hughes broke every last rule and joined Blackman to inspect a brand new de Havilland mock-up at the Hawker Siddeley plant with Clarence Waldron and Jack Real.

These adventures thrilled him; but soon he felt a new anxiety. If he stayed in London any longer than December 26, the day of his arrival the previous year, he would be subject to the very heavy British income tax. No more anxious to pay taxes to a cooperative British government than he had been to the American IRS, he decided to go back to the tax-free Bahamas.

It was a remarkable decision. He could have gone to Grand Cayman, or to Monaco, or to Bermuda, but instead he chose the very place which had so summarily rejected him. The only explanation for his decision can be that he had made a promise through London and the Foreign Office that he would obey the residency laws, obtain work permits for his team, renew his stay every eight months, and employ blacks. Also, he would satisfy the local government by buying property: he settled on the lavish Xanadu Princess Hotel at Freeport, which he had heard was up for sale by Daniel Ludwig. Chester Davis began the negotiations.

In August, 1969, according to columnist Jack Anderson, Hughes had met with Ludwig, his chief rival as the richest American; the location was given as the International Hotel in Las Vegas, but that is impossible; if the meeting did take place, it would have been at the Desert Inn.

Ludwig fascinated Hughes, and had shared with him business interests in Nicaragua. Born in South Haven, Michigan, in 1897, the son of a ship salvage captain, Ludwig was charged with gunrunning during Prohibition, moved into shipping oil, and gradually built a tanker empire. Buying, selling and converting, he cleaned up a fortune in World War II and soon had a fleet that surpassed Onassis's or Niarchos's. Switching, like those rivals, to Panamanian registry, the neutral umbrella that allowed for every kind of business maneuver, he weathered oil slumps by transporting iron ore. Then, in the 1950s, 1960s, and 1970s, he began activities that were of burning interest to Hughes; he plunged deep into investments in the Bahamas.

In 1965, he built the luxurious Kings Inn; in the following year, the Xanadu Princess, an enclave for the very rich. He was a major client of Intertel.

At the beginning of August, Hughes's physicians flew in from Los Angeles to make the aforementioned and ill-fated tests of his ear.

Still intoxicated with the idea of flying, Hughes suddenly announced to Jack Real that he was interested in buying a Concorde from British Aerospace. Luckily, he never went through with the idea.

He attracted the interest of Prime Minister Edward Heath, who was very pleased to note that Hughes was interested in investing in the Lockheed L-1011-2. Heath was so encouraged by Hughes, he wrote to him in a letter that he had ordered the development of a new RB Rolls-Royce engine for use in the crack airplane. He invited him to lunch at 10 Downing Street; Hughes, of course, was forced to decline.

On August 9, Hughes, on a visit to the bathroom in the middle of the night, stumbled over a rug. He fell, striking an occasional table; he lay on the floor in agony, unable to move. The aides heard his cry and rushed to his side. Luckily this was not the United States and doctors made house calls; a physician was located by the management and did a preliminary examination which suggested a broken hip.

In the morning, Dr. William Young, radiologist of the London Clinic, the most exclusive private hospital in London, arrived to take X rays. Hughes received him naked in bed, except for a few paper towels, which Young had the aides remove. He had to be propped up, painfully, so that his legs could be X-rayed; the aides unnecessarily insisted that Young and his team use paper towels to handle both his body and the X-ray equipment. And this for a man who had just made several flights in unsanitized aircraft and had visited a plant filled with floating germs and had shaken hands with five recent visitors! Young was appalled by Hughes's emaciation and parchment skin. His teeth and gums were rotted, and he might easily swallow a tooth. Hughes was forced to undergo a radical operation for his hip—and not in his suite, but at the London Clinic. Dr. Walter C. Robinson, the leading orthopedic surgeon, was selected to insert the steel pin that would enable Hughes to walk. He also was appalled by Hughes's condition.

Within a few days, Hughes rallied sufficiently to sign a lengthy affidavit in the continuing matter of Hughes Tool's investigation of millions squirreled away by John Meier and his partners in the alleged purchase of mining claims. In the affidavit, he denied having any personal knowledge of Meier, or of having any face-to-face dealings with him. This was necessary because Meier was claiming a personal friendship with Hughes that had led to Hughes's authorizing the purchases of the claims and had produced forged memoranda from him, which Hughes needed to expose. Hughes Tool was suing Meier and his partners for $50 million, a prolonged adventure in law as it turned out; Meier at the same time gave secret evidence, still unreleased, in which he stated to the Watergate Committee details of Hughes's links to the Watergate affair.

The deposition was impatient and intensely personal; in clause 7, Hughes burst out with, "I cannot conceive of any manner in which my testimony might be of value in this lawsuit." But he promised to be available for any future depositions. His signature was witnessed by his aide, Levar Myler, who had conveniently become "Commissioner of Deeds for the State of Utah in the United Kingdom."

On September 13, 1973, the deal was at last consummated with Lockheed; Hughes agreed to take an option on the L-1011-2 purchase expiring the following spring. But then a problem arose. The Yom Kippur war broke out; Britain backed Israel against Egypt, and the Arabs in the wake of the conflict put up the price of oil, which included, of course, aviation fuel, from $2.50 a barrel to $10. BOAC and Air Canada were hit so hard they climbed out of their commitments to buy the Lockheed plane and Summa talked Hughes into canceling the deal. The option expired without his taking action. As part of the deal, Hughes could have obtained 10 percent of Lockheed.

After a few days, his aide Gordon Margulis recalls Hughes was restless at the London clinic and ached to return to the womb of the Inn on the Park suite. He was back there, comfortable again, when an industrial strike caused Prime Minister Heath to order all electricity curtailed, and at 10:00 P.M., the power went off, making it impossible to watch television, enjoy central heating, eat cooked food, or even see projected movies. That was the end; Hughes told his aides that, quite apart from the fact that he wouldn't stay long enough to pay United Kingdom income tax, he had to get out.

Although he had "decided" to go back to the Bahamas, he had hit on another idea: he could avoid tax by living entirely on a boat, rather like Scientology guru L. Ron Hubbard. He had close ties to Evelyn de Rothschild, owner of the Inn on the Park, through Chester

Davis, and Jack Real talked with Rothschild's executives, who knew Stavros Niarchos, the Greek shipping tycoon, and promised to do what they could. But the Niarchos yacht, promised for that winter, would not be ready and refitted until the spring. Hughes irritably told Real to forget the idea.

Six days before his tax-free United Kingdom residence expired, Jack Real called up billionaire Adnan Khashoggi, who shared his love of Lockheeds, and borrowed his private TriStar for transport to the Bahamas.

Because Real had advised the Bahamian government that Hughes would be investing heavily in the islands, several prominent dignitaries were at the airport to greet him when he arrived with his aides.

When the party arrived at the Xanadu Princess, an ugly scene took place. The desk clerk informed the group that they would be unable to provide all four promised penthouse suites; it was only when Hughes made clear that he was buying the hotel from Ludwig that they were given the suites at what in 1992 seems the incredibly low total cost of $1,000 a day. Hughes was furious there was no bidet in the bathroom when he checked in; one was supplied in hours.

After a week in the hotel, Hughes had a shock. He was indicted in Las Vegas for criminal stock manipulation in the struggle that resulted in the purchase to buy Air West.

He was protected from fines or arrest by being present in Freeport. He was concerned with Daniel Ludwig's sticky attitude on the Xanadu Princess purchase. When John Holmes advised him that, while negotiations went on for Lots 9 and 10, he would be able to stay on at the hotel at a reduced rent, Hughes drew an arrow against the words "for as long as you want." He added in a scribbled footnote that this would not work at all, that the only way to ensure adequate security was to own the facility, not to rent. Hughes demanded that the closing take place at once.

The negotiations went on.

Chester Davis urged him not to reveal publicly that he was buying the Xanadu as "it would confirm the real reason for your being [in the islands]." Hughes was at the time involved, keeping his promise to Governor O'Callaghan, in planning to plunge the money earned from the victory in the TWA case into expanding Las Vegas to the limit.

He had earlier sold off the Krupp ranch that he had bought for Jean Peters, a strip of land between the Dunes and Caesars Palace, and had rented out the former homes of Robert Maheu, George Francom, and Levar Myler; now he would reverse the trend.

Having rejected Bill Gay's shopping center idea, he planned for the Desert Inn to be under one roof, its buildings connected by covered walkways for pedestrians and electric carts; it was to be his number one property; he would buy back the Black Forest Inn, the Three Fountains, the Travelodge, and the Grace Hayes Restaurant he had previously sold; he would make the Sands the biggest hotel in Nevada; he would build a Sands West, across the street from the Castaways Casino to the south; he would buy property with strip frontage near the Castaways. What all this shows is that, despite the fact that Bill Gay was nominally given power of attorney to run Las Vegas, Hughes was still committed to the city passionately, and in defiance of Chester Davis, who felt he should bail out of Nevada for good.

A serious problem arose in Freeport. The deal to exchange Hughes's two 880 Convairs for a 30 percent share of Somoza's Lanica Airlines had been delayed by the long drawn-out discussions of the Civil Aeronautics Board on whether the deal was appropriate and approvable.

Losing patience at the delay, and acting (according to Hughes's right-hand man Jack Real) without Hughes's approval, the executives of Hughes Tool lost a major opportunity: to buy Texas Air for a modest sum. Regretting the fact that they had acted hastily, they offered Frank Lorenzo, owner of Eastern Airlines, who had bought Texas Air, a substantial sum, plus one-third of Lanica, which they still didn't own, to get the airline. Lorenzo spoke to the press; Somoza saw the offer in print, and was furious. He summoned Real to Managua—Hughes tried to stop him from going—and carpeted him. "Howard treats Lanica like a prize in a Crackerjack package!" Somoza shouted. But, fond of Real's daughter, he relented, and forgave; and now the CAB deal went through. Lorenzo kept Texas Air. Hughes was maddened by the whole matter; and Real was, too. He realized that the Summa bosses were taking matters into their own hands; that Hughes's commands were being ignored. But this was, though Real won't agree, Hughes's own fault; he had, after all, signed over enormous powers to Summa of his own free will. And it is doubtful that, even if he had been in charge, he would have been able, in his state of health, to deal with the countless everyday problems that would have flooded his hotel suite.

The winter, spring, and summer brought Hughes grievous burdens. Day after day in preparing his prolonged suit against Hughes for libel, with Hughes exercising the nonextradition laws of the Bahamas to avoid an appearance as defendant, Robert Maheu exposed Hughes's many sins.

On February 3, 1974, a devastating article, stemming from facts brought to light in Maheu's preparations for the suit, appeared in *The New York Times*. It detailed Hughes's attempts to buy political favors in the Bahamas; how he had made peace with Prime Minister Lynden O. Pindling; the much-quoted phone conversation with Maheu in which he had said, "I will move to the Bahamas if by making large political contributions I can wrap up that government and make it a captive entity in every way."

On May 3, Thomas Bell, one of Hughes's team, gave a sworn statement during the trial that Hughes had tried to block black-white integration in Las Vegas schools. In later testimony, Richard G. Danner mentioned, with manifest omissions, the Rebozo "loan"; on May 14, Maheu testified that Hughes ordered that bankers be followed and harassed when he found they were unwilling to consent to finance TWA jetliner purchases.

Meanwhile, in March, Hughes showed a keen interest in buying WCIX, TV Channel 6, located in Miami; he had much admired the station's programs and had heard it was for sale. He went ahead with the deal later that month, and also concluded the arrangements to buy the Xanadu Princess. He was, as always, busy wheeling and dealing day and night.

Happy about his purchase of the Xanadu Princess, Hughes authorized Jack Real, now in charge of all his eastern affairs, to buy the luxurious Lucayan Beach Hotel. The hotel had lost its gambling license and much influence had to be brought to bear to secure a new one. But Bill Gay's implacable dislike of Real and mistrust of him led to his delaying the deal. Real still hasn't forgiven him.

Hughes had other investment ideas. He wanted to set up a brewery business in the islands, because the water was being successfully desalinated from the ocean. He wanted to buy islands in addition to Cay Sal, which was no longer a CIA military training base. He wanted to buy an airstrip, forty acres of flat country, from millionaire Edward St. George, and start flying again.

By May, the Summa Corporation had a "Bahamian board." John Holmes was a member and a liaison between Summa and the stockholders; Levar Myler was a board member and liaison; the remainder of the team, George Francom, staff executive, Jim Rickard, Howard Eckersley, Chuck Waldron, Eric Bundy, Allen Stroud, Gordon Margulis, Cliff Weissman, and Mell Stewart were all members of Bahamaian Summa. This disproves the theory that somehow Hughes's affairs were being run from Texas; his control of the Bahamian board is attested to by Chester Davis's staff members.

Hughes had more to trouble him at Freeport. On May 11, one Leroy Nickey Barnes was arrested in the Bronx and charged with the murder of Clifford Haynes; he was freed on July 20, on $100,000 bail supplied by Charles Goldfarb, which, he said, he had obtained from the sale of the Frontier Hotel to Hughes in 1967. This was an inconvenient reference to the peculiar character of the individuals Hughes had dealt with in Las Vegas at the time. Then, on June 5, came a more serious matter.

## CHAPTER NINETEEN

# How to Burgle Yourself

The beginnings of this Watergate-like caper can be traced back to December, 1972, when the Securities and Exchange Commission, in its effort to nail Hughes personally for his cheating thousands of shareholders of $60 million in the Air West takeover scam, subpoenaed the relevant documents from Chester Davis, including Hughes's memos to Robert Maheu.

Davis, after consulting with Hughes in Managua, announced that no such files existed. The barefaced lie gave him some breathing space while he figured what to do with them. Instead of destroying them, which might have made more sense, he placed them under lock and key at the Hughes headquarters on Romaine Street, Hollywood.

The SEC made further investigations. An inside contact at Romaine Street told them the files existed. They served a new subpoena on Davis on August 7, 1973, when Hughes was in London. Davis sought angrily to quash this second subpoena when the SEC counsel told him he had evidence that the documents were hidden. Davis failed, but still hid everything.

In collusion with certain Hughes executives he finally allowed the SEC to see a small handful of harmless Air West files—files whose existence he had denied weeks before. The SEC pressed on; unhappy with the crumbs Davis was tossing them, the investigators issued further subpoenas in May and June, 1974. Both were ignored. Davis by now was lying under oath that no other files existed. The SEC tried optimistically to subpoena Hughes in Freeport—to no avail.

Terry Lenzner, Watergate associate counsel, was after Hughes as well. Like Nixon, Hughes had allowed Chester Davis and his friends and aides to remind him that his position was that he knew nothing about Watergate—at least until several months after the break-in occurred.

Consider the following. In March, one of his aides sent the memo to Chester Davis mentioned at the beginning of this book, calling for the shredding of all files relating to Nixon and other political figures.

It is an astonishing document, because it sweeps away allegations that Hughes had no knowledge of his operations at this stage; that he was a brainwashed zombie. In fact, the events that followed, which are fit for the James Bond thrillers he loved, can be traced directly back to this memorandum, whose existence was ignored by the zombie theorists, led by Barlett and Steele.

The only possible interpretation of those events is this.

Davis wasted no time in carrying out Hughes's memoed instructions. He enlisted the aid of CIA operatives, bagmen who were expert in staging fake burglaries to cover the removal of unwanted documents. First, Davis's own office was "raided," and stripped of incriminating papers; Davis told police nothing had been taken. Mullen and Company's records were also removed on Davis's orders; again, the police were told nothing was missing from the Mullen office.

Fake raids were made on the Las Vegas and Encino headquarters of Summa; to dress things up a little, it was stated that a telephone scrambler was missing from Encino; more documents were spirited away.

Suspicious of these imitation break-ins, and furious at Hughes's and Chester Davis's dodging, the SEC counsel memoed the assistant attorney general on June 3, 1974, calling for the prosecution, for felonious conduct, of Hughes himself, Davis, and certain members of the Summa board. Next day, the same counsel subpoenaed a material witness, Gordon Judd. Somebody tried to kill Judd; he fled.

It was essential that all remaining documents be abstracted from Romaine Street, and, along with the others that were sensitive, taken to Hughes's hotel in Freeport. Given Hughes's charter to act,

Davis made sure that the Hughes memoranda and all other relevant papers were to be placed on a conference table, neatly stacked in piles. Next to them would be index cards, making it look as though they were about to be catalogued, and at the same time providing Davis with a guide as to what would be significant.

The approach was similar to that of the Hughes-Mullen-Hunt caper at Watergate. Since Hunt and Liddy were deactivated, Davis engaged a new bagman, probably the same man who had attempted the burglary of Greenspun's safe in September, 1972, and had engineered the fake break-ins of Davis's and Mullen's offices and the Las Vegas and Encino Summa offices.

He worked for both the CIA and the FBI on a free-lance basis, but was authorized in this case by neither. According to CIA specialist William Corson, his control was John Paisley, a double agent for the CIA and the KGB, who had worked for many years for Hughes Aircraft on CIA-connected operations, and was familiar with every aspect of the Hughes empire.

Paisley's motive in getting behind the fake burglary was his need to obtain documents on the *Glomar Explorer,* the Hughes vessel that was at that moment on her way to the Pacific to retrieve the codes from the sunken nuclear submarine. So sensitive was the matter that Chester Davis sent Hughes a fake memorandum, presumably in case it should be found by the press, reminding Hughes that this was no more than a minerals-seeking vessel, years after Hughes had signed the authorization for its actual purpose.

On the evening of June 4, 1974, a staff member obtained the keys to the executive offices and the combination to the front door, known only to six people and changed every thirty days. He got hold of a floor plan, the exact location of the documents, and the construction of the security vaults, safes, and strong rooms, to make torching or peeling them easy. He was not foolish enough to supply the combinations, which would give the game away.

At 12:45 A.M. on June 5, the same hour that the Watergate burglars had made their entry in 1972 and only twelve days short of the same day of the month, the "burglary" team, which was much superior to that of the Hunt-Liddy-Barker operatives, walked through the front door of what was considered to be the most secure office structure in Los Angeles. The batteries of closed-circuit TV cameras had been turned off, the lasers and wire links to police headquarters deactivated, and the alarm bells rendered useless.

Alerted by the SEC's suspicions following the failure of the previous raiders to take objects from the other Summa offices, the men took watches, $68,000 in cash, stock certificates, Nadine Henley's butterfly collection and her Wedgwood and Mongolian bowls, blasted open vaults, picked safes, and then, at last, reached the true objective: the conference room table. They piled the documents into boxes and carried them to a van. They drove to the airport and flew a Hughes private plane to Las Vegas.

The switchboard operator called the police. When they arrived, they were told that no manuscripts were missing—even before they asked. That was a slip nobody cottoned to.

Certain sensitive items were taken to the Xanadu Princess at Freeport and stored there. Witnessed on arrival in boxes by Gordon Margulis and aide Mell Stewart, their presence known to Jack Real, these papers were, Margulis and Real say, not seen by Hughes. *But they needn't have known* that the papers were seen by Hughes.

Typically, Hughes was panic-stricken after the burglary. His awareness of it is clearly shown by a memorandum filled with anxiety about who might be probing into his private vaults—the insurance investigators, who couldn't be bought off. Chuck Waldron wrote, "He wants a full account, step by step, on just how it is intended that [the] search is to be made. He wants these reports before anything is touched."

It was necessary to find a fall guy; the SEC was suspicious of the "break-in," and so were the FBI and the Los Angeles police. An actual "burglar" must be named. The trick was brought off. The chief operator called one Donald Woolbright, who had a police record, and told him exciting news: the St. Louis mob had stolen the papers, and wanted to blackmail the Hughes people for a million dollars to buy them back. Woolbright was to make the contact and get a piece of the loot.

Woolbright fell for the plan. He took a harmless document, a memo from Hughes to Maheu about a casino takeover in Las Vegas in 1968, and put it in an envelope in a trash can on Ventura Boulevard, opposite Nadine Henley's office in Encino. A phone call told her to look out. She saw the envelope, oddly suspected a bomb, called the police, and they found the memo. Later, Woolbright told her that the bulk of the documents were for sale for a million. She checked with one of her bosses, who naturally refused to pay. After all, the hot stuff was in Freeport.

Woolbright got in deeper. He thought he might peddle some papers to *Der Spiegel,* the German magazine, then panicked and gave up.

By now, the CIA was aware that the *Glomar Explorer* documents were missing. In order to deactivate them, somebody told them that the documents had been stolen, the theory being that the moment they learned this, they would discontinue the investigation and the SEC, the FBI, and the LAPD would also. That is exactly what happened; rewards for the recovery of the papers were withdrawn; Woolbright went free and unarrested to his farm in Missouri.

There the matter would have rested, had it not been for some tough investigative journalists at the *Los Angeles Times.* Suspicious of the sudden dropping of inquiries, they managed to winkle out of a police officer the fact that the *Glomar* documents were gone. Just as they were about to publish the sensational story in the *Times,* CIA chief William Colby tried to kill it. But it was too late; *The New York Times* was not far behind. Colby crisscrossed the country, pleading with editors to bury the follow-ups. But after a hiatus, nobody would go on being suppressed. The story made headlines all over the world; to the Soviets' delight, the *Glomar*'s efforts had to be discontinued.

The public screamed for a victim. The Los Angeles D.A. was on the spot; he had failed to arrest anybody for a burglary that hadn't even been in the press for seven months, but now was front-page news. Woolbright was the answer. Indicted by the Los Angeles grand jury, he surrendered at his farm and was shipped back to Los Angeles for trial.

Meantime, a hotshot journalist, Michael Drosnin, who had been arrested in Times Square with Abbie Hoffman for peddling cocaine (he was released when an editor said he was researching an article), put together a piece on the burglary in the liberal *New Times.* He offered the Los Angeles police, according to former Democratic National Committee Chairman Larry O'Brien, information on underground figures if they would give them the inside dope on Woolbright; they refused. He harassed O'Brien on Watergate to the point that O'Brien threw him out of his office. The same day the jury was out in the Woolbright trial, he announced he was offering the Romaine Street documents to New York publishers at a floor price of $100,000. Neither the assistant D.A. prosecuting Woolbright nor defending counsel Richard Kirschner recalled the jury in the light of this new evidence. When Woolbright was found guilty, the judgment was reversed, since the judge was found to have directed the verdict; a year later, Woolbright was tried again. A mistrial was declared when the jury disagreed. Again, Drosnin was not called as a witness.

At least one person involved with the Summa Corporation knew too much and later paid the price for that. Bobby Hill was an expert in electronic eavesdropping who had acted as security agent for Summa and had helped in setting up the systems at Romaine Street; he also worked at the police department, where one of his contacts was Chief Jack Egger, formerly one of Hughes's closest circle of bodyguards.

On a July evening two years and one month after the break-in, he was found shot through the back of his head, two cherries stuck in his mouth, in his Burbank apartment. Two of his partners, working for his security agency under contract to Summa, were charged with the crime. It turned out that they had assisted the fake burglary of at least one of the Hughes offices, in Encino. One of the men went to prison for life.

When Egger was found to be connected to Hill, he resigned from the force; his testimony in court resulted in the murderer's life sentence. Some doubted Egger's truthfulness in the matter; but he was not questioned by the judge.

In obtaining Hill's files, it was found that he had been intimately connected to the Hughes empire in more ways than one; he had been drawing illicit, laundered funds from the Union Bank of Switzerland account of Rosemont, the special Hughes subsidiary set up to protect Hughes's publishing rights. Cash from the account was personally used by Hughes to buy a TWA jet in 1967; some was used by staffers for heroin shipments from Mexico. It was obvious why Bobby Hill had to be disposed of. He was, after two years, about to talk.

Hughes was uneasy in the summer of 1974, after the Romaine Street "burglary" and before it got into the headlines. Maybe John Meier, still being pursued by the law, and Hank Greenspun, still the *Las Vegas Sun* honcho who hated him, might catch on?

All through that year of 1974, according to charges made by cousin William Lummis and the Hughes Estate in 1978, there was a conflict over Hughes's use of drugs. One of his physicians, Dr. Norman Crane, wanted to discontinue them, and wrote to Hughes in January to that effect, saying that the extent of the dosages was above legal limits. Hughes needed them to kill his constant pain, Bill Gay and Kay Glenn told another Hughes physician, Dr. Lawrence

Chaffin. They were concerned about this, and tried to have Chaffin write to all of the physicians on the Hughes payroll to have them continue the supply, but the doctors refused. Why? The charge Lummis made was that Hughes was being drugged beyond painkilling necessity; that he was being manipulated and rendered helpless to control his affairs. Walter Kane, long since off the Hughes payroll, swore out an affidavit in April saying that Gay and Glenn had asked him to set up a Mexican source for the drugs. Finally, Mormon Dr. Walter Thain, brother-in-law of Bill Gay, agreed to help.

Although the interpretation placed on this by Lummis was sinister, an opinion shared by such friends of Hughes as Jack Real, to the objective observer the threat to take Hughes off drugs seems worse. Without codeine and Valium, his suffering would have been indescribable. His nerve endings exposed, his gums and teeth painfully rotting, his muscles twisted and tortured, his tumorous growths and AIDS-like wasting would have been excruciating, and it is likely he would have committed suicide.

In the knowledge of Hughes' agony, Thain agreed to supply Hughes with seven grains daily of codeine. A sealed package would be delivered each Friday at 8:00 A.M. Arriving in Freeport on August 16, 1974, he obtained Hughes's signature on a drug approval document. This, naturally, Hughes agreed to; thus is removed the theory that he was drugged against his will. Given his temperament and suffering, the oft-repeated statement that he would have accepted a drying-out process is unacceptable. Such a process might have killed him.

However, as a result of Dr. Crane's refusal to continue the drugs, Hughes grew testy with him. He accused him of stealing drugs from a closet. He yelled at his aides, "That big clown! I know who took those! That big clown Norman did it and no one can tell me otherwise. I know he took them!" But he didn't fire Crane.

Hughes was so delighted with Thain for giving him the relief he craved that he offered him, on October 22, 1974, the job of head of the Howard Hughes Medical Institute's governing board. But Hughes failed to appoint him to the chairmanship. Fearing that Hughes might dismiss him completely, Thain sensibly obtained a year's contract, beginning January 1, 1975.

For some reason his enemies regarded this request as evil. But why wouldn't a man in agony give the sun, moon, and stars to his painkilling savior? And why wouldn't that doctor mistrust his wretched patient, who seldom kept a promise and changed his mind constantly?

Thain took charge, with the approval of Hughes's aides, of many of the sick man's affairs. He was in Salt Lake City on January 30, 1975, discussing with Bill Gay and Kay Glenn future employment contracts that Hughes must sign. Thain's ledgers show repeated efforts to have Hughes give his approval. What was wrong with that? Hughes would scarcely want to dismiss his executive board, who knew all of his dangerous secrets and were taking care of countless matters he could not. Hughes was nervous that a Pandora's box might be opened if he granted anybody the right to handle his affairs. By approving Thain's special role as his charge, he would keep the box lid firmly shut. Hughes backed out again and again, but finally, in September, yielded to Thain's entreaties for his contract and the other contracts.

Why shouldn't Hughes have been forced? He was capable of leaving everyone contractless and rudderless. The aides had secured $100,000 a year and more from Bill Gay, and if Hughes canceled their contracts or refused to renew them, they would be working as masseurs, garage hands, or carpenters. And didn't they, God knows, earn their money, what with preserving his urine in Mason jars, enduring his deafening movies day and night, played to the limit of sound when Hughes tossed aside his hearing aid, trimming his Fu Manchu nails, cutting his hair, putting up with his stench and his selfishness, with never a question about themselves, their wives, their families—a man without an ounce of interest in these servants' lives?

In the 1978 Lummis suit against Gay, Glenn, and the others, including the aides, it was wrongly stated, "Thain mercilessly manipulated Hughes, forcing him to give employment contracts."

According to allegations made by William Lummis in the 1978 case, and supported today by Jack Real, Gay and the aides set out to dislodge Real from Hughes's bedside. They kept him out—it was said in a deposition under oath from aide George Francom—by changing the locks on the doors. They blocked Hughes's memos to Real. When Hughes asked for Real, they refused to tell him Real was there. Francom balked at this and Bill Gay and Kay Glenn accused him of being "less than a man." But soon Real was back.

How can it be explained that memos exist in the Hughes Estate files showing that from early 1974 until the end of 1975 Hughes was

continually active in issuing orders, was being given sage advice by
Gay and by his aides, and was, rather remarkably, on top of many
things? Consider the following:

On January 27, 1974, Hughes drew up a document appointing
Moses Lasky, James Wadsworth, and Samuel S. Lionel his attorneys
in the Air West case.

Throughout the Air West hearings in June, he was in constant
touch with Chester Davis, and asked him to change the name
Summa to HRH Properties; he repeatedly sought progress reports.
Davis sent him memoranda, which he read, on the continuing matter
of his interest in Lockheed after his option expired on the L-1011-2
deal. He was kept apprised of, and approved, Kay Glenn's move in
buying a corporate JetStar 5118 from Qualitron at a price of
$1,165,000. Glenn advised him against leasing future jets, as he
needed a tax deduction; he obeyed. Glenn also advised him against
grounding the 5118, and he did not. The documents show he was
kept fully advised on aircraft matters.

On January 17, 1975, he approved a long-term land lease with
the FAA for the North Las Vegas control tower; he ordered a legal
problem overcome at the Desert Inn, which was in default. Also on
January 17, Real, Chuck Waldron, and George Francom signed a
document for Bill Gay reporting that Hughes instructed Real to take
action to make sure that the Hughes monopoly was maintained on
his improper control of Las Vegas Airport; Hughes ordered a hangar
for L-1011s and DC-8s and a warehouse, and these were "to be
secretly planned and built on our property, one on each side of the
jetcraft site in order to preclude condemnation proceedings." This
was Hughes pure and simple.

At the time, the sale of the North Las Vegas airport (Thunder-
bird Field) to Hughes was followed by Hughes's snapping up the
existing operators, thereby eliminating sales of Piper and Mooney
aircraft. County officials granted, between 1967 and 1969, 155
acres of McCarran Airport, increasing the monopoly, and Hughes
Tool bought out the Beechcraft dealer and cut out that line of aircraft completely.

By making himself the exclusive dealer in Cessna and cutting
out all other aircraft, as well as getting a corner in aviation fuel,
Hughes, by 1975, controlled Las Vegas's airways operations; laws
were established setting operating standards so high that only
Hughes could reach them.

On February 28, 1975, Hughes again issued instructions to repurchase the Black Forest Inn, the Three Fountains, Travelodge, and Grace Hayes Restaurant, on which he had long exercised options. He wanted to complete the buys before making the Sands the biggest hotel in Nevada. He would build a Sands North, and a Sands West across the street, on the site of the Castaways Casino and south of it. The Desert Inn would expand and become a number one property. These instructions Kay Glenn began to implement.

He removed Mickey West as his attorney in charge of tax matters, and he approved lawyer Larry Sikes as substitute. He authorized Hughes Aviation to buy King Aircraft. This would replace the Cessnas currently flying company personnel from Miami to Freeport. The Cessna planes would be traded.

The same day, Hughes ordered the building of a new KLAS-TV station in Las Vegas. It was to be constructed on the same site for historical reasons; it was to be operated during construction out of temporary quarters which he meticulously specified, showing an amazingly sustained grasp of Las Vegas city geography, either south of a church or on the "Felcher property." He wanted four mobile transmitting stations, all identical; the new structure must be "a standard rectangular office building." It was not to contain an auditorium or stage, as he felt the Desert Inn showroom could be used for that. He approved studios for the building.

In view of his appalling condition, it is amazing that Hughes had this much life in him.

He began showing an interest in going to Acapulco, where he wanted to buy Merle Oberon's house and to buy the Princess Hotel, owned by Daniel Ludwig, as well. But first, since it was clear to him he was dying, there must be a will. And now he became really diabolical.

Yet again, the myth that Hughes was a puppet of his aides can be shattered easily; he double-crossed them all in the matter of his will. It is true that he hadn't been aware of their huge $100,000 a year salaries—in that respect, at least, his executives had pulled the wool over his eyes. But he did deceive them and his doctors when he told them they would be taken care of by him for the rest of their lives.

He teased Nadine Henley with the idea of leaving all his money to the Medical Institute—i.e., free of taxes and essentially to the CIA, for which the Institute continued to be a front. He talked about wills prepared in 1938 and in the 1940s; and said that these replaced his earlier will of 1928, made when his parents died. He sent a lying memo to aide Howard Eckersley that summer, saying that he had drawn up a well-phrased document with the late lawyer Neil McCarthy. He gave Nadine Henley at least two wills for retyping, naming her as a beneficiary, then failed to sign them.

Johnny Holmes memoed him that if he did not sign a will an old one might be found leaving money to Noah Dietrich. Hughes was furious; "Imagine me leaving the son of a bitch a nickel!" he snapped. Chuck Waldron begged him to sign a document making sure he would not suffer, with his family, when Hughes died. What did Hughes care? He enjoyed torturing his aides with his promises. He had never shown an interest in his men's personal lives; he didn't care about their wives and children; when Christmas came, he hated the fact that his men would sometimes leave and join their folks. He was as jealous and puzzled by personal happiness as he had always been; he knew none himself; his life was loveless and empty. When an aide expressed a longing for his wife, Hughes said that he should meet her at some location, spend the night with her in a motel to satisfy his desire, and return the next day. He couldn't imagine that anyone would want more with a marital partner than a quick fuck. "Why," he asked the aide, "should you need more than that?"

But his selfish being knew nothing now of love, of tenderness, of companionship. Even an employee's visit to a dentist or a doctor was incomprehensible to him, because it would take the man away from him. Now that he had no closeness with anyone, why should his aides? He imagined that they slept when they were not with him; often, he would call out, "Wake 'em up!", even in the middle of the day, and couldn't believe it when he found that his men were out having dinner. People didn't exist when they were not in the room with him.

Never once would an aide say to him, "I have to go home." Graduation ceremonies, wives' operations, accidents in the house—none of these did his aides dare bring up to him. They gave up their lives to him as completely as though they were in a monastery. When they did import wives and children, they were never allowed near him; he still dreaded children—and dogs and cats.

Now, he could really show that he cared for nothing: he would make sure that his staff could look forward to nothing when he was gone. George Francom prodded him to say where his will was hidden. "You don't think I'm going to tell you where it is, do you?" Hughes replied. In September, the Summa board met at Chester Davis's estate near Unadilla, New York. Bill Gay, Nadine Henley, Levar Myler, and John Holmes sat around a table with Davis at the head and Kay Glenn and Jack Real further down to figure out the aides' future contracts.

Davis called Hughes (thus proving that the board was not acting without Hughes's knowledge) to have him approve the team's contracts. Hughes objected, but was overruled. Even he didn't dare refuse paying his staff money in the future: they might abandon him; they probably would have. The fact that he even demurred now is, to put it mildly, shocking. Asked by Davis for his will, Hughes lied that there was a signed one. "I'll update it, with a codicil," he teased.

Nadine Henley sent Hughes a letter reminding him that she did have an old unsigned will, naming Noah Dietrich as an executor. Maybe he'd want to change it? He was furious at her pushiness, but promised, malevolently, to alter that document and sign it. He had no intention of doing anything of the sort.

How he must have chuckled to himself in the dark hours of the night! How absolutely he was in control of his executives and aides instead of the other way round! He knew that the will naming Dietrich as executor was invalid without his signature. He knew that his rescinding of the 1928 will would stand. He would leave no will, not ever; these wretches could stew in the juice of their greed till hell froze over. But he might have taken care of Jack Real and Gordon Margulis, at least. Even these good friends he left nothing, and Real would spend the rest of his life shielding Hughes's image.

Bill Gay moved Hughes's personal belongings from Romaine Street to Houston. Hughes had been fretting for some time about the problems raised by the fake burglary in June, and, with Woolbright's trial coming up, something might come to light. His old records, along with nostalgic items and his movie prints and projects and flying trophies, were taken to Houston. The documents that had been carried to Freeport and had not been shredded were locked up in Houston with them.

Hughes was active late that summer. He talked about putting TV receiver stations on most of the Bahama islands; he bought three fishing boats for use by Mrs. Lynden O. Pindling, wife of the prime minister, to bring fish in to her Andros Island refrigeration plant; he let Chester Davis plan a special airport hangar for his own use and a beach house on the grounds of the Xanadu Princess, on an artificial island surrounded by water.

He planned to set up an Air East, a branch of Air West, on Grand Bahama Island, to fly on junkets and tourist excursions, with charters to Europe. He began to think (again) of buying Ludwig's hotels in Bermuda and Acapulco. He would add a casino to the Xanadu Princess. Hughes told Dr. Thain lies about his dreams of the Medical Institute's "doing as much for people as the discovery of penicillin." He said he didn't want Thain to concentrate on research into cancer and heart disease, which were overfunded, but rather into genetics and metabolic diseases, like diabetes. He wanted to establish an award for research comparable to the Nobel Prize.

He broke his usual rule and talked to Thain about his parents and his love for them, and Bo Hughes's invention of the power drill; his flights around the world; the women he loved. He said that he still adored Jean Peters.

Thain encouraged him to move to Acapulco to buy the Princess Hotel there, Thain says, because "every time he moved, it was an activating influence." Thain tried harder than any other doctor, but in vain, to get Hughes into a dentist's office to have his loose, rotted teeth pulled and his gums and jaw treated. He tried to make Hughes walk; Hughes could, but wouldn't. "I treated him just like I would treat any patient in a country hospital who comes in with bad teeth and a broken hip," Thain said later.

Every month, Hughes received profit and loss statements from his companies. As the year neared its end, on December 4, he issued instructions through Howard Eckersley and Chuck Waldron to Bill Gay that no adjustments in salaries were to be made without his approval. If the aides had been controlling him, surely no such memorandum would ever have been sent? Eckersley and Waldron both signed it.

On December 9, he reviewed the floor plans for KLAS in Las Vegas, and made certain stipulations: the new studio would offer twenty-four hour service, seven days a week (he had not forgotten his annoyance at its previous midnight cutoff). There would be a backup power plant and air conditioning, and cable would be installed to the Desert Inn show room. Chuck Waldron signed the memo.

When Hughes's lawyer, cousin William Lummis, sued Thain, Dr. Crane, and several aides over their control of Hughes in Nevada, and then Los Angeles, in the late 1970s, the case did not result in a guilty verdict, but rather in a settlement out of insurance by Lummis's office.

Johnny Holmes said later that Hughes talked about making the flight to Mexico on what he now believed to be his seventieth birthday, December 24, saying that he would make a dry run in a test airplane. Holmes discussed the plan with Real, but Real said he couldn't get an extension on an aircraft that might have been suitable. Chester Davis suggested that Hughes might hold a reunion of old friends at the airport before he took off.

The plan for the party fell through, though Hughes seriously considered inviting Cary Grant. Hughes talked to aide Johnny Holmes of other plans: to return to Vancouver from Mexico and thence to London again and back to Freeport. All of this is documented in a 1977 deposition by Holmes. The authors Barlett and Steele, who examined the document, wrote in their book *Empire,* "Someone in the Hughes hierarchy, for a reason not readily discernible, decided that it would be better for Hughes to spend his last days in Mexico." This is nonsense.

On February 10, 1975, Hughes and his entourage flew in a British BAC II to Acapulco. On January 6, President Somoza had sent him a Happy New Year greeting and a request that he return to Managua. He responded on March 6 with a warm and characteristic note saying that he hoped to explore business opportunities in Nicaragua again. Meanwhile, Hughes settled into the $2,000 a day Princess penthouse, its darkened rooms sealed by plywood and black curtains.

In attendance were George Francom, Chuck Waldron, John Holmes, and Gordon Margulis; Jack Real was no longer locked out, metaphorically or actually, from Hughes's life and was a vigilant presence on the scene. Dr. Wilbur Thain, until he took leave and went to Logan, Utah, and thence to the Bahamas and Miami, was there; Dr. Norman Crane and Dr. Lawrence Chaffin were also present. Hughes would have no nurses in the suite; his misogyny was showing again.

Until at least late March, he was continuously wheeling and dealing, "alert, bright and sassy," according to Thain, despite his grievous condition and weighing less than 100 pounds. He complained around the clock about his physical suffering, despite the fact that he was sedated as much as was possible. For over five years, he had endured the misery of arthritis, whenever the drugs wore off; he had severe nerve pain in his neck and shoulders and back; his compressed spinal discs were excruciating; the ache of his gums and teeth was still gnawing and inescapable. His doctors were locked in a dilemma, afraid to exceed the legal doses of codeine and analgesics, yet unwilling to face his wrath if they took away his needles. In his efforts to inject himself with painkillers when the doctors and the aides looked away, he broke needle after needle in his arms and thighs.

He had never been a good patient, and now he was impossible: commanding, controlling, yelling at everyone. On March 1, he got out of bed without help; he had been told to call the moment he wanted to rise. He stumbled awkwardly and fell, slicing off the ugly tumor that disfigured the top of his head.

The gash bled profusely; he refused to wear a bandage or submit to having the wound sewn. He looked ghastly, the miserable sore a glaring, open red. He begged Crane for another drug to ease the agony. Crane refused it. Then he tried Chaffin, who also refused. Hughes groused to Crane, "Chaffin's a knife, scissors, and hammer man. He doesn't believe in medication and nor do you!"

Next day, Hughes told George Francom he was sorry; Francom in turn told Chaffin, though typically Hughes didn't tell Chaffin himself. But he did call Chaffin in and talk to him about the old days which Chaffin had shared with him: the days of Muirfield Road, the plane crash in Beverly Hills, Katharine Hepburn.

Somehow, in defiance of everyone, Hughes managed to smuggle twenty to thirty aspirins a day into the suite, through an aide. These helped to reduce the pain when his doctors reduced his codeine intake to four ccs. He grumbled louder and louder about the sticky heat that the Princess's inadequate air conditioning system failed to subdue. He never looked out of the window at the lush tropical gardens of the hotel.

At the end of March, Hughes became unusually quarrelsome. He clashed with one of his aides, Chuck Waldron; he had always been fond of Waldron, and when Waldron's little daughter was drowned, he, for once, showed human feelings. But now, every time Waldron reminded him that some documents needed attending to, he would get angry; finally, Waldron snapped at him: "Why should I stay away from my family and try to help you get your business matters in order? I'd rather go home." Hughes shouted at him, and Waldron shouted back.

For Waldron, it had never been easy to get Hughes to take care of anything, not because Hughes wasn't on top of everything (Waldron stated that he was) but because of his procrastinations.

Hughes began talking about buying a multimillion-dollar mansion in Houston and authorized bribes for various politicians.

On April 3, it became obvious that Hughes was failing. He stopped eating after several days of nibbling feebly at his food; his gums were bleeding badly, and he may have swallowed loose teeth.

At 3:00 P.M., George Francom suffered a shock. He found that Hughes was apparently blind. When he waved his hand over his eyes, Hughes gave no flicker of response. One of the most insidious infections of HIV is cetameglo-virus retinitis (CMV) which in some cases causes rapid blindness. It is almost impossible to detect until it has already affected the eyes. Also, Hughes was suffering from delusions and incoherent, babbling speech, followed by lucid intervals, another classic symptom. But there is still no proof he had AIDS.

Francom called Dr. Crane, who gave Hughes a quick examination. He found Hughes in a state of shock, his pulse rapid; his blood pressure was very low (100 over 60); he was sweating, cold, and clammy. Dr. Chaffin prepared an injection of 1,400 ccs. of five percent glucose in water to maintain his sugar level, into his left arm. His pulse slowed, but he still showed no sign of recognition.

At 4:00 P.M., Hughes became delirious, talking nervously, incoherently about a life insurance policy. Was this the common affliction of AIDS-related dementia? He refused water or food; he made a feeble effort to inject himself; Dr. Crane took the needle from him. He begged George Francom to plunge the needle in; Francom would not. Hughes got his revenge; suddenly snapping to, he became his old, sly self. Chuck Waldron walked in with a proxy form, which he was to sign to let all and sundry in his empire use his accounts as they pleased. Hughes refused to sign it. Even if he was dying, and he must have known it, nobody would ever get anything out of him.

Late that afternoon, after much hesitation, the physicians called in a local specialist, Dr. Victor Montemoya, for a diagnosis. Hughes managed to force a trickle of urine for a test; Montemoya found the patient badly dehydrated. He did not recommend hospitalization in Acapulco as the local clinic was badly air conditioned and primitive.

He suggested that Hughes be flown to the United States. Dr. Thain canceled a trip to Guatemala and came at once. It was Sunday, April 4.

When Thain arrived, he saw that Hughes should be gotten to an American hospital at once. He looked ghastly; he was comatose; he was covered in needle marks; the gash on his head was hideous; his skin was grayer and slacker than ever; the muscles were stringy and loose.

Besides glucose and water injections, which had been administered from the moment the coma began, Thain ordered two intravenous shots of Solu-Cortel, to prevent Hughes from dying of a cerebral edema. Thain didn't know at the time that the aspirin doses Hughes was taking were triggering a necrosis of the kidneys which was killing him.

Jack Real was delegated the task of finding a plane to take Hughes to Houston. No aircraft had been rushed in from Los Angeles; when efforts were made to charter a local plane, the owner was unreachable, on a fishing trip, and the pilot couldn't accept the charter. Real rechartered the Learjet that had brought Thain in from Miami.

On the morning of the 5th, Hughes set out on his last journey. His aides carried him on a stretcher to a waiting van, and thence at the airport to the waiting plane.

It is clear that the aides knew Hughes was going to die very soon because only one elected to travel with him to Texas. Doctors Thain and Chaffin and Johnny Holmes were on the final journey. His men simply placed him on his stretcher on the cabin floor. The physicians took turns to monitor his blood pressure, pulse, and respiration. The pilot flew on a direct northwest course, through smooth conditions, in a cloudless, clear blue sky.

At 1:25 P.M., Thain observed that Hughes's eyes were glazing over; his pulse stopped. Thain tried to revive him, without success. He told Dr. Chaffin that there were no vital signs. Mercifully, Hughes had not wakened, and didn't know what was happening. He had not emerged from his coma of two days earlier. It was what he would have wanted; with his money and power, he had fulfilled all of his wishes, except to be freed from pain, and now that wish had come true. It was appropriate he would have died in an airplane cabin; that most antiseptic, lifeless, and charmless of human accommodations was always his favorite habitat. The wheel of his life had come full circle, for he was now, at last, on the way to Houston, where he had spent his childhood. Soon he would be buried next to the parents who had left him in death when he was far, far too young.

# Postscript

Just twenty minutes after life was declared extinguised, the Learjet pilot touched down at Houston Intercontinental Airport. Dr. Thain and Dr. Chaffin had that morning telephoned to have Hughes taken, on arrival, to Houston Methodist Hospital, and that plan wasn't changed. In the hospital's basement morgue, Dr. Jack L. Titus found that the body's limbs were still flexible; rigor mortis had not yet set in, and would not, given the temperature, for some hours. Titus determined that Hughes was down to ninety-three pounds, and was totally dehydrated.

Titus informed Hughes's next of kin, Hughes's mother's sister, Annette Lummis, and her son William; Mrs. Lummis was not certain that the dead man was her nephew, even after the corpse had been identified, and insisted on a full-scale postmortem. Dr. Joseph A. Jachimczyk, in charge, confirmed Titus's belief that acute kidney failure, combined with dehydration, was the cause of death. He found evidence of cancer, not only in the scalp but in the prostate gland, a fact which was never made public then or later. Significantly, he stated that Hughes's brain was not deteriorated, and, oddly, added that its owner was "very smart."

On April 7, Hughes was interred in the presence of Annette and William Lummis, and a handful of others, next to his parents, in a modest grave at Glenwood Cemetery.

His estate was valued at about $650 million; millions more had been lost through mismanagement. Theories were circulated that he had been murdered; that either a physician, or one of his aides, or a CIA agent, had injected a fatal dose of codeine into him when he was comatose. The trouble with this theory is that both physicians and aides had more to gain from his being alive; they were on retainers of $100,000 a year and up—many times that much in 1990s money. The doctors might have obtained similar figures in private practice, but the aides had been humble workmen before Hughes hired them, and, without his support, they would probably be humble workmen again. The CIA theory is equally unfounded. The CIA had every reason to keep its longtime chief supplier of secret weaponry alive.

The truth is that the only injection administered to Hughes in his comatose condition was Dr. Thain's perfectly legitimate Solu-Cortel shot, designed to prevent him from having a fatal edema of the brain.

Marooned in Acapulco, Hughes's aides, Chuck Waldron, Eric Nundy, and Clyde Crow, were charged with forging Hughes's signature on documents required for an entry visa when they arrived in Mexico in January, although the charges were eventually dropped. Once again, nobody would believe Hughes was capable of acting of his own free will; once again, his signature was proven to be genuine. Chuck Waldron was even jailed briefly in the matter, a victim of the myth of a helpless Hughes.

After much wrangling between relatives and lawyers, it was decided that Annette and William Lummis were best entitled to run the tangled estate, and judges in Texas, California, and Nevada so ruled. A desperate search for a valid, signed will took place, consuming scores of thousands of dollars. Hotels, apartment buildings, mansions where Hughes had lived were searched. Psychic Peter Hurkos was hired; he asked for an item of Hughes's clothing, but none could be found, so he gave up. The statement was made (repeated by Barlett and Steele in *Empire*) that Hughes had gone naked for years. The truth is that his filthy rags had been burned; not even his shoes or lucky hat remained. No valid will was located then or later.

Twenty-two of Hughes's cousins began fighting to obtain their share of the fortune; hundreds more joined the fray. Leader of the cousins' contingent was Rupert Hughes's stepdaughter, Avis McIntyre, the former Mrs. John Monk Saunders, who played so significant a role in Hughes's early life. Lawyers popped up all over the map, some of them claiming to represent mentally incompetent persons. Fantastic claims were made that Hughes's father was not his father; that his mother was Annette Lummis, who was a child when he was born; that he was one of triplets, or one-half of one set or two sets of identical twins . . . the nonsense went on and on.

On April 27, before Superior Court Judge Jeil Lake, three granddaughters of Rupert Hughes—Agnes Roberts, Elspeth de-Pould, and Barbara Lapp Cameron—sought to wrest California control of the estate from Richard Gano and have it run by County Administrator Bruce Altman. This was denied. Avis and Rush Hughes put in claims. Then there was a startling development.

On the afternoon of April 27, a will, dated March 19, 1968, was found on a desk of the Mormon world headquarters in Salt Lake City. It was addressed to the late David O. McKay, Church President, with a covering letter purportedly signed by Hughes. Badly spelled, it stated that his assets were to be divided between the Hughes Medical Institute, the University of Texas, the Rice Institute, the Universities of Nevada and California, the Mormon Church, David O. McKay, a home for orphan children, the Boy Scouts, Jean Peters, first wife Ella Rice, William R. Lummis, Melvin DuMar, and his aides; the Spruce Goose was to be given to the City of Long Beach, and Noah Dietrich was to be executor.

The last sentence was the giveaway; Hughes detested the nickname Spruce Goose for his ill-fated seaplane, and he despised and had dismissed Noah Dietrich. If anyone had been his executor in 1968, it would have been Robert Maheu.

Who was Melvin DuMar? He turned out to be Melvin Dummar, a Utah gas station operator, who came up with a fantastic story. In January, 1968, he said he was driving from Tonopah, the site of Hughes's wedding, to Beatty, when he found an ancient, beaten bum lying beside the road, dressed in baggy pants and tennis shoes. The man asked to be dropped off at the Sands Hotel, and Dummar obliged. The man was Hughes.

Overnight, Dummar was famous; a paperback publisher wanted his life story; MCA-Universal talked about a movie, and flew him to Hollywood with his wife for a stay at the Beverly Wilshire Hotel; music publishers chased him for his songs.

Noah Dietrich declared the will genuine. So did the usual number of handwriting experts. But soon the lid came down. It was obvious that Hughes spelled properly and would never have misspelled his own cousin William Lummis's name as Lommis. Yet law enforcement authorities from Texas to Nevada and Utah were lax in nailing Dummar, who sailed on, embattled, but not exposed.

It was not for a year that the FBI began analyzing fingerprints on the will and found they were those of two officials who had examined it. The envelope, however, carried Dummar's thumbprint. Dummar kept changing his story; he said that the will had been left at his service station in Willard, Utah, on April 27, 1976, by a mysterious man driving a blue Mercedes. He steamed the envelope open, found the will, and took it to the Mormon headquarters.

At that stage, one LeVane Forsyth announced that he was the mysterious man. He said he had been a confidential agent and courier for Hughes, had as many as fifty aliases, and, when calling Hughes with secret information, addressed Hughes only as "Ventura." In the summer of 1972, he said, Hughes, in Vancouver, gave him the envelope containing the will. But he made a slip; he said he was driving a Ford or a Chevrolet when he left the envelope with Dummar. Meanwhile, that authority on handwriting, Clifford Irving, added his five cents by saying the will was a fake. The case against Dummar succeeded; the will was shown to be a forgery.

It was found that Hughes had taken at least one action, presumably through his aides, without advising Bill Gay or his other executives. He had deposited enormous numbers of stock certificates, upwards of $100 million, with the Bank of America. There was speculation that he had put them there as liquidateable assets in the event a $70 million bond might be required if he lost the TWA case, but nobody was sure.

The money was his, his alone, and was not made over to Bill Gay or anyone else.

Another will turned up in the office of Probate Judge William Bear, in the Harris County courthouse, Houston; it bequeathed the entire estate to Annette Lummis (misspelled Lunnis) with just $60,000 to one Ellen Pukovich; this was found to be fake. Yet another turned up at Judge Keith Hayes's office at the county courthouse of Las Vegas, dated June 22, 1969, and leaving everything to Summa (spelled Sunna), which was not named or formed until 1972.

More and more wills turned up, the fake beneficiaries buried cunningly in small print. One will left $400 million to Dwayne Clyde Byron Hughes, who said he was Hughes's son and was born in a flying saucer over Oklahoma in 1946; James Robertson, of Groton, Connecticut, sold 2,000 fake Hughes wills over the counter as a gag, although neither of them were ever shown to have directly tampered with the documents. By June 30, thirty wills had been filed.

Some old details emerged: Hughes had borrowed $39.5 million from three Texas banks three months before he died—Texas Commerce, First City National, and Bank of the Southwest—merging part of the money into a cash bond portfolio of $200 million. Apparently, this was for improvements of the Desert Inn, but it was never proven. It also emerged that he was constantly borrowing enormous sums on his collateral because borrowed money could not be taxed.

At the end of 1976, there was a fierce struggle for control of the now drifting Hughes empire. William Lummis tried to fire Chester Davis, without success; he also tried to dislodge Bill Gay. Lummis fought against a Davis-Gay plan to renovate the Desert Inn, as Hughes had long wanted, but very much on the grounds of Gay's plans that Hughes had brutally rejected in London; again and again, Davis, Gay, and Nadine Henley, who was with them, overruled Lummis in majority board decisions.

Finally, on May 26, 1977, Lummis managed, as administrator, to strip Davis, and aides Johnny Holmes and Levar Myler, of their positions on the board. He kept Bill Gay on for a time, but Gay soon resigned of his own accord, amid strong recrimination. At the same time, litigation continued, which resulted, in July, in the provisional settlement of the estate, ratified two years later: it would be divided between Avis Hughes McIntyre and her brother Rush, Annette Lummis, Barbara Lapp Cameron, Rupert Hughes's granddaughter, and eighteen other cousins.

It was ruled that the Hughes Medical Institute must at last justify itself; no longer sole owner of Hughes Aircraft, it must increase its spending. In March, 1987, it paid $35 million in back taxes. On January 25, 1978, Samuel Lionel, Las Vegas attorney, filed the unsuccessful suit on behalf of the First National Bank of Nevada, William Lummis, the Summa Corporation, Hughes Air West, and Hughes Properties, charging Bill Gay, Chester Davis, and numerous others with siphoning off $50 million from Hughes by manipulating and isolating him for the last years of his life. The case dragged on for years and got nowhere; Summa settled out of the insurance money. Robert Maheu was awarded an out-of-court settlement of $17.3 million in his libel suit (he had shrewdly filed it against

Hughes Tool, not Hughes himself) but later lost the lot at the appel-late level. By June, twenty-two relatives were fighting for control of the Hughes companies; Summa had rallied under Lummis and gone from losses of $17 million in 1976 to pretax profits of $31.1 million in 1977. A battle over where Hughes was resident when he died dragged on for years.

By 1980, the empire was beginning to crack open. Borg-Warner bought a 20.5 percent stake in Hughes Tool that year. In 1986, General Motors snapped up Hughes Aircraft. Today, the Hughes Medical Institute is an ironical monument to the memory of a man who used it only as a tax dodge; its ten-year program calls for an expenditure of $500 million for education in the medical and biolog-ical sciences. Howard Hughes, wherever he is, must surely have appreciated the joke.

# Author's Note
# and Acknowledgments

I originally embarked on this book in 1971, without a contract; but I became perhaps forgivably diverted by the idea of a book on Ava Gardner, and wrote that instead. I began it again in 1974, also without approaching a publisher; then Katharine Hepburn agreed to cooperate with me on a biography of her, and the idea evaporated once more. I revived the idea in 1992, and, encouraged, proceeded with the book for Putnam and Berkley. I am grateful for the enthusiasm of my editor, George Coleman; and of my agent, Dan Strone, of William Morris, who never lost his faith in the project. Dorene Suter was my intrepid typist.

Because of the odd, broken course of the research, many individuals have died in the intervening years. Of these, Hughes's right-hand man, Noah Dietrich, was the prime source. He gave me long, exhaustive interviews in his Gothic castle overlooking Sunset Strip, his energy unabated although he was then very old. He had a detailed knowledge of Hughes's bisexual nature; he made an unforgettable impression. I also enjoyed the raffish Johnny Meyer, whom I met at his favorite watering place, the Drake Hotel bar in New York, where he once consorted with Hughes and pimped for him; unabashed, amoral, he was a great, gossipy source; his death—he was run over by his own car—is still unexplained. Ted Carpentier was Hughes's little-known friend, who for years was in touch with him;

he also is much missed, and so is the macho, manic producer, Jerry Wald.

Of those happily alive, I owe a special debt to Robert Maheu, Noah Dietrich's successor as Hughes's right-hand man, whose loyalty to Hughes is remarkable, given the billionaire's ill-treatment of him, and who has survived years of exhausting litigation, a heart attack, and other burdens with charm, courtliness, and unstinting kindness. I treasure our meetings in Los Angeles and Las Vegas. Jack Real, best friend of Hughes and aeronautics authority, was another fine source. Gordon Margulis gave me hours of invaluable interviews on tape at the Desert Inn in Las Vegas, where he first went to work for Hughes and where I stayed. Mell Stewart filled out more details; so did Jim Golden, formerly of Intertel. The depositions of the other Hughes aides were indispensable. I enjoyed the cooperation of Hughes Estate administrator Bill Miller and William Lummis; Bernard Barker, chief burglar of Watergate, was a main source; Dr. Wilbur Thain, Dr. Howard House, and the late Dr. Verne Mason were richly revealing on Hughes's medical condition. The following individuals filled in more: the late Don Siegel, director; the late Lucien Ballard, cameraman; the late Norman Foster, director; Bill Feeder, Hughes publicist; Linwood Dunn, RKO special effects genius; Stanley Rubin, producer; Richard Fleischer, director; David Hooks, ace Houston researcher; Jeff Hearn, prince of Washington sleuths and archival research whiz kid; Ted Hamilton and Nile Coates, diligent Los Angeles diggers into books and records; Burton Hersh, authority on the CIA and contact maker; Barbara Howard, finder of rare Dallas documents; Scott Lichtig, owner of Rupert Hughes's Moroccan mansion; Richard Bissell, formerly of the CIA; Robert McKay, Madison, Wisconsin, expert; Patrick McGilligan, writer; Dr. Brian Miller, psychotherapist, expert on bisexuality; Henry Rogers, publicist and author; Charles Rappleye, chronicler of Johnny Rosselli, friend and mentor; Lawrence Quirk, author and irreplaceable source on the wayward stars; Anthony Slide, historian; Kevin Thomas, film critic; Stuart Thompson, art dealer and friend; Dr. Michael Stefan, valuable answerer of many medical questions; Christopher Ely, researcher; Julio Vera, who arranged for me to talk to Bernard Barker and did much other background work; Marc Wanamaker, archivist; Dudley C. Sharp, son of Hughes's boyhood friend of the same name; Sandra Garrett and Sarah Clark, Austin, Texas, researchers; Brigitte Koepus, curator of the UCLA Special Collections Department, keeper of the RKO production files; Bruce Oudes, Nixon authority; Tom Pollock, head of MCA/Universal, who, despite a heavy schedule, had his staff locate Hughes's legal files for me; Al Levitt, writer; Bertrand Tavernier, friend, famous director, and authority on the blacklist; Michel Ciment, critic and friend; Peter D. Gordon, lawyer; Jim Hougan, author and journalist; Diane Finstad, lawyer and writer; W. C. Allen and O. Delton Harris, Shreveport bigwigs; Christian Harper and Stephen Sorrentino of HarperCollins; Miles Kreuger, keeper of musical movie treasures, wise friend; Howard Kohn, authority on Intertel; Jim Appleby and Jim Farmer, aeronautics experts; Anita Bouziane, New York researcher; my close friend Todd McCarthy of *Variety;* Leland W. Warner, associate of the late Ambassador Turner Shelton; Mrs. Turner Shelton; Francois du Sardou, expert on all things Latin American; Mina Nelson, friend of the late President Somoza; Don Carlos Rodriguez, Somoza publisher and newspaper owner; Philippe and Pamela Mora, director and his life partner, friends; Jerry and Milton Pickman, of the RKO years; Judge Harry Shafer, of the Superior Court; Mrs. Rosick Cravens and Mrs. Edward Kelley, childhood friends of Howard Hughes; June Lang, Hughes's early girl friend; John Sturges, director (who died during the writing of this book); Milo and Sally (Forrest) Frank, witty producer and star; Jamison Handy, Hughes honcho; Peter Maheu, powerful private eye; William Corson, John Prados, and Victor Marchetti, CIA experts; Howard Hunt, peripatetic spy, whose refusal to talk about Hughes was more eloquent than words; Dennis Tomlin, lawyer; Abe Hershberg, anecdotalist; Lucille Turner and Ruth Ellen Taylor, mainstays of the Hughes empire; Jimmy Zacharakos, assistant to Chester Davis; Taylor Branch, biographer; George Parnham, lawyer; Robert Mundy, writer; Barbara Greenspun and former Governor O'Callaghan, of the sturdy *Las Vegas Sun;* John Farquhar, executive; Jack Real, Hughes friend, aeronautics authority; Jim Phelan, biographer, veteran journalist; Anson Thacher, school friend; Professor Stephen Ambrose, distinguished Nixon biographer, who confirmed in a taped interview my findings on the nature of the Watergate operation, and Hughes's and Nixon's role in it; Philip Klass, authority on satellites; Mrs. Lawrence O'Brien; Clarence Lyons, archivist; Jane Greer, actress; Katherine Pradt, copy editor.

Sworn depositions by the following individuals, in the public domain, were obtained by David Hooks, in Houston, from the files of the Hughes Estate litigations, and have been used extensively in this book (listed here in the order filed): Barbara Lapp Cameron; Noah Dietrich; Rush Hughes; Avis Hughes McIntyre; Marie Miller, Thacher School librarian; Robert Maheu; Johanna Madsen; Fred Wilson; Gordon Sawyer; Charles Moran, waiter; Ralph Winte; Macy Todd; Dr. Jack Titus; Frank W. Gay; Dr. Homer Clark; Howard Eckersley; Perry Lieber; Terry Moore; Robert Poussin, chef; James Richard; Clarene Waldron; Vernon Olsen; Ron Kistler; Ben Lyon; Frank McCulloch; Levar Myler; Greg Bautzer; Milton West; John Holmes; Thirza Ebdon; Dr. Lawrence Chaffin; Jack Egger; George Francom; Dr. Norman Crane; Hank Greenspun; Jean Peters (Mrs. Stanley Hough); Walter Kane; Glenn Odekirk; Jack Real; Richard Dreher; Patricia Mason, daughter of Verne Mason; Roy Crawford.

In addition, I should like to acknowledge the following documentary sources: the little-known Final Report of Howard Baker's Select Committee on Presidential Campaign Activities, U.S. Senate, Pursuant to S. Res, February 7, 1973, which depicts the CIA links to Watergate; Larry DuBois's and Lawrence Gonzalez's two-part series in *Playboy*, September-October, 1976, entitled "The Puppet . . . Uncovering the Secret World of Nixon, Hughes and the CIA"; Bruce Oude's *From the President: Richard Nixon's Secret Files;* Howard Kohn's *The Hughes-Nixon-Lasky Connection: The Secret Alliances of the CIA from World War II to Watergate,* published in *Rolling Stone* on May 20, 1976; the complaint of the *First National Bank of Nevada v. Frank William Gay, etc.,* Case No. 185995, 1982, filed in Las Vegas, followed up in Los Angeles, which contains Dr. Wilbur Thain's diary notes; the Securities and Exchange Commission report on the Romaine St. break-in, contained in the files of the case *California vs. Woolbright,* 1976, and the CIA report on the burglary; Peter Dale Scott's *Crime and Cover-up: The CIA, the Mafia and the Dallas-Watergate Connection,* published by Westworks, Berkeley, California, in 1977; hearings before the Committee on Internal Security, House of Representatives, 93rd Congress, October 17 and 18, 1973, which contain statements by Dr. Manuel Reyes; records of Watergate Special Prosecution Force, including an important statement by Robert F. Bennett (August 11, 1973, etc.); Fred D. Thompson's *At That Point in Time,* Quadrangle, New York, 1978, which first revealed the now forgotten Democrat plot; *The CIA,* by Brian Fremantle, published by Stein and Day, New York, in 1984; Stephen Pendo's *Aviation in the Cinema,* published by the Scarecrow Press, Metuchen, NJ; hundreds of Hughes's memoranda found in Houston in the Hughes Estate files in 1985; and, very importantly, Mary Smith Fay's genealogy of Hughes (though she missed his correct birthdate) published in *The National Genealogical Society Quarterly*, March, 1983.

There follow notes on sources and a select bibliography of works consulted; in all, millions of words and some 55,000 documents were read for the book.

# Notes on Sources

## CHAPTER ONE

The correct details of Howard Hughes's birth were obtained by David Hooks in Houston, Texas, and in my correspondence with St. John's Episcopal Church, Keokuk, Iowa, which sent the register entry. The Gothic rumors surrounding the birth were determined from Diane Finstad, historian and former Hughes Estate attorney; Miss Finstad and the late Noah Dietrich supplied information on Rupert Hughes. The facts concerning Bo Hughes's wildcatting experiences were drawn from several thousand pages of oral histories with pioneer oilmen, preserved at the Barker Center of the Texas State Archives in Austin, Texas, and accessed by Sandra Garrett. The material on the Ganos was assembled at the Dallas Historical Society by Barbara Howard; the wedding was described in the Dallas newspapers. Secretary Charlie Lane's oral history at Barker was a main source on the Hugheses' honeymoon and its aftermath. The descriptions of the Buffalo Bayou and of Shreveport were drawn from the records of the Louisiana and Texas historical societies. Allene Hughes's experiences were gleaned from the Barker collection. The oral histories there of Charlie Lane and of Granville Humasson were especially useful on the invention of the tool bit. Addresses were obtained from city directories. Veteran Louisianans O. Delton Harrison, W. C. Allen, and Eleck Taylor were detailed on the Shreveport period. Hughes's hearing problem was described for me by leading Los Angeles hearing specialist Dr. Howard House at his home in the Los Feliz district of Los Angeles. The Houston Education Board supplied material on Mrs. Eichler's "University." The Rice murder case was headlined in *The New York Times* in 1900. The former Mary Cullinan was a major source on Hughes's childhood. The Prosser period was covered in letters from teacher Richardson to Sherman Thacher, found in the Hughes Estate files in Houston. The Burlington matter is recorded in the same collection. The records of the Camp Dan Beard stay are found in the collection of the Beard Outdoor School housed in the Library of Congress, and include letters to and from Allene and Howard Hughes, Rush Hughes, Victor Aures, and Dan Beard. Dudley Sharp II was interviewed for supplementary information.

## CHAPTER TWO

The information on Fessenden School was supplied by the present head teacher and library staff and was obtained by Mr. and Mrs. Christopher Ely. The yacht registration and details were in Lloyd's Register of American Yachts. Eleanor Boardman spoke to me in 1971 at her home in Santa Barbara of her affair with Bo Hughes and of Allene Hughes's final, tragic note. Lawrence Quirk was the source on the incestuous seduction of Howard by Rupert Hughes. The material on Thacher is from Hughes's friend Anson Thacher and from family correspondence in the Hughes Estate files. John Monk Saunders's background was supplied by Fay Wray, in 1971, at her Tiger Tail Road, Brentwood, home. The Saunders/Avis wedding was in the *New York Herald-Tribune.* The death certificate and obituary of Allene Gano Hughes were obtained by David Hooks from County Records Offices. The movements of Annette and Sonny, etc., are to be found in family correspondence in the Hughes Estate files. Bo Hughes's death details were obtained by David Hooks; probate files of Bo's estate are in the Houston archives. Houston estate files are the source of the Ella Rice engagement and marriage, the latter reported in *The Houston Post.* I discussed the Rossmore ménage in the early 1970s with the late Rush Hughes and with the late Noah Dietrich, who were also the chief sources on the Hugheses' unhappy marriage. Dietrich and the late Johnny Meyer were sources on Hughes's sexual habits then and later, as was Ted Carpentier.

CHAPTER THREE

In 1971, Noah Dietrich spoke of his experiences with Hughes at length at his Gothic castle above Sunset Strip. The Hughes files of the Academy of Motion Pictures Arts and Sciences are rich with information on Hughes's early film ventures. My friend Lewis Milestone in joyous conversation in the 1970–71 period kept me agog with tales of working with Hughes, all given here. So did Mary Astor, at her home in Fountain Valley, California, in 1971, and on board the S.S. *Arcadia* in the South Pacific, in 1968. The details of *Hell's Angels* were drawn from Academy files; from interviews with Jim Farmer, Hugh Wynne, Jim Appleby, Bob Boder, and Lawrence Quirk; from conversations with my neighbor and boyhood friend Ben Lyon at Dolphin Square, London, in the late 1940s; from files preserved at MCA/Universal and supplied courtesy Tom Pollock, its president and CEO. Files of Lincoln Quarberg, publicist, including the "obscene" picture, are at the Academy; I drew from *Los Angeles Times* files, *Motion Picture Herald, Variety,* etc., etc. The vice king parallels were in the *Los Angeles Times* and *Variety;* the Jean Harlow gangster information was from Ben Lyon and Irving Shulman. The breakup of the Hughes marriage is from a confidential Houston source; the lockup of the room is from depositions of household staff members Richard Dreher and Johanna Madsen. The *Dawn Patrol* story was given me by Hal Wallis at his home in Trancas, California, in 1985.

CHAPTER FOUR

On the matter of Billie Dove, I spoke to Miss Dove in 1971 in Palm Springs and to her chronicler and friend, DeWitt Bodeen, in Hollywood, and Irvin Willat, at his Hollywood home, also in 1971; the Warner Bros. file was consulted in Burbank at that time, courtesy of the late Carl Shaefer, formerly Warner's foreign publicity chief. The *Ranger* details came from Lloyd's Register. Marc Wanamaker, archivist, was the source on the *Hell's Angels* premiere, backed up by the opening night deluxe program (courtesy the Academy of Motion Picture Arts and Sciences). Lewis Milestone described the opening to me and so did Howard Hawks and George Jessel. For the promotions, see the Quarberg files; the London opening was recorded in the London *Daily Mail.* The Quarberg files were detailed on the other films of the time; Milestone gave me particulars of *The Front Page* and so did Jed Harris, at the Waldorf-Astoria Hotel, New York, in 1974. *Scarface,* more than any other picture, can be traced from start to finish in the Quarberg documents at the Academy, including Hughes's telegrams and ship-to-shore wirelesses. Todd McCarthy is writing a book on Hawks and is a main source on him, as are my interviews with Hawks in 1971, in Palm Springs, for Time-Life Books; Hawks told me of Hughes's emphasis on incest; the bootleg story was from Noah Dietrich and was told, slightly differently, in his memoirs; the George Raft matter is in his biography; a London *Daily Mail* series dealt with *Queer People.* A startling exposé of the matter was obtained at the Library of Congress.

## CHAPTER FIVE

The Glenn Odekirk material was drawn from Odekirk's depositions in the Hughes Estate papers in Houston; the *Rover* details were recorded in Lloyd's Register of shipping; the FBI files on Axel Wenner-Gren are in the author's collection at USC; Ida Lupino described her romance with Hughes at lunch with me in Hollywood, 1968; the journeys as photographer and tramp are described in Omar Garrison's *Howard Hughes in Las Vegas;* the 1934 air race was reported in *The Miami Herald.* Corinne Griffith told me of her affair with Hughes in Beverly Hills in 1968, also of her fight against taxes. The *Sylvia Scarlett* story came from my interview with Katharine Hepburn at her home in West Hollywood in 1974; interviews with George Cukor, also in West Hollywood, in 1968, 1969, 1970, 1972; and interviews with Brian Aherne, Santa Monica, 1974. The flight of the H-1 racer was reported in the *Los Angeles Times* and *Los Angeles Herald Examiner* and *The New York Times.* Lewis Milestone and Noah Dietrich told me of the attempted sabotage.

## CHAPTER SIX

Sources on the Hepburn romance were Miss Hepburn herself, at her home in West Hollywood in 1974, and depositions by Johanna Madsen and Richard Dreher. The air flight on a bet was in *The New York Times* and the *Chicago Tribune;* also the car crash. Ginger Rogers's account is based in part in her memoirs, in part on Madsen; Noah Dietrich supplied more information, as did my former secretary, the RKO contract actress Frances Mercer, Pandro S. Berman, RKO production chief in Beverly Hills, and director George Stevens, late and much-missed companion of many Hollywood lunches. The *Jane Eyre* tour was described to me by Hepburn; the Harmon Trophy Award is documented at the Roosevelt Memorial Library, Hyde Park; the affair with Barbara Hutton in London was described by David Heymann in *Poor Little Rich Girl,* the life of Barbara Hutton, from whose diary he quoted; the Bette Davis affair was described to me by Miss Davis in Beverly Hills in 1968 and by her business manager, Carlyn Wood, who saw the check stubs and made the financial transactions in Hollywood; in a recent book on Hayworth, Barbara Leaming inaccurately denied the story, without talking to me, or to Wood. Parts of the story preceding the world flight are in Hepburn's *Me,* supplemented from a wide variety of sources including *Time, Newsweek, Aviation Monthly, The New York Times* and *Los Angeles Times,* etc., etc., as well as Glenn Odekirk's depositions; Madsen/Dreher added more. The Smithsonian Institution had some information on the flight as well as on the plane itself; the particulars of the flight were determined through research conducted in part by Jeffrey Hearn in Washington; in State Department files; Department of Commerce and Air files; CAA files; *Le Matin,* Paris; *Le Monde;* the St. Paul, Minnesota, *Pioneer Press;* Lockheed files; Civil Aeronautics Board files, Russian newspapers, including *Moscow News* in English; *The Houston Post* and the *Houston Chronicle;* Fairbanks, Alaska, Historical Society files; and the memoirs of Grover Whalen. Fay Wray described her dating Hughes, and her visits with him, in her memoirs *On the Other Hand;* in my interview with her in 1971 she told me of the fatal effect on John Monk Saunders. The hurricane story was in *Me,* by Hepburn. Joan Fontaine wrote of Hughes in her memoirs, *No Bed of Roses.* In 1968, I spoke to Olivia de Havilland at the Beverly Wilshire Hotel about Hughes's interest in her.

## CHAPTER SEVEN

On TWA, Robert Serling's *Howard Hughes' Airline* was a good source; the Wenner-Gren matter is, as stated, in the FBI files; the affair with Gene Tierney is described in her memoirs and in those of Igor and Oleg Cassini; the Power affair with Hughes is from Lawrence Quirk; Lana Turner's romance with him is in her autobiography. *The*

*Outlaw* story I gleaned from Lucien Ballard in West Hollywood in 1984 and from Howard Hawks in Palm Springs in 1972; other sources were the Breen office files of the Motion Picture Code, Academy of Motion Picture Arts and Sciences, Beverly Hills; Lawrence Quirk (the Jack Buetel matter); Jane Russell's memoirs. The Santa Claus/Rogers story was in Johanna Madsen's depositions. The prolonged series of briberies of government beginning in 1942 were documented in the Senate hearings of 1947 and in the FBI files on Hughes; in the Department of Commerce files; in *The New York Times, The Washington Post,* and *The Wall Street Journal;* in *Time* and *Newsweek;* in conversations with Hughes lawyer Gregson Bautzer in Beverly Hills in 1984 and with Johnny Meyer at the Drake Hotel, New York, and at the offices of the Onassis Corporation, 1972; and in the White House files of presidential secretary Stephen Early, Franklin D. Roosevelt Memorial Library, Hyde Park, New York.

## CHAPTER EIGHT

Hughes's S and M experiences were related to me by William Haines at his decorators' shop in Beverly Hills, 1970; by Ted Carpentier in Hollywood in 1978; and by Ramon Novarro in the Hollywood Hills in 1965. Lawrence Quirk was the source on Richard Cromwell, Russel Gleason, and Robert Taylor. Johnny Meyer's story was that Flynn and Hughes met for the night, but Quirk gives a different outcome. The Hughes FBI files disclose the Darnell affair; Nunnally Johnson, writer and director, also told me of it. The Ava Gardner matter is dealt with in her memoirs and those of Mickey Rooney. I interviewed Rooney in Sydney, Australia, in the 1960s. Yvonne De Carlo's memoirs detail her romance with Hughes. The 1945 scams were a weekly feature of Westbrook Pegler's syndicated columns. For TWA material, see Serling, op. cit. For the Preston Sturges matter, see James Curtis's life of Sturges. Diane Finstad and the *Los Angeles Times* were the best sources on Mrs. Rupert Hughes's suicide; the Constellation flight was recorded in the FBI files and in the *Los Angeles Times.*

## CHAPTER NINE

Noah Dietrich was the chief source on the Shreveport episode, supported by the aforementioned Shreveport sources; Ted Carpentier was a major source on the XF-11 and on the plane crash. I consulted depositions by Jean Peters, Glenn Odekirk, Richard Dreher, and Dr. Lawrence Chaffin in the Hughes Estate, Houston; and drew from interviews with Ted Carpentier and Johnny Meyer and from files of the hearings of the Senate War Committee.

### CHAPTER TEN

Flying boat information came from John J. McDonald's history of the plane. The story of the buying of RKO is contained in the Jacqueline Cochran biography; other sources were interviews with Richard Fleischer and Stanley Rubin in Bel Air and Beverly Hills; the late Raquel Torres, the former Mrs. Stephen Ames (Malibu); William Feeder (telephone); Jane Greer (telephone); the late Norman Foster (Beverly Hills); and Robert Wise (telephone). Dore Schary's memoirs and his papers at University of Wisconsin, Madison, Wisconsin, have been useful. The maid Macy Todd's deposition, Hughes Estate, Houston, was a mine of information on the Hughes-Peters relationship; Barbara Leaming wrote of Hayworth's abortion in her biography. Terry Moore's intriguing and little-known *The Beauty and the Billionaire* dealt with her prolonged affair with Hughes; skeptics please note that she repeated most of her story under oath in depositions that are in the Hughes Estate files; her statements on her German experiences were confirmed by Elia Kazan. The *Jet Pilot* production files, exhaustively detailed, are at the UCLA Research Library; the *Stromboli* matter was best recorded in *Variety;* Judge Harry Shafer was the source on the Hughes affair with a man in San Francisco; Ted Carpentier was the source on the gay arrest in Los Angeles; details of the male bordello came from a confidential source. Hank Valdez is a pseudonym for a still living Hollywood figure; Mario Zamparelli, Richard Fleischer, and Vincent Price were main sources on *His Kind of Woman;* the two anonymous actresses spoke on the understanding they not be given as sources.

### CHAPTER ELEVEN

More Terry Moore material came from *The Beauty and the Billionaire;* Stewart Granger's memoirs and two interviews Roy Moseley conducted with him in 1990 are the chief sources here. Production files on *The Big Sky* are at UCLA, the details filled out by

Hawks's biographer Todd McCarthy; other material on RKO was supplied by the Jerry Wald files at USC and by himself in 1961; the Quarberg memo is in his collection at the Academy. The story of trying to buy Elizabeth Taylor is from a confidential source, a close friend and associate of Gregson Bautzer. The Senate War Hearings detail Hughes's hiring of Air Force generals and his war profiteering; Clark M. Clifford refers to Hughes's hiring him in his memoirs. Noah Dietrich discussed Hughes's affair with Barbara Payton; Granger, again, was the source on the Simmons matter.

## Chapter Twelve

Jerry Wald told me the "shoes" story at his house in Beverly Hills in 1961; the proxy fight was discussed in *The Wall Street Journal.* Paul Jarrico is the source on *The Las Vegas Story* matter; it has been documented in many books on politics in Hollywood. The Zizi Jeanmaire matter was recorded by Hughes's chef, Robert Poussin, in depositions in files in the Hughes Estate, Houston. Walter Kane, in 1971, in Beverly Hills, and in his depositions, testified to Hughes's sexual ritual of clothing; also Poussin, under oath, testified to Hughes's eating habits at the time; Granger discussed wanting to kill Hughes in his memoirs. Prints of *The French Line* have been examined and compared with the script and with the Breen censorship files at the Academy; also, *Underwater!* The Linda Darnell material is in her files at the Academy; the Hayward details are in *Red,* by Robert La Guardia and Gene Arceri; files on *The Conqueror* are at MCA/Universal; the facts concerning it were discussed with me by John Wayne, in his studio dressing room in 1972, and with Agnes Moorehead, at her home in Beverly Hills that year. A file on the nuclear waste poisoning episode is at the Academy. On *Son of Sinbad,* I consulted Vincent Price, its star, Sally Forrest, and the Breen files, and saw the film. As for the Medical Institute, Barlett and Steele's *Empire* exposed it as a tax dodge and gave ample documentation of the TWA management problems.

## Chapter Thirteen

Ava Gardner and Terry Moore discussed their relationships with Hughes in their memoirs; Jean Peters testified in a lengthy deposition in the Hughes Estate files, Houston; Stuart Thompson, a mutual friend, was a valuable source. Hughes's fantasies about flies were described to my by Noah Dietrich; a fine source here was Ron Kistler's wonderfully entitled *I Caught Flies for Howard Hughes.* The Hughes-Nixon loan was documented in the Watergate hearings and in the book titled *The Nixon-Hughes Loan.* The description of Hughes at the time is from Kistler's and from aide Jerry Bell's memoirs; they, and Johnny Meyer and Noah Dietrich, described Hughes's housing of girls under his control. Robert Maheu's memoirs describe his hiring and the subsequent business dealings; John Holmes's depositions in the Hughes Estate, Texas, describe the situation in Montreal, and also in Nassau; Maheu told me more.

CHAPTER FOURTEEN

The memoranda from Hughes to his aides are in the Hughes Estate, Houston. Barlett and Steele in *Empire* were reliable on the history of Hughes Aircraft; the aforementioned friend and associate of Greg Bautzer was the source on Bautzer's dealings with Hughes; John Holmes's richly detailed depositions describe Hughes's life with Jean Peters in Rancho Santa Fe. Cay Sal was described in *The Miami Herald,* August 25, 1963. The Rosselli matter is best dealt with in Charles Rappleye's biography of him and in the *Senate Report on Alleged Assassination Plots against Foreign Leaders,* November, 1975; also in Maheu's memoirs. The TWA matter is in *TWA vs. Hughes* in U.S. District Court files, New York. The hearing matter was recorded by Dr. Howard House in the interview I conducted at his Los Feliz, Los Angeles, house in 1992. Bernard Barker was the source on E. Howard Hunt's early association with Hughes; John Prados was the expert on Hunt and lasers; the information on Hughes's ripping off NASA is in a little-known book, *JPL and the American Space Program,* by Clayton R. Koppes (Yale University Press, 1982); the matter of Hughes's book deals was in *The New York Times* and *The Wall Street Journal;* Greg Bautzer discussed them with me in Beverly Hills in 1980. The trip to Boston was described to me by Peter (son of Robert) Maheu and, in more detail, was discussed in John Holmes's depositions. Robert Maheu filled me in on Hughes's arrival in Las Vegas; Gordon Margulis was a prime source on those years; I interviewed him in Las Vegas. The ice cream anecdote and other materials concluding this chapter are from Margulis.

## CHAPTER FIFTEEN

The description of Hughes's life at the Desert Inn is drawn from interviews with Robert Maheu, Gordon Margulis, and Mell Stewart; the Sinatra episode was described by Kitty Kelley in her biography of the star; Bob Wearley's testimony in the Watergate hearings described the founding of the private air service; Robert Maheu discussed the TV station sale, confirmed by Mrs. Hank Greenspun, whom I interviewed at her offices of the *Las Vegas Sun;* Maheu was the source on the Easter egg hunt episode and the problems with show room attractions. The Mary Carter Paints story was explored in files of the Watergate hearings; the Bayer matter was documented in the *New York Herald Tribune* on August 3, 1947; the helicopter matter is best dealt with in Barlett and Steele; the TWA matter was again dealt with in their pages; the ABC matter is to be found in *ABC vs. Hughes,* U.S. District Court for the Southern District of New York, 1968. Maheu was the source on the bomb scare matter and on Hughes's response to Bobby Kennedy's death; the pertinent memorandum is in the Hughes Estate files, Texas. Files on the Air West matter are in *Anderson vs. Air West* (U.S. District Court for the Northern District of California) and *The Securities and Exchange Commission vs. Howard Hughes* (same court), both 1968; Maheu wrote of the case in his memoirs and spoke to me of it. The silver claims in Nevada were described by Maheu; the Meier affair is documented in Barlett and Steele.

## CHAPTER SIXTEEN

The matter of bribing the president and Hubert Humphrey was amply documented in the Watergate Final Report; Robert Maheu's memoirs; and reports prepared by Leon Jaworski, Special Prosecutor, obtained by Jeffrey Hearn in Washington, D.C. The Watergate Final Report analyzes the details of monies paid and the fact that certain dates of checks do not fit. The Hughes memo is in the Hughes Estate, Texas. The attacks on Maheu were described in his memoirs and in conversation with me; details of Intertel are in the Watergate Final Report ancillary documents, prepared by the Republican Committee to Re-Elect the President. The nerve gas story was in Maheu, confirmed by Intertel's Jim Golden, whom I interviewed in Las Vegas; particulars of Operation Jennifer are to be found in the

Securities and Exchange Commission Annual Reports of Global Marine, Inc.; I interviewed Victor Marchetti, former CIA agent and author, on the subject, on the telephone to his offices in Washington, D.C. The Bud Wheelon matter is recorded in the Senate Subcommittee on Appropriations for Technical Espionage, 1966. The Hughes-Maheu exchange is in the Hughes Estate, Texas; the subsequent dealings with Hughes are from Maheu's memoirs and conversations with him; and from documents in the case of *Maheu vs. Hughes Tool Co.*, 1974. The move to Nassau was described to me by Gordon Margulis and Jim Golden; Dr. Joseph Choi and Gordon Margulis discussed Hughes's AIDS-like condition with me; the memos concerning Maheu are in the Hughes Estate, Texas.

## CHAPTER SEVENTEEN

The attempt to rescue Hughes was documented in Maheu's memoirs; it was also recounted by Peter Maheu to me in Los Angeles and by Jim Golden; the memos are in the Hughes Estate, Texas. Hughes's medical condition was recorded in depositions from his aides John Holmes, Chuck Waldron, and Levar Myler, and in statements made to me by Gordon Margulis; the Chaffin report is in the Hughes Estate, Texas; *The New York Times* covered O'Callaghan's efforts to have Hughes authorize the power of attorney; O'Callaghan granted me an interview in the offices of the *Las Vegas Sun*. The Irving affair is best described in his memoirs and in *The New York Times;* the press conference was featured in all media; the Somoza political dealings are found in his book *Nicaragua Betrayed;* I talked to Jack Real at length by telephone to his home in Hollywood and to publisher Don Carlos Rodriguez and Somoza's friend Mina Nelson at the latter's home in the Rossmore district, Hollywood, on Hughes's dealings in Nicaragua; the leading publicist for Latin America François Du Sardou talked to me of these matters. The Hughes memo on Somoza is in the Hughes Estate, Texas; the stories of Hughes's flight and his arrival in Managua are from Gordon Margulis, also from Jim Golden, both interviewed in Las Vegas; I am indebted to Mrs. Turner Shelton in the matter. Mrs. Barbara Greenspun filled in particulars of the attempted burglary of her safe; the Watergate subcommittee, headed by Howard Baker, investigated the Greenspun matter, but its findings were left out of the Final Report. The quotation from Jim McCord came from his book *A Piece of Tape;* the memo to Somoza is in the Hughes Estate, Houston; the Flame Enterprises matter was in *The New York Times;* Nadine Henley described her visit to Hughes in her deposition in the Hughes Estate; *The New York Times* and Irving's memoirs provided the material on the Irving affair; Don Carlos Rodriguez was the source (confirmed by Jim Golden) on the reasons for the move to Vancouver; Gordon Margulis and Jim Golden both describe the airplane farewell.

## CHAPTER EIGHTEEN

Jim Golden and Gordon Margulis described Hughes's arrival in Vancouver; the North-Broome book was discussed in *The New York Times,* as was the Eckersley affair; the ITT matter was discussed in the House Intelligence hearings, 1974; Hughes's contribution to CRP was recorded in Gordon Liddy's book *Will* and overlooked at the time; the Watergate Final Report dealt with other money sources; Larry O'Brien described the attempts on his property in his Oral History housed at the University of Texas in Austin and at the Kennedy Library, and in his important and overlooked memoir, *No Final Victories;* the Barker matter is based on interviews with him by telephone to his home in Miami; Liddy's *Will;* E. Howard Hunt's statements to the Watergate Committee; the entrapment story was related in H. R. Haldeman's memoirs and largely overlooked, and in Victor Lasky's and Fred Thompson's accounts of the affair. The memo from McCord to Alch is in the Watergate Second Final Report (on CIA links); I talked to William Corson by telephone to his Washington home; Jeff Hearn searched the papers in the Nixon collection at the National Archives; much significant data emerged. The late Fawn Brodie's biography of Nixon was a good source, as were the memoirs of H. R. Haldeman, John Dean, Jeb Magruder, and Charles Colson on different aspects of Watergate; the life of Richard Helms, *The Man Who Kept Secrets,* was a valuable source; and Fred Thompson's *At This Point in Time.* The sale of Hughes Tool is documented in *The New York Times* and in the Securities and Exchange Commission files; Jack Real was the main source on Hughes's aircraft interests in Vancouver and Jim Golden supplied more data; the Oil Tool Division matter was best dealt with by *Fortune* magazine; Mrs. Julius Sedlmayr was the prime source on her husband's meeting; the Hughes-Eckersley memos are in the Hughes Estate, Houston. Gordon Margulis, Jack Real, and Mell Stewart described the Managua earthquake to me at first hand; the IRS report, dated January 5, 1973, is in the author's papers; the events in Florida are in John J. Olszewski's IRS Intelligence Division memo, dated January 5, 1973. The Inn on the Park material was drawn from Gordon Margulis, Jack Real, and depositions by Levar Myler and Chuck Waldron; Governor O'Callaghan gave me a first-hand account of the meeting with Hughes in London.

## CHAPTER NINETEEN

The Securities and Exchange Commission documents are in the *California vs. Woolbright* files at the County Courthouse, Los Angeles; the reconstruction of the true facts of the Romaine Street break-in have been assembled from a reexamination of all the evidence and from interviews with Donald Woolbright's attorney Richard Kirschner, Jack Real, William Corson, Victor Marchetti, Gordon Margulis, Mell Stewart, and a secretary in the Romaine Street office who wishes to remain anonymous; I also consulted the depositions of Chuck Waldron. The Hughes memoranda on the matter are in the Hughes Estate, Texas; the aides' memorandum on Hughes's ordering the destruction of documents was cited, in another context, in an article by Larry DuBois in *Playboy,* and is missing from the Hughes Estate files; the Woolbright attempted blackmail plot is in the transcription of the Woolbright grand jury hearings in *The New York Times;* William Colby's memoirs provide a valuable source; the Drosnin clash with O'Brien is in O'Brien's oral history at the Kennedy Library and the University of Texas in Austin; Drosnin's arrest in Times Square was reported in *The New York Times;* the murder of Bobby Hill is in *Spooks,* by Jim Hougan; Jack Egger's deposition is in the Hughes Estate, Houston. The drug matters are dealt with in the depositions in the Hughes Estate by doctors Norman Crane, Lawrence Chaffin, and Wilbur Thain and aides Chuck Waldron and John Holmes; the Thain diary excerpts are from his deposition; I interviewed Dr. Thain by telephone to his home in Arizona. The aides' memorandum is in the Hughes Estate; also the subsequent memos of instruction from Hughes; his attitudes of selfishness were described to me by Gordon Margulis in Las Vegas in 1992 and by Mell Stewart on the telephone from Utah; the plans for the party are in Holmes's deposition; the journey to Acapulco is described in the oral histories of George Francom, Chuck Waldron,

John Holmes, and doctors Crane, Thain, and Chaffin; statements made by Dr. Montemoya have been drawn from. Hughes's death was described to me by Dr. Thain. *The New York Times, The Wall Street Journal* and the *New York Post* covered the material discussed in the postscript. The autopsy files and interrogatory reports were consulted in Houston.

NOTE: In addition to the above, Peter Dale Scott's *Crime and Cover-up: The CIA, the Mafia and the Dallas-Watergate Connection,* published by Westworks, Berkeley, in 1977, is much the best and most closely documented book on the Hughes/crime/CIA links, and is recommended to all scholars.

# Selected Bibliography

*Alleged Assassination Plots Involving Foreign Leaders.* An Interim Report of the Select Committee to Study Government Operations with Respect to Intelligence Activities. U.S. Senate. Washington, D.C.: Government Printing Office, 1975.

Ambrose, Stephen E. *Nixon: The Education of a Politician, 1913–1962.* New York: Simon and Schuster, 1988.

——. *Nixon: Ruin and Recovery, 1973–1990.* New York: Simon and Schuster, 1991.

——. *Nixon: Triumph of a Politician, 1962–72.* New York: Simon and Schuster, 1990.

Barlett, Donald L., and Steele, James B. *Empire: The Life, Legend and Madness of Howard Hughes.* New York: W. W. Norton, 1979.

Bell, Jerry. *Howard Hughes: His Silence, Secrets and Success!* New York: Hawkes, 1976.

Block, Alan A. *Masters of Paradise.* New York: Transaction, n.d.

Brodie, Fawn M. *Richard Nixon: The Shaping of His Character.* Cambridge, Massachusetts: Harvard University Press, 1983.

Cassini, Igor. *I'd Do It All Over Again: The Life and Times of Igor Cassini.* New York: G. P. Putnam's Sons, 1977.

Cassini, Oleg. *In My Own Fashion: An Autobiography.* New York: Simon and Schuster, 1987.

Ceplair, Larry, and Steven Englund. *The Inquisition in Hollywood: Politics in the Film Community, 1930–1980.* New York: Anchor Press, 1980.

Clifford, Clark, with Richard Holbrooke. *Counsel to the President: A Memoir.* New York: Anchor Books, Doubleday, 1992.

Cochran, Jacqueline, with Maryann Bucknum Brinley. *Jackie Cochran.* New York: Bantam, 1987.

Colby, William, with Peter Forbath. *Honorable Mention: My Life in the CIA.* New York: Simon and Schuster, 1978.

Corson, William R., Susan B. Trento, and Joseph J. Trento. *Widows.* New York: Crown, 1979.

Davenport, Elaine, Paul Eddy, and Mark Hurwitz. *Howard Hughes' Final Years.* London: Andre Deutsch, 1977.

Davenport, Joe, and Todd S. J. Lawson. *The Empire of Howard Hughes.* San Francisco: Peace and Pieces Foundation, 1975.

Dean, John. *Blind Ambition: The White House Years.* New York: Simon and Schuster, 1976.

De Carlo, Yvonne, with Doug Warren. *Yvonne.* New York: St. Martin's, 1971.

Dietrich, Noah, with Bob Thomas. *Howard: The Amazing Mr. Hughes.* New York: Fawcett, 1972.

Drosnin, Michael. *Citizen Hughes.* New York: Holt, Rinehart and Winston, 1985.

Fay, Stephen, Chester Lewis, and Magnus Linklater. *Hoax: The Inside Story of the Howard Hughes–Clifford Irving Affair.* New York: Viking, 1972.

Finstad, Suzanne. *Heir Not Apparent.* Austin, Texas: Texas Monthly Press, 1984.

Gardner, Ava. *Ava: My Story.* New York: Bantam, 1990.

Garrison, Omar V. *Howard Hughes in Las Vegas.* New York: Lyle Stuart, 1970.

Genevoix, Sylvie. *HRH.* Paris: Plon, 1972.

Gerber, Albert B. *Bashful Billionaire.* New York: Lyle Stuart, 1967.

Graham, Don. *No Name on the Bullet: A Biography of Audie Murphy.* New York: Viking, 1989.

Granger, Stewart. *Sparks Fly Upward.* New York: G. P. Putnam's Sons, 1981.

Haldeman, H. R., with Joseph DiMona. *The Ends of Power.* New York: Times Books, 1978.

Hecht, Ben. *A Child of the Century.* New York: Primus; Donald I. Fine, 1954.

Hatfield, D. D. *Howard Hughes H-4 Hercules Airplane.* Los Angeles: Historical Airplanes, 1972.

Heymann, C. David. *Poor Little Rich Girl: The Life and Legend of Barbara Hutton.* New York: Random House, 1983.

Hepburn, Katharine. *Me: Stories of My Life.* New York: Alfred A. Knopf, 1991.

Hougan, Jim. *Spooks: The Haunting of America—the Use of Secret Agents.* New York: William Morrow, 1978.

*Investigations of the National Defense Program.* Hearings before a Special Committee Investigating the National Defense Program, U.S. Senate, 77th Congress, First Session, Parts I 40 and 43. Washington, D.C.: Government Printing Office, 1948 *(Senate War Hearings).*

Irving, Clifford, with Richard Suskind. *What Really Happened: His Untold Story of the Hughes Affair.* New York: Grove Press, 1972.

Jewell, Richard B. and Vernon Harbin. *The RKO Story.* New York: Arlington House, 1982.

Johnston, Marguerite. *Houston, the Unknown City.* College Station, Texas: Texas A and M University Press.

Kaminsky, Stuart M. *The Howard Hughes Affair.* New York: St. Martin's, 1979.

Keats, John. *Howard Hughes.* New York: Random House, 1966.

Kistler, Ron. *I Caught Flies for Howard Hughes.* Chicago: Playboy Press, 1976.

Klein, Herbert G. *Making It Perfectly Clear: An Inside Account of Nixon's Love-Hate Relationship with the Media.* Garden City, New York: Doubleday, 1980.

Lacey, Robert. *Little Man: Meyer Lansky and the Gangster Life.* New York: Little, Brown, 1991.

La Guardia, Robert, and Gene Arceri. *Red: The Tempestuous Life of Susan Hayward.* New York: Macmillan, 1985.

Lasky, Betty. *RKO: The Biggest Little Major of Them All.* Santa Monica, California: Roundtable, 1989; Englewood Cliffs, New Jersey: Prentice-Hall, c. 1984.

Lasky, Victor. *It Didn't Start with Watergate.* New York: Dial Press, 1977.

Leaming, Barbara. *If This Was Happiness: A Biography of Rita Hayworth.* New York: Viking, 1989.

Leigh, Janet. *There Really Was a Hollywood.* Garden City, New York: Doubleday, 1984.

Liddy, G. Gordon. *Will: The Autobiography.* New York: St. Martin's, 1980.

Lukas, J. Anthony. *Nightmare: The Underside of the Nixon Years.* New York: Viking, 1976.

MacDonald, John J. *Howard Hughes and the Spruce Goose.* Blue Ridge Summit, Pennsylvania: TAB Books, 1981.

Magruder, Jeb Stuart. *An American Life: One Man's Road to Watergate.* New York: Atheneum, 1974.

Maheu, Robert, with Richard Hack. *Next to Hughes: Behind the Power and Tragic Downfall of Howard Hughes.* New York: HarperCollins, 1992.

Mailer, Norman. *Harlot's Ghost: A Novel.* New York: Random House, 1991.

Mankiewicz, Frank. *Perfectly Clear: Nixon from Whittier to Watergate.* New York: Quadrangle, 1973.

———. *U.S. vs. Richard M. Nixon: The Final Crisis.* New York: Quadrangle, 1975.

March, Joseph Moncure. *The Wild Party.* New York: Citadel Press, the Carol Publishing Group, 1979.

Marchetti, Victor, and John D. Marks. *The CIA and the Cult of Intelligence.* New York: Knopf, 1974.

Mathison, Richard R. *His Weird and Wanton Ways.* New York: Morrow, 1977.

McComb, David G. *Houston: A History.* Austin: University of Texas Press, 1981.

Moore, Terry. *The Beauty and the Billionaire.* New York: Pocket Books, 1984.

O'Brien, Larry. *No Final Victories.* Garden City, New York: Doubleday, 1974.

Parrish, James Robert. *The RKO Gals.* London: Ian Allen, 1974.

Phelan, James. *Howard Hughes, the Hidden Years.* New York: Random House, c. 1976.

*Presidential Campaign Activities of 1972.* Hearings before the Select Committee on Presidential Campaign Activities of the U.S. Senate, 93rd Congress, Second Session. Washington, D.C.:

U.S. Government Printing Office, 1976 *(The Watergate Hearings).*

Rappleye, Charles, and Ed Becker. *All American Mafioso: The Johnny Rosselli Story.* New York: Doubleday, 1991.

Rhoden, Harold. *High Stakes: The Gamble for the Howard Hughes Will.* New York: Crown, 1980.

Russell, Jane. *An Autobiography: My Path and Detours.* New York: Franklin Watts, 1985.

Schary, Dore. *Heyday: An Autobiography.* New York: Little, Brown, 1979.

Schell, Jonathan. *The Time of Illusion.* New York: Knopf, 1976.

Scott, Peter Dale. *Crime and Cover-up: The CIA, the Mafia, and the Dallas-Watergate Connection.* Berkeley, California: Westworks, 1977.

Serling, Robert. *Howard Hughes' Airline: An Informal History of TWA.* New York: St. Martin's/Marek, 1983.

Somoza, Anastasio, as told to Jack Cox. *Nicaragua Betrayed.* Belmont, Massachusetts: Western Islands, 1980.

Sturges, Preston, adapted and edited by Sandy Sturges. *Preston Sturges.* New York: Simon and Schuster, 1990.

Tierney, Gene, with Mickey Herskowitz. *Self-Portrait.* New York: Wyden Books, 1978.

Tinnin, David B. *Just About Everybody vs. Howard Hughes: The Inside Story of the Hughes-TWA Trial.* Garden City, New York: Doubleday, 1973.

Whalen, Grover A. *Mr. New York.* New York: G. P. Putnam's Sons, 1955.

Whiting, Charles. *Hero: The Life and Death of Audie Murphy.* Chelsea, Michigan: Scarborough House, 1990.

Wray, Fay. *On the Other Hand.* New York: St. Martin's, 1988.

# Index

*Adventure in Baltimore,* 137
*Affair with a Stranger,* 169
*Age for Love, The,* 53–54, 60
Aherne, Brian, 69–70, 90
Air Canada, 301
Air Trans Canada, 194
Air West, 11, 236–39, 242, 246, 277, 281, 302, 306, 314, 318, 329
Alamo Airways, 229
Alch, Gerald, 286
Alexander, J. B., 40
Allenberg, Bert, 160, 161
*All the President's Men,* 287
Altman, Bruce, 327
Amato, Giuseppe, 173
American Aircraft Company, 40
Anderson, Jack, 188, 285, 299
Anderson, Merry, 181
*Androcles and the Lion,* 161–62
*Angel Face,* 168, 173–4
Annabella (French actress), 93
Annenberg, Walter, 244
Argosy Pictures, 144
Armendariz, Pedro, 175, 233
Arnold, H. H. (Hap), 101, 105, 115
*As It Really Happened,* 289
Astor, Mary, 38–39
Atkinson, Brooks, 93
Aures, Victor, 21–23
Ayres, Lew, 76

Babcock, Howard, 261
Ball, Lucille, 137, 183
Ballard, Lucien, 96–98
Banco Internacional, 254, 269, 282
Bank of America, 328
Bank of the Southwest, 329
*Barefoot Mailman, The,* 151
Barker, Jess, 173
Barker, Lex, 154
Barnes, Leroy Nickey, 305
Barrett, Wilton A., 61–62
Barry, Eddie, 140
Barry, Philip, 90
Barrymore, John, 62
Batista, Fulgencio, 61, 92, 204, 230
Bautzer, Greg, 156–57, 162, 163, 169, 199, 204, 211–13
Bayer, Albert W., 231
Beach, Rex, 44
Bear, William, 328
Beard, Dan, 20–21, 23–24, 230
Beard, Dita, 282
Behn, Harry, 39
Belisle, David, 248
Bell, Jerry, 189
Bell, Thomas, 304
Bell Helicopters, 231
Bergman, Ingrid, 146, 183
Bernadotte, Count, 119
Bernstein, Carl, 287
Best Books, 266
Better Business Association, 194

Bez, Nick, 236–38
*Big Sky, The,* 153–54
*Big Steal, The,* 138
Birdwell, Russell, 92, 100, 101, 102, 117, 128
Bishop, Joey, 226
Bizet, Georges, 183
Black, Caroline, 44–45
Blondell, Joan, 139
*Blue Veil, The,* 154
BOAC, 301
Boardman, Eleanor, 25–26, 29, 31, 51
Boc, Joe, 221
Boldt, Charles, 51
Boldt, Mrs. Charles, 51
Bonafede, Don, 211
Bond, Lilian, 69
Borah, Charlie, 24
Borax, Don, 221
Borden, Lizzie, 117
Borg-Warner, 330
Boyd, William, 38–39, 54
*Boy with Green Hair, The,* 137
Brandi, Fred, 198
Breech, Ernest R., 201
Brewster, Owen, 115, 127, 128, 157, 179
*Bride for Sale,* 144
Bridges, Harry, 144
Brontë, Charlotte, 76
Brown, S. T., 30
Bryan, Frederick, 213
Buckley, Robert, 215–16
Buetel, Jack, 96, 103, 109
Bullitt, William, 83
Bundy, Eric, 305
Burgess, Carter, 197
Burr, Raymond, 149
Byoir Associates, Carl, 265

Caddo Company, 51, 121
Caddo Field, 40, 42, 44
Cagney, James, 123, 159
Cagney, William, 123, 126
California Studios, 116
Campbell, Judith, 202
Cameron, Barbara Lapp, 326, 328
Capone, Al, 44, 55–57, 58, 62
Carpentier, Ted, 122, 147, 187, 276
Carroll, Harrison, 154
Carter Paints, Mary, 230–31, 248
*Casanova's Big Night,* 164
Cassini, Oleg, 93, 94, 112, 152, 160
Castro, Fidel, 261, 269, 275
  Hughes and 203–4, 209–11, 218, 220, 230, 269, 272, 279, 282–85, 288
Cay Sal, 210–11, 250, 269, 304–5

Cerf, Bennett A., 212–13
Chamorro, Pedro Joaquin, 271, 277
Chaplin, Charlie, 52
Chase, Borden, 137–38
Chester, Lewis, 276
*Chicago Tribune,* 266
Chickering, Henry, 24
Choi, Joseph, 256
CIA, 181, 185, 285, 287
  Hughes and, 11, 193, 201–3, 209, 211, 220, 230–31, 238, 242, 248–52, 255, 262, 269–71, 275, 281–83, 288, 304–5, 308–10, 316
*Citizen Hughes,* 311
Clarke, Frank, 42, 44
*Clay Pigeon, The,* 137
Clifford, Clark M., 159, 268
Clift, Montgomery, 156
Cline, Bill, 104
Cochran, Jacqueline, 74, 78, 133, 204
Cochrane, Paul, 145
*Cock of the Air,* 54, 60
Cohn, Harry, 59, 118, 133, 141, 155, 183
Colbert, Claudette, 144
Colby, William, 310
Collins, LeRoy, 179
Columbia Pictures, 59, 133, 141, 155
*Confessions of a Muckraker,* 188
*Conqueror, The,* 173–75, 233
Constantine, Mortimer, 281–82
Conterno, Dominic, 45
Converse, Edmund, 236–38
Cook, Raymond, 232
Corson, William, 286, 308
Courtland, Jerome (Cojo), 141, 142, 151, 166
Cowan, Barry, 294
Coward, Noel, 161
Cramer, Stuart, III, 181, 182, 185, 193
Crane, Norman, 312, 320–23
Creel, George, 28
Cromwell, Richard, 108–9, 125
Crow, Clyde, 326
Cukor, George, 70
Cullinan, Joseph, 19, 20
Cullinan, Mary, 19

Dalitz, Morris (Moe), 217–19, 231, 262
Damon, Ralph, 179
*Dangerous Profession, A,* 143
Danner, Richard G., 240, 243–44, 304
Darnell, Linda, 100, 109–10, 113, 118–19, 125, 172–73
Darrow, John, 42
Davies, Marion, 50
Davis, Bette, 79–81, 88, 109, 115

Davis, Chester C., 11, 12, 204, 211, 212, 233, 237–38, 248–49, 268, 270, 271, 275, 276–77, 280, 283, 292–96, 299, 301–2, 303, 305, 306–8, 314, 317–18, 319, 329
  hired by Hughes, 204
  Maheu power struggle and, 249, 252–54, 259–62
Davis, Glenn, 152, 155, 156
Davis, Jim, 121
Davis, Sammy, Jr., 226, 230
Davison, F. Trubee, 87
Dean, John, 263, 287, 289
De Camp, Rosemary, 124
De Carlo, Yvonne, 112–13, 143, 173, 176, 279
de Havilland, Olivia, 89–90
de Havilland Company, 179
Depinet, Ned, 135, 136
de Rothschild, Evelyn, 301
*Der Spiegel*, 310
Desert Inn, 217–19, 224–26, 228, 230, 238, 296, 299, 303, 314, 315, 319, 329
*Destination Murder*, 144
de Varona, Manuel Antonio, 204
Devlin, C. J., 136–37
Dewey, Thomas, 230
Dial, Elizabeth Patterson, 30, 32, 118
DiCicco, Pat, 187, 194
Diehl, Jack, 274
Dietrich, Marlene, 111, 144, 155
Dietrich, Noah, 35–37, 47, 48, 50, 51, 57, 64, 67, 70, 91, 101, 125, 157–59, 170, 171, 181, 187, 193, 265, 316, 317
  fired by Hughes, 187, 327
  hired by Hughes, 35
  memoir, Hughes and, 265, 266, 276–77
Dillingham, Elizabeth, 19
Dillon, Read, 198, 199, 204
Disney, Walt, 143–44, 164
Dolenz, George, 117
Domergue, Faith, 113, 117, 148, 152, 155
Dominguin, Luis Miguel, 181, 182
*Double Dynamite*, 155
Douglas Aircraft, 74, 101, 179
Dove, Billie, 50, 51–52, 53–54, 57, 60, 62, 66
Dowling, Beatrice, 77
Dozier, William, 142
Drake, Betsy, 137
Drosnin, Michael, 310–11
D-2 aircraft, 101, 102, 104, 105
Dulles, Allen, 230, 251, 269–70
Dummar (DuMar), Melvin, 327–28
Dunes Hotel, 242, 245, 246, 248, 304

DuPont, Marian, 69
Durkin, Bill, 124
Dvorak, Ann, 55, 56, 62

Eaker, Ira C., 157–58, 170
Earhart, Amelia, 36–37, 71
Early, Stephen, 102
Eastern Airlines, 273, 303
*Easy Living*, 137
Echols, Oliver P., 101, 105
Eckersley, Howard, 221, 264, 280–81, 288, 292, 295, 305, 316, 318
*Eddie Cantor Story, The*, 164
Edward, Sheffield, 203
Egger, Jack, 188–89, 311
Ehrlichman, John D., 240
Eichler, Jenny M., 19
Elizabeth II, queen of England, 53
Ellington, Duke, 187
Ellsberg, Daniel, 283
Emerson, Faye, 104, 105, 114, 211
*Empire*, 319, 326
Entratter, Jack, 220, 226–27
Equitable, 206
Ernst, Morris L., 61, 62
*Escape to Burma*, 176
Estabrook, Howard, 46
Evans, Robert, 184
*Everybody's Acting*, 38
*Every Girl Should Be Married*, 137

Fairchild, Sherman, 66, 76, 87, 122
Fairbanks, Douglas, Sr., 50, 52
Farnsworth, Arthur, 115
Farrow, John, 148–49
Farrow, Mia, 148, 226
Fawcett Books, 276
Fay, Stephen, 276
FBI, 109, 116, 118, 219, 308
Feeder, William, 134, 138
Felt, Dick, 104
Ferguson, Homer, 127–28
Fessenden School, 24
Fife, John, 25
*Film Daily*, 61
First Boston Corporation (FBC), 197
First City National Bank, 329
First National Bank of Nevada, 329
Fleischer, Richard, 134, 137, 139, 149
Flexner, Simon, 24
*Flying Leathernecks*, 154
Flynn, Carl (Jock), 66, 143
Flynn, Errol, 90, 109
*Follow Me Quietly*, 137
Fontaine, Joan, 90, 94, 142
Forrester, William, Jr., 197–98

Forsyth, LeVane, 328
Fortas, Abe, 206
*Fortune,* 267
Foster, Norman, 138
Fox, Francis, 237
Francis, Lee, 148
*French Line, The,* 171–72, 177, 181
Frontier Hotel, 220, 243, 244, 288–89, 305
*Front Page, The,* 54–55
Furthman, Jules, 95, 99, 117, 145–46
Fry, Helen, 183
Fry, Jack (husband of Helen), 183
Frye, Jack (airline head), 91–92

*Gambling House,* 151
Gano, Richard, 327
Gardner, Ava, 110–13, 148, 152, 155, 173, 181–83, 185, 193, 204, 227
Gardner, Bappie, 111–12
Gay, Bill, 132, 194, 215–17, 218, 247–49, 264, 265, 280–82, 289, 296, 303, 304, 312–14, 317–18, 328, 329
  Maheu power struggle and, 249, 252–54, 259–62
Gaynor, Mitzi, 183
Gener, Rafael (Macho), 203–4
General Motors, 330
General Service Studios, 136
General Teleradio, Inc., 182–83
General Tire and Rubber (GTR), 182–83
Genghis Khan, 173–75
George, Harold L., 157–58, 267
George VI, king of England, 53
Giancana, Sam, 202, 204, 226, 231
Gleason, James, 109
Gleason, Russel, 109
Glenn, Kay, 197, 221, 276, 279, 280, 312–14, 317
*Glomar Explorer,* 251, 252, 308, 310
*Glomar II,* 250
Goddard, Paulette, 118
Godfrey, Peter, 144
Gold, Harry, 116
Goldenson, Leonard, 232–33
Goldfarb, Charles, 305
Goldwyn, Sam, 55, 143–44, 164, 190
Goldwyn Studios, 27, 99, 134, 137, 139, 142, 165, 190
Goodman, Ezra, 211–12
Grable, Betty, 148
Grace, Dick, 43–44
Granger, Stewart, 152–53, 160–62, 169
Grant, Cary, 69, 70, 77–78, 79, 118, 125, 127, 133, 136, 137, 139, 153, 189, 223, 319

Grauman, Sid, 51–52
Grauman's Chinese Theater, 51–52, 62
Graves, Ralph (movie star), 37
Gray, J. Richard, 218–19
Greene, David J., 164
Greenspun, Hank, 220, 227, 234, 237, 274–75, 282, 289, 302, 308, 312
Greenspun, Mrs. Hank, 275
Greer, Jane, 135, 138–39
Griffith, Corinne, 68–70
Griffith, D. W., 117, 212
Guevara, Che, 284
Guild, Leo, 211
Gwynne, Edyth, 69

H-1 aircraft, 66–68, 70–71, 91–92, 124
H-2 aircraft, 92, 102, 124, 130, 266
Haberfeld, Stephen A., 245
Haddad, William, 285
Haines, William, 58, 108
Haldeman, H. R., 240, 287
Hall, Robert, 211
Hand, Lloyd, 243
Hanna, Keith, 215
Hanna, Mrs. Keith, 215
Hannah, Richard, 266, 267
Harbin, Vernon, 176
Harding, Lana, 81
Harlow, Jean, 45–47, 49, 52, 58–59
Harmony, Sally, 282
Harris, Jed, 54
Harris, Marion, 32
Haskin, Byron, 145–46
Hawker Siddeley, 298–99
Hawks, Howard, 55–57, 59, 62, 78, 89, 95–98, 137–38, 153, 154, 267
Hayes, Keith, 328
Hays, Will, 44, 54, 58–63
Hayward, Susan, 173–76, 181, 183, 185, 233
Hayworth, Rita, 25, 100, 139, 141, 169, 183
Heath, Edward, 300, 301
Hecht, Ben, 54–56
*Hell's Angels,* 39–49, 51, 53, 55, 58, 89, 98, 117, 139, 154
Helmsley, Harry, 217, 219, 226
Helmsley, Leona, 217
Henley, Nadine, 132, 143, 207, 245, 265, 271, 276, 309, 316–17, 328
Hepburn, Audrey, 161
Hepburn, Katharine, 69–70, 73, 75–83, 86–90, 93, 110, 122, 133, 141, 320
Hepburn, Richard, 81
*Hercules* (Spruce Goose), 12, 105–6, 115, 120, 121, 130–32, 134, 296, 327

Herter, Christian A., 194
*High Heels,* 152, 164
Hill, Gladwin, 266
Hilton, Nicky, 156, 162, 183–84
*His Kind of Woman,* 149
Hitchcock, Alfred, 118, 282
Hoffman, Abbie, 310
Hoffner, Erich, 17
Holmes, Johnny, 188–89, 194, 197, 201,
    214–15, 227, 272, 279, 281, 302,
    305, 316, 317, 319–20, 322, 328
Holt, Rinehart and Winston, 311
Hopper, Hedda, 115, 161
Hoover, J. Edgar, 108, 115, 116, 133,
    202
House, Howard, 12, 207–8
*Houston Post,* 24
Howard Hughes Medical Institute
    (HHMI), 177–78, 179, 185, 188,
    198, 210–11, 232, 234, 251, 255,
    262, 263, 276, 313, 316, 318,
    327, 329, 330
Howard Hughes Productions, 105
Howard Hughes Research Laboratory, 33
HRH Properties, 314
Hubbard, Chauncey, 24
Hubbard, L. Ron, 301
Hughes, Adelaide (aunt), 26, 27, 29, 30,
    33
Hughes, Adella (aunt), 32
Hughes, Allene Gano (mother), 13,
    15–17, 143, 185, 325
    death of, 28–30, 125, 178, 323, 325
    relationship with son, 13, 16–26,
    28–30, 33, 79, 120, 178, 185,
    226, 318, 320, 323
Hughes, Dwayne Clyde Byron, 327
Hughes, Ella Rice (first wife), 19, 31, 36,
    38, 47, 327
    divorce, 47, 50
    wedding, 32–33
Hughes, Felix (judge, grandfather),
    13–16, 24, 29, 291
Hughes, Felix (son of above, uncle), 14,
    31, 32
Hughes, Howard, Jr. (Sonny)
    autobiography, authorized, 276
    autobiography hoax (Irving), 265–68,
    276, 277, 280, 289, 292
    Bahamas, permanent move to,
    255–58, 261, 270
    bank accounts, secret, 210, 311
    birth of, 13, 16
    blackmail attempt against, 194
    bootlegging, 57, 66
    boyhood years, 16, 40,
    Cay Sal, 201, 210–11, 250, 269,
    304–5
    education of, 19–22, 24–32, 40
    estate, battle over, 164, 325–30
    father, relationship with, 16–18,
    20–22, 24–26, 120, 318, 320, 323
    FBI and, 109, 116, 118, 219, 308
    Mafia and, 45, 58, 202, 217, 226, 255
    Mormons and, value to Hughes, 12,
    132–33, 175
    mother, relationship with, 13, 16–26,
    28–30, 33, 79, 120, 178, 185,
    226, 318, 320, 323
    as vagabond, 37, 67, 120–21
    wills, 70, 165, 316–17, 325–30
Hughes, Howard: aviation, 24, 32, 37,
    42–43, 64
    Air West, 11, 236–37, 239, 246, 277,
    281, 302, 314, 318, 329
    Alamo Airways, 229
    Caddo Company, 51, 121
    Caddo Field, 40, 42, 44
    D-2 aircraft, 101, 104–5
    *Hell's Angels,* 39–49, 51, 53, 55, 58,
    89, 98, 117, 139, 154
    H-1 aircraft, 66, 68, 70–71, 91–92,
    124
    H-2 aircraft, 92, 124, 130
    Hughes Aircraft, 91, 101–2ff.
    King Aircraft, 315
    Lanica Airlines deal, 270, 277, 290,
    303
    Las Vegas airports controlled, 40, 314
    Lockheed deal, 296, 298–99, 301, 314
    Los Angeles Airways, 248
    NASA and, 209
    Northeast Airlines, 206
    Rolls Royce engines deal, 296
    Surveyor spacecraft, 209–10
    TWA, 91–92, 107, 111, 113, 115–16,
    118, 127, 152, 157, 179, 182,
    188, 197–200, 204–7, 217, 232,
    242, 245–46, 254–55, 289, 295,
    303, 311, 328
    XF-11 aircraft, 105, 120, 121, 123–24
Hughes, Howard: business, 35–36. *See
    also* Hughes, Howard: aviation;
    Hughes, Howard: Hollywood;
    Hughes Tool Company
    Better Business Association, 198
    Desert Inn, 217–19, 224–26, 228, 230,
    238, 296, 299, 303, 314, 315,
    319, 329
    Dunes Hotel, 242, 245, 246, 248, 304
    Frontier Hotel, 220, 243, 244, 288–89,
    305
    *Glomar Explorer,* 251, 252, 308, 310
    *Glomar II,* 250
    Howard Hughes Medical Institute,
    177–78, 179, 185, 188, 198, 210,

211, 232, 234, 251, 255, 262,
263, 276, 313, 316, 318, 322,
329, 330
Howard Hughes Productions, 105
Howard Hughes Research Laboratory,
33
HRH Properties, 314, 329
Intertel, 248–49, 255, 261, 262, 270,
283
IRS and, 178, 232, 255, 261, 266,
279, 280, 288, 293, 299
ITT, 281–82
Mary Carter Paints, 236–37, 254
Oil Tool Division (OTD), 289, 290–91
Operation Jennifer, 250–51
Pan American Mines, Ltd., 280–81
Paradise Island Casino, Hotel and
Ocean Club, 230, 248, 255
Resorts International, 248
SEC and, 11, 239, 306–9
Summa Corporation, 12, 289,
296, 301, 303, 305, 311, 317,
329
Tonopah land purchase, 229, 239, 241
WCIX-TX (Miami), 304
Xanadu Princess Hotel, 11, 299, 304,
318
Hughes, Howard: health, 11ff., 25, 36,
115, 256–57, 263–64, 291–92,
312–13
blindness, 321
AIDS, 256–57, 321
anemia, 256
death of, 12, 323–30
delirium, 257, 321
diet, 34, 107, 140–41, 168, 189, 191,
194, 195, 215, 223–25, 247, 256,
280, 321
drug use, 12, 199, 205, 228, 247, 254,
263, 296, 298, 312–13, 320–22,
326
hypochondria, 21–24, 33, 189, 230,
233–35
incompetent, attempt to have him
declared, 215–16, 218, 248–49,
254
mumps, 25
pneumonia, 254, 256
polio, 271
spinal meningitis, 36
vasectomy, 185
Hughes, Howard: Hollywood, 27–28,
116ff. *See also* Hughes, Howard:
mistresses
*Adventure in Baltimore,* 137
*Affair with a Stranger,* 169
*Age for Love, The,* 53–54, 60
*Androcles and the Lion,* 161–62

*Angel Face,* 168–69, 173
*Big Sky, The,* 153–54
*Big Steal, The,* 138
*Blue Veil, The,* 154
*Boy with Green Hair, The,* 137
*Bride for Sale,* 144
*Carmen,* 165, 183
*Casanova's Big Night,* 164
*Clay Pigeon, The,* 137
*Cock of the Air,* 54, 60
*Conqueror, The,* 174–76, 233
*Dangerous Profession, A,* 143
*Destination Murder,* 144
*Double Dynamite,* 155
*Easy Living,* 137
*Eddie Cantor Story, The,* 164
*Escape to Burma,* 176
*Everybody's Acting,* 38
*Every Girl Should Be Married,* 137
*Flying Leathernecks,* 154
*Follow Me Quietly,* 137
*French Line, The,* 171–73, 177
*Front Page, The,* 54
*Gambling House,* 151
*Hell's Angels,* 39–49, 51, 53, 55, 58,
89, 98, 117, 139, 154
*High Heels,* 152, 164
*His Kind of Woman,* 149
*Jet Pilot,* 144–46, 153, 163
*Las Vegas Story, The,* 164–65
Loring Theater Corporation and, 144
*Lusty Men, The,* 173
*Macao,* 164
*Mating Call, The,* 44
*My Forbidden Past,* 155
*Narrow Margin, The,* 163–64
*Outlaw, The,* 95–100, 103, 118–19,
137, 144, 146, 170
*Out of the Past,* 135
*Outrage,* 151
*Passion,* 176
*Payment on Demand,* 154
*Queer People,* 58
*Rachel and the Stranger,* 138
*Racket, The,* 44, 55, 154
*Rancho Notorious,* 155
*Riders on the Range,* 143
RKO Pictures and, 133–41. *Also see*
RKO Pictures
*Scarface,* 55–62
*Second Chance,* 170, 172–73
*Secret Heart, The,* 144
*Set-Up, The,* 139
*She Wore a Yellow Ribbon,* 144
*Sins of Rome,* 176
*Sky Devils,* 54
*Son of Sinbad,* 176–77
*Split Second,* 174, 185

*Stromboli*, 146–47
*Susan Slept Here*, 176
*Swell Hogan*, 37–38
*Tarzan's Peril*, 154
*Thing, The*, 154
*Threat, The*, 143
*Two Arabian Knights*, 38–39
*Underwater!*, 172, 173
*Vendetta*, 117
*Wagonmaster*, 144
*Where Danger Lives*, 148, 155
*Woman on Pier 13, The*, 143
Hughes, Howard: homosexual lovers, 34, 96, 113
   Buetel, Jack, 96, 103, 109
   Cromwell, Richard, 108–9, 125
   Darrow, John, 42
   Grant, Cary, 69, 70, 77–78, 79, 118, 125, 127, 133, 136, 137, 139, 153, 189, 223, 319
   Hughes, Rupert (uncle), 14, 15, 18, 21, 25–32, 56, 108, 118, 133, 326, 327, 328
   Power, Tyrone, 93, 94, 100, 109–10, 125, 126
   Scott, Randolph, 48, 69
Hughes, Howard: marriages. *See* Peters, Jean; Hughes, Ella Rice
Hughes, Howard: politics
   bribes/manipulations, 105–8, 115–16, 127–29, 158–59, 188, 194, 227, 229, 231, 233–37, 239–52, 262–63, 268, 269, 280–82, 288, 297, 308
   Castro, plots against, 202–4, 210–11, 269, 272, 279, 282, 284–85
   CIA and, 11, 193, 202, 209, 211, 230–31, 248, 250, 251–52, 255, 263, 269–75, 281, 283, 285, 288, 304–5, 307, 308–11, 316
   1968 election, 235–37, 244
   1972 election, 282–87, 292
   Nixon and, 11, 187–88, 194, 234, 240–46, 261, 270, 272, 284, 287–89, 292, 294, 307
   Somoza and, 271, 273, 275, 277–78, 290, 293, 297, 307, 319
   Watergate and, 11, 12, 219, 275, 284–86, 287–89, 308, 310
Hughes, Howard: sex life, 27–28, 34, 45, 56–57, 104, 105, 107, 148, 208. *See also* Hughes, Howard: homosexual lovers;

Hughes, Howard Robard (Bo, father), 13–18, 20, 32, 33, 40, 102, 120, 318, 320, 323
Hughes tool bit, 17–18

Hughes, Jean (Mimi, grandmother), 29–32
Hughes, Rupert (uncle), 14, 15, 18, 21, 25–32, 56, 108, 116, 118, 133, 326, 327, 329
Hughes Aircraft. *See* Hughes, Howard: aviation
Hughes Tool Company, 30, 36, 70, 107, 116, 127, 156, 191, 202, 207, 211, 216, 218, 224, 233, 237–38, 236, 245, 247, 250, 251, 253, 261, 262, 263, 289, 290, 291, 301, 315, 330. *See also* Hughes, Howard: Summa Corporation
   HRH Properties, 314, 329
   Oil Tool Division (OTD), 289, 290–91
Humasson, Granville (Granny), 18
Humphrey, Hubert, 234–35, 242–43
Hundley, William, 248
Hunt, E. Howard, 209, 255, 269, 270, 271, 274, 281–85, 287, 308
Huston, Walter, 97
Hutton, Barbara, 77, 153

Intertel (International Intelligence), 248–49, 255, 261, 262, 270, 283
IRS, 261, 266
   Hughes and, 178, 238, 255, 261, 266, 279, 280, 288, 293
Irving, Clifford, 265–68, 289, 328
Irving, Mrs. Clifford, 277–78, 290
ITT, 281–82
Ivey, Courtney, 291–92

Jachimczyk, Joseph A., 325
Jarrico, Paul, 164–65
Jaworski, Leon, 243, 245
Jeanmaire, Zizi, 165–66, 183
*Jet Pilot*, 144–46, 153, 163
Jewell, Richard D., 176
Johnson, Edwin C., 146
Johnson, Lyndon B., 211, 234
Jones, Jesse H., 101, 102
Jones, Phil, 44
Judd, Gordon, 307

Kaiser, Henry J., 102, 113
Kane, Walter, 167–68, 312
Kazan, Elia, 166
Keaton, Buster, 84
Keats, John (biographer), 212, 213
Kefauver, Estes, 154
Kenaston, Robert, 62
Kennedy, John F., 188, 202, 204, 210, 211, 269

Kennedy, Joseph, 65, 269
Kennedy, Robert, 220, 231, 234–36, 248
Kennedy, Rose, 65
Khashoggi, Adnan, 302
King, Alan, 230
Kirk, Claude, 249
Kirschner, Richard, 310
Kistler, Ron, 187–89, 191–2, 193
Kolod, Ruby, 218
Korda, Alexander, 50
Kotchian, Carl, 232
Krasna, Norman, 154, 163, 164
Krupp, Alfred, 220, 303
Krupp, Vera, 220, 303
Kuldell, R. C., 31

Ladies' Home Journal, 265
La Follette, Robert, 61
La Guardia, Fiorello, 77, 86–87
La Jotte, Chuck, 40
Lake, Jeil, 327
Lambagh, E. C., 20
Lane, Charlie, 16
Lang, Fritz, 154–55
Lang (Vlasek), June, 63, 202
Lanica Airlines deal, 270, 277, 290, 303
Lansbury, Angela, 109
La Prensa, 271, 277
Lasky, Jesse L., 37, 38, 44, 46
Lasky, Mrs. Jesse L., 37
Lawford, Peter, 226
Laxalt, Paul, 11, 119, 219, 229, 235, 244, 260, 264, 280, 307
Leigh, Janet, 144, 145
Lenzner, Terry, 307
Lesser, Sol, 116
Leventhal, A. R., 267, 268, 276
Levitt, Al, 137
Lewis, Sinclair, 88
Lichtman, Al, 62
Liddy, Gordon, 246, 274–75, 281–85, 286, 308
Lieber, Perry, 138, 154, 218
Life, 189
Linklater, Magnus, 276
Lionel, Samuel S., 314, 329
Lobo, Julio, 204
Lockhart, Bicknell, 136–37
Lockheed, 101, 232, 266, 280
  Hughes deal with, 296, 298–99, 301, 314
Loew, Arthur, 145
Lombard, Carole, 36–37, 41, 43, 44, 49
Loomis, Robert, 212, 213
Lorenzo, Frank, 303
Loring Theater Corporation, 144
Los Angeles Airways, 248

Los Angeles Times, 62, 266, 310
Losey, Joseph, 137
Loving, Rush, Jr., 291
Ludwig, Daniel K., 270, 271, 299, 302, 315
Lummis, Annette Gano (aunt), 29–32, 36, 64, 125–26, 262, 325–29
Lummis, Frederick (uncle), 29–33, 36, 64, 125–26
Lummis, William (cousin), 312, 319, 325–330
Lupino, Ida, 66, 68, 151
Lurie, Louis R., 164
Lusty Men, The, 173
Lyon, Ben, 41–42, 44–46, 49, 52, 53, 58

MacArthur, Charles, 54
McCall, Mary, Jr., 165
McCarey, Leo, 116
McCarthy, Eugene, 234
McCarthy, Joe, 127, 128
McCarthy, Mary, 170
McCarthy, Neil S., 50, 289, 316
McCord, James, 274–75, 285–86
McCulloch, Frank, 265–66
McGovern, George, 282, 283
McGraw-Hill, 265, 267, 276–77, 289
McInerney, James, 188
McIntyre, Avis Hughes Saunders (cousin), 28, 32, 36, 326, 329
McIntyre, Marvin H., 102
McKay, David O., 327
MacKenzie, Joyce, 170
Madden, Owney, 57
Maheu, Peter, 215, 249, 254–55, 261
Maheu, Robert, 193–95, 201–5, 208, 218, 225, 230–33, 236–44, 249, 259–62, 286, 303, 304, 306, 311, 329
Maheu Associates, Robert M., 193
Mantz, Paul, 71, 89
Marchetti, Victor, 251, 252
Marco, Albert, 45
Margulis, Gordon, 12, 221, 222, 256, 266, 272–73, 277–78, 279, 294, 296–98, 301, 305, 309, 317, 319
  hired by Hughes, 220
Marley, Peverell, 110
Marsh, Marian, 63, 66
Martin, Dean, 226
Marx, Chico, 96
Marx, Groucho, 96
Marx, Gummo, 96–97
Marx, Harpo, 96
Mason, Jackie, 226–27
Mason, Verne, 125, 166, 183, 207
Mating Call, The, 44

Mature, Victor, 151, 165
Mayer, Louis B., 58, 59, 95, 118, 123, 133, 139, 164
MCA-Universal, 327
Meigs, Merrill C., 103
Meier, John, 239–41, 244, 277, 300–1
Menjou, Adolphe, 54
Metropolitan Studios, 41, 51
Meyer, Johnny, 101, 104–5, 109, 113–19, 123, 125, 128, 131, 141, 167, 186, 231
Meyers, Bennett E., 105, 107
Michael, George, 159
Miles, Marvin, 266
Milestone, Lewis, 38–39, 41, 43, 44, 54
Millard, Oscar, 173
Miller, Marilyn, 41
Mitchell, John, 245, 246, 283, 288, 289
Mitchell, Thomas, 97
Mitchum, Robert, 135, 138, 148–49, 155, 164
Monroe, Marilyn, 126
Montemoya, Victor, 322
Montez, Lola, 112
Moore, Terry, 25, 139, 141–43, 145, 147, 151–52, 155–56, 159, 160, 162, 166, 167–68, 173, 181–86, 193, 230
Moorehead, Agnes, 175, 233
Morgan, Edward P., 188, 218, 220, 245
Morley, Karen, 55
Morris, Chester, 60
Morrissey, Margaret, 140
Motion Picture Herald, 62
Motion Picture Producers and Distributors of America (MPPDA), 58, 60, 63, 119
Mullen and Company, Robert R., 255, 274, 282, 283, 307, 308
Muni, Paul, 55, 56, 58–60, 62
Murphy, Audie, 123, 126
Murrin, Lee, 244
Muskie, Edmund, 274
My Forbidden Past, 155
Myler, Levar, 280, 292, 301, 303, 305, 317, 329

Narrow Margin, The, 163–64
NASA, 209
National Aviation Association, 71
National Board of Review, 61–62
NBC, 266
Neal, Roy, 266
Neal, Tom, 160
Neil, Robert, 160
Neilan, Marshall, 38, 41
Nelson, Ham, 80–81

New Times, 310
Newton, Wayne, 230
The New York Times, 62, 266, 274, 304, 310
Niarchos, Stavros, 193, 299, 302
Nigro, Edward H., 228, 238, 290
Nissen, Greta, 41, 45
Nixon, Donald, 11, 187–88, 240–41, 242, 244, 268, 280, 288
Nixon, Hannah, 188
Nixon, Richard, 246, 275, 294
    Hughes and, 11, 187–88, 234, 240–47, 255–57, 261, 263, 283–84, 287, 288, 292, 294, 307
    Watergate, 11, 12, 209, 243, 246, 274–75, 282–88, 292, 301, 304, 306–8, 312
Nixon-Hughes Loan, The, 187–88, 280
North-Broome, N., 280
Northeast Airlines, 206
Northrup, 74
Nosseck, Max, 191
Nundy, Eric, 326

Oberon, Merle, 315
O'Brien, Larry, 235–36, 244, 255, 281–82, 285–89, 310
O'Brien, Pat, 54
O'Callaghan, Mike, 11, 264, 280, 292, 296, 302–3
O'Connell, James, 202–3
Odlum, Floyd, 74, 78, 134, 139, 204, 206
Odekirk, Glenn (Odie), 64–66, 68, 69, 71, 79, 82, 122, 123, 125, 276, 290
O'Keefe, Dennis, 124
Oliver, Robert, 283
Oliver, Spencer, 283, 285–87
Olszewski, John J., 293
Onassis, Aristotle, 193, 299
O'Neil, Tom, 182–83
Ophuls, Max, 117
Orsatti, Frank, 116–17
Oswald, Lee Harvey, 204
Outlaw, The, 95–97, 99–100, 116–19, 144, 146, 170
Out of the Past, 135
Outrage, 151

Pacific Air Transport, 92
Paget, Debra, 183
Paley, William, 229
Palmer, Dick, 68, 69, 71
Pan American Airways, 117, 198
Paradise Island Casino, Hotel and Ocean

Club, 230, 255
Paramount, 37, 44, 48, 184
Parker, John, 237
Parsons, Louella, 89, 115, 146
Pascal, Gabriel, 162
*Passion,* 176
*Payment on Demand,* 154
Payton, Barbara, 159–60
Pearson, Drew, 188, 220
Peck, Gregory, 159
Pegler, Westerbrook, 115, 116
Peloquin, Robert, 248, 249, 261
Perlin, Creighton, 137
Peters, Jean (second wife), 123, 126–27,
    139–43, 147, 155, 185, 190,
    191–92, 195, 196, 200, 220, 229,
    257, 303, 318, 327
  divorce, 247
Phelan, Jim, 265, 280
Pickford, Mary, 38, 52
Pindling, Lynden O., 268, 304, 318
Pindling, Mrs. Lynden O., 318
Pistell, Vi Strauss, 133–34
Post, Mrs. Wiley, 85, 267
Post, Wiley, 77, 85, 267
Poussin, Robert, 165–67
Powell, Dick, 173–75
Power, Tyrone, 93, 94, 100, 109–10,
    125, 126
Powers, Mala, 151
Prados, John, 209
Preminger, Otto, 168, 190
Preyssing, Louis, 78, 79
Price, Vincent, 176–77
Priest, Doug, 261
Production Code Administration, 171
Pukovich, Ellen, 328
Putnam, George, 36–37, 71
Putnam's Sons, G. P., 36


Qualitron, 314
Quarberg, Lincoln, 53, 55, 59–61, 63,
    154, 267
*Queer People,* 58
Quirk, James, 26, 108
Quirk, Lawrence, 26, 42, 96, 108, 109,
    118


Raborn, William, 251
*Rachel and the Stranger,* 138
*Racket, The,* 44–45, 55, 154
Raft, George, 56, 57
*Rancho Notorious,* 155
Random House, 212–13, 276
Rank, J. Arthur, 160
Ray, Johnnie, 160

Real, Jack, 12, 270, 289, 290, 293–94,
    296–300, 302, 303–5, 309, 314,
    317, 319, 322
Rebozo, Charles C. (Bebe), 240, 243–45,
    270, 274, 288, 304
Reed, Harry G., 67–68
Rehak, Bob, 272
Reiner, Phillip, 187
Reventlow, Lance, 153
Reyes, Manolo, 284
Reynolds, Debbie, 160
Rice, Ella, 19, 31
Rice, Peter, 19
Richter, Paul, 92
Rickard, Jim, 293, 305
Riddle, Major A., 220
*Riders on the Range,* 143
RKO Pictures, 76, 78, 81, 133–41, 142,
    154, 164–65, 170, 183, 185, 202,
    267
Roberts, Agnes, 327
Robertson, Dale, 177
Robertson, James, 328–29
Robinson, Edward G., 118
Robinson, Walter C., 300
Rockefeller, Laurance, 178
Rogell, Sid, 134, 136–39, 144, 157
Rogers, Ginger, 76–78, 80, 89–90, 99,
    113, 133
Rogers, Lela, 76
Roland, Gilbert, 172
Rooney, Mickey, 112
Roosevelt, Elliott, 104–6, 108, 115, 128,
    231
Roosevelt, Theodore, 21
Rosselini, Roberto, 146–47
Rosselli, Johnny, 202–4, 218–20, 227
Rothschild family, 270, 294
Rowland, Richard, 60
Russell, Gail, 113
Russell, Jane, 97–100, 103, 113, 149,
    164, 170–72


St. George, Edward, 305
Saunders, John Monk, 28, 32, 36–37,
    47, 88–89
Sawyer, Gordon, 267
*Scarface,* 56–62
Schary, Dore, 135–36
Schaub, V. T., 280
Schemmer, Benjamin F., 257
Schenck, Joseph, 43, 51, 53–55, 58, 61
Schenck, Nicholas, 133
Scott, Randolph, 48, 69
Screen Writers' Guild, 165
Seaman, Marjorie, 37
Sears, Peter Gray, 33

SEC, 11, 239, 306–9
*Second Chance,* 170, 172–73
*Secret Heart, The,* 144
Sedlmayr, Julius, 291–92
Sedlmayr, Mrs. Julius, 291–92
Sennett, Mack, 36
*Set-Up, The,* 142
Shafer, Harry, 147
Sharp, Dudley, 19, 22–24, 27, 32
Sharp, Jim, 15, 18, 95
Sharp, Mary, 19
Sharp, Walter, 15–20, 22
Sharp-Hughes Tool Company, 18
Shaw, Artie, 113
Shelton, Turner, 270, 273, 277, 278, 293
Sherwood, Robert, 61
*She Wore a Yellow Ribbon,* 144
Shore, Dinah, 230
Shurlock, Geoffrey, 96
Siegel, Don, 141–42, 145
Sikes, Larry, 315
Simmons, Jean, 152–53, 160–62, 168–69
Sinatra, Frank, 155, 193, 226–28
Sinatra, Nancy (wife of Frank), 155
*Sins of Rome,* 176
*60 Minutes,* 268
*Sky Devils,* 54
Slater, Leonard, 211
Small, Edward, 137–38
Snyder, James (Jimmy the Greek), 236
Somoza, Anastasio, 269–71, 273, 275, 277–78, 281, 290, 293, 294, 297, 303, 319
Somoza, Luis, 269
Sonnett, John, 205, 206
*Son of Sinbad,* 176–77
*Split Second,* 174, 185
*Hercules* (Spruce Goose), 12, 105–6, 115, 120, 121, 128, 130–32, 134, 296, 327
Stanwyck, Barbara, 176
Starr, Jimmy, 154
Stassen, Harold, 194
Stewart, James, 113
Stewart, John, 285
Stewart, Mell, 12, 225, 292, 293, 296, 305, 309
Stolkin, Ralph E., 169–70, 174
Stonehouse, Ruth, 32
Strickling, Howard, 153
*Stromboli,* 146–47
Stroud, Allen, 305
Stuart, Lyle, 211–12
Sturges, Preston, 67, 116–17
Surveyor spacecraft, 209–10
*Susan Slept Here,* 176

Susskind, Richard, 268
*Swell Hogan,* 37–38
Swiss Credit Bank, 268

Talbott, Harold E., 170
*Tarzan's Peril,* 154
Taylor, Elizabeth, 156–57, 160–61
Taylor, Robert, 109
Taylor, Ruth Ellen, 207
Taylor, Sara, 156–57
Telemundo, 271
Texaco, 15
Texas Fuel Oil Company, 15
Texas National Bank of Commerce, 227, 244, 329
Thacher, Anson, 26–27
Thacher, Sherman, 26, 29
Thain, Wilbur, 12
Theater Guild, 76
*Thing, The,* 154
Thomas, Charles S., 197, 199
Thomas, Wayne, 266
Thompson, Tommy, 212
Thorkelson, Lawrence, 71
*Threat, The,* 143
Tierney, Gene, 93–94, 99, 110, 113–14, 125, 142
Titus, Jack L., 325
Todd, Macy, 139–41
Todd, Mike, 184
Toland, Gregg, 98
Tomick, Frank, 40, 42, 43
Tone, Franchot, 159–60
Tonopah land purchase, 185–86, 229, 239
Totter, Audrey, 139
Tracy, Spencer, 54
Trafficante, Santo, 202
Trippe, Juan, 115, 127, 179, 198
Turner, Lana, 94, 118, 119, 148
TWA, 91–92, 107, 111, 113, 115–16, 118, 127, 152, 157, 179, 182, 188, 197, 200, 204–7, 217, 232, 242, 245–46, 254–55, 289, 295, 303, 311, 328
*Two Arabian Knights,* 38–39

*Underwater!,* 172, 173
Uris, Leon, 204

Valdez, Hank, 148
Vallee, Rudy, 135
*Vendetta,* 117
Von Rosenberg, Charles W., 103–4
von Sternberg, Josef, 144, 146, 164

*Wagonmaster,* 144
Waldron, Clarence (Chuck), 297, 299,
    305, 309, 314–16, 318, 319–22,
    326
Wales, Prince of, 53
Wallace, Jean, 159
Wallace, Mike, 268
Wallis, Hal, 47
*Wall Street Journal,* 34, 164, 170
Walsh, Raoul, 145
Warner, Harry, 133
Warner, Jack, 51, 62, 133
Warner Bros. (studio), 51, 62, 133
Warren, Earl, 206
Watergate, Hughes and, 11, 12, 219,
    275, 284–86, 287–89, 308, 310
Watkin, William Ward, 22
Wayne, John, 133, 144, 145, 154, 173,
    175, 233
Wearley, Bob, 228, 262, 290, 296, 298
Webb, Del, 218
Weissman, Cliff, 305
Welles, Orson, 141
Wenner-Gren, Axel, 92, 122, 266
Whale, James, 45, 47, 49
Whalen, Grover, 80, 81, 86–87
Wheelon, Albert (Bud), 251–52
*Where Danger Lives,* 149, 155
Whitney, Jock, 87
Whitney, Mrs. Jock, 87
Wilde, Cornel, 176, 177
Wilding, Michael, 153, 160–61
Willat, Irvin, 50

Winchell, Walter, 61
Windsor, Duchess of, 92
Windsor, Duke of, 92
Winte, Ralph, 274
*Woman on Pier 13, The,* 143
Wood, Carlyn, 80
Wood, Vernon, 80
Woods, George, 197
Woods, Rose Mary, 246
Woodward, Bob, 287
Woolbright, Donald, 309–11, 329
Woolstone-Smith, A. J., 284–85
Woulfe, Michael, 152, 174, 175, 181
Wray, Fay, 88–89, 141
Wynn, John S., 17

Xanadu Princess Hotel, 11, 299, 302–3,
    318
XF-11 aircraft, 120–24, 140

Yeager, Chuck, 146
Young, Robert, 137
Young, William, 300

Zamparelli, Mario, 149–50
Zanuck, Darryl F., 93, 100, 126, 154,
    167, 174, 177
Zeckendorf, Bill, 178
Zwillman, Abe (Longy), 58–59